P9-ECN-077

Philip and Alex's Guide to Web Publishing

"The Web is not just about looking at pages of text, it is about interacting with live information, sorted and organized the way you want. To do this, your Web server has to be a database server. But that is only the first insight. A database server is not just about downloading product information from online retail catalogs, it is about update too— a framework where a community of like-minded people can build a structured repository of shared information. That is the second insight. The third insight? It does not take millions of dollars to do this. It can be done cheaply enough that anyone can operate a Web server with a database. Read the book and learn how."

—Dave Clark, Chief Protocol Architect of the Internet, 1981–1989

"Greenspun fearlessly tells all from his extensive experience in the Web's trenches. You can save at least $100,000 by avoiding the software he warns you against. But more important, you can avoid wasting millions of dollars if you follow his advice on designing useful Web sites rather than cool Web sites. This is a how-to book about business survival in the network economy."

—Dr. Jakob Nielsen, Web Usability Guru, *www.useit.com*

"IBM has been working for 20 years to build high performance relational database management systems. This book gives you field-tested ideas and techniques to unlock the data and deliver it to users across the Internet."

—John R. Patrick, Vice President, Internet Technology, IBM Corporation

"Smart companies are using the Web to support collaboration. Smarter companies will be using the Web to support computer-to-computer transactions. Philip Greenspun has written the first book that explains how to do both elegantly."

—Mort Meyerson, Chairman of Perot Systems Corporation

"Philip Greenspun interfaced our 60 GB Oracle medical record database to the Web in 1994. It took him three weeks and all it cost me was a 4 GB hard disk and some SIMMs for his Macintosh. Since then, Greenspun has become too rich and famous to write Perl anymore. I'm going to use this book to train some high school kids to replace him."

—Isaac S. Kohane, M.D., Ph.D., Director, Children's Hospital Informatics Program

"Caught up in the frenzy of just being there, we have all been enticed by the possibilities the Net offers in a one-to-one world of idea and transactional commerce. Many have planted expensive seeds on the Net with the hope that they will germinate into something of value. Greenspun has thoroughly captured the logic of what can win from the viewpoint of both the creator, who may be, and the viewer, who is, king. Information and ideas can serve lofty purposes but without organization, tools to easily mine and find, and an audience to share and view, there is no purpose."

—Mark Miller, Executive Vice President & General Manager, Hearst Magazines

"This is the first book on RDBMS-backed Web sites that an intelligent programmer can enjoy." **—Doug McKee, Manager, Web Server Development, America Online, co-developer of AOLserver**

"There are a lot of books that will tell you how to design a web site that looks like something else—a computer game, or a print magazine—which would be great if web pages were computer games or print magazines. They aren't. Read this book to find out what they are."
                                                                    —Robert S. Thau, author of the Apache Web server

"Greenspun's prize-winning and colorful Web publishing experience is as old as the Web and a must for all aspiring Web publishers."
                            —Michael L. Dertouzos, Director MIT Laboratory for Computer Science, author of *What Will Be*

"I've been buying and reading books on the Web and books on Databases and any combination, trying to get to the bottom line on how to publish text and multimedia on the Web. This is the book I've been waiting (and looking) for. Buy it!"
                                                                    —Mark Kelly

"[This book] was the most entertaining technical book I've ever read. Come to think of it, it's the only technical book that I've ever read from cover to cover."
                                                                    — J. Piscioneri

"We have distributed this book throughout our organization because it not only gives details on Web publishing, but also gives the reader a feel for the 'social environment' of the Web. It is much more than a book about Web databases, although that is what is really driving Web development."
                                                                    —Mark Samis

"There's much more to Greenspun's work than Dilbert/Dogbert's recycled truisms; don't compare them just because Greenspun's writing is witty and often very amusing. The difference is that Greenspun's book has *content*: real, useful, and very well presented (and yes, the humor does help)."
                                                                    —Cris Pedregal Martin

"The best general book on web publishing I have seen yet. A 900-word review can be found at *http://www.anatomy.su.oz.au/danny/book-reviews/h/Database_Web.html*."
                                                                    —Danny Yee

"If you buy one book on the web this year and you already know HTML, make this book the one, because you're not going to learn anything from the other ones anyway."
                                                                    —Faisal Jawdat

"While there are many things to love about this book, I think the best part is that Philip places the emphasis on putting yourself in the user's shoes. He avoids the narrow focus of the "Teach Yourself To Be A Dummy In 21 Days" books. He talks about the whys as well as the hows. And he's funny as hell. I love this book!"
                                                                    —David A. Buser

"I can't think of anyone in the web industry—engineers, content producers, advertising sales, etc.—that wouldn't benefit from the remarkably common-sensical (yet somehow lucidly revealing) presentation that Greenspun's spun. I spent 2.5 years writing a book of my own, yet I feel this is one of the best books I've ever read."
                                                                    —Jeffrey Friedl

"Excellent book. I hope some marketing people read it."
                                                                    —Paul Wilson

Philip and Alex's Guide to Web Publishing

Philip and Alex's Guide to Web Publishing

Philip Greenspun

Morgan Kaufmann Publishers, Inc.
San Francisco, California

Senior Editor: Jennifer Mann

Director of Production & Manufacturing:
Yonie Overton

Editorial Assistant: Karyn Johnson

Composition/Art Management:
Proctor-Willenbacher

Scanning to Kodak PhotoCD:
Advanced Digital Imaging, Boston Photo

Color Space Conversion: Alpha CD Imaging

Cover Designer: Ross Carron

Cover Photograph: Elsa Dorfman,
http://elsa.photo.net

Photographs of the author (Chapter 5): Rob Silvers,
http://photomosaic.com

Text Design: Studio Star

Illustration: Mina Reimer, Cherie Plumlee

Proofreaders: Leslie Tilley, Sarah Burgundy

Printer: Courier Corporation

Photographs, other than those designated above, were taken by Philip Greenspun, scanned to Kodak PhotoCD by Advanced Digital Imaging and Boston Photo, converted from YCC to CMYK color space by Alpha CD Imaging, digitally delivered to press by Proctor-Willenbacher, and printed computer to plate by Courier Corporation in Kendallville, Indiana.

The haiku at page 208 first appeared in *Salon,* an online magazine at *http://www.salonmagazine.com,* and is reprinted with permission of the magazine and the author. An online version remains in the *Salon* archives.

Designations used by companies to distinguish their products are often claimed as trademarks or registered trademarks. In all instances where Morgan Kaufmann Publishers, Inc. is aware of a claim, the product names appear in initial capital or all capital letters. Readers, however, should contact the appropriate companies for more complete information regarding trademarks and registration.

Morgan Kaufmann Publishers, Inc.
Editorial and Sales Office
340 Pine Street, Sixth Floor
San Francisco, CA 94104-3205
USA
Telephone   415 / 392-2665
Facsimile   415 / 982-2665
Email   *mkp@mkp.com*
WWW   *http://www.mkp.com*
Order toll free 800 / 745-7323

© 1999 by Morgan Kaufmann Publishers, Inc.
All rights reserved
Printed in the United States of America

04   03   02   01   00   5   4   3   2

No part of this publication may be reproduced, stored in a retrieval system, or transmitted in any form or by any means—electronic, mechanical, photocopying, recording, or otherwise—without the prior written permission of the publisher.

Library of Congress Cataloging in Publication Data
Greenspun, Philip.
    Philip and Alex's guide to Web publishing / Philip Greenspun.
      p. cm.
    New ed. of: Database backed Web sites / Philip Greenspun. 1997.
    Includes index.
    ISBN 1-55860-534-7
    1. Web sites—Design.   2. Databases.   3. Web publishing. I.
Greenspun, Philip. Database backed Web sites. II. Title.
    TK5105.888 .G75 1999
    005.2 ' 76—dc21   99-21939
                                                                 CIP

CONTENTS IN BRIEF

Contents

Chapter 9

User Tracking

Chapter 14
ecommerce   **399**

Chapter 16
Better Living Through Chemistry   491

PREFACE

This book is a catalog of the mistakes that I've made while building more than 100 Web sites in the last five years. I wrote it in the hopes that others won't have to repeat those mistakes.

In a society that increasingly rewards specialists and narrowness, Web publishing is one of the few fields left where the generalist is valuable. To make a great site, you need to know a little bit about writing, photography, publishing, Unix system administration, relational database management systems (RDBMSs), user interface design, and computer programming. I have thus assumed no specific technical background among my readers and have tried to make the text self-contained.

I knew that I'd succeeded with my previous book, *Database Backed Web Sites,* when I happened to sit next to a Harvard M.B.A on a flight to San Francisco. He grabbed the book from my hands and read it from cover to cover during the six-hour flight. When he finished he said, "I learned from every page. I don't have any technical background but I found all of the explanations very clear. The book was funny and easy to read all the way through." I was adjusting my position so that I could pat myself on the back when he commented on the cover: "I never would have bought this book if I'd seen it in a bookstore."

Mercifully, that previous book is out of print, though the lessons I learned from the people who used it are incorporated here.

For the manager in charge of a Web publication or service, this book addresses the big picture. It is designed to help you to affirmatively make the high-level decisions that determine whether a site will be manageable or unmanageable, profitable or unprofitable, popular or unpopular, reliable or unreliable. I don't expect you to be down in the trenches typing Oracle SQL queries. But you'll learn enough from this book to decide whether in fact you need a database, whom to hire as the high database priest, and whom to allow anywhere near the database. You'll be able to have a conversation with a database expert. If you get bogged down in some of the tech chapters, I encourage you to skip to the end, where I present a vision of the future informed by my 22 years at the same email address.

For the literate computer scientist, I hope to expose the beautiful possibilities in Web service design. I want to inspire you to believe, as I do, that this is the most interesting and exciting area in which we can work.

For the instructors who've been using my book as a course text, I've added "More" sections at the end of each chapter, pointing to in-depth reference material.

For the student, I've thrown in lots of my photos so that when the class is over, you'll have a nice coffee table book.

For the working Web designer or programmer, I want to provide a new vocabulary and mental framework for building sites. There can be more to life than making a client's bad ideas flesh with Photoshop and Perl/CGI.

What's Different from the Old Book

In case you were unfortunate enough to struggle all the way through *Database Backed Web Sites* back in 1997, you might want to know what is different about the new book, especially since the chapter titles are so similar.

This book has about 60 percent more words than the old book. To the extent that material was cut and pasted from the old book, it was generally revised and rethought. Thus only about 30 percent of the text in this book is the same as in the old book.

A fundamental difference is that I've taken off my "magazine-style" Web site blinders. The new book reflects my current focus on how to make Web services that replace desktop applications. If you're interested in how people charge for these services, then the brand new ecommerce chapter will appeal to you. I learned things about credit card processing that I never wanted to know. The all new chapter, Better Living Through Chemistry, talks about some sophisticated applications that I built with the Environmental Defense Fund.

If you took all of my advice from the first book and built yourself a million-hit-a-day community Web service, then you're probably shaking your fist at me right now. As you might expect from a member of the MIT Class of '82, the advice that I dispensed scaled up fine as far as software and hardware were concerned but fell a little short along the human dimension. The software that I gave away made it easy for a wimpy computer to solicit, collect, and organize into a relational database tens of thousands of contributions from readers. However, it didn't give publishers much help in terms of dividing responsibility for moderation, excluding high-cost users, and identifying content that needed updating. In an all new chapter on community, this book describes a comprehensive technical and social approach to building community sites in which the database works harder so that the moderators can relax.

Many of the case studies are new. I still like the old ones, but since the full text of my old book is online at a permanent URL, I felt that I could just ask people to

read the relevant sections from the old book. The new case studies include my useful Uptime server-monitoring service and the infamous Brutal Truth Industries game site (the source code to which will be useful if you want to do online quizzes and surveys).

I've sat in more conference rooms with people struggling to put together brand new sites. This has made me think more about the management processes necessary for building a maintainable Web service. I've set forth my ideal workflow in the chapter, Static Site Development. Note that this chapter is probably useful even for folks who are building dynamic Web sites, but I couldn't think of a better chapter title.

There are some minor differences between the editions. Throughout the book, the SQL examples are given in Oracle8 syntax. This is partly because Oracle is the most popular RDBMS on the market but mostly because Oracle8 is what I use every day behind my Web sites, and it was therefore easy to cut and paste code from my running systems. I'm giving away more free software with this book, and folks who want to download it will probably have the best results by coming to the online edition at *http://photo.net/wtr/thebook/*, finding the relevant chapter, and clicking through to the .tar files.

The photographs in the hard copy edition are new. They came out of some discussions with Jennifer Mann and Mike Morgan at Morgan Kaufmann. We decided to experiment by making the world's first coffee table computer book. The idea is that people who buy the paper edition should get something better than if they'd simply downloaded the online edition and printed it out. High-quality color printing and binding are things that are tough to do even in modern offices. If you're curious to know more about a photo, just visit the online edition, click on the thumbnail of the photo, and you'll find the caption underneath the enlarged version.

Finally, if you've liked my tech writing well enough to read both books, I want to make sure that you've seen my "The book behind the book behind the book…" story at *http://photo.net/wtr/thebook/dead-trees/story.html*. You'll laugh, you'll cry, and you'll never agree to write a book!

ACKNOWLEDGMENTS

In *Database Backed Web Sites,* I declined to acknowledge anyone in the front of the book. If someone had given me an idea, I thought it was more honest to work their name into the main text. Also, I couldn't resist reprinting my friend Olin's acknowledgments for the *Scheme Shell Reference Manual:*

> Who should I thank? My so-called "colleagues," who laugh at me behind my back, all the while becoming famous on my work? My worthless graduate students, whose computer skills appear to be limited to downloading bitmaps off of netnews? My parents, who are still waiting for me to quit "fooling around with computers," go to med school, and become a radiologist? My department chairman, a manager who gives one new insight into and sympathy for disgruntled postal workers?

> My God, no one could blame me—no one!—if I went off the edge and just lost it completely one day. I couldn't get through the day as it is without the Prozac and Jack Daniels I keep on the shelf, behind my Tops-20 JSYS manuals. I start get-

ting the shakes real bad around 10 am, right before my advisor meetings. A 10 oz. Jack 'n Zac helps me get through the meetings without one of my students winding up with his severed head in a bowling-ball bag. They look at me funny; they think I twitch a lot. I'm not twitching. I'm controlling my impulse to snag my 9mm Sig-Sauer out from my day-pack and make a few strong points about the quality of undergraduate education in Amerika.

If I thought anyone cared, if I thought anyone would even be reading this, I'd probably make an effort to keep up appearances until the last possible moment. But no one does, and no one will. So I can pretty much say exactly what I think.

Oh yes, the acknowledgements. I think not. I did it. I did it all, by myself.
—Olin Shivers, Cambridge, September 4, 1994

I was convinced that there would never be a more entertaining acknowledgments page for any technical book. Then I opened *Who's Afraid of Java* (Steve Heller, 1997; Academic Press):

Besides those who have directly helped me with this book, I'd like to acknowledge two of the greatest benefactors of mankind in general and myself in particular. The first of these is the greatest writer I know, Ayn Rand. She had the ability to explain complex philosophical concepts in language so simple that anyone could understand them; if I can explain programming half as clearly, I will consider myself a great success. Even more important, she laid the foundation for solving what is possibly the greatest conundrum of philosophy: how to connect what is with what ought to be.

Finally, I want to thank L. Ron Hubbard for his discoveries and inventions in the field of the mind and spirit. Even a small fraction of his myriad contributions to knowledge would qualify him for the first rank of friends of mankind; in total, they elevate him without question to the top of the list.

Seeing Olin so completely upstaged has given me hope that I too can write a memorable acknowledgments page. Here's my attempt....

THE REAL ACKNOWLEDGMENTS

I'm not going to thank my friends and family. I don't have any friends left after spending nearly two years writing this book and its predecessor. My family is sick of hearing me answer "How are you doing?" questions with "Check my Web server to see how the book is going." I'm going to limit myself to people who more or less directly helped with this book, in chronological order.

Bruce Lewis, my Corvette-driving eighth grade English teacher, brought New Yorker articles to class, heaped scorn on inarticulate and complacent critics, and introduced me to the idea that writing matters. A whole generation of kids in Bethesda, Maryland is richer for his work (though since he was openly gay, I'll bet that, had he not died from a heart attack, he'd have a tough time getting a job in a modern school system).

Curt Roads, editor of MIT Press's Computer Music Journal, actually taught me how to write. He wore out red pens obliterating "obviously" and "in my opinion" from my text. He made me incorporate footnotes into the main flow. He kept the red ink flowing even as I quoted Gene Fowler to him: "An editor should have a pimp for a brother, so he'd have someone to look up to."

This book and the experience that underlies it wouldn't exist if not for my personal Web site. The Web site wouldn't exist if not for

- the Web-interested community on the fourth floor of the MIT computer science building back in 1993: Hal Abelson, Brian LaMacchia, and Jonathan Rees
- the technology and generosity of Hewlett-Packard, on whose Unix machines my content is developed and served
- the photo labs who've scanned my images to Kodak PhotoCD: Advanced Digital Imaging and Boston Photo

The Web site wouldn't be an interesting technology case study if not for

- the wizards who built AOLserver: Jim Davidson and Doug McKee
- the Hearst Corporation, whose server farm I used from 1995 through 1997 for my collaboration experiments
- the reliability and speed of the Oracle relational database management system, which I'm able to use thanks to the efforts of Jack Haverty and David Saslav
- the support and ideas of people at Hewlett-Packard, notably Ira Goldstein, Ho John Lee, Saul Marcus, and Carol Peck

Speaking of my personal site, I should thank Terry Ehling of MIT Press. After reading a couple of draft chapters from my first book, she noted:

There are more than quite a few references to Philip . . . . Not everyone wants to know this much about the author. The examples are sound but the self-citations are actually off-putting. This is an instructional text not a biography. There are ways of being personal without showing home movies.

Ouch! The truth hurt but it was useful and made for a better final product. Apparently I didn't learn my lesson, though, because Edward Tufte independently came to the same conclusion after reading drafts of the first two chapters of this book: "the phrase 'self-indulgent' will occur to [readers]."

Let me say in my defense that the only sites that I can write about authoritatively and specifically are the ones that I've built. Those are the ones for which I have source code, for which I know how much and what kind of user confusion was generated, and for which I know the cost to build and operate.

Simon Hayes was the guy who originally convinced me to set down what I'd learned about Web publishing. Angela Allen, Jin Choi, and Paula Hardin told me what was wrong with the draft of my first book, of which 30 percent of the text has survived in this one. Mina Reimer did the napkin drawings that everyone loved. I've never met Bruce Lundquist or Janet Piercy, but Macmillan says that they did the (tasteful) interior design and page layout for that book. Joe Wikert was gracious about giving me back the rights so that I could take this book to Morgan Kaufmann.

As for the MK crew . . . Karyn Johnson made it painless for me to publish this book both on the Web and in print. Jennifer Mann, my editor, called me every day and shamed me into finishing the manuscript. Mike Morgan was willing to risk real money publishing the first coffee table Web nerd book; I'm not sure whether to thank him or try to have him committed.

Uber-designer Yonie Overton and Rad Proctor made the finished four-color work a reality. They treated my words and pictures with far more care than I would have myself. Yonie read the whole manuscript three times and rooted out more solecisms than any professional copy editor. For that alone, I want to have her baby.

The hardcopy book has been improved by hundreds of folks who read the online version and sent pages and pages of email corrections. This truly has been a collaboratively developed work.

For more on the gestation of this book, see *http://photo.net/wtr/thebook/dead-trees/story.html.*

Since 1976, it has been my privilege to be part of the MIT computer science community, physically rooted at 545 Technology Square. Although we've spent most of the past three decades trying to figure out how to get the ventilation system to stop hissing (with nobody except Tom Knight having any success), it is tough for most people to imagine a building where a young nerd can walk out of his office on the fourth floor, argue with the guy who started the free software movement (Richard Stallman), annoy the authors of the best computer science book ever written (Abelson and Sussman), walk up one floor to run a few ideas past Dave Clark, Chief Protocol Architect for the Internet from 1981–1989, and walk down two floors to talk to Tim Berners-Lee, developer of the World Wide Web.

philg@mit.edu

1

Envisioning a Site that Won't Be Featured at suck.com

Why did the world buy 20 million expensive computers and connect them together? Was it really so that a kid in Botswana could look at a flashing GIF 89a logo from a Honda repair shop in Sunnyvale, California? And if we don't think that is true, what kinds of Web services should we build?

An alternative formulation of this question is, "How can I design a site that won't be featured at *http://suck.com*?"

In this book, I'll cover two broad categories of Web sites. The first is *Web Publishing*. These are sites that are vaguely magazinelike and include, as a degenerate case, the typical corporate product catalog site. The second broad category is *Web-based Services*. These are sites that do a job for a user, such as a site that keeps a dog's medical record and sends out email reminders when the dog needs immunizations. The first category is older and more familiar, so let's talk about Web Publishing first.

YOU CAN'T SAY "WEB PUBLISHING" WITHOUT THE WORD PUBLISHING

When you put up a magazine-like site, you are publishing. Virtually all of the important decisions that you must make are publishing decisions. Eventually you will have to select technology to support those decisions, but that is a detail.

Start by putting yourself in your users' shoes. Why are they coming to your site? If you look at some Web sites, you'd presume that the answer is, "User is extremely bored and wishes to stare at a blank screen for several minutes while a flashing icon loads, then stare at the flashing icon for a few more minutes." Academic computer scientists refer to this process of fitting software systems to people as "user modeling."

Slightly more content-rich sites are based on the user model of "user wants to look at product brochures" or "user wants to look at fancy graphics." After pulling the server logs for the sites that reflect these user models, though, it is tough to have much faith in them.

Think about it for a minute: If users wanted a flashing computer screen and a confusing user interface, they could stuff a CD-ROM into the drive. They could get an even more enticing show without the crummy user interface by picking up their television remote control and flipping channels. If users wanted product brochures, they could get them by calling manufacturers or visiting shops. If users wanted fancy graphics, they could flip through dozens of pages' worth in a print magazine in the amount of time it would take to load a single corporate Web page.

Users come to magazine-like Web sites because they have questions. They are not bored losers. We are not doing them a favor by putting product brochures online or showing them huge logo GIFs. Users are doing us a favor by visiting our Web sites. They are paying to visit our servers, if not exactly with money, then at least with their time. We have to give them something of value or they will never come back.

Ever.

If you can anticipate user questions and make sure that your site answers them, then you will be a successful Web publisher.

Example 1: Personal home page

Suppose that you are building a humble personal home page. Why would a user come to your page? Someone might be trying to contact you or send you a package. So you obviously need to include your phone number, mailing address, and possibly fax number. Perhaps you've invited people to your house for a party and they don't know how to get there; they can't call you because you're out shopping for bagels. So you should have a map to your house (I just made my home address a hyperlink to the Yahoo map server; see *http://photo.net/philg/contact-info.html*).

Imagine that a friend of yours is at a party talking to Dale, a beautiful member of whatever sex you happen to fancy. Your friend is describing your charity, great humanity, and kindness to animals. Dale, however, won't agree to meet you without seeing a photo first. So you'd better hope that there is a portrait of you somewhere on your home page before Dale and your friend stroll over to the WebTV.

Or imagine that you've given an interview to a reporter who is on deadline. It is 2:00 A.M. when the reporter realizes he forgot to ask you for some background biographical information. You'll be getting a wake-up call unless you remembered to put a copy of your résumé online.

At this point, some people might object that this information is too, well, *personal* for a personal home page. The Internet frightens them. Sure, their phone number is listed, and the price they paid for their house is public information. And their credit record is open to almost anyone who cares. But they think that if their name is known to an Internet search engine, suddenly all of the privacy that they supposedly formerly had will evaporate. Well, my home phone number has been available via the Internet for 20 years, and my personal site gets about 20,000 visitors a day. I include a picture of myself naked with my old dog George and maps to my house and office on my site. And just as I typed that last period, sitting in what I thought was the privacy of my own home, someone I didn't know called me up. At 8:20 P.M. on a Monday. Would I make a donation to the March of Dimes?

Probably about 1 percent of my unsolicited phone calls are from readers of my Web site. Surprisingly enough, people who find me on the Internet seem to send email instead. Go figure.

Note: "What makes an effective personal home page?" is a different question than "Why put effort into a personal Web site?" I can answer the latter question for myself. I've been immersed in the MIT programming culture since 1976. One of the most painful things in our culture is to watch other people repeat earlier mistakes. We're not fond of Bill Gates, but it still hurts to see Microsoft struggle with problems that IBM solved in the 1960s. Thus, we share our source code with others in the hopes that programmers overall can make more progress by building on each other's works than by trying blindly to replicate what was done decades ago. If I learn something about the publishing industry, about cameras, about computers, or about life, I want to share it with as many people as possible, so that they can benefit from my experience. Wasting time isn't wasteful anymore if you can write it up and keep other people from wasting time.

Example 2: Camera manufacturer

Consider *www.nikon.co.jp*. Why would a photographer come to this site? Possibly to look at brochures, so it might be nice if advertising literature were on the site. But the most important users are existing customers, such as someone who is traveling with a fancy Nikon single-lens reflex camera and has forgotten how to work the flash. Caught without the owner's manual, this customer has surfed in from an Internet café hoping to find the full text online.

Someone with a broken camera will want to know how to get it fixed and how much it will cost. They'll be looking for maps to service centers, warranty details,

and prices for out-of-warranty repairs. The site is a natural focal point for customers to meet, interact, and share experiences with each other. So *www.nikon.co.jp* should have moderated Q&A forums, bulletin boards, and classified ads where customers can contribute.

The preceding advice sounds trivial, but try to find a product manufacturer who is following it. If you visit the average company's Web site, you find lots of advertising to potential customers but virtually no services or documentation for existing customers. In this sense, the Web is kind of like early television. People didn't understand the new medium, so they stuck a camera at the back of a live theater, recorded the movements and speech of the actors, and broadcast the result. On the Internet, companies have produced Web sites by sticking a camera in front of their marketing and sales brochures.

As of August 1998, *www.nikon.co.jp* was amply stocked with advertising. If you were at an Internet café and needed to review the instruction manual for your Nikon camera, you'd find instructions for going to the post office, purchasing six International Reply Coupons, and mailing them to Japan. Upon receipt of the coupons, Nikon would mail you the relevant manual. There were no tools for collaboration among customers, but you could send Nikon email. First they asked you to read the following disclaimer:

```
Nikon Corporation (" Nikon ") has no obligation for monitoring any ideas,
concepts, suggestions or comments (hereafter collectively called " Ideas " )
you transmit to this Site (" the Site ") by electronic mail or otherwise.
Nikon understand that you abandon all rights regarding the Ideas at the time
when you transmit the Ideas to Nikon, and Nikon has no obligations to keep
the Ideas confidential.
Nikon has no responsibility for any problems or issues resulted from the Ideas.
```

For a glimpse of what a corporate site looks like when a company thinks about existing customers, look at *www.ge.com.* They have advertisments, yes, but also owner's manuals and installation guides for every GE product. If you have moved into an apartment with a GE appliance, but the previous tenants did not leave you the instructions, you can grab a PDF file from the GE site and print it.

Example 3: Software company

Everything that works for GE or could work for Nikon should work for a software company as well, but the bar is higher for a software vendor. A camera maker such as Nikon is under no obligation to demonstrate an understanding of the Internet. But someone in the computer business can't afford to have customers say, "My 10-year-old built a better Web site than that last week."

All of a software vendor's documentation must be online and current. Demonstration programs, ideally running on the server or as Java applets, should be available. Customers should be able to purchase and download everything that is for sale. If a software company can't use the Internet effectively, then why would anyone believe it was capable of doing anything with computers effectively?

Compare the Web sites for AOLserver (*www.aolserver.com*) and Oracle (*www.oracle.com*). Since 1995, you have been able to go to the AOLserver site and learn how to program in Tcl, learn how to build a Web site in Tcl with their particular set of API calls, download the latest version of the software, get the installation instructions for 10 different operating systems, and find pointers to applications built on top of the AOLserver and developer discussion groups. They had one full-time documentation person on staff.

By contrast, in visiting Oracle's site on July 29, 1998, I found announcements of a product that I could buy in 1999 (the Oracle RDBMS on Linux), reports of Oracle Applications having won "ERP/MRP Product of the Year" from *Managing Automation* magazine, and a bunch of articles about how other people love Oracle products. Yet a person who'd already purchased Oracle's core relational database management system could not use *www.oracle.com* to learn how to install the software or how to write programs using Oracle's version of the SQL language. The product has been on the market for 20 years and the documentation was available a couple of years ago in HTML format on a CD-ROM. Yet folks at Oracle are only now thinking about possibly parking it on the Web site for open public access.

Example 4: University research lab

I work at the MIT Laboratory for Computer Science (LCS). Some folks in the building came to me with their plan for a new *www.lcs.mit.edu*. The site would have a mission statement from the lab director and a list of all the groups in the lab. For each group, we'd indicate which professor was in charge and the mission statement for that group. The overall goal was to attract undergraduates at other universities to apply here for graduate school and to attract graduate students at other universities to apply here for faculty jobs. The site would be produced through four levels of management with the directors telling the PR staff what they wanted to say, the PR staff telling a writer what to write, and the writer's words going to a graphic designer for formatting into HTML.

My comments?

It would be a nice 20-page site that would cost about $100,000 a year to maintain because every change would have to go up and down this four-level management chain. Assuming we had the budget to do it, I could only see one little problem.

"What's the problem?" asked the PR folks.

"If you walked out of this building and spent the rest of your life searching the planet, I don't think you'd find a single person who cared about the names of the groups at LCS or who is running them."

My suggestion was first to think about Jane Nerd, a computer science undergraduate at the University of Michigan. She is interested in network protocols. She should be able to type "network protocols" into a search box and learn something interesting about the history, practice, and future of computer networks. In the process, she would probably discover that our very own Dave Clark was Chief Protocol Architect for the Internet from 1981 to 1989 and that the Advanced Network Architecture Group at LCS is tackling the problem of making one Internet protocol work simultaneously for real-time control, video conferencing and other forms of interactive collaboration, plus traditional data transfer. If she is curious about encryption, she should find the Internet's best tutorial on the workings of the RSA algorithm. In the process, she might learn that LCS employs Ronald Rivest (the "R" in RSA) and that Ron is part of the Theory of Computation Group.

Next, we should think about Joe Maxinerd, finishing his Ph.D. in computer science at Stanford. Joe's thesis is on computer graphics. He should have been visiting one of our Web servers every day or two, because we are operating a community Web site where the world's leading experts in graphics algorithms meet to exchange research results, talk about new ideas, and teach students. As a participant in forums and from reading comments on research papers, he would be intimately familiar with all the MIT LCS folks who work in the Computer Graphics Group.

We should think about teaching. A quick review of our server logs will reveal that the entire world doesn't come here every day desperate to find out what we're doing. If we want traffic, we'll have to give something back to the Internet. Fundamentally, there are two ways of teaching a scientific or technical subject. The standard textbook takes the "here's the way it is" approach. You don't learn about how people struggled to understand electric and magnetic fields over 2,500 years; you get Maxwell's equations. It doesn't have to be this way. At St. John's College (*www.sjca.edu*), students learn physics by reading original writings by Aristotle, Newton, Kepler, Maxwell, Einstein, Heisenberg, and Millikan.

Nearly all computer science tutorials take the "here's how you do it" approach. With such a short history behind the field and instructors who tend to be ignorant of that history, colleges generally just show students a point-in-time snapshot of thinking about computing. LCS is 35 years old this year, so we're one of the few institutions that has been around long enough to talk credibly about the history of the field.

What would make a great LCS site is a collaboratively produced, collaboratively taught history of computer science. Journalists, historians, and other casual users might wish to read the timeline of technological advances and click through to see explanations of what each advance brought in terms of applications. Thus, for example, an entry on early bitmap displays (Stanford, Knight TV, Xerox PARC) would be linked to an explanation of how they led to the MIT Lisp Machine, the Macintosh, and then Microsoft Windows. Computer science students would be able to learn all of computer science by following hyperlinks from the timeline to original papers and software. In doing so, they would note that much of the innovation in computer science happened at MIT and perhaps become inspired to apply for positions here.

Because we would farm out responsibility for each section of the timeline to a professor and the responsibility for running community sites in research areas to the various groups, the overall cost of this kind of site would probably be similar to that of the 20-page site produced with a four-level management hierarchy.

The point of this example? A publisher's internal structure is of no interest to Web users. People come to Web sites trying to get a job done or a question answered. The first thing the guys at *www.fedex.com* did was publish a Web interface to their package tracking database. That was back in 1994. Today, if you want to find out about FedEx the company, you find a subtle hyperlink to a separate site: *www.fdxcorp.com*.

Note: I asked Edward Tufte to read this book, and he asked, "How is it different from the old one?" I said that I had much better ideas and lots of great new examples. I'd just finished writing up the preceding example and recited it to him as an example of my brilliant originality. "Oh yes," he said, "design recapitulates bureaucracy. I wrote that at the back of *Visual Explanations*" (1997, Graphics Press). Check page 148 of Tufte's book to see how original my ideas actually are.

How do you know when you are done?

You can objectively measure how well your site meets user needs. Are you getting a lot of email questions? As soon as two users ask the same question, you should beef up your site to answer it unattended: Build a page, fix the navigation model, or tune your search engine.

Every competently run site runs a local full-text search engine. Why not go the extra mile and hack the CGI scripts so that the search engine sends you email when

a query results in zero matches? Given information about which user queries are failing, you can add content or keywords as appropriate.

At this point you can relax. You aren't a loser with a big budget, a lot of ugly graphics, and no traffic. Users are not leaving your site in frustration, shaking their heads, and saying "They just don't get it." Now that you are safe from the wags at suck.com, what can you do to make your magazine-like site fulfill its potential?

BECOME ILLITERATE: PRESENT MULTIPLE VIEWS

Look up "Bomarzo" in the *Michelin Green Guide to Italy:* "Extending below the town is the park of the 16th-century Villa Orsini (Parco dei Mostri) which is a Mannerist creation with a series of fantastically shaped sculptures." Compare that description to these photos showing just a tiny portion of the Parco dei Mostri (Park of Monsters).

Do these not suggest a somewhat richer place than the sentence in the Michelin guide? Yet the sight of a tourist slavishly following the Michelin guide is a commonplace. Something really fascinating and unexpected is happening in front of him, but he has his nose buried in the guide, trying to figure out what the next official point of interest is. The tourist is *literate.* Not literate in the "I read Classics at Oxford" sense, but literate in the "knowledge is closed" sense. Everything about Italy can fit into a book. Perhaps the 350 pages of the *Green Guide* aren't enough, but some quantity of writers and pages would suffice to encapsulate everything worth knowing about Italy.

Oral cultures do not share this belief. Knowledge is open-ended. People may hold differing opinions without one person being wrong. There is not necessarily one truth; there may be many truths. Though he didn't grow up in an oral culture, Shakespeare knew this. Watch *Troilus and Cressida* and its five perspectives on the nature of a woman's love. Try to figure out which perspective Shakespeare thinks is correct.

Feminists, chauvinists, warmongers, pacifists, Jew-haters, inclusivists, cautious people, heedless people, misers, doctors, medical malpractice lawyers, atheists, and the pious are all able to quote Shakespeare in support of their beliefs. That's because Shakespeare uses multiple characters in each of his plays to show his culture's multiple truths.

In the 400 years since Shakespeare, we've become much more literate. There is usually one dominant truth. Sometimes this is because we've truly figured something out. It is kind of tough to argue that a physics textbook on Newtonian mechanics should be an open-ended discussion. Yet even in the natural sciences, one can find many examples in which the culture of literacy distorts discourse.

If you were able to stay awake long enough to read through an academic journal for taxonomic botanists, you'd learn that not all botanists agree on whether Specimen 947 collected from a particular field in Montana is a member of species X or species Y. But you'd see quite clearly that everyone publishing in the journal agreed on the taxonomy—on how to build a categorization tree for the various species.

However, if you were able to stay awake long enough to get through a cocktail party in a university's department of botany, you'd discover that even this agreement is illusory. There is widespread disagreement on what constitutes correct taxonomy. Hardly anyone believes that the taxonomy used in journals is correct, but botanists have to stick with it for publication because otherwise older journal articles would be rendered incomprehensible. Taxonomic botany based on an oral culture or a computer system capable of showing multiple views would look completely different.

Open today's *New York Times*. A Republican politician is arguing for relaxed regulations on widgets. A Democrat is quoted arguing in favor of tightened regulations. There is a vote; widget regulations are tightened. On the surface, it looks like multiple perspectives. Yet at a cocktail party, your friend Sue argues that the government shouldn't be regulating widgets at all. Joe interrupts her to say that widget regulation

Note:
I learned all of this interesting stuff about taxonomic botanists from Peter Nürnberg from Texas A&M University. But as much as he educated me about botany, I failed to educate him about Web publishing. He broke the link that I had to his Webnet '96 paper.

is a canard; we really ought to talk about flag burning. Dana brings up the *Simpsons* episode in which Bart went on a school field trip to the widget factory. Alan tells his grandfather's widget factory stories from World War II. Elizabeth talks about how she was surprised to see that they had no widgets in New Zealand and apparently did not miss them. Compared to the texture of the cocktail party, the *New York Times* article sounds like two rich, old, white guys saying more or less the same thing.

Some people like a one-truth world. If you have a huge advertising and PR budget, then you can control your public image very effectively in a literate world. Ford Motor Company has enough money to remind you 2,000 times a year that "Quality Is Job One"; unless your friend was roasted in a Pinto gas tank explosion, you possibly will eventually agree. Microsoft, via the genius of Bill Gates, invented the mouse-windows user interface, reliable operating systems, affordable computing, and the Internet; if you don't think all that is true, ask someone who has never used a computer and whose only exposure to the industry is through mass media.

Perhaps it is because I'm a few billion dollars short of the necessary funds to create a one-truth world of my own, but I think the greatest artistic achievements hold the mirror up to a multiple-truth life.

The Internet and computers, used competently and creatively, make it much easier and cheaper to collect and present multiple truths than in the old world of print, telephone, and snailmail. Multiple-truth Web sites are much more interesting than single-truth Web sites and therefore will get a lot more traffic. For example, the car manufacturers' sites are mostly collections of product brochures tarted up with flashing graphics. They get minimal traffic compared to the plain-text rec.auto.* newsgroups, which present the real experience of car owners from around the world. The newsgroups don't have pictures, animation, sound, or video clips, but they have multiple truths.

Okay, enough philosophy and Shakespeare. This is the point in the infomercial where the guy wearing the CAT Diesel cap asks, "Do I need a college education to build one of these here multiple-truth Web sites?" The answer is, "No."

> **Step 1: Put up some magnet content.** The Internet has reduced distribution cost to zero. So take every document that you've ever distributed to anyone and put it on your site. In my case, I wrote a 30-page story about Berlin and Prague, illustrated with 60 photos, and stuck it at *http://photo.net/bp/* before inviting people to contribute their experiences.

> **Step 2: Develop technical means for collaboration.** *http://photo.net/photo/* has a question-and-answer forum, a classified ad system, a stolen equipment registry, a neighbor-to-neighbor recommendation service, and an add-a-comment link at the bottom of every article. Users are helping each other build a great repository of photographic knowledge. I try to be diligent

about responding to questions in the forum, but my happiest hours are spent watching users answer each other's questions.

You don't have to be a traditional publisher to benefit from the collaboration systems that you'll learn how to use by reading the rest of this book. Manufacturers can collect and redistribute consumer comments about dealers who carry their products. Academic researchers can collect comments, ideas, and questions sparked by their writings.

Step 3: Be prepared to interact with users. This means that if you have a question-and-answer forum, spend the time to answer the questions. It also means moderating the forum to delete uninteresting threads. It means killing idiotic comments on the comment server but keeping the relevant ones, even those that savagely disagree with your point of view.

Does this sound like too much work? If your site is commercial and you claim to be a smart businessperson, then you ought to be able to figure out a way to interact with users more cheaply over the Internet than via 800 numbers. If you are a writer or a photographer who has built a noncommercial site, disintermediating the publisher means total artistic freedom. User feedback might be annoying at times, but if you want to be insulated from your readers, why publish on the Web at all?

What happens if you take these steps? Sometimes magic. Here's a passage from Part 2 of my Berlin/Prague story (*http://photo.net/bp/part2.html*):

Die Neue Synagoge on Oranienburger Strasse had a tired Oriental look and was under restoration. This building demonstrates the power of a single person of conscience. When the Nazis rolled around on Reichkristallnacht *and set fire to the synagogue, a lone policeman decided that it was a valuable historical building. He got a fire brigade to put the fire out and then arranged an all-night guard for the place. His efforts were ultimately in vain, for the Nazis had learned something from the Turks in Athens: when you want something to be destroyed, e.g., the Parthenon, put a lot of explosive stuff inside and wait for an accident. Thus the building was used as an ammo dump and an Allied bomb blew the place to smithereens in 1943.*

I'd cribbed the facts from a guidebook and would never have realized that they were wrong if I hadn't put in a comment link (*http://db.photo.net/com/philg/bp/part2.html*) and waited a year:

I read your article about Berlin with great interest. For the sake of accuracy, the Nazies did not place ammunition in the Neue Synagoge. It was used as a warehouse. The basement was used as an office. The place was bombed and the main sancturary was burned out, only the front part and the walls were kept standing. After the War, the East Germans blew up the the remains of the sancturary, "Safety Reasons". The front was left to decay. The front part has been rebuilt, and now it is beeing used as a learning center. How do I know. I lived in the Synagogue from before the War until my arrest and eventual incarceration to Auschwitz May 7. 1943. After my Liberation in 1945, I came back there and visited the place. In 1994, I went back to Berlin on a visit, and naturally I went to see the place. At that time they were rebuilding the place. In the rubble they had found papers of mine from 1937 to relating to my Barmitzwah. A year later, I was invited to the rededication ceremony.
—Harry S. Rowe (April 26, 1997)

It seems safe to assume that people are likely to accept his version of the facts as authoritative. No paper book is ever going to collect a story like this.

It turns out to be fairly tricky to engineer and maintain systems for collaboration like this, and that is partly what this book is about. But I feel so strongly that every site should work this way that I am letting other publishers use my software and even Web/database server merely by filling out forms from *http://photo.net/philg/services .html.* It takes about 10 minutes to set up a question-and-answer forum or a comment server and link to it from your site (see Figure 1-1). Try it out right now if you've got a Web site comprising static HTML pages.

THINK OF THE WEB AS PRIMARY

A site that exists primarily to tease people off the Internet to buying something almost always cries out to be ignored. Web sites should stand alone.

Figure 1-1: The question-and-answer forum in *http://photo.net /photo,* which contains more than 25,000 archived messages. Answers are emailed automatically to the user who posted the question, even months later. Users can choose to be notified of new messages by email, instantly, daily, or weekly. If you'd like to run a similar forum on your own site, just visit *http://photo.net /philg/services.html* and fill out a form. The software is free, and you can even use one of my Web/RDBMS servers for free.

Joe Greedy puts up a site showing the cover of his book and a headline: Buy Me For $17." You'd think that this would be the lamest possible Web site. But Mr. Greedy manages to earn extra suck points by making sure that the only ordering option is by telephone. That way the modem crowd will be forced to write down the number on a Post-it and then disconnect before they can order their pile of processed tree carcass.

Jane Clever puts the full text of her book online. With several hundred pages of text instead of one, her content will be several hundred times more likely to attract users of search engines. By enabling online ordering for those dead-tree huggers, Ms. Clever will sell more copies of her book than Mr. Greedy. Also, with 100,000 hits per day, Ms. Clever can sell ads on her site, links to other Web publishers, and consulting services to people who would not have found out about her if she were only an author stuck in the back of a bookstore.

Sites that are adjuncts to physical events or off-the-Web creations almost always disappoint. Millions of dollars are spent by Hollywood studios on companion Web sites for movies. When was the last time you visited one or heard anyone talking about a movie-adjunct site?

Pathfinder did a companion to a traveling museum show by well-known photographers such as Annie Liebowitz. The biggest available pictures on the Web site were tiny, occupying about 1/100th of my 20-inch screen. The editor of the site asked me to add a link from photo.net to the Pathfinder site. I said I'd be happy to add a link if he

put up some larger images so that readers didn't just get frustrated. He replied that the museum show photographers were concerned about copyright infringement. I said, "Well, maybe they shouldn't be on the Net. They are getting plenty of promotion in bookstores, museums, and magazines. Why don't you find some less-known photographers for whom the Web is primary?"

The site could be bad because the people running it only thought of it as an advertisement for the physical show. As long as the show itself was adequate, they didn't feel any shame about having a bad Web site.

In October 1995, the MIT Media Lab threw itself a tenth anniversary party. The physical event was fabulous: little gifts for everyone, cleverly packaged; a Photomosaic poster by Rob Silvers; women in plastic pants. As an adjunct to the physical event, the Media Lab was going to create the best Web site ever: *www.1010.org*. They got NYNEX to bring in a dedicated 45-Mbps T3 network connection; you wouldn't want packets requested by millions of users to get slowed down working their way through MIT's backbone before getting to the wider Internet. Hewlett-Packard donated a huge pile of multiprocessor machines with disk arrays. The Media Lab hired expert consultants to plug all the computers in and hook them up to the network. They hired professionals to do graphic design and site layout for *www.1010.org*.

The site launched without any magnet content. Nobody had written any stories or taken any pictures. Every day a Media Lab editor posed a question and then sat back to watch a USENET-style discussion evolve. There were only a handful of postings in each area. One user contributed a smiley face: colon/dash/right-paren. That was his entire message. This didn't really shock me until I noticed that on a scale of 1 to 7, this posting had been rated 4.3 by other users. Yes, several other users had taken the trouble to rate this three-character posting. When the 10-day Web event was over, the massive disk arrays held almost enough user-contributed data to fill two 3.5-inch floppies.

How could so much money and hardware have resulted in a site that an elementary school would have been embarrassed to make public? Because the Web site wasn't primary; the party was the important thing. The Media Lab, one of the last groups at MIT to put up a Web site, had no real Internet culture. They wanted to reach corporate managers and bring them into the physical space of the Lab. Since corporate managers in 1995 didn't tend to have a TCP/IP connection on their desktops, it wasn't obvious how the Internet would be useful in attaining the Media Lab's goals.

Don't try to visit *www.1010.org*. The Media Lab eventually got Web-savvy enough to realize the embarrassment value of such a site and pulled the plug on the server.

Money is nice. Bandwidth is nice. Graphic design is occasionally nice. But if you treat your Web site as a pimple on the butt of something much larger, then it will probably be ripe for suck.com.

So that you don't have to break into tomorrow's Prozac supply, let me close this section on a happy note: *http://www.dannen.com/szilard.html*, Gene Dannen's biography of Leo Szilard, the Hungarian-Jewish theoretical physicist who made the atomic bomb work and then tried to stop Roosevelt from using it. Dannen says that he is writing a book, but surely the Web is a richer place because he got distracted from finishing it and did this site instead. Since there isn't a "Szilard, the Movie" or "Szilard, the Book" or "Szilard, the Museum," Leo Szilard Online has ended up a rich and fascinating site.

Let's shift gears now from the first site category, Web Publishing, and consider the second category, Web-based Services.

YOU CAN'T DO WEB-BASED SERVICES WITHOUT PROGRAMMING

The crux of Web-based Services is inevitably server-side programming of some kind. That shouldn't be a problem for me because I've been a programmer since 1976, but sometimes I have crises of faith that make me wonder whether there is any dignity left in programming. I seriously considered quitting the industry in 1997 when Apple Computer was concluding its acquisition of NeXT. Imagine if in 1997 the president of General Motors had said, "It has come to my attention that our cars are kind of clunky and unreliable. Don't worry, though. We're rectifying this problem by licensing the blueprints to the 1985 Toyota Camry." Everyone would laugh. Maybe GM cars aren't state of the art, but certainly a 1997 Chevy is better than a 1985 Toyota. Car making is a mature industry, yet not so moribund that a company can compete by offering 12-year-old technology.

People assume that computer technology moves forward at a rapid clip, yet no eyebrows were raised when Apple said that its big step forward was going to be licensing the NeXT OS. This is Steve Jobs's late 1980s facelift of Carnegie-Mellon University's early 1980s rewrite (Mach) of Bell Lab's early 1970s Unix operating system. Maybe it is better than Windows NT, but if so, that only makes it a more damning condemnation of the software industry.

Shortly before Apple acquired NeXT, I'd had a foot operation. I disclosed in the pre-op interview that I'd been taking aspirin. The hospital wanted to make sure that my blood would clot adequately so they brought in a phlebotomist who applied what looked like a self-inking rubber stamp to my forearm. Blood soon began to flow. I'd been a regular blood donor and had never fainted or thrown up, but somehow the sight of my blood just oozing out onto my arm was more sickening than that of it collecting in a bag. I managed to control my nausea for the first five minutes but then the phlebotomist got bored and asked me what I did for a living.

"Oh, you're in computers? Do you know that really smart guy?"

I thought for a moment. "Do you mean Bill Gates?"

"Yes, that's the one. What did he invent?"

Our industry is an embarrassment. When a Honda engineer goes to a party, it would be rare for another guest to say, "Oh, you design cars for Honda? You know, last Friday my husband's Accord just exploded while he was pulling out of the garage." But admit that you're a programmer and you can't get out of the room without hearing about somebody's crashed Macintosh or Windows machine. Furthermore, to the extent that there have been any software innovations in the last 40 years, the Microsoft Monopoly either gets credit for them or keeps them from getting into users' hands.

What keeps me from chucking it all and becoming a tire salesman? I love the power that Web service development gives the individual programmer. My epiphany came thanks to Hewlett-Packard. I was supposed to fly out to HP's Corvallis, Oregon factory and give a talk. I figured that, being *Fortune 500* types, these guys would demand overhead slides or even some kind of animated display from a laptop. My laptop had been gathering dust since I'd parked all of my important files on my Web server. Nor did I really know how to use any presentation software. At MIT, the students are forced to listen to us, even if we arrive to lecture with no more impressive equipment than a piece of chalk. I guess you're also supposed to have a fancy presentation if you get invited to speak at an academic conference, but I'd written enough nasty things about credentialism in my Web site that nobody was inviting me to speak anywhere (and then I drove another few nails in the coffin of my academic career with *http://photo.net/philg/school/tuition-free-mit.html*).

I was all set to install and learn PowerPoint, a classic desktop bloatware package for making slides. But then I worried that I'd have to transport my presentation out to Corvallis on a floppy disk and hope that the HP guys had the same version of PowerPoint. It hit me: Why not just make the slides HTML files on my Web server? Every HP desktop and conference room would surely have a Web browser and Internet access. I created a directory and built a few files, and then the data modeler in me rebelled. All of these slides have the same structure: title, preamble, bulleted item, bulleted item, bulleted item, postamble, standard footer. It is always a bad idea to take structured data and put them into an unstructured text file that a computer program can't read. What if one day I wanted to reformat my slides to look pretty?

The slides should really be in a relational database with a Web front end. Why should I have to know how to use any tool other than Netscape Navigator to edit my slides? Once it was all in a database, I should be able to collaborate with other people. I should be able to authorize my friend Ellen at Mills College in Oakland to edit a presentation. If I wanted something pretty, the system ought to be able to grind out the slides in PDF or PostScript for a transparency printer. If I wanted something pretty on screen, the system ought to be able to serve the slides with a reference to a cascading style sheet. I should be able to lose my laptop and my desktop hard disk and still come back five years later to find my presentation intact in the database.

There is a point to this story. It took only a few days of programming to build WimpyPoint (*http://wimpy.arsdigita.com*) up to the level that it was more useful to

me, and people like me, than PowerPoint. The Web and the idea of Web-based services is so powerful that a few days of work by a good programmer is sufficient to make something better than Microsoft has managed to produce in 10 years using the "herd of losers building desktop apps" approach. In this case I designed the system in a sufficiently clean and perspicuous manner so that I don't have to charge people for using it. After all, if I'm already maintaining a Unix box running Oracle on the Internet, the marginal cost of dealing with WimpyPoint users is minimal.

THE USERS WILL REBEL

Users will get sick of being turned into system administrators. One day they will be on the phone when Microsoft tech support determines that their registry is corrupt. They will patiently listen to the suggestion that they reinstall Windows and then all of their apps. They will toss their PC into a swamp and buy a network computer (NC) that will run a Web browser right out of the box. Instead of puzzling out how to configure their machine to fetch email via POP or IMAP, they'll switch their email over to Hotmail, a Web-based email service. Instead of shopping for a calendar application, they'll use *http://www.arsdigita.com/remindme/* when they want to be sure they don't forget Mom's birthday.

Network computer users will burst onto the Web looking for server-based solutions to the computing problems that they formerly solved with desktop apps. You can't be successful in the Web services business unless you are a good engineer. Bad engineering in the desktop app business is costly for users. Given that Microsoft has a monopoly, a bug in Word might waste a lot of user time, but it isn't going to cost Microsoft any sales. But if I screw up the user interface design or the back-end database programming for WimpyPoint, I'll have 100 email messages a day from upset users and I'll be inspecting my Unix box's entrails until the problem is fixed.

Many of the following chapters in this book are directed at helping you engineer Web-based services in such a way that users have a pleasant experience, while minimizing your costs.

22

SUMMARY

The stuff in this chapter isn't meant to be the one final truth. I'm not a great writer like Shakespeare (yes, I know that I could write this observation up for *Duh* magazine; you don't have to send email) and hence I'm unable to transcend the medium of the printed page and present multiple truths. My hope is that I have provoked you into doing the following:

- putting yourself into your user's shoes before planning your site's content. Why would they come to your site and what can you do to make sure their visit is rewarded?

- thinking seriously about the Web's potential as a medium for collaboration. In intelligent, thoughtful hands, the Internet is more powerful than the printed page.

- creating new ideas for interesting Web-based services

- working to liberate users from the hell of system administration into which Apple and Microsoft have plunged them

This chapter is about people talking to computers and people talking to each other with a computer mediator. The next chapter is about how computers talking to each other can finally deliver all of the benefits that the Computer Age was supposed to have conferred on us (and, if you insist, how you can make a buck off of it).

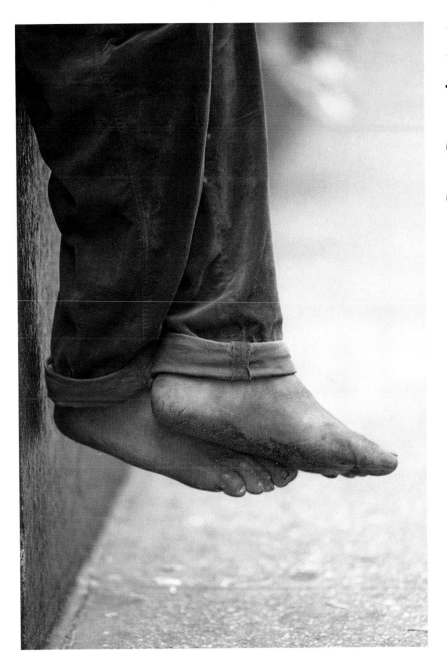

2
The World's Grubbiest Club: Internet Entrepreneurs

"The guy with the Web site." That's how my friends introduce me at parties. I guess that says something about what a rich, multifaceted, textured personality I've developed by spending 17 out of my 35 years at MIT. Yeah. Anyway, the response from my new acquaintances is invariably the same: "How are you going to make money off your Web site?"

If they'd been told I'd spent $15 on a copy of *The Forsyte Saga,* they wouldn't ask how I intended to make money off that. If they knew I'd splurged for a $5,000 Viking stove, they wouldn't ask if I was going to start charging my brunch guests $5 each. If I told them I dropped $27,000 on a Toyota minivan, they wouldn't ask if I was going to charge my dog $10 for every trip.

Web publishing can cost less than any of these things; why does everyone assume that it has to make money? I did not set up my site to make money. I set up my site so that my friend Michael at Stanford could see the slides I took while driving from Boston to Alaska and back. It turns out that my site has not made money. Yet I do not consider my site a failure. My friend Michael at Stanford can look at my slides anytime he wants to by typing *http://photo.net/samantha/.*

I'm not saying that this should be everyone's goal. After all, you might not know my friend Michael at Stanford. Or, if you do know him, you might not like him. But keep in mind that if you are destined to lose money on your site, it is much less humiliating when you can say that making money wasn't the idea.

For those who've forgotten that greed is one of the seven deadly sins, I've written this chapter about how to make money on the Internet.

First, let's ask why we think that there *is* money to be made off the Internet. Karl Taylor Compton, former president of MIT, said it best in 1938: "In recent times, modern science has developed to give mankind, for the first time in the history of the human race, a way of securing a more abundant life which does not simply consist in taking away from someone else."

I believe that *computers* will secure a more abundant life for the human race. Mine would not have been a controversial statement in 1960, when IBM was just beginning to saturate corporate America with mainframes. It was obvious to everyone in 1960 that computers were going to usher in a new Age of Leisure. In 1998, my statement seems absurd. Computers have been around for 50 years now without having done much for the average person. In fact, it is a commonplace among economists that computers have reduced the productivity of American business.

Computers by themselves are a liability. Getting information into and out of them is so expensive that using paper and file cabinets is probably less trouble. Sure, in 1998 we don't see too many people manually writing payroll checks or calculating artillery shell trajectories. But most people get through most parts of their day without relying on a computer. Why don't I think that this lifestyle will be possible in another 50 years? Because of the network.

THE STEAM ENGINE AND THE RAILROAD

James Watt's 1765 steam engine didn't change your life unless you were pumping water out of coal mines. A steam-powered factory could have produced enough goods to supply an entire nation, but since there was no way to distribute that output, there wasn't much point in building such a factory. With the railroad came the ability to serve a national market with one factory. Factories grew enormous and pulled people out of the countryside to work inside the Satanic Mills. It was the mounting of the steam engine on rails and the spreading of railroads across nations that transformed society, not the steam engine, per se. The computer is the steam engine of our times; the network is the railroad.

With a ubiquitous network, all of the information that you consume will arrive in a machine-readable form. If the information is structured appropriately, as with standards like Electronic Document Interchange (EDI), it will arrive in a form that is immediately applicable to your internal databases without human intervention. Your computer will truly be able to handle routine transactions on your behalf.

When the network infrastructure is powerful enough for most houses to enjoy video-rate bandwidth, the computer will be able to support your collaboration with other people. If you had TV-quality video and audio links to your collaborators and a shared workspace, you wouldn't have to commute to work or fly around from city to city so much. Though I don't like to predict the demise of a 3,000-year-old trend toward urbanization, it indeed seems possible that collaboration tools might enable some people to move out to the country yet still keep their urban jobs.

The Internet will change society. Some people will get rich off that change. I guess you might as well be one of them. Probably your safest bet is to figure out where all those telecommuters are going to end up living and open a little mall there with a McDonalds, MicroCenter, and Trader Joe's. If you're a nerd, then you'll probably make the most money building intranet sites that sit inside corporate firewalls

and let workers collaborate in new ways. However, since there is such a popular obsession with making money from public Web sites, let's start by considering how to turn hits into revenue.

Four Ways to Make Money from Your Public Site

The previous chapter divided all Web sites into either magazine-like Web Publishing or Web-based Services. That is a useful division for thinking about whether off-the-shelf technology is going to be helpful to build a site, but when estimating the profit potential of a consumer-oriented Web site, I think one needs a separate set of four categories. If you are starting a new site for the purpose of making money, it is worth considering which categories your planned Web operations fall into and how hard it is to make money in those categories.

Here are the categories (see Figures 2-1 through 2-4):

1. **Sites that provide traditional information.** This is the type of site that requires the least imagination but also the most capital investment. Find bodies of information that consumers in the 1980s bought offline and sell them online. This includes movies/videos/television, newspapers, magazines, weather reports, and stock market information. Revenue comes from

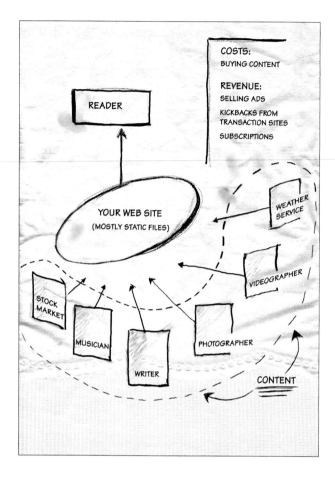

Figure 2-1: A Category 1 site simply provides bodies of information that consumers in the 1980s obtained offline. A classical example is an online magazine or newspaper. Putting up a Category 1 site requires almost no imagination, technology, or investment, but it will cost you a fortune in the long run as you keep buying content to keep it fresh.

advertising, links to sites that do retail transactions and give you a kickback, and occasionally subscriptions.

2. **Sites that provide collaboratively created information.** This is information that was virtually impossible to collect before the Internet. A dead-trees example would be the *Consumer Reports* annual survey of automobile reliability. They collect information from their readers via mail-in forms, collate the results, and publish them once a year. The Internet makes this kind of activity less costly for the provider and gives the user much more immediate and in-depth information. Revenue comes from the same sources as in Category 1, but production expenses are lower.

3. **Sites that provide a service via a server-side program.** An example of this would be providing a wedding planning program. The user tells you how much he or she wants to spend, when and where the wedding is, who is invited, and so on. Your program then figures a detailed budget, develops an invitation list, and maintains gift and thank-you lists. You are then in a position to sell an ad to the Four Seasons Hotel that will be delivered to couples getting married on June 25, who live less than 100 miles away, are inviting fewer than 80 guests, and have budgeted more than $17,000. A familiar example of this kind of site is Hotmail.

4. **Sites that define a standard enabling a consumer to seamlessly query multiple databases.** For example, car dealers have computers managing their inventory, but such data are imprisoned on the dealers' computers and are unavailable to consumers in a convenient manner. Suppose you define a standard that allows the inventory computers inside car dealerships to download their current selection of cars, colors, and prices. You get the car dealers to agree to provide their information to you. Then your site

becomes a place where a consumer can say, "I want a new dark green Dodge Grand Caravan with air conditioning and antilock brakes that's for sale within 60 miles of zip code 02176." From your query to the dealers' multiple databases, your user can get a list of all the cars available that match their criteria, and can then jump right to the relevant dealer's Web site.

In terms of bang per dollar invested, the most expensive type of site is Category 1. To create a site like this, you have to hire writers, pay photographers and editors, and scrupulously maintain your site. If you stop updating for one day, people may turn away to a competitor's site.

A Category 2 site is very cheap to start up. You spend a little bit of money for programming, a data model, and "anchor content." Thereafter, the site expands itself.

A Category 3 site requires much more investment and effort, particularly in selling ads and working with advertisers, but it has potentially much higher payoffs since you know so much more about your users. An advertiser won't pay too much for an ad on the Netscape home page, perhaps a few cents per impression. All that anyone knows about the readers is that they haven't changed their browser's default first page. An advertiser will pay a lot more for an ad on a search engine's site, if it's delivered only to those people who've entered query words relevant to the product advertised. For example, Century 21 would pay a lot to have its ad delivered to people who include "real estate" in their query string. If you learn enough about your readers, you might be able to charge an advertiser several dollars just to display one banner ad to each one.

Category 4 is probably the most lucrative because it harnesses the full power of the Internet. Entering this area requires having the right connections and making the proper business arrangements. It is the Category 4 sites that will change the way

Figure 2-2: A Category 2 site provides collaboratively created information. Each user tells you how frequently his car has broken down, and you end up with a valuable database of car reliability statistics to give back to users collectively. Even a humble classified ad system falls into this category. It costs money to establish your server as a forum for users to exchange data. You have to buy some magnet content and write some programs. But once established, the site can grow in popularity with very little additional investment on your part.

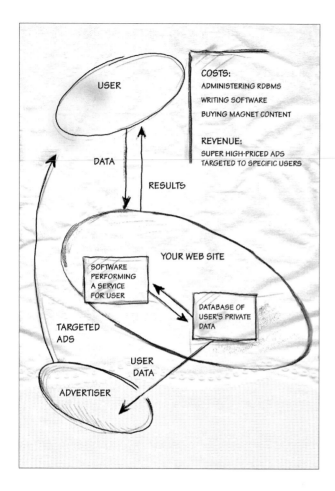

USER

COSTS:
ADMINISTERING RDBMS
WRITING SOFTWARE
BUYING MAGNET CONTENT

REVENUE:
SUPER HIGH-PRICED ADS
TARGETED TO SPECIFIC USERS

DATA

RESULTS

YOUR WEB SITE

SOFTWARE
PERFORMING
A SERVICE
FOR USER

DATABASE OF
USER'S PRIVATE
DATA

TARGETED
ADS

USER
DATA

ADVERTISER

Figure 2-3: Category 3 sites provide a service to the user via a server-side program. For example, suppose that you can convince people to use your server to fill out their income tax returns. Why should they go to the trouble of installing a program on their computer that they are only going to use once? Your Web site is so much more convenient! Meanwhile, as they are filling out their taxes, you are building up a database of information that they would ordinarily be reluctant to give you, such as how much money they made last year. Armed with this information, you can sell very expensive and highly targeted advertising. Did the user make more than $350,000 per year? Rolls-Royce might pay you $10 to show him an ad for the Corniche IV. Did the user cheat on his return? VARIG would probably pay you $25 to run a page with Brazil's extradition laws and fares to Rio.

the computer is seen. In a Category 3 car site, you offered users a new car planning service. You know what kinds of cars they need, their budgets, and where they live. You can charge car manufacturers and local dealerships quite a bit to display banner ads that might tempt particular users. But in a Category 4 site, you know which user is about to drive to which dealer to buy which car with which options. You can demand a commission from the selling dealer. You can charge $50 to a competing dealership to run an ad that says, "Just wait two days and Joe Foobar Toyota will have that same color sedan in stock. The price will be $75 lower and Joe Foobar Toyota is 10 miles closer to your house than the dealer you're planning to buy from."

Let's consider how we'd use these categories to build services for a variety of fields.

Travel example

A lot of money dangles from the travel tree. Vendors and consumers are separated by vast distances and numerous intermediaries. Each intermediary extracts a commission. It is the sum total of those commissions that is potentially available to Web travel sites.

Traditional publishers do their best to capture these commissions with guidebooks, magazines, advertising supplements, and plain old brochures. Despite the vast forests that are chopped down in this valiant attempt, dead-trees publishers aren't satisfying travelers. A subscriber opens a travel magazine and finds the articles either much too long, because he or she isn't planning to visit the city described, or much too short, because he or she has a definite trip planned and is hungry for detail. Travel books are better, though they generally suffer from the "one-voice" problem, and the best-written books usually don't have any pictures because the expense of color printing can't be justified when there aren't any ads.

Traditional travel publishers don't even try to give consumers the most critical information, like, "How did the last 100 people who went there like it?"

An Internet travel site starts off with a huge relevance advantage. Search engines consistently deliver travel URLs to people who are about to book a trip or leave for a destination. No other advertising-carrying medium comes close, except perhaps the airplane and hotel magazines that consumers get after they've started their trip.

The most important Category 1 service for a travel site is magnet content that will attract people to Category 2, 3, and 4 services. You can organize all kinds of Category 2 services around magnet content. For example, suppose that your magnet content in an Italian site says, "I went into the cathedral at Assisi to reload my camera; there were some pictures on the walls. I think somebody next to me said they were painted by a guy named Joe." Somewhere out there on the Net there is a guy who did his art history Ph.D. on those frescoes by Giotto. Your magnet content's function is to draw that expert into surfing your site and contributing a few paragraphs via your comment server.

You will also want to have classified ads for vacation homes and tour packages, Q&A forums, and a quality rating system for tour operators and hotels. What makes all this more useful than rec.travel.europe is that the magnet content gives structure to the user-contributed thoughts.

Check out *http://photo.net/webtravel/* for a glimpse at my idea of what a Category 1 and 2 travel Web site should be like.

The obvious Category 3 service for a travel site is a trip planning system. Your database will know where the consumer intends to be at every hour of every day of his trip. With that kind of information about your readers, if you can't sell high-priced ads for delivery to specific people, it won't be my fault!

Figure 2-4: Category 4 sites define a standard for cooperation among databases and then let users seamlessly query them all. Just about every bank has a computer database of the interest rate it pays on a certificate of deposit. But these data are not in any standard form. You engineer a standard that lets bank computers tell your Web server what CDs are available and at what rate. Then when a consumer visits your site and indicates an interest in six-month CDs, your server can display a list of the banks, ordered by interest rate offered. If the consumer clicks through to a bank and buys a CD, you collect a commission.

The obvious Category 4 application is a hotel room booking system. Your server queries all the hotel reservation computers and the consumer can query you: "Show me the available hotel rooms in Paris for September 15th to 20th, sorted by distance from the Louvre and then by price. Oh, and convert the prices to U.S. dollars, please."

Real estate example

Real estate agents in the United States collect a 6 percent commission every time they connect buyer and seller. This leads to musings like, "Why does New York have so much garbage and Los Angeles so many real estate agents?" Standard answer: "Because New York had first choice." This kind of humor would hurt realtors' feelings if they weren't raking in $142 billion each year (source: 1992 Census).

Realtors are precisely the sorts of intermediaries that Internet technology is supposed to eliminate. If you were trying to capture a share of this $142 billion, you'd want to start in Category 1 with articles about moving or character sketches for neighborhoods. This content would attract search engine users. Moving into Category 2, you'd run a commission-based classified ad system to connect renters with landlords and buyers with sellers. For a Category 3 service, perhaps you could create a moving planner. You'd get the old address, the new address, and the moving date from the user. You could use these data to help the user disconnect and hook up utilities, compute cost-of-living differences, and arrange travel. Meanwhile, you'd be bombarding the person with ads from competing communications, furniture, and appliance vendors in the new locale. For a Category 4 application, you'd cut deals with other real estate sites to query their databases. If a user made a transaction on that foreign site, you'd split the commissions.

Medical example

Joe Schmoe is treated at five different hospitals over a three-year period. Each hospital has a sophisticated computer medical record system. When Mr. Schmoe visits hospital number six, the clerks create a record for him on *their* big database. But even though Joe's entire medical record is available in electronic form, the new hospital has no way to import it from the previous five hospitals. So the doctors don't realize that Joe is allergic to an obscure drug. Joe dies.

You could have saved Joe's life. You could have built a Web site where Joe can store and control his own medical record. When he goes to a new hospital, he can authorize the staff to retrieve portions of his record and to store their findings back on his personal server. Then when Joe has an accident while traveling and is rushed to a Parisian hospital, the doctors there can download his record and find out just which drugs will provoke a life-threatening allergic reaction.

This is a Category 4 site with a vengeance. All of the challenge is in figuring out how to make disparate databases talk to each other. The data models on the hospital systems can be radically different. Even trivial differences, such as different abbreviations for the same disease, can prevent databases from understanding each other. You have to find a way to get these databases to cooperate, even though they were never designed to do that.

Big companies do this all the time, of course. They'll decide that starting July 1, everyone is moving to the big, new central database system and everyone will use the same part number for a number 8 machine screw. They have the money, resources, and authority to make this happen. On the Internet, there are many more organizations who could benefit from data exchange, but there is much less trust, less money, and no central authority. This creates a huge technical challenge to figure out a cheap automated or semiautomated method of integrating databases (see Chapter 17, A Future So Bright You'll Need to Wear Sunglasses).

That's a whirlwind tour of the four ways to break down consumer Web services. Assuming you run with one of my ideas or come up with a great one of your own, then you'll be on your way to achieving the Holy Grail of the Web: traffic.

We Lose Money on Every Hit, But Make It Up on Volume

If nobody ever visits your site, then you won't make any money. Advertisers don't like to place ads where nobody will see them. You can't sell stuff to nobody. Collecting a middleman's commission on no transactions is not very attractive. If you have visitors, then at least you have a chance to make money, even if you didn't have a specific plan when you set up the site.

Internet commerce is the most obvious method of making money from a popular site, but it may not be the best. Internet commerce appeals deceptively to a particularly male fantasy. Guys like the idea that after a short initial period of programming, a computer will tirelessly slave away for them, making them money 24 hours a day. Set up the site, walk away, and watch the money pile up in your bank account.

You can feed this fantasy by reading articles in the business press about *http://amazon.com,* the perennial poster child for Internet commerce. They set up what is essentially a front end to a wholesale book distributor's database, and now they are selling books every few seconds. It sounds like they are rolling in money.

Well, it turns out that I know some people who work at amazon.com. The customers don't always fill out the forms exactly right. The books aren't always in stock like they should be. The customers send email asking when their books are going to be shipped. So instead of one Unix box and a big vault for the cash, the company has hundreds of employees sucking all the money out of it (they lost $34 million on $307 million in sales during the 12 months ending June 1998, according to *quote.yahoo.com*). And remember, this is the best that anyone has really done: high expenses and high sales. More typical is an Internet store with high expenses and low or no sales.

So did the Amazon founders lose their shirts? Uh, not exactly. In fact, as of July 30, 1998, the company had a market capitalization of $5.3 billion. Does that mean investors are idiots and will buy any stock with an Internet angle? Maybe. Amazon isn't worth buying for its unique technology. The MIT Press Web site (*mitpress.mit.edu*) is functionally similar and was built by two programmers in a few weeks.

The MIT Press site publishes a catalog from a database table. There is a full-text search engine through titles, author names, and book descriptions. Readers can place public comments on any book. The software can collect reader orders on a secure server. It can collect names and addresses of readers who are interested in particular books or categories of books. There is a back-end admin interface so that the MIT Press staff can view or spam their customer list. The cost for programming the core site was $9000 (see Chapter 14, ecommerce, for more on this experience). In an efficient world, the management of Barnes & Noble and Borders would have surfed the

Amazon site early in 1995, had clone sites up on the Web by July 1995, and put Amazon out of business by December 1995.

How can the investors who bid Amazon up to $5.3 billion possibly make money? It took more than three years for Borders to put up a Web site with online ordering. The nimbler management of Barnes & Noble was able to clone amazon.com in just 30 months, but they forgot to include any provision for capturing the voices of readers, the key thing that an Internet site can do better than a physical bookstore.

Look at the Amazon page for the first edition of this book, *Database Backed Web Sites,* which has Macmillan's marketing copy, written by someone who never read the book. The page has my own comment on the book. I'm not sure if it is more effective than Macmillan's marketing copy, but at least it was written by someone familiar with the contents. It has 37 reviews contributed by readers (my favorites are always the negative ones, for example, "The author is certainly a knowledgeable person and does a good job telling you what's wrong with the current tools. Unfortunately, he doesn't tell you how to fix them"). They have an interview with me. They have all of this stuff because they spent some time programming their Oracle system. Now they can just sit back and let content accumulate.

Contrast the Amazon page with the page at *http://www.barnesandnoble.com.* In their site's first incarnation, Barnes & Noble had the title, the author name, the price, and a scan of the jacket. It was inconceivable to me that anyone would buy the book from its site. The saddest thing about the Barnes & Noble site was that B&N had swallowed whole a dollop of MIT Media Lab hype and bought the Firefly system, an approach to personalization whose naivete is discussed in Chapter 9, User Tracking. Amazon cleverly queries their database to figure out that buyers of Book A also bought Book B, and therefore if buyers are interested in A, then they should probably look at B.

Note: I went over to the Barnes & Noble site in January 1998 to make sure that I wasn't being unfair. I laboriously registered to become part of their community and then submitted to the Firefly system's questions. I said I was interested in Fiction and Literature. Here are some examples of Fiction and Literature, according to the B&N site: *Letters to Penthouse V* (Penthouse Magazine), *100 Best Careers: Writers and Authors* (no author cited; dead link from title), *There and Back Again: The Map of the Hobbit* (Brian Sibley, no description), but according to Amazon it's, "The companion map to the highly successful *The Map of Tolkien's Middle Earth,* this beautifully designed and annotated, full-color, 30" × 28" map of the lands of the Hobbit describes important areas and highlights the fascinating topography necessary for a complete understanding of Tolkien's books"). MIT Media Lab technology working for me!

Why is so much money and effort being put behind online bookstores? The idea of people using our vast, modern computing system to purchase information that is finally mailed to them in a fifteenth-century form is kind of absurd. Yet amazon.com's sales are tripling every year. One thing that makes online bookselling work is that books are the ultimate commodity. If you know the ISBN of a book, you know exactly what you're going to get, right down to the binding. Furthermore, there is nothing so great about the average physical bookstore, which is generally stocked with the books that publishers think you need and the marketing copy that publishers want you to have (mostly on book jackets). At amazon.com, they have their finger much more directly on the pulse of the market. They can quickly feature books that readers say they need. Amazon has the publishers' marketing copy but, much more importantly, it has become the de facto repository for actual consumer experience with books. Even people who read my old book online or bought a copy at a local, physical bookstore went to the Amazon site to place their comments. You'd think that the natural respository would have been my own blurb server, associated with the cover page for the online edition (*http://photo.net/wtr/dead-trees/*). However, for some reason, people preferred to leave their comments with Amazon.

WE LOSE MONEY ON EVERY HIT BUT GET SOME KICKBACKS FROM OTHER GUYS WHO LOSE MONEY TOO

Another thing that makes amazon.com interesting as an ecommerce case study is that they pioneered the payment of referral fees. If a reader clicked from your site to Amazon and he bought something, Amazon would kick back a commission to you. This should be encouraging to publishers of deep content. Instead of tarting up your site with banner ads, just put in a few discreet links to transactional commercial sites.

You become an "Amazon.com Associate" by adding encoded links from your pages to Amazon's. In my case, I could go through *http://photo.net/photo* and replace every occurrence of

```
You should check the Kodak Professional Photoguide
```

with

```
You should check the
<a href="http://www.amazon.com/exec/obidos/ISBN=0879857986/photonetA/">
Kodak Professional Photoguide</a>
```

When a user clicks on the link, he is presented with an order form from amazon.com. Should he complete the order, Amazon theoretically will kick back to me some percentage of the price of the book. In a perfectly competitive, commodified environment, the owner of the reader (me) would eventually capture all of the profit to be derived from the book sale. Assume there is a $10 profit in selling someone a book. If Amazon was paying me $3 a transaction when altbookstore.com offered me $5 a transaction, I'd write a Perl script to grind over my .html pages to change all of the Amazon references to altbookstore references. If books.com were to then offer me $7 a transaction, I'd run the Perl script again to retarget the links to books.com. Eventually, I'd be getting almost all of the $10 in profit, and the online bookstore would be just barely able to pay for their network connections.

How does all of this work in practice? In 1996, I set up links from my site to Amazon and Computer Literacy, asking them to write referral fee checks payable to Angell Memorial Animal Hospital (see *http://photo.net/photo/donationlist.html* for the story behind the choice of this charity). It turned out that just as our tangible economy isn't perfectly competitive, neither is the Internet economy. Computer Literacy's pages were barren of content, their brand name recognition was low, and I suspect that most of my readers eventually bought a book from Amazon and therefore their browsers got persistently cookied for 1-click ordering from Amazon. Amazon sales were 5 or 10 times better than Computer Literacy's when links were placed in parallel.

The process by which sales and referrals grew was interesting. I'm maintaining an archive of selected Amazon reports at *http://photo.net/wtr/thebook/amazon/* and invite you to check it periodically. Here's a summary of what happened:

Week Ending	Clickthroughs	Sales	Referral Fee
September 28, 1996	2,872	3	$ 5.76
May 3, 1997	1,943	10	$32.57
July 25, 1998	1,829	17	$82.56

The first thing to observe is that this is a much more cost-effective way for Amazon to get customers than buying banner advertisements, which typically cost several dollars for each person delivered to a site. Even in the most expensive week, Amazon's cost per clickthrough is 4.5 cents.

The second thing to observe is that the trend is positive. Though users aren't clicking through to Amazon much more than they did, the dogs at Angell are getting more money. Partly this is because amazon.com has changed its policies. They used to exclude books purchased that referring sites didn't recommend, books purchased that referring sites recommended but that weren't purchased on the very first click, or books purchased that referring sites recommended but that were hard for them to get. Gradually, they've expanded their commision payment scheme, but it might also be that consumers are buying more impulsively online now that they are used to Internet shopping and now that their browsers are cookied out for 1-click ordering.

A third thing to observe is that you have to trust your referral partner. A publisher could use my clickthrough.net system (see *http://photo.net/philg/services.html*)

to verify Amazon's clickthrough count, but there is really no way to know whether Amazon is telling the truth about how many readers are actually buying. Here's a sequence of stats from Amazon that don't look quite right to me:

Week Ending	Clickthroughs	Sales	Referral Fee
November 22, 1997	3,768	24	$ 75.26
November 29, 1997	2,934	17	$ 58.39
December 6, 1997	2,356	0	$ 0.00
December 13, 1997	3,177	2	$ 5.99
December 20, 1997	3,772	0	$ 0.00
December 27, 1997	2,619	2	$ 7.19
January 3, 1998	3,079	67	$183.54
January 11, 1998	3,855	36	$128.93
January 17, 1998	4,021	32	$ 84.49
January 24, 1998	3,933	17	$ 61.30

Had the entire Internet visited *www.adbusters.org,* absorbed its anticonsumerist message, and resolved to purchase nothing through the Christmas season? Was the Christmas shopping volume too taxing for Amazon's Oracle database administrators and programmers? Was Amazon trying to cheat the dogs at Angell? I'll never know for sure.

Note: Another interesting amazon.com anecdote relates to the very book that you are reading now. I contributed an author review saying what I thought was good about the new book, closing with a note that the full-text was available at *http://photo.net/wtr/thebook/.* Amazon posted the review a couple of days later, but with the final paragraph removed. So instead of me burnishing my public image as a generous person happy to share his ideas with those too poor to pay $45, it looked like I was running a scheme with Amazon to bilk the clueless who stumbled on the Amazon page without realizing that they could read the thing for free online. I complained to Amazon about the removal and about their completely transforming my words without asking my permission, but they refused to restore the paragraph offering readers the opportunity to read (or at least examine) the book for free.

My Site, the Cash Cow

```
Date: Wed, 29 Jul 1998 16:05:37 -0700 (PDT)
From: "Joe Business Genius" <genius7529@aol.com>
To: philg@MIT.EDU
Subject: promoting photo.net

Your photo.net site looks pretty good.  I can sell banner ads on your
site and split the revenue with you.  ...
```

Part of the reason that I'm able to answer all of my email is that I read it in Emacs, a programmable text editor. With a couple of lines of Lisp code, I was able to program a two-keystroke shortcut response to such questions:

```
Thank you for an interesting idea.  Before taking my site out of MIT
Net and making it commercial, I'd like to see a more fully developed
business plan.  Here's a statement of expenses and revenue for my site
today.  Perhaps you can complete it for me by adding the new revenue
sources that you envision.  Then let's see how much profit there
actually is.

Capital Expenses
----------------
Hewlett Packard K460 server:      $500,000
(incl. 36 disk drives, 4 GB
of RAM, 4 CPUs)
Sun Microsystems E5000 server:    $150,000
(incl. 4 CPUs, 1.25 GB of RAM,
14 disk drives)
Quad PentiumPro server:            $25,000
(incl. 8 disk drives)
Oracle RDBMS 4-CPU license
with ConText Option for K460:     $500,000
Oracle RDBMS 4-CPU license
with ConText Option for E5000:    $500,000

Operating Expenses
------------------
HP K460 service contract:          $38,000/year
Sun E5000 service contract:        $15,000/year
Oracle support:                   $200,000/year
10 Mbit network connection:       $120,000/year
Unix system administrator:        $100,000/year
(including benefits, overhead)
Oracle db administrator:          $100,000/year
Web programmer:                   $100,000/year

Revenue
-------
amazon.com referral fees:           $3,000/year
(currently donated to charity)
orders for prints                  $10,000/year
(currently donated to charity)

I look forward to your reply.
```

A Surefire Way to Make Money (for Other People)

Actually, photo.net *does* make a lot of money. I just don't get any of it. The manager of the Hotel Milvia in Costa Rica tells me that his nine-room hotel gets two or three bookings a week because of a recommendation in *http://photo.net/cr/*. B&H Photo is mentioned in *http://photo.net/photo/* as a good place to buy a camera. The clickthrough server reports that 150 to 250 people *per day* are following the link from my site to theirs.

I suppose the lesson here is that it is easy to sell people what they already want. People who read my Costa Rica story are about to go to Costa Rica. People who read the photo.net "where to buy a camera" page are very likely about to buy a camera.

A Final Plea for those with Public Sites

If your tastes in hardware aren't as luxurious as mine or you can fleece some naive investors into buying shares in an initial public offering, I suppose that it is possible to make money with what might otherwise be a personal Web site. But before you build your site, take a moment to think about the things that you went into because you thought you could make money. How many of them proved satisfying in the long run? How many actually made money?

You could start your Web site by asking, "What can I get from this right now?" Alternatively, you could start out by asking, "What can I give people?" I expect that in the long run, you'd be about equally likely to make money with either approach. I started with the latter.

I gave away my pictures. I gave away my stories. I gave away to "competitors" my advice and software. The Web gave me back a large and growing audience for my work. The Web gave me back some money, to be sure. But I actually do place a higher value on some of the email that I've gotten:

> *Thanks for getting me thru some sloooow weekends at work.... I have been working all the holiday weekends here at Directory Assistance & I wouldn't have made it out alive without your book. Thanks for sharing.*
>
> —Mary in Wisconsin

> *I love your book for two reasons. First, it's great, the story is fresh and honest. The second is of course that it is the kind of thing that this technology has been building for—it somehow makes all those millions of dollars spent on computers, on the Net, on decades of development seem like there might have been a reason for it all. Thanks for the warm glow.*
>
> —Jonathan in New Zealand

Let's Get Real

As my partner Jin says, "Get with the 90s, Philip; they're almost over." Poverty sucks. If you claim to be an expert on modern information systems and you aren't rich, then most people will infer that you are stupid.

Why then do so many Internet entrepreneurs, amply stocked with greed and capital, fall flat? They are going after discretionary time and discretionary dollars. For example, a lot of people want to get rich by entertaining folks over the Internet. Step back and think for a moment. How much money did you spend on CDs, video rentals, and movies last year? How much did you spend on your car?

In a calendar year, America's entire recorded music industry has revenues roughly equal to one month's sales by IBM. I guess we can be proud of our cultural exports, but we'd make more money if we figured out ways to help people in other countries get to work and accomplish their tasks once at work.

What about desperately going after shoppers? Since people are spending money while they shop, it seems natural to hope that you can get a slice. The success of amazon.com and computer parts vendors demonstrates that selling physical objects over the Internet works pretty well if (1) the user already wants exactly what you have, such as "a copy of *The Marriage of Cadmus and Harmony* to be shipped to a friend in Greece, or "a Seagate 23 GB 3.5-inch SCSI hard drive with SCA connector"; (2) the item is a commodity and doesn't need to be physically inspected before purchase; (3) the item is kind of painful to find and buy at a traditional shop; and (4) it is easy for the consumer to find you online, with AltaVista, for instance.

Unfortunately, there are millions of other people thinking exactly the way you do. Economists can demonstrate that under perfect competition no vendor will earn more than an average return on investment. Unless you can rely on all one million of your competitors being incompetent, you won't be doing much better than the S&P 500.

If I wanted to get rich, I'd figure out a way to capture people during the time they spend in Microsoft Office rather than during the time they spend reading the newspaper or shopping.

Friends of Mine Who Will Be Way Rich

My head is full of great ideas for getting rich by applying Internet technology. Unfortunately, I didn't think of any of them. My friend Brian was the tenth employee at a company that builds a system to automate the workflow of corporate purchasing. Big companies use Brian's software to formalize all their rules for who has authority to buy how much and what the chain of approval must be. Then an employee can go to a Web page and click on a new computer that he would like for his desktop. If he has authority to purchase an item of this cost, the order gets pumped into the company's purchasing system (e.g., SAP). If an order of this cost must be approved by two levels of management, the relevant people are alerted to come to their Web browsers and approve or deny the request. A basic version of a system like this is easier to build than most of the public Web services described in this book. Ariba's prices for an intranet installation start at $1 million. Their customers so far? Bristol-Meyers, Chevron, Cisco, FedEx (according to *www.ariba.com* on August 1998).

Brian is going to get rich because Ariba Technologies watched for a bunch of corporate employees standing around doing something inefficiently. The guys at Savera (*www.savera.com*) are going to get rich because they watched for a bunch of corporate employees doing something that they shouldn't be doing at all.

Suppose that you run a telephone company. You need software to keep track of your customers and how many calls they've made, and whether they've paid their last few bills. You need software to generate monthly bills. You need software for your customer service folks to use when people call and say, "I didn't make that call to Mongolia, please remove it from my bill."

Can you buy a good off-the-shelf package to do all of these things? No. You have to hire a bunch of programmers and wait until they implement these functions, then suffer along with your customers as those programmers fix their bugs over the next decade. How much will this cost you? Phone companies spend about $12 billion every year on this kind of information system.

The biggest reason that there isn't a mature market for turnkey phone-company-in-a-box software is that, for so many years, telcos were monopolies. Would you want to write a software product for which AT&T was the only potential customer?

With deregulation, somewhere in the world at least one telephone, cellular phone, or cable TV company starts up every week. Savera is building a packaged application that can get these guys operational in less time than it might take them to figure out what brand of computer to purchase. To established companies, Savera can ask the question, "Why are you paying 100 programmers to nurse along the bugs in your legacy system when we have this whizzy packaged application? Customers will be able to get to their accounts from any Web browser. Your customer service folks can toss their desktop applications and just use a browser also."

HOW TO GET SORT OF RICH

You like these cars? You like these beautiful women? They can be yours!...
Come to my seminar ... you have nothing to lose...."

This is the point in the infomercial where Tom Vu drives out in his Rolls-Royce. What's my plan for getting sort of rich? Consulting.

Oddly enough, I didn't go into consulting to make money. I went into it because the MIT computer science labs didn't have the equipment to support my research.

This seems surprising if you recall that MIT, Stanford, and Carnegie Mellon had state-of-the-art computing facilities as recently as the mid-1980s.

A tenured computer science professor these days generally wants to do the following things:

- Write technical papers and progress reports for federal agencies that give him $1 million research grants.

- Teach students who pay $150,000 and physically show up on campus.

- Teach people who purchase his book in a bookstore.

It turns out that you don't need modern computing systems to do these things. Since you're working alone on monolithic documents, you don't need relational database management systems, the building blocks of current corporate information systems. Since you have airplanes to bring students to your classrooms and trucks to take your books to bookstores, you don't need the Internet. All of the problems faced by a computer science academic in 1998 were nicely solved by the desktop tools perfected at Xerox PARC in 1975. The killer application for a computer science professor is Microsoft Word.

Wait a minute. Wasn't the World Wide Web developed by academics interested in sharing research results? Yes. By particle physicists. Physics is a science. You don't want to spend a year with your head underneath a linear accelerator discovering a particle that someone else already discovered. Thus, you must keep current with research done at other institutions. Thomas Kuhn, author of *The Structure of Scientific Revolutions,* would have called computer science pre-paradigmatic. Since we don't agree on enough fundamentals, it isn't possible to make progress with papers describing incremental discoveries. Progress in computer science is made with the distribution of revolutionary software systems and the publication of revolutionary books. We don't need a fancy information system to alert us to these grand events; they will hit us in the face.

Another good excuse for ignoring the literature is that, since everyone has strong beliefs about fundamentals, but can't support those beliefs rationally or consistently convince nonbelievers, computer science is actually a religion. The people at Stanford are heretics; why would we want to read what they have to say?

The bottom line: When I proposed that our lab move into the 1970s and hire a part-time relational database administrator so that researchers could build Web applications, the senior faculty responded, "Why do we need a database management system? We don't have any data."

I didn't want to take on the thankless and difficult job of maintaining a reliable Oracle database server myself, so I started teaming up with companies who were interested in Web-based collaboration software. They got to use my code, they paid me some money, I got to use their modern computing infrastructure for experiments.

In the software development world, it turns out that finishing a project on schedule or under budget is so rare that if you do it even once, your (big, rich *Fortune 500*) customer will tell all of his (big, rich *Fortune 500*) friends. People were offering me $250 an hour and I had to turn them down because there simply weren't enough hours in the day. In early 1997, I looked around at my friends and realized, hey, all of these people are nerds. Any of them could learn to do what I was doing, and then they could make $250 an hour, too. Between my site and the book that Macmillan was about to publish (*Database Backed Web Sites*), I figured that I had enough marketing exposure to generate work for four or five full-time consultants. But what was the point in having a company? Why not just work as individual consultants? I came up with the following reasons for banding together:

- We can do better, bigger sites that have more impact on the world.

- We can share the responsibility for maintaining a server and an RDBMS.

- We can convince people to hire us for larger jobs and hosting; customers have to know that Philip can cover for Ben or Jin can cover for Philip.

- We can support each other with complementary expertise; for example, Ulla knows a lot about design but nothing about how long it will take an Oracle server to handle a particular query. We want her to be able to draw on any of the techier people without the customer needing to know or hire someone else.

- We can share the work and PR that is brought in by all the Web/db tutorial content on the photo.net site.

- We can go on vacation for a few weeks without calling in every day to make sure that a server hasn't melted.

- We can develop a great toolbox, a kind of "SAP for the Web" (see Chapter 3, Scalable Systems for Online Communities), that we can give away or sell.

Terence already owned the arsdigita.com domain, a pun on the fourteenth-century musical period, Ars Nova, that nobody seems to appreciate, so we decided to call ourselves ArsDigita and lifted a motto from Brancusi: "Create like a God, Command like a King, Work like a Slave."

One of the great things about startup companies is that you can debate how to split up money that you haven't seen and probably never will. Here's what we decided:

We do not skim money from each other. The ArsDigita name, server, and reputation are available to all members equally. If an ArsDigita member does a complete project by him or herself, then all the money goes to that member. If N people work together on a project and all contribute equally, then the revenue for that project is split equally.

We needed a bit of capital to purchase servers, software, and bandwidth, plus the usual accounting and legal overhead for a small company. Since I was already sort of rich and the goal was to make my friends richer, I decided to just pay for these out of my own pocket.

Note:
By the time this
book went to press,
ArsDigita had grown
to $2 million per year
in revenue; rented
1,800 square feet
of office space,
and acquired a fax
machine.

How has it worked out? After a year and a half, with most of us working only part time, we're up to about $1 million a year in revenue. That might not sound impressive, but consider that we have no office, no phone line, and no fax machine, and have had less than $30,000 in capital, legal, and accounting expenses. More importantly, we have no sales force, no marketing department, no advertising, no brochures, no business cards, no letterhead, no press releases, no corporate communications department. We have no clerical, administrative, or purchasing staff.

It looks as though every ArsDigita software developer who is willing to work full time will grow into a $500,000 a year job. Yet, paradoxically, we're usually able to build a working Web service at a much lower cost than other software consulting firms.

The first reason we end up being cheap is that we never take any technology risk. We ignore press releases from Web technology startups. We ignore Windows NT. We use the same relational database management system and operating system that we were using to build sites in 1994 (Oracle on Unix). We use the same Web server that we've been using to build sites since 1995 (AOLserver, which America Online uses to answer several hundred million requests a day). We have done so many sites by now that we can almost always cut and paste ideas, approaches, and code fragments from previous projects.

The second reason we can be cheap is that we don't waste time setting up new systems. We like to build a new Web service on top of an already running Web/RDBMS server. This, plus our extensive toolkit, lets us get up and running with a prototype within a few days, before most Web developers would have figured out how to install the relational database management system.

The third reason that we can be cheap is that we can do any project with a team of two or three programmers. There are two basic approaches to successful software development. If you have mediocre programmers, you need to have lots of them. If you have lots of people working on a project, you need first-rate management practices to keep the programmers coordinated and on schedule. One problem with this approach is that there is a limit to how responsive a team of 100 people can be. They might be able to build an impressive site, but it will take them three months just to get organized. Another problem is that specifications have to go from the customer through a layer or two of management before reaching a programmer. This costs time and money and may result in the specification being corrupted. The second basic approach to successful software development is to have really good programmers and second-rate management. With only a few people on the team, they can all work together in one office and holler out design changes. The customer can show up in that office and tell the programmers what is needed. A request to change a live ecommerce site can be handled immediately by a programmer who leaves behind a comment in the Web server script and a note in the core design document.

Which approach did ArsDigita take? Given that our management skills are nil and our management staff is nil, we're more or less forced to take the second approach: great programmers, bad management.

What's the problem with this approach? It doesn't scale. I brought in Ben, my top student from the MIT intro computer science section that I taught in 1995. In fact, he was the top student out of 400 people who took the class that term. That's great for Ben and great for ArsDigita today, but where does it leave ArsDigita tomorrow when we need more programmer power? There aren't too many more people like him and most of them already have jobs that they like.

What's wrong with not being able to scale? The only people who can afford to pay $250 an hour are groups within big companies or well-capitalized startup companies with good ideas. Groups within big companies talk to other groups. Startup companies grow. Everyone for whom we've ever built a site now wants us to build three more, and we don't have the time or nerdpower.

We'll also need to scale up if we want to stop our friends who've taken their companies public from laughing at us: "You can't go public if you can't demonstrate that your business has the potential to grow to $100 million in revenue."

Growing ArsDigita the easy way: Skim

We can just bring in more people. Here's a message from a friend of a friend who wants to join ArsDigita:

> ** long list of accomplishments as Web developer **
>
> . . .
>
> So, now that I've extolled my virtues, you might wonder why I am not a zillion-aire myself! I guess I've always focused more on my work instead of selling myself or searching for really high-profile clients. . . . one of the things the company could provide me is the services of Phil Greenspun, web superstar, who can seemingly drum up business without breaking a sweat. . . .

With our no-skimming philosophy, note that this is a proposal that I act as unpaid salesman, invoicer, and check writer for someone who doesn't even know me well enough to realize that I go by "Philip" rather than "Phil"!

"Skim, skim, skim!" my friends say. "You should take something for getting work for these guys."

First, I don't want to spend more time selling, invoicing, and writing checks, even if I get paid for it. I want to spend time creating interesting Web services and documents. Second, even if I wanted to get paid for doing business-y stuff, skimming becomes a slippery slope. This guy is currently earning $30 an hour and I know I can bill him out at $125. Should I take 10 percent? That's more than fair. He'd be earning $80 an hour more than if he were on his own. Now that I think

about it, I could skim 30 percent. He'd still be making twice what he's actually worth in the marketplace . . . .

Eventually, I'm skimming 50 or 70 percent and ArsDigita becomes just like any other contract software shop: a bunch of losers who can't program because the people who could all quit to work independently, plus one guy who used to know how to program but can't anymore because he's trying to whip the losers and mollify the customers.

That's nothing to be proud of.

Growing ArsDigita the annoying way: Sell software

We give away our best software to thousands of Web developers and publishers every year. We could instead put our toolkit in a fancy "WebWare 2000" package, stick a $50,000 price tag on it, sell four copies to big companies, and go public on the strength of a fanciful spreadsheet. Then we could use the money from the public offering to hire a full staff of management, HR, PR, support folks, testers, programmers, and so on.

We never considered this idea. Trying to fleece customers, venture capitalists, investment bankers, and the public is a wearisome activity. Witholding our toolkit from the world wouldn't bring us more business, since we couldn't possibly grow large enough to support more than a tiny fraction of people developing Web sites. Finally, there was a pretty good chance that the whole company would tank, which is kind of pathetic considering that we each could have made $500,000 a year risk free, making customers happy rather than investors miserable.

Growing ArsDigita the sustainable way: Teams

In less time than it took me to write this book, my friend Rajeev managed to start and finish an MIT Ph.D. thesis, start a company and sell it to Microsoft, and get engaged to the perfect woman.

I think the only reason that he still talks to an underachiever like me is that walking the dog around campus with me gives him a chance to duck into Toscannini's for ice cream, normally forbidden him by his fashionably thin fiancée.

We were walking over to the Student Center one night when Rajeev said, "Teams. That's how you take ArsDigita public."

Rajeev's central idea is that we grow the company by building independent teams of developers. Each team is four or five people. These teams can locate themselves in any city where a team leader wishes to live. Half of the revenue collected by a team goes to the central company and the other half to the team members themselves.

We classify each team member as either an Apprentice, Developer, or Team Leader. After each project, the apprentice and his or her coworkers on the team decide whether or not the new person should continue as a team member. Thus, the company never bears "the bozo risk" for more than one project.

After one year, an apprentice can graduate to developer. This status brings with it the responsibility to train new apprentices, take ownership of large portions of a project, and make commitments to customers.

After one year as a developer, a person can, but will not necessarily, move into team leadership. Note that the ability to be a team leader does not mean that one will always be functioning as such. The actual leadership role is assigned per project. A very difficult project might have three people qualified to be team leaders, plus two developers (and zero apprentices).

Nobody who hasn't personally built several high-volume DB-backed sites with our toolkit can join ArsDigita as a team leader. This is insurance against delivering sites that fall below our standards.

Recall that the teams are coughing up half their revenue to the core organization. What does this core do?

- maintains the canonical version of the ArsDigita Community System with a team of great programmers who merge enhancements contributed by all the teams (and external users of the software) into new versions of the software

- runs training classes for new employees and customers

- takes a leading role in operating free public services that demonstrate our ideas and technology

- runs the Unix and Oracle servers that are the backbone of the business

- bills customers

- certifies and decertifies team leaders

The core organization is not responsible for marketing, sales, or approving contracts. Every team is expected to develop a worldwide reputation for excellence and take primary responsibility for feeding themselves.

How fast can an organization like this grow? We assume that each four-person team can bill approximately $1,000 an hour and bill 2,000 hours per year, for a total of $2 million a year per team. Assume that each team of four people grows into four teams of four after two years (i.e., the company doubles every year). We have enough people for two teams right now. We could therefore have eight teams in two years. That's $16 million in annual revenue. Pathetic by real company standards, but it would actually make us one of the more successful Internet startups.

Could ArsDigita grow faster? Sure, but it would be hard work. There is a natural growth rate for a company like this. The more people we have, the easier it is to recruit new ones, since each employee has friends. The more projects we've done, the easier it is to sell new ones, since our clients will recommend us to potential customers. Forcing the company onto a steeper growth curve would cost a lot of time, money, and effort. It is also pointless. The world is not suddenly going to become filled with expert, well-managed Web/DB developers.

What did we decide?

We haven't decided. We're reasonably happy with the work that we're doing now, which is always interesting and varied. Some of it brings us lots of cash (see Chapter 14, ecommerce). Some of it is lots of fun (see Chapter 16, Better Living through Chemistry). We give away what we think are useful ideas, services, and software.

The most attractive thing about the team business plan is having the core group of developers improving the community system that we use internally as a toolkit, and distribute externally as a .tar file. The least attractive thing is having either to manage the business or to turn it over to managers who wouldn't run things "our way."

Note that one feature of the team business plan is that every reader of this book can execute it without reducing ArsDigita's (or each other's) profits. When I lived in Silicon Valley, my friends all went off to work at startup companies with business plans so great they had to be kept secret. I never found out how any of them were planning to get rich until after their companies went bankrupt. Looking back, I'm surprised that I didn't see the folly of the top secret business plan. How could it be reasonable to base all of your hopes and your family's financial future on the assumption that nobody would find out what you were doing? My personal metric for every project now is: If I give this idea away to 100,000 people on my Web site and they all run with it, is it still worth doing?

Under the giveaway free metric, it is still worth writing a novel. Even if everyone agrees that *Gone with the Wind* was the greatest novel ever written, they can't just read it over and over. Some of them will have to read *Lives of the Monster Dogs* (Bakis, 1997; Farrar Strauss & Giroux). It is still worth making a movie or a Web site. It is not worth making a word processor or an operating system. There is only going to be room for one or two of those in the market. That turned out great for Bill Gates, of course, but not for the 10,000 other people who were contemporaneously working on operating systems and word processors for personal computers.

Summary

Money is the universal language of the 1990s and hence I've felt free to range over disparate topics in this chapter. Here's what I hope you take away:

- The Web is a powerful medium for personal expression, for sharing knowledge, and for teaching. It has also made a lot of people very wealthy, but that doesn't mean you can get rich by adding banner ads and referral links to what started out as a beautiful noncommercial site.

- If you want to get rich, focus your efforts on building applications for businesses.

- If you are a good information designer or Web/DB developer, you can easily make enough money to live better than 95 percent of Americans, but it is unclear how to make enough to push past an additional 4 percent to become obscenely wealthy.

MORE

- *www.eyescream.com* has some good examples of effective banner ads.

- Read *A Random Walk Down Wall Street* (Malkiel, 1996; W.W. Norton) before investing money in someone else's Internet company (or any stock for that matter).

- If you want to make sure that you don't miss any of the Internet business banalities being ingested by B-school graduates, read *net.gain* (Hagel and Armstrong, 1997; Harvard Business School Press), where a couple of management consultants will tell you how the ultimate way to get rich is to build an online community like photo.net. The authors have so much confidence in the plan they have set forth that they have kept their jobs at McKinsey. *Webonomics: Nine Essential Principles for Growing Your Business on the World Wide Web* (Schwartz, 1997; Broadway Books) is sort of the same idea. Alternatively, check *www.mckinsey.com* to see the best ideas that Corporate America's money can buy.

3

Scalable Systems for
Online Communities

As a society gets richer and better-equipped with machines, people spend less time grubbing out the basics of food and shelter and more time on education. Some of this time is spent in a setting that everyone recognizes as educational, for instance, a college classroom. Most education, however, occurs in nontraditional settings.

Our media does not portray the Michigan Militia (*militia.gen.mi.us*) as a primarily educational institution. Yet a new member must learn where and when to meet, a body of Constitutional law, field communication skills, firearm safety, and marksmanship. To rise in the organization, a member must learn how to lead and educate other members.

Suppose that you decide to adopt a dog. You have to *learn* about the characteristics of different breeds. After choosing a breed, you have to *learn* about good breeders in your region. After choosing a puppy, you have to *learn* about training and *learn* about good vets in your city. You have to *learn* what brand of dog food is best and where to buy it. You have to *learn* where it is safe and legal to let your dog off the leash so that he can

run and play with other dogs. Virtually all of this education will happen through informal contacts with more experienced dog owners, none of whom will set up a classroom or expect to be paid.

If you go to work as a computer programmer in a big company, the more experienced employees will have to *show* you where to find the water cooler, *explain* to you the significance of the project on which you're working, *tell* you how much of the work has been done so far, *teach* you how to use the software development tools, and *demonstrate* the fine points of the relational database management system on which the system you're building relies.

WHAT IS A COMMUNITY?

What common features can we extract from the above examples? A *community* is a group of people with varying degrees of expertise in which the experts attempt to help the novices improve their skills.

This definition embraces the traditional physical university. Professors and Ph.D. students work with undergraduates to help them learn enough to graduate. This definition is not large enough to embrace a physical small town or city neighborhood, which is what most people usually mean when they use the word. Newcomers to a residential community will need to learn how to get to the supermarket, but otherwise are not likely to be pursuing a productive goal in common with other residents.

WHY WOULD WE WANT ONLINE COMMUNITIES?

If you've ever strolled among the beautiful buildings of Oxford or been awed by Manhattan's skyscrapers, you might ask why anyone would want an online community. If we can have the real thing, why settle for an ersatz electronic version?

One answer is that not everyone *can* have the real thing. Many people wish to learn who cannot afford Ivy League tuition. Many people wish to learn who cannot afford to stop working for four years. Many people wish to learn whose responsibilities or disabilities prevent them from traveling to a university campus.

Companies *can* have pretty much whatever they want. Certainly they have plenty of money to build lavish offices. Yet, isn't there something odd about a workaday world at the turn of the millennium that Melville's Bartleby ("Bartleby the Scrivener," 1853) would find utterly familiar? Workers come in from their homes each morning to settle into individual offices, where they find the paper documents necessary for their work. With better technology and management techniques, perhaps it would be possible to benefit from contributions by part-time workers or workers who don't leave their houses. Perhaps projects could be finished sooner by workers cooperating in rooms devoted to the project, rather than isolated in offices mostly devoted to storing paper documents from previously completed projects.

If you still feel that physical communities must always be superior to electronically linked communities, let me ask you to ponder three words: *junior high school.*

Junior high school throws people together who have nothing in common besides parents who chose to locate in a particular neighborhood. Unless you're very adaptable, it is tough to find good friends. High school is more or less the same idea, but the pool of people is usually larger, so it is more probable that kids with uncommon interests will find soul mates. In college, not only is the pool larger, but there can be a concentration by personality type. Nerds find each other at Caltech and MIT; hippies find each other at Bard and Reed; snobs find each other at Harvard and Princeton; skiers find each other at state schools in Colorado and Vermont. When students graduate and go to work, they usually don't make as many friends. They aren't meeting as many people and the common thread of "do not want to starve in street" doesn't tie them very tightly to other workers.

What we can infer from this is that people make the best friends when the pool is large and the interests are common. Enter the Internet, which affords instant communication among millions of people worldwide. It isn't possible to find a pool on a comparable scale except in the world's largest cities. Given the Internet's raw communication capability and huge pool of potential friends, if you want to make a really great friend you just need a means of finding someone who shares your interests and then a means of collaborating with him or her.

To summarize, here are the new things that we can do with online communities:

- We can teach other people without becoming part of a university or secondary school bureaucracy.

- We can teach other people without having to teach full time.

- We can learn without paying $40,000 a year to a college.

- We can learn without quitting our jobs.

- We can learn without leaving our houses.

- We can learn from people who have broader experience than full-time teachers.

- We can work without having to be in the same building.

- We can contribute to a company's or nonprofit organization's projects without having to work full time.

- No matter how unusual our personality or interests, we can make like-minded friends (Rush Limbaugh met his wife on CompuServe.)

Anyway, these are the things we could theoretically do with online communities. In practice, we have to do some programming work first if the communities are to remain useful as they grow. The evolution of public communities is instructive.

EVOLUTION OF PUBLIC COMMUNITIES

The Ancient World. People got information from personal communication and groups meeting face-to-face. The influence of government and commercial interests on information was limited.

The Modern World. With the invention of movable type (popularly credited to Johannes Gutenberg in 1450, whose printing system incorporated a number of practical refinements, but actually Pi Sheng, a Chinese alchemist, was using

movable type in 1041), information became susceptible to government and commercial control. The mass media exclude information that will offend advertisers. Governments have powerful systems with which to distribute propaganda.

The Early Internet. Most of the information that users got from the ARPAnet and early Internet was personal communication. Users got personal email letters, mailing list letters, discussion group postings, documents written by individuals working without a publisher, and computer programs that expressed individual ideas. There was no advertising. There was little or no participation by major commercial interests. People reading a USENET discussion of Chrysler versus Toyota cars would get information from owners and none from the manufacturers.

The Internet Circa 1999. With the Web, the Internet finally became comprehensible to corporate PR departments. The best organized and most heavily used Web services are thoroughly corrupted by banner advertising and kickback

arrangements. Some of the bones of the early Internet are still visible, but they haven't scaled well. In the old days, you could read about Chrysler versus Toyota in the USENET discussion group rec.autos. Now, it isn't really clear where that discussion should go. rec.autos is no longer a group; it is the top of a hierarchy. You could read rec.autos.makers.chrysler, but you might get tired of wading through the 100-plus postings a day, especially as much of it might be spam from auto dealers or spam from generic commercial advertisers ("make money fast"). With nobody to organize the content, it is unlikely to be very useful. You're more likely to do your research at *autos.yahoo.com,* a beautifully organized service, admittedly (I bought my Toyota minivan clicking through from there), but one whose content consists of information from commercial sources punctuated by banner ads.

What do we conclude from these observations? Technology profoundly affects the type of community that can be sustained and the extent to which information flows from few to many or from many to many.

THE BIG PROBLEM

Thousands of people are operating public community–style Web services. Virtually all of them are using simple standalone software packages to handle things like discussion forums or classified ads. When one of these sites becomes popular, the publisher begins to devote 80 hours a week of free labor to moderating discussions, weeding out redundant classified ads, deleting alerts for users whose email addresses have evaporated, answering questions from the confused, keeping content up-to-date, developing new content in response to user questions, and so on. The beautiful thing about this is that so many people are willing to devote 80 unpaid hours a week toward helping their fellow human beings. The ugly thing about this is that 80 hours a week turns out not to be enough.

Site growth can outstrip the capacity of any person, no matter how dedicated or efficient.

One typical reaction on the part of the publisher is to turn the formerly noncommercial site into a showcase for whoredom. Users return to find six banner ads

on the home page and links to kickback-paying referral partners obscuring content that had formerly been highlighted. With all of the money flowing in, at least the publisher's scaling problems are history. More users means more page loads means more banner ads served means more revenue. The publisher can hire a discussion forum moderator and a customer service staff. Money can be used to hire writers and a webmaster to organize their contributions. The content may be bland and tainted by commercial interests, but at least the publisher is making a fat profit.... Oops! In practice, nearly all commercial community site publishers are losing money because the cost per user to maintain the site is too high.

Corporate intranet communities also need to scale. It really would be sad to have to hire a new moderator, webadmin, or sysadmin for every new employee. Yet the intranet community should be as vital as any public community site. If an employee sends another employee private email asking a how-to question, that should be regarded as a failure of the intranet community software. Why wasn't it more efficient for these folks to collaborate using a Web service that would then archive the discussion?

THE BIG SOLUTION

The big solution is a configurable set of software packages that will

1. keep a database of users, how to contact them, and how private they want their personal information kept

2. keep a database of site content, who contributed it, and how each piece relates to the others

3. keep track of which users have looked at which pieces of content

4. keep track of which users are costing the community time and money

5. keep track of how users are coming into the site and which external links they are selecting (clickthroughs)

6. (if a commercial site) keep track of which advertisers' banner ads have been served and to whom and whether or not they were effective

7. help the site maintainers keep in contact with different classes of users

What are some of the ultimate goals of having all of these software packages installed and set up? Here are a few things I'd like to be able to do with it on my personal site:

- If Joe User asks whether he should buy a Nikon F5 or a Canon EOS-1, I want to know whether or not he's read *http://photo.net/photo/what-camera-should-I-buy.html* (requires modules 1 and 3; if it turns out that he's asked this question without bothering to read a reasonable subset of the Canon versus Nikon threads in the Q&A forum or the static content on this subject, then we record that behavior in module 4).

- An expert on photography should be able to come to photo.net, have the system show him the content areas about which users are currently the most confused, and register to write an article on a subject (requires modules 2, 3, and 4).

- Someone contemplating buying a camera from the classified ads (*http://photo.net/gc/domain-top.tcl?domain=photo.net*) should be able to see the ad author's history as a community member, including registration date, previous ads posted by the same person, Q&A forum activity, and comments on static articles.

- Someone who has answered 100 questions in the discussion forums should be automatically put forward for co-moderation status. If the site administrator does not squash the promotion, the user should then be offered the option of weeding out duplicate threads.

A seven-module software system that offers the preceding capabilities is going to be expensive to design, expensive to program, and expensive to maintain. Our new innovative community software system will require an underlying relational database management system that, though not innovative, also tends to be expensive to purchase and maintain (more on that in Chapter 12, Database Management Systems).

Before any Web publisher contemplates running an online community, it is probably worth stepping back to ask which components of the software should be built, which developed cooperatively with other publishers, and which can and should be purchased off the shelf.

BUY OR BUILD?

Someone who wants a community site with at least the basic capabilities above has to do the following:

1. Choose NT or Unix.

2. Choose a relational database management system (RDBMS).

3. Choose a Web/DB integration tool.

4. Write SQL data models.

5. Design a user interface to the legal transactions.

6. Write dynamic pages that pull information out and stuff data into SQL tables (i.e., implement the user interface to the transactions).

Suppose that the new publisher makes all of these decisions correctly. It will still take six months and $500,000 in programmer time to reproduce the community software that I had working at *http://photo.net/photo/* in 1995 (software that scaled reasonably well but not so well that it didn't need a substantial rewrite in 1998). In fact, in terms of management attention, hourly wages, and lost time to market, it generally costs at least $100,000 just to make the operating system/RDBMS/Web tool decision: Managers who don't know SQL will sit in meetings with salespeople

who don't know SQL, trying to figure out whether Oracle, Informix, Sybase, or DB2 is best.

Most publishers will not make these decisions correctly. In fact, most won't even choose a reliable raw substrate of OS/RDBMS/HTTPD (see my diatribe against junkware in Chapter 11, Sites That Are Really Databases). If they somehow randomly succeed in picking a decent infrastructure, then surely they will overlook some things at the data modeling stage. And they definitely will come to grief with their user interface and have to hire a bunch more people to support users until they figure out how to make the site's forms 99 percent self-explanatory.

Bottom line: A fortune will be spent on programming; schedules will slip; the users will get reamed by all the bugs. Just as with any other custom software development effort.

Will this always be true? No. My basic argument: The Web server-side software industry's development has and will continue to recapitulate the development of the business data processing software industry.

History of business data processing

In the 1960s, people who needed to do business data processing bought "iron," mainframe computer hardware. They hired programmers to write what today we would call a database management system. The same programmers would then build data models and application programs to put data into and pull data out of those data models.

In the 1970s, people would buy a commercial database management system plus some kind of iron on which to run it. They were tired of suffering with bugs in their programmers' ad hoc database management schemes and figured that their data storage needs weren't any different from hundreds of other computer users. Now company programmers were used only to write data models and application programs.

In the 1990s, people buy an enterprise software system such as SAP or Oracle Financials. They then buy an RDBMS to support it. They finally buy some iron to support the RDBMS. Company programmers are used only for some customization of the canned data models and apps.

Note that over these 40 years, there has been a huge transfer of power from iron vendors to data model/app vendors. Savvy companies realized this and adapted. IBM, for example, went heavily into the DBMS software business and then into business apps. On some days, you can go to the Oracle Web site and never learn that they make an RDBMS; the whole front page is given over to promoting the packaged business applications that they also sell. Not-so-savvy makers of iron or DBMS software have been nearly destroyed (e.g., Digital and Sybase).

Why the big shift from custom programming to packaged apps?

Given that business managers pride themselves on being innovative, why the huge rush to have everyone using the same handful of enterprise software systems? Wouldn't they be better off with custom-written programs that have a lot of embed-

ded knowledge about their particular products and the way that they like to deal with customers or vendors? Possible Answer 1 is that popular programming tools aren't really any better than they were in the 1960s but system requirements are more complex, thus making custom software development more expensive and perilous. Possible Answer 2 is that managers have figured out how to pay programmers so little that only stupid or lazy people are willing to work these days as programmers, thus making custom software development more expensive and perilous. Possible Answer 3 is that business managers are in fact no more innovative than a herd of sheep. They all read the same business literature. They all think about purchasing, invoicing, and payroll in exactly the same way. So they'd no more write custom information systems for their company than they would write a custom word processor.

Maybe it is a combination of all three. In any case, if your company handles payroll exactly the same way that Wombley's Widgets, Inc. does and they have a working program to do it, then you might as well use Wombley's software. If you hire programmers to build it from scratch, the best case is that you'll spend some money and get a working system. In the expected case, you'll spend a few years and millions of dollars working through all the bugs that Wombley's Widgets worked through five years before. The worst (and surprisingly common) case is that you'll spend ten years and tens of millions of dollars before having to scrap the whole project.

How about the Web?

In the early days of the Web, publishers started with iron, usually a desktop machine running the Unix operating system. Then they'd hire a programmer who'd write a Perl/CGI script that pulled data out of and stuffed data into a Unix file in a custom format, namely, *their own database management system.* By 1995, publishers had noticed that such programs tended to have a lot of strange mutual exclusion bugs; for instance, if two users simultaneously entered orders, the little custom database table would get corrupted. So publishers started building on top of a standard RDBMS such as Oracle, moving to where business data processing folks were in the 1970s. That's more or less where we are now (in March 1999).

A packaged solution?

Could one develop and distribute a packaged solution to Web publishing as one does for word processing or corporate purchasing? It depends on one's level of intelligence and cunning. Suppose that we have a CD-ROM containing an "enterprise software system." Here are a couple of possible descriptions for the same software:

Described by the engineers who built the software	Described by the marketing department
Here's a collection of hacks that we've assembled after building data processing systems for 15 companies. We're sorry that we never really finished it, and that it doesn't do everything you need, and that it will take 50 programmer-years to fill in the cracks and make it work for your business. But when you're done you'll probably have fewer bugs than if you'd started from scratch.	This is a comprehensive turnkey business data processing system already in use by 15 large and sophisticated companies. It does absolutely everything you need and is so flexibly designed that it will *only* take you 50 programmer-years to customize for your unique business practices.

Whose description is accurate? They both are. Which description do you think results in $35 million in software license revenue, plus another $100 million for consulting?

THE ARSDIGITA COMMUNITY SYSTEM

One of the dangers of writing a book like this is that the author may start to believe his own theories: I actually designed a packaged community Web software system and sat down with Tracy Adams, Ben Adida, and Jin Choi to build it (it might be more accurate to say "rebuild it," since many of the subsystems date back to 1995 or 1996). The system described in this chapter will be downloadable, with source code, for free from *arsdigita.com*.

Even if you decide to build everything from scratch rather than download our source code, I expect that this chapter will prove useful as a design aid.

Fundamentals

The ArsDigita Community System (ACS) is based on the Oracle 8 RDBMS, connected to the Internet via the AOLserver Tcl API. I'm currently serving more than 100 requests per second using this infrastructure and know that it works (America Online successfully handles hundreds of millions of requests per day with an almost identical architecture: AOLserver + Sybase + Unix).

I'm hoping to find partners who wish to maintain a version based on Microsoft's popular Active Server Pages system and a version that uses the easy-to-administer Solid RDBMS. Beyond that, it is too time-consuming to implement a system that works with any Web server and any RDBMS. I don't think Web publishers should really care what operating system or database management system they are running; the important decisions all have to do with data modeling and site philosophy. It is best to quickly pick an infrastructure that is known to work and thereafter focus on decisions that relate to the business.

At the risk of alienating the casual reader, let's plunge into describing the seven modules:

1. User Database
2. Content Database
3. User/Content Map
4. Member Value
5. Referer/Clickthrough
6. Banner Ads
7. Publisher/Member Connections

I apologize for inflicting SQL code on you so early in the book, but it is the most practical way to express a data model. Without a precise data model, it isn't possible to say anything interesting. If you're not a programmer and can't infer the meaning of the table definitions, then please skim ahead to the database chapters (Chapters 11–13 and 15), read the brief database/SQL tutorial, and come back.

Module 1: User database

This is the heart of the ArsDigita Community System (ACS). All the tables in other modules will refer to rows in the user's table:

```
create table users (
    user_id                 integer not null primary key,
    first_names             varchar(100) not null,
    last_name               varchar(100) not null,
    priv_name               integer default 0,
    email                   varchar(100) not null unique,
    priv_email              integer default 5,
    email_bouncing_p        char(1) default 'f'
                            check(email_bouncing_p in ('t','f')),
    password                varchar(30) not null,
    url                     varchar(200),
    on_vacation_until       date,
    last_visit              date,
    second_to_last_visit    date,
    registration_date       date
);
```

First note the privacy columns that permeate the community data model. For each piece of information collected from members, there is an associated privacy column, preceded by "priv_". There is a 0 through 9 privacy scale for each item:

- 0 means "show to everybody."
- 5 means "show to other registered users."
- 9 means "show to nobody except maintainers."

In the user's table, the email and name columns have associated privacy columns. The default for email address privacy is "show only to other registered users". This prevents SPAM crawlers from harvesting email addresses from public Web pages.

Note that in addition to storing the user's name, we provide space for a home page URL. This will allow the system to present member names as hyperlink anchors to their respective Web sites.

A community site with moderately clever programmers inevitably has lots of nooks and crannies in which email is sent automatically to members. For example, joe_56K@aol.com user can tell my photo.net server to alert him via email if a classified ad containing the word Linhof is placed by another user. A Linhof is an $8,000 camera with which a good photographer can take two pictures per day, and is thus not very popular. The server might first collect an ad containing the string "Linhof" one month after the alert was placed. By that time, joe_56K@aol.com might have decided to get a cable modem and has become joe_wayfast@mediaone.net. America Online does not forward email for members who abandon their service, so my server's mail to joe_56K @aol.com will bounce back to me and I'll have to shut off his alert manually. This didn't seem like too much of a burden when I built my software in 1995, but by 1998 there were thousands of email alerts in the database and my inbox would fill up with 50 or more bounced messages on some days.

I guess I learned that referring bounces back to the site maintainer is not a scalable system.

My new code therefore includes an `email_bouncing_p` flag. Note that the `_p` suffix is an old Lisp programming convention for naming a variable whose only possible values are true or false; sadly Oracle 8.0 does not offer a Boolean data type, so I'm forced to represent true and false as the characters "t" and "f". Anyway, the column starts out as false. Messages are logged as they go out and are sent in such a way that bounced email ends up in the hands of a little Perl script that opens up Oracle, logs the bounce, and checks to see if all mail sent to this user in the last ten days has bounced. If so, the user is flagged with `email_bouncing_p` and no more email will be sent until the user comes back to the site and changes or verifies his email address. Why ten days rather than, say, five? If a user has a weekly email alert, you want to allow his server to hiccup once without causing the user to be delisted.

If a member tells the system that he is going on vacation, the `on_vacation_until` column is filled with the date on which he expects to return. This way, a member does not return from vacation with a hundred useless discussion forum alerts.

In many areas of a community site, we will want to distinguish "new since your last visit" content from "the stuff that you've already seen" content. The obvious implementation of storing a single `last_visit` column is inadequate. Suppose that a user arrives at the site and the ACS sets the `last_visit` column to the current date and time. HTTP is a stateless protocol. If the user clicks to visit a discussion forum, the ACS queries the `users` table and finds that the last visit was three seconds ago. Consequently, none of the content will be highlighted as new.

The ACS stores `last_visit` and `second_to_last_visit` columns. We take advantage of the AOLserver filter facility to specify a Tcl program that runs before every request is served. The program does the following:

> IF a request comes with a user_id cookie, but the last_visit cookie is either not present or more than one day old, THEN the filter proc augments the AOLserver output headers with a persistent (expires in year 2010) set-cookie of last_visit to the current time (HTTP format). It also grabs an Oracle connection and sets

```
last_visit = sysdate,
second_to_last_visit = last_visit
```

> We set a persistent second_to_last_visit cookie with the `last_visit` time, either from the last_visit cookie or, if that wasn't present, with the value we just put into the `second_to_last_visit` column of the database.

We do something similar for unregistered users, using pure browser cookies rather than the database.

If you're taking the time to administer a relational database, then your site or service ought to offer extensive personalization. You can start with a very simple common table:

```
create table users_preferences (
    user_id                 integer not null references users,
    prefer_text_only_p      char(1) default 'f' check
                            (prefer_text_only_p in ('t','f'))
);
```

Publishers will alter this table to add columns as appropriate.

Other tables in this module are users_demographics and users_contact. If publishers elect to solicit age, sex, income range, geography, snailmail addresses, or phone numbers from users, the data go in these tables. The obvious way to do this is to demand all the fields at initial registration time. However, suppose that Jane Newcomer has come to a site to read a single document. She has an interesting alternative perspective to contribute and clicks on the "add a comment" link. We'll have to hammer her with a new user registration page. If we ask for more than name and email address, it seems likely that she'll simply back up.

The ArsDigita Community System incorporates software to progressively solicit desired information from users. A publisher can specify that on the tenth registered visit the system should ask for demographic data, or that on the twentieth registered visit, if the data have not already been entered (perhaps because the user purchased something), the system should ask for address and phone number.

Module 2: Content database

We want some support from the content database module of our publishing software in the following areas:

- helping community experts figure out which articles need revision and which new articles would be most valued by the community at large

- helping contributors work together on a draft article or a new version of an old article

- collecting and organizing reader comments and discussion, both for presentation to other readers and to assist authors in keeping content up to date

The kneejerk Web/DB reaction to this set of requirements is to say, "Let's store all the HTML pages in the relational database; then we can easily keep consistent metainformation about documents." I've seen a bunch of commercial Web content management systems that do just this. Publishers are then supposed to edit pages

with Web forms. There are a bunch of problems with this kind of system. First, Netscape Navigator is a good browser, but there are better text editors than its rendering of an HTML TEXTAREA. Not only is editing a Web document in a Netscape TEXTAREA inconvenient, but the last time I checked, Netscape 4.0 could only support about 33,000 characters in a TEXTAREA. Many of my Web documents are longer than this. For example, the previous chapter of this book is about 70,000 characters long. This doesn't stress my everyday text editor, GNU Emacs, into which I routinely load 80-*million*-character server log files.

A raw operating system file system, such as that provided by Unix, Windows, or the Macintosh, is not a powerful database management tool, but there are lots of client programs that talk directly to it. For example, data in a Unix file system can be

- edited by a novice using Netscape 4.0 and HTTP PUT
- updated via FTP by a graphic designer using Fetch on a Macintosh
- updated via Emacs by a sysadmin logged into the Web server
- updated en masse by a Perl script looking for regular expressions

- grabbed by any Web server program and delivered to users worldwide, even when the finicky RDBMS is offline

- full-text indexed by a variety of off-the-shelf products

Folks who build whizzy content management systems fall in love with their ideas and never bother to think about how these daily tasks will be accomplished under their shiny new regime.

I don't have the energy to build interfaces to all the software on which Web publishers are currently relying. So my shiny new system for content management is the moldy old Unix file system. Static HTML documents stay in a hierarchical file system, where they've always been. The ArsDigita Community System uses the relational database to manage data about those static documents and to manage data (e.g., comments) that augment those static documents. One advantage of this system is reliability. I can program AOLserver to deliver a static page from the Unix file system, then try to connect to Oracle and augment the page with comments and links pulled from database tables. However, if an Oracle connection isn't available, then the AOLserver thread can simply terminate after delivering what was in the file system.

Even though the content in the Unix file system remains primary, we need a rich set of data in a relational table:

```
create table static_pages (
    page_id             integer not null primary key,
    url_stub            varchar(400) not null unique,
    original_author     integer references users(user_id),
    -- generally PAGE_TITLE will be whatever was inside HTML TITLE tag
    page_title          varchar(4000),
    -- the dreaded CLOB data type; we're forced to use
    -- in Oracle when we want strings longer than 4000 characters
    page_body           clob,
    draft_p             char(1) default 'f' check (draft_p in ('t','f')),
    -- force people to register before viewing?
    members_only_p      char(1) default 'f' check (members_only_p in ('t','f')),
    -- if we want to charge (or pay) readers for viewing this
    price               number,
    -- for deviations from site-default copyright policy
    copyright_info      varchar(4000),
    -- whether or not this page accepts reader contributions
    accept_comments_p   char(1) default 't' check (accept_comments_p in ('t','f')),
    accept_links_p      char(1) default 't' check (accept_links_p in ('t','f'))
);
```

Note that we use a generated integer page_id key for this table. We could key the table by the url_stub (filename), but that would make it very difficult to reorganize files in the Unix file system (something that should actually happen very seldomly on a Web server; it breaks links from foreign sites).

After talking the talk about leaving the page in the Unix file system, we stuff the full content into the page_body anyway. Why? Keeping a copy of the site's static content in the database allows us to use the RDBMS's full-text search engine (see Chapter 12, Database Management Systems) and search static pages in a fashion consistent with the way that we search discussion postings or comments. Having a copy also allows the ACS to provide a "notify me when a page has been updated" service to readers.

If a page has the draft_p flag set, we hide it from all users except authors of static pages on the site. We also know to look for it in the Unix file system with a ".draft.html" extension rather than the usual ".html".

If there is a file in the Unix file system ending in ".new.html", we know that there is a proposed new version of this document. The proposed new version is only served to authors of this document. We keep track of authorship via the following table:

```
create table static_page_authors (
    page_id            integer not null references static_pages,
    user_id            integer not null references users
);
```

If we're ever going to help users find new articles that interest them, we need to tag files with categories. We will keep a table of content categories for the entire site, categories we can use for tagging static content, organizing Q&A forums, and recording user interests:

```
create table categories (
    category_id        integer not null primary key,
    category           varchar(50)
);
```

We then reference this table from a table that maps static pages to categories:

```
create table static_categories (
    page_id            integer not null references static_pages,
    category_id        integer not null references categories,
    unique(page_id, category_id)
);
```

Note:
SQL nerds will note the unique constraint that keeps a page from being put in the same category twice.

We will fill this table automatically by parsing META tags in the HEADs of the static files on the server.

The ArsDigita Community System collects reader comments on static pages. The most important reason to do this is to collect alternative perspectives and experiences from those of the page's primary authors. However, we also need to find out whether static pages are meeting users' needs or not. To that end, we divide reader feedback into the following categories:

- `alternative_perspective`
- `private_message_to_page_authors`
- rating (0 through 10)
- `unanswered_question`

Note that only the comments of type `alternative_perspective` are generally presented to readers. If you've been naive enough to swallow the hype of various collaborative filtering companies, then you might think that the ratings were of some value for public presentation. However, my experience with photo.net leads me to believe otherwise. During an 18-month period in which many thousands of text comments were received, people only wished to rate content 632 times, despite the fact that it was easier and faster to type in a rating of "5" than the average comment received (900 characters in length). You'd think it might not be too much of a waste of folks' time to at least show users the top-rated pages on a site and the administrators the bottom-rated, but in practice this information isn't useful. The average rating of a page on my server is 8.27. The page that has the most 10 ratings is my photo tour of Graceland (*http://photo.net/summer94/graceland.html*), which is in fact likely to be of little interest to anyone except the Elvis fans who've already found it. The page that has the most 0 ratings is my Career Guide for Engineers and Scientists (*http://photo.net/philg/careers.html*), which is intentionally not what people might have expected if they did an AltaVista search. Why then collect ratings at all? A user who is able to rate a page via a Web form is a user who is presumably less likely to send a "what a great page" email message to the publisher. Such messages may be confidence-building at first but are always burdensome to answer.

Here's the data model to support this system:

```
create table comments (
    page_id          integer not null references static_pages,
    user_id          integer not null references users,
    comment_type     varchar(30),
    message          clob,
    -- null unless comment_type is 'rating'
    rating           integer check (rating = 0 and rating <= 10),
    originating_ip   varchar(50),
    posting_time     date
);
```

Note that we keep the IP address from which a comment was added. In the event that a malevolent person adds a lot of irrelevant comments, it will generally be adequate to bulk-delete comments by `user_id`. However, if the spammer also has access to a range of `user_id`'s and passwords, then being able to bulk-delete by IP address is also useful.

Another form of user-contributed content is the related link. Essentially each community Web site is a micro-Yahoo. Authors and readers will find interesting sites on the wider Internet and note that they provide relevant information on the same topic. Having an automated facility frees the publisher from having to read dozens of daily "please add my site as a link" messages. Keeping the links in a structured database allows the publisher to run a nightly link checker script to remove the dead links from the site.

Here's the data model:

```
create table links (
    page_id           integer not null references static_pages,
    user_id           integer not null references users,
    url               varchar(300) not null,
    link_title        varchar(100) not null,
    link_description  varchar(4000),
    -- contact if link is dead?
    contact_p         char(1) default 't' check (contact_p in ('t','f')),
    status            char(10) default 'live' check (status in
                            ('live','coma','dead','removed')),
    originating_ip    varchar(50),
    posting_time      date,
    unique(page_id,url)
);
```

What if Joe Pathetic thinks his GeoCities site, complete with animated "under construction" sign, is a related link to one of your static documents? As soon as he adds it, email will be automatically sent to those page authors who've requested to be notified of changes. Page authors and the site owner will also see Web page summaries of new links, comments, and so forth when they log in. The static page authors or site owner can remove the link if they don't like it.

What if Joe Spammer adds his commercial site as a related link to every document on your server? For him, there is The Blacklist:

```
create table link_kill_patterns (
    page_id          integer references static_pages,
    -- who added the kill pattern
    user_id          integer not null references users,
    date_added       date,
    glob_pattern     varchar(500) not null
);
```

Adding a `glob_pattern` such as `*microsoft.com*` to the blacklist removes all links to URLs that match this pattern, either on one page or sitewide. Furthermore, any attempt by the spammer to add a link matching this pattern will be rebuffed by the software.

By recording related links and comments, we've covered virtually the entire territory of user contributions that are tightly coupled to static site pages. On a standard community site, we still have to consider user-to-user communications that are only loosely coupled to static pages. For example, on my personal Web site, I have about a thousand .html pages but only six Q&A forums, my personal favorite brand of discussion group. A few of the questions in the "photo.net" forum are explicitly related to one of my static pages on photography, but most of them come from readers' day-to-day experiences. User-contributed answers to these questions are then almost completely unrelated to the original static content on the site.

Covering the data model and workings of a database-backed threaded discussion system would take a whole chapter by itself. See the operating forums at *http://photo.net/photo/* to get a feel for the user experience; see Chapter 13 of my last book (*http://photo.net/wtr/dead-trees/53013.htm*) for an explanation of the data model and software.

Another form of user-to-user communication is classified advertising. Note that a classified advertisement need not be narrowly construed as "an offer by a user to sell something to another user." Instead we can think of a classified ad as "any user-contributed content that is unrelated to a static article, to which we normally do not expect a public response, that may be categorized."

The classified ad system included in the ACS would be useful for implementing the following applications:

- a personal ad service with five categories: men seeking women, women seeking men, men seeking men, women seeking women, other

- a big company's "jobs available" page where the public could view all the listings but only existing employees would be able to post

- an exhibit calendar affiliated with an art Web site; postings would be categorized by city and would expire after the show described closed

- scientists posting descriptions of their work; categorization would be by conference

Of course, some publishers may elect to use the classified ad system in the most obvious way: to facilitate readers selling items to each other. This creates a great demand for assistance, with the question, "How do I know which other readers I can trust?" At photo.net, readers find assistance from a "neighbor-to-neighbor" service.

After buying or selling an item in the classifieds, readers are encouraged to record their experience with the other party. Thus far, the database contains only 320 such records. Yet there have been tens of thousands of classified ads posted. Rather than demanding that users enter their story, can we be clever about using information that is already in the database? Absolutely. One of the things that buyers most wish to know is whether or not the seller is a professional camera dealer. There is a belief that camera dealers have higher prices and less integrity than photographers who want to unload a spare item. Do we ask each person posting an ad whether he or she is a camera dealer? If so, do we have the administrative resources to monitor these self-reports?

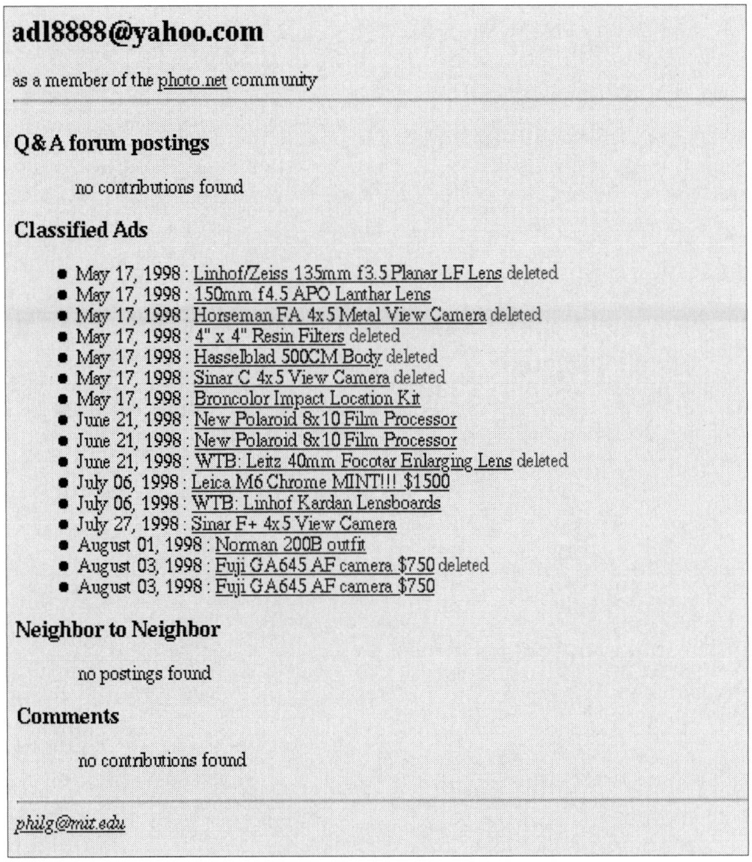

adl8888@yahoo.com

as a member of the photo.net community

Q&A forum postings

> no contributions found

Classified Ads

- May 17, 1998 : Linhof/Zeiss 135mm f3.5 Planar LF Lens deleted
- May 17, 1998 : 150mm f4.5 APO Lanthar Lens
- May 17, 1998 : Horseman FA 4x5 Metal View Camera deleted
- May 17, 1998 : 4" x 4" Resin Filters deleted
- May 17, 1998 : Hasselblad 500CM Body deleted
- May 17, 1998 : Sinar C 4x5 View Camera deleted
- May 17, 1998 : Broncolor Impact Location Kit
- June 21, 1998 : New Polaroid 8x10 Film Processor
- June 21, 1998 : New Polaroid 8x10 Film Processor
- June 21, 1998 : WTB: Leitz 40mm Focotar Enlarging Lens deleted
- July 06, 1998 : Leica M6 Chrome MINT!!! $1500
- July 06, 1998 : WTB: Linhof Kardan Lensboards
- July 27, 1998 : Sinar F+ 4x5 View Camera
- August 01, 1998 : Norman 200B outfit
- August 03, 1998 : Fuji GA645 AF camera $750 deleted
- August 03, 1998 : Fuji GA645 AF camera $750

Neighbor to Neighbor

> no postings found

Comments

> no contributions found

philg@mit.edu

Figure 3-1: Member profile page of a camera dealer.

What distinguishes a camera dealer from a person selling a camera? Volume, volume, volume. The ArsDigita Community System includes a community member profile page that, for an individual user, shows

- a (hyperlinked) list of the user's discussion forum contributions
- a (hyperlinked) list of current, expired, and deleted classified ads
- a (hyperlinked) list of neighbor-to-neighbor postings by or about this user
- a (hyperlinked) list of comments on static pages contributed by this user

A camera dealer's profile will generally have a long list of classified ads and little else. For example, see Figure 3-1.

I happen to know that Russ Arcuri is not a camera dealer. Almost anyone viewing his profile page would come to the same conclusion. It shows 430 Q&A forum postings (going back to December 1996), ten comments on static pages, two neighbor-to-neighbor postings, and only three classified ads (see Figure 3-2).

arcuri@borg.com

as a member of the photo.net community

Q & A forum postings

- December 20, 1996 : Response to This one's for sports photogs...
- December 24, 1996 : Response to Sunrise Photos
- December 30, 1996 : Response to Portrait lens
- December 30, 1996 : Response to Why does my Elan II select 1/60 when flash sync

.. removed 400 lines for clarity ...

- July 24, 1998 : Response to What medium- or large-format system will let me take long-focal-length portraits for under US$1000 (used)?
- August 03, 1998 : Response to Where to go in Mid-Summer
- August 03, 1998 : Response to Where to go in Mid-Summer
- August 03, 1998 : Response to Which tripod for a tall person?
- August 03, 1998 : Response to White spots on prints: dust or what?

Classified Ads

- May 12, 1998 : Mamiya TLR & accessories for sale deleted
- May 12, 1998 : Canon EF 28-105 lens Mint-/Ex+ $210 deleted
- July 21, 1998 : Mamiya TLR & accessories for sale - price reduced!

Neighbor to Neighbor

- March 16, 1998 : B&H Photo : Numerous orders, most without a hitch
- March 16, 1998 : Camera World of Oregon : Numerous orders, all good except for o

Comments

- March 17, 1997 : This is just a quick note to address a particular ...
- April 07, 1997 : I've gotten a couple questions via e-mail about p ...
- April 07, 1997 : I also should have noted that the ECLIPSED moon ca ...
- April 25, 1997 : I just wanted to second the recommendation someone ...
- May 19, 1997 : Jim, Basically I think we agree here. Phili ...

Figure 3-2: Member profile page of a photographer.

For brevity, the data model is omitted here because Chapter 13 of my last book (*http://photo.net /wtr/dead-trees/53013.htm*) gives detailed instructions for building a Web-based classifieds/auctioning system.

Chat is one of the more popular Internet services, but it is a bit tough to think about how to tightly weave it into a Web service. I've no personal experience operating a chat server, but I've seen enough panicky "the ichat server is down" messages on commercial Web publishers' sysadmin mailing lists to be wary of the idea. Furthermore, I think that users will balk at downloading chat client software or using clunky Java applets when they can use the instant messaging software that they're already running. ICQ has millions of users and their desktop client program is already capable of functioning as a chat room server. America Online's instant messaging system (AIM) is bundled with Netscape Navigator on the Internet side and, in addition to working between two Internet users, provides a seamless bridge to the 11 million AOL system users. AIM currently does not support multiuser chat. On both ICQ and AOL, it can be tough to find out the "screen name" of a user. So we have `aim_screen_name` and `icq_number` columns in the `users_contact` table. We can use this to help registered users chat with each other using other folks' infrastructures.

More interestingly, it is technically feasible for a Web server to pump a message into the AOL instant messaging or ICQ networks. If your Web server is capable of sending instant messages, then the information that users traditionally get via email could be optionally receivable via AIM instead.

The bottom line is that chat isn't particularly difficult, but it's tough to imagine what good it is unless your community site has a product support dimension. In that case, chat-type software can be great for collapsing the distance between a

support technician and the user. For example, if the product is a computer program and the chat software lets the support technician drive the user's machine to some extent, the support technician can put up Web pages, bring up commands in the program that generated the confusion, and give audio or text suggestions.

Note: Don't forget that, amidst all of this chat "technology" hype, there is nothing stopping you from setting up an Internet Relay Chat (IRC) channel and pointing your users to it (see *http://www.yahoo.com/Computers_and _Internet/Internet/Chat/IRC/*).

Module 3: User/content map

We want to know which users have read which pieces of content. This information is useful when an expert is trying to assist a novice. Note that this is different from the aggregate Web activity statistics I discuss in Chapter 9, User Tracking. Logging fine-grained user activity into a relational database imposes a huge load on the publisher's servers, so we try to make sure that we log as little as possible and do it for good reasons.

We don't even consider database logging of thumbnail or larger image requests. We focus our attention on page views. However, even those statistics can be unrealistically large. In 17 months (through August 1998), my photo.net server cookied more than 1.5 million unique browsers. Assuming that each browser grabs an average of 20 unique pages, that's 30 million potential records. If it takes us 100 bytes to store each record, that's 3 GB of data. In a world of 18-GB disk drives, 3 GB doesn't sound like too much data. However, if logging and querying are going to be fast, all of our user profiling data are going to have to fit into RAM. My Web server has only 4 GB of RAM. It seems like a bad idea to give over 75 percent of the memory to these data.

What if I were to affirmatively decide that I don't care about casual surfers? And that I don't need to log site activity that occurs before a casual surfer has converted to a registered, interested member of the community? Now my data requirements are somewhat more reasonable. At photo.net, there are probably only about 50,000 regular users who've bothered to add comments, Q&A forum messages, or classified ads. Assume further that we don't need to record the fact that User X has grabbed Document Y more than once. Our data storage requirements become more modest, despite the fact that we probably have to assume at least 100 pages per user: only 5 million records total. At 100 bytes per record, this still would be a healthy 500 MB of data, but that's only $2,000 of RAM as of June 1998.

Instead of limiting the number of users, we could limit the number of documents. A site like photo.net contains more than 100,000 documents, but most of them are user-contributed fragments such as classified ads or discussion postings. We're very unlikely to be able to infer anything from the fact that User X has grabbed Ad 35623. What if we limited ourselves to the consciously authored static pages, of which there are only about 1,000? We then need only 1,000 bits per user to keep track of which users have read which documents. For example, if my bit vector started out with "11001...", it would mean that I'd read the documents with page_ids 1,2, and 5 but had not read documents 3 and 4. With this scheme, we could keep records for 1.5 million browsers and 1,000 documents in less than 200 MB of memory.

What's the downside of doing things this way? Relational databases are happy to store binary data as binary large objects (BLOBs), but these data aren't available for indexing, ad hoc querying in SQL, report generation with standard tools, and so on. Your software would be difficult to port to other RDBMS software. For example, to make this kind of system work in Oracle 8, you'd probably end up writing a bunch of code in Oracle's proprietary PL/SQL language, plus some custom C or Java (Oracle 8.1) code running on the server side, plus some custom code in database client software (e.g., AOLserver).

Complicating matters to some extent is the development of commercial Web activity analysis and user-profiling software such as Andromedia's ARIA (*http://www.andromedia.com*). In a new application area like Web publishing, it is generally easier to write software from scratch than to integrate packaged software. However, since I haven't figured out myself what the best way to do this is, I designed the ArsDigita Community System so that the other modules don't intimately depend on the details of this module.

Flexibility and abstraction are great, but ultimately someone has to write some code. So here's what the ACS has by default:

- Information is stored in a standard table relation, i.e., we do not use bit vectors.

- Information is only kept for registered users, i.e., those who've contributed content or signed up for email alerts.

- Information about repeat loadings of pages is not kept.

- Detailed information about activity within classified ad systems or discussion groups is not kept.

There is one exception to the last point. For publishers who want to offer readers an email "summary of discussion group postings that you haven't seen," the system has to log at least a week's worth of user/posting download data.

Module 4: Member value

Commercial publishers and service operators are interested in how much customers are worth to them because they expect to get money from them. However, noncommercial and intranet communities also need to know which members are valuable and which are imposing a burden on the community.

Even if you're a classically greedy commercial publisher, pricing user activity on the Web presents some paradoxes. Traditionally people are willing to pay to run classified ads in magazines. So obviously, you should charge people for every classified ad posted. But once you've installed the ArsDigita Community System, the marginal cost of letting a user post a classified is $0. If people come to your site to look at this classified ad and also view banner ads, then actually you should be willing to *pay* the reader for posting a classified ad! That seems logical until you think about the fact that every classified ad user presents a statistical chance that you will need to invest customer support resources in (1) deleting a duplicate ad, (2) editing an ad, (3) assisting the user if he can't figure out what you thought were self-explanatory forms, and (4) dealing with bounced email to that user, and so forth. I explicitly designed the ACS classifieds to have a zero support cost, but in practice operating the photo.net classifieds seems to have chewed up about 30 minutes of my time for every 1,000 ads posted.

In the offline world, it is tough to set "pain-based prices." The publisher is expected to charge all the users equally and spread customer support costs among them. In the online world, there is no technological reason not to charge people for the costs that they impose, though it may seem confusing to customers. For example, if I place a classified ad in a newspaper and then call to cancel it, I wouldn't expect to be charged. Yet in the online world, a user who places an ad and then telephones your customer service number has cost you 100 times as much as a user who merely places an ad. It makes sense to charge people according to how much customer service time they've burned up, and you might even be able to explain that to them.

In the offline world, recognizable contributions from customers come almost exclusively in the form of money. If Jane Smith recommends her Ann Taylor jacket to a friend, neither the Ann Taylor manufacturer nor retailer is likely to ever find out. In the online world, a customer can contribute to an online community by posting an interesting question in a discussion forum, answering someone else's question, buying something from a merchant that gives the community a kickback, writing a static article, or filling out a form recommending the community to a friend (who will then receive an email invitation to join).

With a public community site you might decide to charge users for viewing certain pieces of content, even though the marginal cost of them doing so is nearly zero. You could make this decision to charge simply because you're greedy or because you're trying to defray the high average cost of producing content. The ArsDigita Community System lets you attach prices to individual pages. Note that these prices can be negative—you can pay users to read pages that are important to you or the community.

The ArsDigita Community System doesn't impose any business model on a Web service. A publisher need not be greedy or open-handed or open to the public or closed to all except employees. The ACS merely defines a comprehensive set of events that could conceivably lead to a user's account being debited (or credited). The publisher decides whether and how to price these events. The publisher decides whether or not to use "real money," that is, to ultimately bill people. The publisher decides whether or not to bill credit cards online or pipe a report of charges to an existing accounting system. The publisher decides whether to bill periodically or when users hit a configurable threshold.

Here is a partial list of chargeable events:

- User downloads static page where price is not null.
- User posts classified ad.
- Administrator has to delete or edit user's classified ad.
- User posts question that is deemed "good" by moderators.
- User posts answer that is deemed "good" by moderators.
- User posts comment.
- Administrator has to delete user's comment.

The actual billing of charge cards is handled by software lifted from the ArsDigita Shoppe system, described in Chapter 14, ecommerce.

Module 5: Referer/clickthrough

In general, we want to have a public Web service where registration is not required
to view most community content. In order to avoid buying a 10,000-pound database server, we refrain from keeping detailed data on unregistered users. On the
other hand, we want good data on how people are getting to our site and we want
good data on how many people are following links to external sites from our pages.

Since a publisher can't control who links to his or her site, the referer data (misspelled as "referer" in the HTTP standard) are logged by a completely general purpose
system. An AOLserver Tcl filter runs after any page on the system is requested by a
user. It looks for an external referer header and, if a database connection is available,
increments a counter in the `referer_log` table:

```
create table referer_log (
    -- relative to the PageRoot, includes the leading /
    local_url       varchar(250) not null,
    -- full URL on the foreign server (including http://)
    foreign_url     varchar(250) not null,
    entry_date      date,      -- we count referrals per day
    click_count     integer default 0
);
```

An example entry in this table:

local_url	/photo/
foreign_url	http://www.yahoo.com/Arts/Visual_Arts/Photography/Magazines/
entry_date	1998-06-12
click_count	24

This tells us that 24 folks came from Yahoo to photo.net. We'll not easily find out how many come from AltaVista, though, because each one will end up in a separate row:

local_url	http://photo.net/photo/point-and-shoot-tips.html
foreign_url	http://altavista.digital.com/cgi-bin/query?pg=q&kl=XX&q =point+and+shoot+photography+techniques
entry_date	1998-06-12
click_count	1

The referer header in this case contains the user-entered query string. If we want to lump these together, we need to keep a collection of lumping patterns. For example:

```
http://altavista.digita.com* maps to http://altavista.digital.com
```

will cause all the AltaVista queries to be logged as if the referer header had read "http://altavista.digital.com". We can keep these in a table:

```
create table referer_log_glob_patterns (
    glob_pattern                varchar(250) primary key,
    canonical_foreign_url       varchar(250)
);
```

and have the AOLserver pull them from the database every 30 minutes (and then cache them in RAM). Oddly enough, we probably *do* want to keep track of user query strings that lead people to the community. So we augment the glob_patterns table to include a Tcl regular expression. If it isn't null, the logging filter will try to find a query string in the referer header:

```
create table referer_log_glob_patterns (
    glob_pattern                varchar(250) primary key,
    canonical_foreign_url       varchar(250),
    -- not NULL if this is here for a search engine and
    -- we're also interested in harvesting query strings
    search_engine_name          varchar(30),
    search_engine_regexp        varchar(200)
);
```

```
-- strings entered by users, either on our site-local search engine
-- or at Internet-wide servers

create table query_strings (
    query_date                  date not null,
    query_string                varchar(300) not null,
    -- if they came in from a public search engine and we
    -- picked it from the referer header
    search_engine_name          varchar(30),
    -- if we know who they are
    user_id                     integer references users,
    -- not null if this was a local query
    n_results                   integer
);
```

Note that the final table (query_strings) is very important when the query string was typed locally and the number of results returned was zero.

Tracking clickthroughs to foreign sites is very similar. See Chapter 9, User Tracking, for a detailed explanation of the clickthrough tracking system, which is unchanged from the 1996 version.

Module 6: Banner ads

Back in 1995, banner ads were the cornerstone of Internet entrepreneurs' dreams. Now people recognize them for what they are: mostly an annoyance. So why do we include an ad server in the ArsDigita Community System? Because it is too painful to watch publishers shell out $50,000 for packaged junkware ad servers that don't work. Here's our $50,000 ad server:

```
create table advs (
    adv_key         varchar(200) primary key,
    adv_filename    varchar(200),
    target_url      varchar(500)
);

create table adv_log (
    adv_key         varchar(200) not null references advs,
    entry_date      date,
    display_count   integer default 0,
    click_count     integer default 0
);
```

The advs table keeps a list of banner GIF files and the URLs to which users who click on them should be redirected. The adv_log table counts the number of times

a day that ads were displayed and clicked on. A reference in my review of the Nikon
300 mm lens (*http://photo.net/photo/nikon/300-2.8.html*) to the ad server looks like

```
<a href="adhref.tcl?adv_key=pfizer">
<img src="adimg.tcl?adv_key=pfizer">
</a>
```

Assuming that the advs table was appropriately stuffed, the adimg.tcl script would
deliver a GIF explaining the benefits of sildenafil citrate. While the user is studying
the pixels, the adimg script stays alive to record the display in the adv_log table.
Were the user to click on the image, he would invoke the adhref.tcl script and be
redirected to *http://www.pfizer.com*. The adhref.tcl script continues to run after the
user has been redirected. It will update the adv_log table to reflect the clickthrough.

For publishers who want to realize the grand 1994 dreams of marketing executives
worldwide, we provide a layer of tables and logic on top of the basic ad server. The
idea is to serve users those ads in which they are most likely to be interested, on which
they are most likely to click, and that they have not seen too many times. We drive the
user interest model from the same categories table that we use for the rest of the site.

We can infer user interest in categories by looking at the tables built up by Module 3 (User/Content Map) or by looking at the `users_interests` table, augmented when a user explicitly requests notification of new content in a particular category.

We keep our user/ad history in a log table:

```
create table adv_user_map (
    adv_key          varchar(200) not null references advs,
    user_id          integer not null references users,
    event_time       date not null,
    -- will generally be 'd' (displayed) 'c' (clicked through)
    event_type       char(1)
);
```

Note that we aren't bothering to capture this information for casual surfers, only for registered users. Suppose we combine data in `adv_user_map` with ad categorization data:

```
create table adv_categories (
    adv_key          varchar(200) not null references advs,
    category_id      integer not null references categories,
    unique(adv_key,  category_id)
);
```

Now we can ask, "What is the probability that User X will click on a health care product ad?" We can use data from `adv_categories` to build Tcl procedures that "serve the user a randomly selected health care ad" or "serve the user the health care ad that he hasn't seen" or, if he has seen all the ads categorized as health care, then "serve him the one he has seen the least often."

This module includes a large set of password-protected reporting pages, some for the publisher and some for individual advertisers.

Note: My favorite day in Internet banner advertising was September 20, 1998. CNN's NetGravity server delivered a banner ad depicting a new BMW zooming through a blurred landscape. The article underneath was indeed automobile-related: "Duchess of York's mother dies in car crash."

Module 7: Publisher/member connections

One reason people are willing to waste so much money building and maintaining Web services is the possibility of direct contact with users/customers. The connections module in the ArsDigita Community System serves the following functions:

1. suggesting to the publisher those members who are due for promotion, from novices to co-maintainers, for instance

2. allowing the publisher to selectively spam groups of members

Promoting members is one of the trickiest parts of the ACS. Each discussion forum may develop as a standalone subcommunity. Thus the fact that Jane Treehugger has answered 100 questions in the Nature Photography forum ought to put her forward for co-moderation there, but wouldn't affect whether or not she can co-moderate a forum on studio photography. There may be participants in the Studio Photography forum who've never seen any postings by Jane Treehugger.

When choosing a group of members to spam, the publisher ought to be able to include or exclude people along the following axes:

- activity in discussion groups
- has read a particular static page
- has commented on a particular static page
- has authored a static page
- length of membership in community
- has expressed an interest in a category of content

So one could say, "Send email to people who've posted at least 10 messages in the discussion groups this month but who've not read *Travels with Samantha*" or "Send email to people who've said that they were interested in large-format cameras."

NOW THE HARD PART

Suppose that one has implemented the preceding seven modules, taking a huge leap forward in the engineering of a Web service. They involve so much data modeling and programming that it is tough to imagine a harder engineering challenge. Yet actually, the system sketched above only represents the beginning of the effort in building the kinds of Web systems that the world needs and wants. It is a reasonable start and collects enough data that a publisher can begin to do interesting computation. Here's an example:

> Assume a Web site with 1,000 static .html files, a discussion forum, and all the services and information above. An expert shows up at the site and begins to participate in the discussion forum and comments on some of the static pages. I want the software to automatically recognize that this person is an expert. If the expert asks, "What 1,001st static document can I write that will help the community the most?" I want the software to be able to suggest some topics.

This example is as hard as the entire artificial intelligence problem and could occupy brilliant computer scientists for decades.

Brilliant computer scientists? The same ones that brought Microsoft Blue Screen of Death™ to your desktop and "server not responding" to your favorite ecommerce site? Or perhaps you'd rather trust the authors of the code that delayed the opening of Hong Kong's new $20 billion airport, then crippled operations and left stranded passengers smelling dead fish and rotting fruit from the stalled cargo terminal.

On second thought, maybe we should try to let the community users handle some of the programming themselves. Most of the Web technology that you can buy off the shelf presumes a mainframe-style "priesthood that develops what users need" world, complete with the three-tiered architecture that shut down the Hong Kong airport. The ArsDigita Community System, on the other hand, is built in such a way that genuinely hard things are left to a standard commercial relational database management system. Things that don't have to be hard are done in a safe interpreted computer language so that novice programmers running the community can modify and extend the software.

If we're smart enough to develop safe and effective languages, the power of programming need not be limited to the maintainers of a community Web site. The most useful and innovative services of all are often algorithms specified by users that

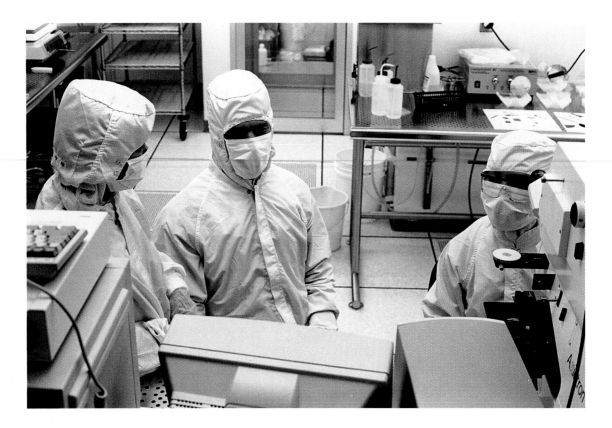

run on the publisher's server: "Send me mail every Monday and Thursday nights if there are any new articles by my friend Judy."

The programming chapters of this book illustrate the power and reliability of this software architecture for ecommerce and Web applications that replace desktop apps.

SUMMARY

Collaboration technology can shape the way people work, learn, and live. Until the advent of the telephone, for example, the largest manageable companies had only a few hundred employees and had to be more or less in one building. Truly effective technology to support online communities will change assumptions that we don't even realize we've been making for the last 100 years.

MORE

- Herman Melville understood everything important about modern office work in 1853 when he wrote "Bartleby the Scrivener." Bartleby's modern counterparts are the office workers in Nicholson Baker's novels *La Fermata* and *The Mezzanine*.

- If you're sick of USENET and feeling nostalgic for the great physical community you had growing up, rent *Welcome to the Dollhouse* (1996) and relive those great junior high school years.

- Check out *net.gain* (Hagel and Armstrong, 1997; Harvard Business School Press) and learn how to get rich running an online community (from two authors who've never built or operated an online community).

- If you got lost among the table definitions, read *The Practical SQL Handbook* (Bowman, Emerson, Darnovsky, 1996; Addison-Wesley).

- If you want to see what academic computer scientists have done in this area, see *Readings in Groupware and Computer-Supported Cooperative Work* (edited by Baecker, 1993; Morgan Kaufmann) and *Computer-Supported Cooperative Work: A Book of Readings* (edited by Greif, 1988; Morgan Kaufmann). You'll find that the Web was nearly fully conceived by Vannevar Bush in 1945 and nearly fully implemented by Douglas Engelbart in the late 1960s. In late 1994, I talked to 600 career researchers at the ACM Computer-Supported Cooperative Work Conference. None of them really knew what the Web was or were taking steps to put their ideas on the Web ("How would we charge for them?"). When I got back to MIT, I asked Tim Berners-Lee whether he'd found any papers by people from this conference or community helpful when he was implementing the World Wide Web. He said that he had never heard of the conference or any of the professors.

4

Static Site Development

The preceding chapter set forth **The Right Way** to do a Web site using a massive database management system and tens of thousands of lines of computer software. This approach is not the best fit for every publisher's budget and system administration skills. Certainly it is much simpler to operate a Web site that is merely a set of files in a Unix or Windows NT file system, in other words, a *static site*. Do people need a formal methodology for developing a static Web site? I never thought so. After all, a six-year-old with Claris Home Page or Netscape 4.0 can build a working Web site.

Why don't these what-you-see-is-what-you-get (WYSIWYG) HTML editors enable everyone to become a competent Web publisher? They solve the wrong problem. In the early-ish days of the Web, say 1994, it was observed that college undergraduates who were Unix users could build themselves a Web page in about 30 minutes, even if they were English majors who had never taken a programming class. Users of desktop PCs were unable to produce Web pages at all. Software developers set out to solve what they thought was the desktop user's problem: HTML "programming" is too hard to learn.

It turns out that HTML "programming" consists of sticking "<I>" and "</I>" around a word that you want to appear in italics. Secretaries worldwide were successfully using word processors like this all through the 1970s. Had the average person really become so stupid and lazy in the succeeding 20 years that he couldn't learn that "the I tag is for italics, the B tag for bold"?

In Alan Cooper's interesting book on user interface design, *About Face* (1995, IDG), he makes the claim that users don't understand the difference between RAM and disk, and further, that they don't understand the file system or directory hierarchies. Somehow people struggle along and get a letter printed, but they are confused when they close a document and their word processor asks them if they'd like

to save their changes. Save them where? Why weren't they saved before? Why is there a "file" menu on a typical program at all? Shouldn't I just be working on a document and be offered the chance to revert to older versions?

Building a Web site exposes and exacerbates all of the problems that users have with their computer systems. No longer are they just trying to print out a letter. They have to organize and link together a set of documents. So if you give someone a WYSIWYG editor for HTML, he will usually just get stuck 30 minutes deeper into the task of building a site.

Furthermore, there is the problem of *sample bias.* Suppose that you go to the airport to try to estimate the percentage of vacant seats on that day's flights. You decide to stand in the arrival area and ask folks how many vacant seats there were in their row. Sample bias skews your statistics because planes that were full contain more passengers than planes that were relatively empty. So you're likely to encounter a lot of people who will tell you that their rows were full and unlikely to find people who were on a nearly empty plane. You'll conclude that planes are 80 percent full, when in fact they are closer to 60 percent full.

If you're working with someone who has never published anything on the Web, be conscious of sample bias. In 1992 a user of a NeXT computer could browse an HTML document, edit it without seeing the HTML tags, and press a button to publish it back to the server. By early 1995, someone with a Mac or a PC could do this in NaviPress (subsequently purchased by AOL and renamed "AOLpress," downloadable for free from *www.aolpress.com*). If a person had something to say and was facile with organizing documents in a computer file system, why in 1998 would they not already have a Web site? The sample bias inherent in working with people on their first Web site in 1998 is that you're likely to encounter someone who has nothing to say or has never understood computer tools. Either way, you are in deep trouble.

The static site development plan here is intended first to expose the need for formal thinking and to bring everyone on a project into sync over the fundamentals. Here's a sketch of the plan:

- Draw a site map.

- Assemble and structure content.

- Make a text-only site.

- Hire a graphic designer.

- Establish a maintenance plan.

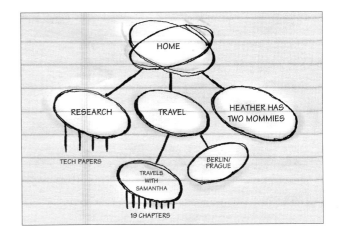

Figure 4-1: Site map for photo.net circa 1994.

DRAW A SITE MAP

The goal of putting the site map down on paper is to communicate to others on the project what the ultimate goals are. Areas that are expected to grow should be identified and perhaps given their own directory in the file system. Remember that these directory names become permanent once a site is public and can never be changed without breaking precious links from other sites. Figure 4-1 is an example of a site map from my personal site circa 1994.

It turns out that the site map immediately forces you to make decisions about whether the site is temporal or not. In other words, if you have an online cooking magazine, do you have blobs for November 1998 and December 1998 that then link to articles, or do you have blobs for Desserts and Main Courses? If the site is a mirror of a paper publication, then perhaps the temporal structure will make the most sense to readers. Otherwise, perhaps it would be more Web-centric to organize by subject. Whichever is best, drawing the site map forces you to make a decision.

The site map also gives you a chance to make the one-time versus anchor service site design choice. Most graphic designers are inclined toward building one-time Web sites. These have a bunch of lead-in pages (entry tunnels) with introductory text and fancy graphics. This is the equivalent of the GeoCities 10-year-old's "Welcome to my home page on the Web." The implicit assumption is that you've come here for the first time and that you will never return. A lot of programmers, on the other hand, are naturally inclined to build Internet anchor sites. Look at *http://www.yahoo.com.* The very first page is lean and is essentially a menu of over 100 functional links. There is no entry tunnel. There are no custom link colors. There are no frames. The Yahoo folks assume that you've been there before, that you know what Yahoo is, that you want to get a task accomplished, and that you don't want to waste time figuring out how to get to the functions. There is a company

info link at the very bottom of the page that will give you some background about Yahoo if you're confused.

I guess if you have a huge advertising budget and a one-time event, then perhaps the one-time Web site makes sense. But personally, I think it is almost always a mistake. In fact, users have caught on and develop an itchy Back button as soon as they suspect that they've landed on a one-time site. Life is too short to surf someone's advertisement. If you care about traffic, your site *structure* should send the message that you expect visitors to return frequently to accomplish a task.

Discussing a site map is a good way to figure out if anyone on the team has a CD-ROM fixation. The useless welcome page that links to another useless welcome page that leads to another useless welcome page, as mentioned above, is a strong hint that someone has a CD-ROM fixation. But the clincher is the appearance of an owner's manual/user's guide on the site map.

Let's step back for a moment and think about the CD-ROM, something in which readers have a big investment. They go to the shop, they pay $50, they transport it home, they disable their computer by ejecting whatever useful CD-ROM was already in the drive. At this point, the user has a huge investment in the multimedia work and will be delighted with a two-minute introduction complimenting him on what a smart purchase he has just made. Futhermore, the user might be willing to go into some control panels and change his monitor settings or do whatever else is necessary to make the CD-ROM work properly.

The problem with the entry tunnel is that it isn't necessarily safe to assume that the site under development will be one of a tiny handful of delightful sites on the Web or that users will be slavering with anticipation to see the priceless content and therefore be happy to wait a few minutes to get past the entry tunnel.

The user's manual is an even more troubling sign that someone is not thinking, even a subtle user's manual such as "this site is best viewed in Netscape 4.0." People go out and buy $500 printers and won't read the manual. Why does a new Web

publisher with a tiny site imagine that a user is going to read his user's manual and then go out and spend a few hours tuning up his software installations?

If you're the Web nerd on a project, this is the time to remind the novices that Web users don't have any investment in particular sites, that they don't have much patience, and that AltaVista does not send people to site entry tunnels.

Speaking of AltaVista, this is also the time to make sure that the navigation strategy is sound. If a user got dumped by a search engine into a randomly chosen page on the map, would he be able to find his way back to the table of contents?

Let's get concrete. If I were building *http://photo.net/photo/* from scratch, what would my site map look like?

Site map for photo.net

Overall principles:

- This is an anchor site, not a one-time site. The cover page will therefore have links to as many sections and services as possible.

- photo.net will not be temporal. There will be no notion of a "January issue."

Directories:

- **/doc/** for documentation on the server itself, e.g., this directory spec

- **/pcdNNNN/** for JPEG and FlashPix versions of images from the Kodak PhotoCD numbered NNNN (there will be several hundred of these directories as the site grows). All the .html files will reference images in these directories, so that an image may be used in multiple sections.

- **/tutorial/** for a textbook for new photographers, with its own index page and links from each chapter back to the index

- **/travel/** for travel guides to various photography destinations. Multi-document guides with custom illustrations, such as maps, will have their own subdirectories.

- **/technique/** for specialized how-to documents, e.g., taking photographs of star trails or macrophotography. Any article that needs helper drawings will be in a subdirectory.

- **/nikon/**, **/canon/**, etc. will contain reviews of products from those various manufacturers

- **/equipment/** for reviews of miscellaneous photo items that aren't manufacturer/system-centric, e.g., camera bags or tripods

- **/digital/** for articles about digital imaging, digital printers, scanners, etc.

- **/workshops/** for reviews of photography workshops

- **/studio/** for studio photography, especially controlled lighting

- **/about/** for general credits (a masthead), explanations of how the site works, and editorial/submission policy

- **/optics/** for tutorials on lens design

- **/career/** for articles on photography as a career or business

- **/legal/** for information about copyright and whether releases must be obtained from models or property owners

- **/contributors/**username**/** will be a private FTP-writable directory for people who aren't part of the core photo.net team. The file index.html in this directory will contain some biographical information and a link to the person's main site.

- **/new.html** for a human-generated reverse chronological description of new content

File naming/organization conventions:

- Figures go at same level as articles; e.g., foo-f01.gif is Figure 1 for foo.html.

- Audio clips are kept in RealAudio format, in the same directory as the .html file that references them. If the audio clips are associated with a particular image on a PhotoCD, then they go in the pcdNNNN directory.

Collaboration links:

- Q&A forum served by *www.greenspun.com*

- comment link from the bottom of every article, served from *www.greenspun.com*

- related links at the bottom of every article, served from *www.greenspun.com*

- mailing list, served from *www.greenspun.com*

Note:
I wish I could say that this is what photo.net in fact looks like, but it is actually a mess that evolved over six years while I was groping around at 3:00 A.M. trying to understand all of this stuff myself.

ASSEMBLE AND STRUCTURE CONTENT

Once everyone is happy with the site map, the nodes should be given filenames (e.g., foobar.html). Then people must create these files and stuff them with the content that they are ultimately to hold, not worrying whether or not the content is in HTML format.

You can see whether everyone is up to speed merely by looking in the file system and seeing how many .html files have been written. If you're not a programmer, this is a good time to bring one in. If there are a few dozen pages that have nearly identical structure, then it might be more cost-effective and reliable to have the content authors organize things into a flat file or RDBMS, and have the programmer either (1) write a custom Perl script to grind out all the .html files or (2) write a CGI or API script to generate the .html files on the fly.

MAKE A TEXT-ONLY SITE

Assuming that the people assembling the content are completely incapable of "programming" HTML, one person should sit down and turn each content file into a legal HTML document with navigation, page ownership signatures, titles, headlines, and the like. When this is done, everyone will be able to get a feel for the site and holler before big money is invested in this particular site map.

This is also the time to add links to collaboration services. If you've decided against the full-out RDBMS-backed site described in Chapter 3, you're going to

have to use services running on other folks' machines. I have a bunch of these that I offer free to other Web publishers (see *http://photo.net/philg/services.html*).

Questions to the site owner: Do you want readers to be able to discuss content? In one forum for the whole site or in subforums? Do you want to configure a comment server to collect page-specific comments? Are you going to ask readers to join a mailing list? If it turns out that you want collaboration out the wazoo, then maybe it is time to reconsider your reconsideration and go back to the whole-hog RDBMS-backed site.

HIRE A GRAPHIC DESIGNER

Note:
See Edward Tufte's second and third books, *Envisioning Information* (1990, Graphics Press) and *Visual Explanations: Images and Quantities, Evidence and Narrative* (1997, Graphics Press), for some examples of how graphics may be used effectively.

This step is optional. Remember that some of the most popular Web sites are essentially plain text, such as Yahoo, and that bad graphic design is far harder on the user than no graphic design. Also remember that nobody will laugh at a plain-text site and say, "Look at these losers who spent $50,000 on design for a content-free site."

A graphic designer who is a careful and creative thinker about information presentation may be able to help give a site a clean look. The ultimate goal is to make sure the graphics version of the site, which will inevitably be slower to load than the text-only version, offers the user something extra. Graphics should be used to help users absorb, interpret, and understand data. If it is the same information with additional decoration, then users aren't getting much return on their increased investment of time.

How to work with a designer? It is best first to make some decisions about what kind of user queries you can afford to answer. If you can't afford to pay people to respond to email wondering about browser incompatibilities and crashes, then you probably can't afford to publish JavaScript or Java, even if the initial programming is free. Here's an example of a set of requirements I might give to a designer:

- No frames, JavaScript, or Java—I don't want to think about browser compatibility beyond telling people they need Netscape 1.1 or better.

- You can't make pages that are just one big HTML table (that start with a <TABLE>). Browsers have to wait until all of a table is received before they can show any of it to the user. If the page depends on a bunch of RDBMS queries, then the user will have to wait for all of them to complete *and* all of the data to be transmitted before even one word shows up on screen.

- No custom link colors—I want users to find my hyperlinks in blue, just like at most sites.

- We're going to use RealAudio and FlashPix because streaming audio and ability to zoom up on a photo are critical for this publishing project.

- Don't tart up my HTML too much with formatting stuff (e.g., no FONT tags); use a cascading style sheet if you want to control appearance that carefully—I want to be able to edit my HTML by hand.

Please don't construe the above as saying that designers shouldn't be given any scope. On the contrary, I think a graphic designer worthy of the name should be given maximum scope to develop user interface hints. For example, suppose you want older photos on your site to be distinguished from newer ones. You could ask the designer to come up with a way to stick a gold-leaf-frame–type graphic around all the old photos, but you'd probably be happier with the results if you asked the designer to come up with a graphical or text-y way to remind readers that they are looking at an old photo rather than a new one.

COME UP WITH A MAINTENANCE PLAN

A lot of big companies, at least for awhile, will spend millions of dollars every year paying graphic designers to perform clerical functions, basically, pasting new text into HTML templates. Oftentimes both the publisher and designers get upset on a site like this. The publisher is frustrated because he has to holler into a telephone to get a page looking the way he wants. The graphic designer is frustrated because he is being used as a typist. If you don't have the budget or patience to maintain a Web service this way, then you need some plan for direct maintenance of the site by the publisher.

With a database-backed site, this is straightforward. There are admin pages in which authors enter or update text fragments. Computer programs weave these together at run-time into complete HTML pages.

With a static site, you have to give the author some kind of tool—AOLpress, Adobe Site Mill, Claris Home Page, Microsoft Front Page, or Netscape 4.0—that can do HTTP PUT and support simple edits of a page. Alternatively, the author could spend a few hours learning enough HTML to simply edit the pages directly.

Most desktop tools are so badly engineered and they put in so much crud (e.g., " " all over the place) that they are more trouble than they are worth. The extra crud makes it very hard for a Web expert to ever edit the pages manually. It also makes it tough to extract the content from the static files into a relational database. Editing raw HTML on remote PCs is quite easy. Tell the authors to edit their Netscape Composer preferences to register a standard text editor as their preferred way of working with HTML. Then they just use Netscape 4.0 to do the HTTP GET of the page they want to update. As soon as they pull down the "edit page" command from the File menu, Netscape will launch Notepad, SimpleText, Emacs, or whatever. When the authors are done editing, they can use Netscape 4.0 to

HTTP PUT or FTP back the document. You can then add a little item to your page that says "this site engineered with Notepad."

Overall Pitfall 1: Version/Source Control

Version or source control is necessary to prevent lost updates. Here's how a lost update can happen:

- Joe grabs Version A of a document at 9:00 A.M. from the Web site and spends a day editing it.

- Mary grabs Version A at noon and fixes a typo, writing it back at 12:05 P.M. (call this Version B).

- Joe finishes his edits at 5:00 P.M. and writes the document back to the server (call this Version C).

Unfortunately, Version C is an edit of Version A and hence does not include Mary's typo fix. So Mary's update is lost.

Programmers and technical writers at large companies are familiar with the problem of lost updates when multiple people are editing the same document. But Web publishing is the first time that the average person has to confront the problems of version/source control. You have to educate contributors maintaining a site via HTTP PUT or FTP that, if they aren't careful to grab the page just before editing and then save it right back, there is a serious risk that they will be overwriting someone else's edits.

If you're using an RDBMS-backed system to run your Web site, it is relatively easy to add in a version control to check in/check out documents. It is also easy to keep historical versions around. But if you're keeping everything in a file system and expecting novice users to maintain the content via FTP, version control becomes tough. You have to encourage people to use email and telephone calls to check out documents or directories of documents. Oddly enough, if people used decades-old free software such as Emacs on Unix, this would be a solved problem. With zero set-

up effort, Emacs will automatically warn a user that "The file you're about to edit has been changed on disk. Are you sure you want to edit the old version?" There are standard, free, and source code–available version-control systems for Unix that allow authors to conveniently check out and lock files (if the author forgets to check a file back in, another authorized author can steal the lock). We can only hope that, by the year 2000, commercial magic-wonder Web tools will catch up to where the freeware world was in 1980.

OVERALL PITFALL 2: OVER-OPTIMISM ABOUT COMPUTERS

Academic computer science and the software industry have been remarkably unsuccessful at producing reliable or functional systems for users. Though the programmers may have failed, their PR counterparts succeeded brilliantly. Casual computer users believe that computers are intelligent. It would never occur to them that a computer can't handle a special case or that the batch image conversion scripts in the images chapter need exactly one line per image and that an extra carriage return or left-out vertical bar will abort the process. (See Chapter 6, Adding Images to Your Site, for more on batch processing.)

If you are the most technical person on the project, at some point I think it is worthwhile to stand up in front of the whole team and try to educate folks into realizing how stupid computers are and therefore that formal thinking up front can pay huge dividends in the long run. For example, I briefly helped some friends build a catalog site for a clothing manufacturer. The garment-maker's staff was very proud of their all-electronic fabric design and catalog publishing system, which they'd been using for a few years. So there were photos or sketches of all the styles available in digital form. The manager of the desktop publishing shop thought we'd have no trouble making a Web site out of these. However, though they had numerical style or product IDs for their products, the graphics files weren't named "97-04561.tif". The files had names like "new spring jacket.tif" and were of all different sizes. It would have been impossible to write a computer program to fetch the right image file when a user was looking at a page for a particular product ID. Each file would have to be opened by a human, identified, and then renamed, a process that would take hundreds of hours.

ARE YOU FAILING?

If the project is a failure and you haven't been able to educate contributors into doing things sufficiently formally, then you need to impose structure on them. Budget $20,000 to $50,000 to rebuild the site as a database-backed system, to which people can contribute only content via Web forms. The site's structure will be a little rigid, but at least you won't have broken links, illegal HTML, etcetera.

ARE YOU SUCCEEDING?

I like to think my site is a success. It gets a lot of traffic and I get positive user feedback:

> *I've spent a good portion of the last 36 hours navigating through your web pages....*
> *I have just spent two and a half hours with you....*
> *Oh my god, I just spent three hours reading your site....*

On second thought, are these in fact positive comments? Suppose these users all came to my site looking for my mailing address? Should I then feel proud that it took them an average of 14 hours to find it? Perhaps what I need to do is a usability study.

For a proper usability study, you go to a special facility equipped with living room, classroom, and office sets. You sit the subjects at a computer on those sets and start them out on your Web site with a few tasks to accomplish or questions to answer. The proud parents of the Web site stand behind one-way glass and observe the floundering subject, who is encouraged to talk as he or she ponders the potential fruitfulness of the various links on a page.

The easiest kind of site to build and test is an ecommerce site. Everyone can agree on the goal: Make it fast and easy for the user to buy something. So a usability test might be to send a user to *www.amazon.com* and ask them to

- Buy a copy of *Lives of the Monster Dogs*.

- Given only the information "a recent and popular book about a race of super-intelligent dogs who move to New York City," find out that the title of the work is *Lives of the Monster Dogs*.

- From an uncookied browser, find and buy the cheapest edition of *The Forsyte Saga*.

- From an uncookied browser, but as someone who has previously ordered from amazon.com and remembers his account password, find and buy the cheapest edition of *The Forsyte Saga*.

- From a cookied browser enabled for 1-click ordering, find and buy the cheapest edition of *The Forsyte Saga*.

When you get to a product company's site, the goals are a little less clear. Do you want to help existing customers trying to use the product in new ways? Get people to download software and try it out? Get people to purchase something? Consider doing a usability test with *www.oracle.com* by asking a subject to use the site to answer the following questions:

- Does the Oracle RDBMS server run on Linux?

- Does the Oracle RDBMS client library run on Linux (i.e., can one run an application program on Linux that connects to an Oracle database on another computer)?

- I'm running Oracle 8.03 on HP Unix. Is a more recent version available for this operating system? If so, how do I download the upgrade or order an upgrade CD-ROM?

- What is the correct syntax for extracting the month out of a column of type date in Oracle SQL?

- I want to add Oracle to my Web site, currently running on a SPARC/Solaris machine. How much will it cost? How do I download a trial copy?

When you are testing a personal site, the goals are much less clear. I can't really remember why I set up *http://photo.net/philg/*. Suppose I did a usability test and asked subjects to start at my home page and

- Find my photographs of the Sierra Nevada.

- Determine the identity of Samantha in *Travels with Samantha*.

- Find out how much wealth Bill Gates has accumulated.

- Find out how old I am.

The results might show that someone who wanted to know only my age or mailing address got lost and distracted, and read all of *Travels with Samantha* before giving up on the original query. Or that folks looking for the heavily used Bill Gates Personal Wealth Clock never found it, and instead read my comparatively obscure 1994 proposal for standards to make Web pages understandable to computer programs before moving on to The Game. Or that people originally interested in *Travels with Samantha* got sucked into the photo.net community.

Should I change my site in response to these findings? Not necessarily. I set up my personal Web site in order to share my documents, photos, and programs. If

people are getting distracted from their original task because they are being engaged by my ideas or photos, then I'm not sorry.

As noted in Chapter 2, the "making money" chapter, my personal site costs close to $1 million a year to operate. I should probably take a step back once every year and ask, "What do I want this site to do?" and "Does the current site effectively accomplish that objective?"

SUMMARY

Here's what you should have learned from reading this chapter:

- Some formal thinking before you build a site will save a lot of grief and broken links later.

- Plan to add collaboration to a static HTML site by taking advantage of the free services offered at *http://www.greenspun.com*.

- Come up with a set of problems that you want addressed before consulting a graphic designer; "make it look pretty" is not a plan.

- Make sure that you have a way to keep content fresh without going through an expensive intermediary.

- Periodically allocate a week to do a usability test.

- Periodically allocate a day to ask fundamental questions about what you want your site to do and measure your current site against those goals.

MORE

- *http://www.usableweb.com* is an up-to-date list of the best resources on Web site usability.

- *http://www.useit.com,* Jakob Nielsen's personal site. Nielsen is also the author of *Multimedia and Hypertext: The Internet and Beyond* (1995, Academic Press Professional), which will give you more history and perspective than most designers have.

- *Information Architecture for the World Wide Web* (Rosenfeld and Morville, 1998; O'Reilly). This is a good book to give to neophytes. If nothing else, reading it will force them to pause long enough before doing major damage to a project.

- Everyone on the project should agree that well-organized information is the sine qua non of a useful Web site. At a minimum, everyone should have read Edward Tufte's classic troika: *The Visual Display of Quantitative Information* (1983, Graphics Press), *Envisioning Information* (1990, Graphics Press), and *Visual Explanations: Images and Quantities, Evidence and Narrative* (1997, Graphics Press). Pages 146 to 149 of the last book contain everything that is truly important about designing a traditional Web site.

- If my discussion of sample bias has gotten you interested in probability or statistics, read my favorite text, *Fundamentals of Applied Probability Theory* (Drake, 1967; McGraw-Hill).

5

Learn to Program HTML in 21 Minutes

One night *Hardcopy* featured a 10-year-old boy whose psychotic mother wouldn't take her meds and was beating him up. He wanted to live with his father, but the judge wouldn't change his custody arrangement. So the 10-year-old kid built a Web site to encourage Internetters to contact the judge in support of a change in custody.

I tell this story to my friends who ask me for help in building their static HTML Web sites: "The abused 10-year-old got his site to work; I think you can, too."

If they persist, I tell them to find a page that they like, choose Save As in Netscape, then edit the text with the editor of their choice. I've never known anyone who couldn't throw together a simple page in under 21 minutes.

"ONE OF OUR LOCAL WEBMASTERS"

Having said all of that, now I'm going to explain how to write HTML. Why? It all started the day that Jim Clark, Chairman of Netscape, came to MIT to give a Laboratory for Computer Science Distinguished

Lecture. In previous years, the lecturers had been grizzled researchers who'd toiled anonymously for decades at places like Bell Labs and Stanford. In 1996, we had two billionaires: Bill Gates and Jim Clark. Before the lecture, Michael Dertouzos, the director of our lab, was touring Clark around the CS building. Clark stopped in the hallway outside my office to ask some questions about a framed photograph. The official hosts came into my office and dragged me away from my terminal so I could tell Jim Clark how I'd taken a picture of a waterfall in New Hampshire.

This was my big moment; I was being introduced to the one man in the world with enough power to fix everything wrong with the Web standards. I was sure that Dertouzos would tell him what a computer science genius I was. He was going to talk about my old idea to add semantic tags to HTML documents, about the work I'd done to make medical record databases talk to each other to support Internet-wide epidemiology, about all the collaboration systems I'd built that hundreds of Web sites around the world were using.

"This is Philip Greenspun," the lab director began, "one of our local webmasters."
Yeah.

Anyway, part of a real webmaster's job is to assist new users in getting their pages together. So, in that spirit, here is my five-minute HTML tutorial.

YOU MAY HAVE ALREADY WON $1 MILLION

Then again, maybe not. But at least you already know how to write legal HTML:

```
My Samoyed is really hairy.
```

That is a perfectly acceptable HTML document. Type it up in a text editor, save it as index.html, and put it on your Web server. A Web server can serve it. A user with Netscape Navigator can view it. A search engine can index it.

Suppose you want something more expressive. You want the word *really* to be in italic type:

```
My Samoyed is <I>really</I> hairy.
```

HTML stands for Hypertext Markup Language. The <I> is markup. It tells the browser to start rendering words in italics. The </I> closes the <I> element and stops the italics. If you want to be more tasteful, you can tell the browser to *em*phasize the word *really:*

```
My Samoyed is <EM>really</EM> hairy.
```

Most browsers use italics to emphasize, but some use boldface and browsers for ancient ASCII terminals (e.g., Lynx) have to ignore this tag or come up with a clever rendering method. A picky user with the right browser program can even customize the rendering of particular tags.

There are a few dozen more tags in HTML. You can learn them by choosing View Source from Netscape Navigator when visiting sites whose formatting you admire. This is usually how I learn markup. You can learn them by visiting *http://photo.net/wtr/* and clicking through to one of the comprehensive online HTML guides. Or you can buy *HTML: The Definitive Guide* (Musciano and Kennedy, 1997; O'Reilly).

DOCUMENT STRUCTURE

Armed with a big pile of tags, you can start strewing them among your words more or less at random. Though browsers are extremely forgiving of technically illegal markup, it is useful to know that an HTML document officially consists of two pieces: the *head* and the *body*. The head contains information about the document as a whole, such as the title. The body contains information to be displayed by the user's browser.

Another structural issue is that you should try to make sure you close every element that you open. So if your document has <BODY> at the beginning, then it should have </BODY> at the end. If you start an HTML table with <TABLE> and don't have an ending </TABLE>, Netscape Navigator may display nothing. Tags can overlap, but you should close the most recently opened one before the rest, for example, for something that's both boldface and italic:

```
My Samoyed is <B><I>really</B></I> hairy.
```

Something that confuses a lot of new users is that the <P> element used to surround a paragraph has an optional closing tag </P>. Browsers by convention assume that an open <P> element is implicitly closed by the next <P> element. This leads a lot of publishers (including lazy old me) to use <P> elements as paragraph separators.

Here's the source HTML from which I usually start a Web document.

```
<html>
  <head>
    <title>New Doc</title>
  </head>
  <body bgcolor=white text=black>
    <h2>New Doc</h2>
    by <a href="http://photo.net/philg/">Philip Greenspun</a>
    <hr>
    introductory text
    <h3>First Subhead</h3>
    more text
    <p>
    yet more text
    <h3>Second subhead</h3>
    concluding text
    <hr>
    <a href="mailto:philg@mit.edu">
      <address>philg@mit.edu</address>
    </a>
  </body>
</html>
```

Note:
I use lowercase tags, which isn't technically legal in HTML, but it looks better and browsers are forgiving in this regard.

Let's go through this document piece by piece (see how it looks rendered by a browser in Figure 5-1).

The <HTML> element at the top says "I'm an HTML document." Note that this tag is closed at the end of the document. It turns out that this tag is unnecessary. I've saved the document in the file "basic.html". When a user requests this document, the Web server looks at the .html extension and adds a MIME header to tell the user's browser that this document is of type text/html.

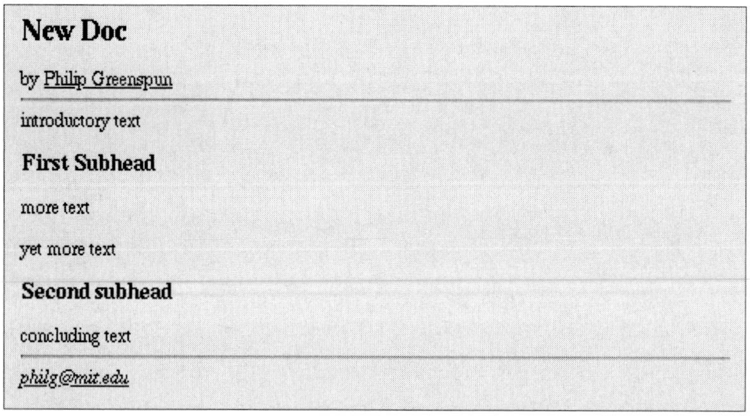

New Doc

by Philip Greenspun

introductory text

First Subhead

more text

yet more text

Second subhead

concluding text

philg@mit.edu

Figure 5-1: Our Web
document rendered
by a browser.

I put in a <HEAD> element mostly so that I can legally use the <TITLE> element to give this document a name. Whatever text I place between <TITLE> and </TITLE> will appear at the top of the user's Netscape window, on his Go menu, and in his Book-marks menu, should he book-mark this page. After closing the head with a </HEAD>, I open the body of the document with a <BODY> element, to which I've added some parameters to manually set the background to white and the text to black. Some Web browsers default to a gray background; the resulting lack of contrast between background and text offends me so much that I change the colors manually. This is a violation of most of my principles, since it potentially introduces an incon-sistency in the user's experience of the Web. However, I don't feel too guilty about it, because (1) a lot of browsers use a white background by default, (2) enough other publishers set a white background that my pages won't seem inconsistent, and (3) it doesn't affect the core user interface the way that setting custom link colors would.

Just below the body I have a headline, size 2, wrapped in an <H2> element. This will be displayed to the user at the top of the page. I probably should use <H1>, but browsers typically render that in a font too huge even for my bloated ego. Underneath the headline, I'll often put "by Philip Greenspun" or something else indicating authorship, plus perhaps a link to the full work. The phrase "Philip Greenspun" is a hypertext *anchor,* which is why it is wrapped in an A element. The <A HREF= says "this is a hyperlink." If the reader clicks anywhere from here up to </A>, the browser should send him to *http://photo.net/philg/*.

After the headline, author, and optional navigation, I put in a horizontal rule tag: <HR>. I wish I could say that the best thing I'd learned from Dave Siegel was how to reel in women via a popular Web site (see *http://photo.net/wtr/getting-dates.html*). Unfortunately, the only thing of practical value that I learned was not to overuse hor-izontal rules: Real graphic designers use white space for separation. I use <H3> head-lines in the text to separate sections, and only put an <HR> at the very bottom of the document.

Underneath the last <HR>, I sign my document with philg@mit.edu, my email address, unchanged since 1976. The <ADDRESS> element usually results in an italics rendering. I think that all documents on the Web should have a signature like this. Readers expect that they can scroll to the bottom of a browser window and find out who is responsible for what they've just read. Note that this one is wrapped in an anchor tag. If the user clicks on the anchor text (my email address), the browser will pop up a "send mail to philg@mit.edu" window. I think it is almost always bad to publish an email address on a Web page and not wrap it in a "mail-to" tag.

TARTING UP YOUR PAGES

Netscape and Microsoft have introduced a whole raft of tags with which you can tart up your pages. Instead of saying "this is a headline, level 3," you can say "stick this in 18-point Helvetica Bold and make it red." Instead of "emphasize this," you can say "stick this in 14-point Times Italic." There are a bunch of problems with filling up your document with tags like FONT:

- Older browsers will ignore them; Netscape 1.0 knows how to render a headline, level 3. But it doesn't understand the Microsoft font directives.

- Newer browsers will ignore them; WebTVs and palmtops are some of the most interesting devices attached to the Web, and they only understand basic HTML.

- When you change your graphic designer, you have to edit 10,000 .html documents.

If you can't "just say no" to formatting your documents instead of working on the content, then you might want to consider developing a sitewide cascading style sheet. Here's the cascading style sheet for the online version of this book (*http://photo.net/wtr/thebook/*):

```
P { margin-top: 0pt; text-indent : 0.2in }
P.stb { margin-top: 12pt }
P.mtb { margin-top: 24pt; text-indent : 0in}
P.ltb { margin-top: 36pt; text-indent : 0in }

p.marginnote { background-color: #E0E0E0 }
p.paperonly { background-color: #E0E0E0 }

li.separate { margin-top: 12pt }
```

Each line of the style sheet gives formatting instructions for one HTML element or a subclass of an HTML element. My first directive is to tell browsers not to separate paragraphs with blank lines (margin-top: 0 pt), but rather simply to indent the first line of a new paragraph by 0.2 inches (I tried 3em but it didn't look right). So now my paragraphs will be mushed together like those in a printed book or magazine. Books and magazines do sometimes use white space, but mostly to show thematic breaks in the text. I therefore define three classes of thematic breaks and tell browsers how to render them. The first, "stb" (small thematic break), will insert 12 points of white space. A paragraph of class stb will inherit the 0.2 inch first-line indent of the regular P element. For medium and large thematic breaks, I specify more white space and override the first-line indent.

How do I use this style sheet? I park it somewhere among my pages in a file with the extension .css. This extension will tell the Web server program to MIME-type it as text/css. Personally, I chose to place this cascading style sheet right at the top level of my Web content directory, because I think that I will eventually use it for all of my writing. Inside each document that uses the cascading style sheet, I put the following LINK element inside the document HEAD, just above the TITLE:

```
<LINK REL=STYLESHEET HREF="/philg.css" TYPE="text/css">
```

Note the leading "/" at the beginning of the HREF. This causes the user's browser to come back and request "http://photo.net/philg.css" from my server before rendering any of the page. Note that this will slow down page viewing a bit, although if all of my pages refer to the same sitewide style sheet, users' browsers should be smart enough to cache it. If you read 15 chapters from this book online with Netscape Navigator 4.0, the browser would request the philg.css style sheet only once.

Okay, now the browser knows where to get the style sheet and that a small thematic break should be rendered with an extra bit of white space. How do we tell the browser that a particular paragraph is "of class stb"? Instead of <P>, we use

```
<P CLASS="stb">
```

right before the text that starts a new theme.

Book designers have all kinds of clever ways of setting off margin notes, body notes, and footnotes. But I'm not a book designer, so I just defined a couple of styles that get rendered with a gray background (`"p.marginnote { background-color: #E0E0E0 }"`). This alerts readers that margin notes aren't part of the main text.

My final new subclass (`"li.separate { margin-top: 12pt }"`) was directed at making lists with white space between each bulleted item. It worked nicely in Internet Explorer 4.0 but failed in Netscape Navigator 4.0, so I don't use it; instead, I use two line-break tags,

.

For a complete guide to all the Cascading Style Sheet directives, look in *HTML: The Definitive Guide* (Musciano and Kennedy, 1997; O'Reilly) or check the online guides that I reference at *http://photo.net/wtr/*.

Now that You Know How to Write HTML, Don't

Owing to the neglect of our defences and the mishandling of the German problem in the last five years, we seem to be very near the bleak choice between War and Shame. My feeling is that we shall choose Shame, and then have War thrown in a little later, on even more adverse terms than at present.

—Winston Churchill in a letter to Lord Moyne, 1938
(*Churchill: A Life*, Gilbert, 1991; Holt)

HTML represents the worst of two worlds. We could have taken a formatting language and added hypertext anchors, so that users had beautifully designed documents on their desktops. We could have developed a powerful document structure language, so that browsers could automatically do intelligent things with Web documents. What we actually *have* with HTML is a hybrid: ugly documents without formatting *or* structural information.

Eventually the Web will work like a naive user would expect it to. You ask your computer to find you the cheapest pair of blue jeans being hawked on the World Wide Web and 10 seconds later you're staring at a photo of the product and being asked to confirm the purchase. You see an announcement for a concert and click a button on your Web browser to add the date to your calendar; the information gets transferred automatically. More powerful formatting isn't far off, either. Eventually there will be browser-independent ways to render the average novel readably.

None of this will happen without radical changes to HTML, however. We'll need *semantic tags* so that publishers can say, in a way that a computer can understand, "This page sells blue jeans" and "The price of these jeans is U.S. $25." Whether we need them or not, we are sure to get new formatting tags with every new generation of browser. (Personally, I can't wait to be able to caption photographs and figures, a common feature of word processing programs in the 1960s.)

Back in 1994, so long ago that I still believed an academic conference was an effective way to distribute an idea, I wrote a paper titled "We have Chosen Shame and Will Get War" (*http://photo.net/philg/research/shame-and-war.html*), presenting a scheme for embedding semantic markup in HTML documents so that it wouldn't break old browsers (such as NCSA Mosaic!). More importantly, I suggested that we needed to develop a common set of document classes—"advertisement", "novel", "daily-newspaper-article"—so that programmers could write software to make life easier for authors and readers.

My idea was too radical and forward-looking for its time. The idea of semantic markup in documents had barely been tested. Charles Goldfarb, Raymond Lorie, and Edward Mosher tried it out in 1969 with Generalized Markup Language (GML). They got their company to use it for about 90 percent of its document production. But this was only at one little company, so not too many Web standards experts would have noticed. Oh, yes, the company name was International Business Machines.

The American National Standards Institute (ANSI) published its first draft of Standard Generalized Markup Language (SGML) in 1980. A few small organizations, such as the United States Department of Defense, the Internal Revenue Service, and the Securities and Exchange Commission, began using the semantic markup features of the new language.

The most bizarre thing about HTML is that it borrows the (uninteresting) syntax of SGML:

```
<element> ... stuff being marked up ... </element>
```

but it doesn't have the (interesting) semantic markup or document-type definition capability of SGML.

As a Web publisher and Web user, it seemed natural to me that the folks who set the Web standards would see the importance of semantic markup and machine processing of documents on behalf of users. A student of Max Weber, however, would not have been surprised that my paper was rejected and that the whole semantic markup issue was ignored for six years. People who write Web standards and go to Web conferences are not doing it because they have a passion for Web publishing or Web surfing. They have a passion for sitting on conference committees, sitting on standards committees, and escaping the boredom of their home-towns by going on company-paid trips to wherever these committee meetings happen to be taking place (note that nobody ever points out the absurdity of putative Internet experts physically flying their bodies around the globe, rather than using some kind of DB-backed Web site and video conferencing to support collaboration). The people who are passionate about publishing are busy building online magazines and services. The people who are passionate about surfing are at home with their cable modems.

It has been four years since I wrote my "Shame and War" paper. Has there been any progress since then? Yes and no. The Extensible Markup Language (XML) is being standardized by the World Wide Web Consortium (W3C). It addresses the need for semantic markup but not the requirement that publishers agree on a common set of classes for semantic markup to be useful. With XML, each publisher or community of publishers can agree on some new document types and concomitant sets of tags. Microsoft and Netscape have agreed to make their browsers render XML. A variety of server-side tools are becoming available for parsing XML, generating XML from databases, converting XML to HTML, and authoring XML.

If you are publishing structured data, does it make sense to use HTML or XML files? Neither. XML will let you store and exchange structured data. But that doesn't mean it addresses the same problems as *database management* systems. With XML, you can certainly keep a catalog of products for sale in a file system directory and easily write a computer program to pull out the price of an item. But you can't easily build an index to facilitate rapid retrieval of all the blue items or all the items available in size 6. XML lets you store how many items are left in inventory, but you won't get any support for writing a program that subtracts 1 when an order is placed (and, more important, making sure that 10 simultaneous subtractions from different users won't collide). An XML document is like one record in a database management system. XML is therefore useful if you want to ship a record from one database to another, but it doesn't really help you build the entire database.

If I were publishing structured information, I would keep the information in a database and write scripts to generate either HTML or XML pages. Then I wouldn't have to edit 1,000 XML or HTML files when either the language standards or my publishing requirements changed. A database? Does that mean a scary, huge relational database management system as discussed later in this book? No. If you aren't updating your data in real time, an ordinary text file is fine.

For example, suppose that you are putting a company phone directory on the Web. You can define a structured format like this:

```
first name|last name|department|office number|home number|location
```

There is one line for each person in the directory. Fields are separated by vertical bars. So a file at MIT might look like this:

```
Philip|Greenspun|eecs|253-8574|864-6832|ne43-414
Rajeev|Surati|athletics|253-8581|555-1212|dupont gym
...
```

In less than an hour, you can write a simple computer program to read this file and generate:

- a public Web service offering names and office phone numbers for everyone at the university

- a public Web page for each department showing names and office phone numbers

- a private Web page for each department showing names and home phone numbers

If you decide to start using a new HTML feature, you don't have to edit all these pages manually. You just need to change a few lines in the computer program and then run it again to regenerate the HTML pages.

When the XML wave hits and someone comes up with a document type for phone listings, you can generate a set of private and public XML files containing names and phone numbers. People downloading an XML file will be able to tell their computer to dial the phone number automatically, since the number will be encased in a VOICE_PHONE_NUMBER element.

The high-level message here is that you should think about the structure of the information you are publishing first. Then think about the best way to build an investment in that structure and preserve it. Finally, devote a bit of time to the formatting of the final HTML or XML that you generate and ship to users over the Web.

IT'S HARD TO MESS UP A SIMPLE PAGE

People with limited time, money, and experience usually build fairly usable Web sites. However, there is no publishing concept so simple that money, knowledge of HTML arcana, and graphic design can't make slow, confusing, and painful for users. After you've tarted up your site with frames, graphics, and color, check the server log to see how much traffic has fallen. Then ask yourself whether you shouldn't have thought about user interface stability.

CD-ROMs are faster, cheaper, more reliable, and a more engaging audio/visual experience than the Web. Why then do they sit on the shelf while users greedily surf the slow, unreliable, expensive Web? Stability of user interface.

There are many things wrong with HTML. It is primitive as a formatting language and it is almost worthless for defining document structure. Nonetheless, the original Web/ HTML model has one big advantage: All Web pages look and work more or less the same. You see something black, you read it. You see something gray, that's the background. You see something blue or underlined, you click on it.

When you use a set of traditional Web sites, you don't have to learn anything new. Every CD-ROM, on the other hand, has a sui generis user interface. Somebody thought it would be cute to put a little navigation cube at the bottom right of the screen. Somebody else thought it would be neat if you clicked on the right-hand page of an open book to take you to the next page. Meanwhile, you sit there for 15 seconds feeling frustrated, with no clue that you are supposed to do anything with that book graphic on the screen. The CD-ROM goes back on the shelf.

The beauty of Netscape 2.0 and more recent browsers is that they allow the graphic designers behind Web sites to make their sites just as opaque and hard to use as CD-ROMs. Graphic designers are not user interface designers. If you read a book like the *Macintosh Human Interface Guidelines* (Apple Computer, Inc., 1993; Addison-Wesley), you will appreciate what kind of thought goes into a well-designed user interface. Most of it has nothing to do with graphics and appearance. Pull-down menus are not better than pop-up menus because

they look prettier; they are better because you always know exactly where to find the Print command.

Some of the bad things a graphic designer can do with a page were possible even way back in the days of Netscape 1.1. A graphic designer might note that most of the text on a page was hyperlinks and decide just to make all the text black (text=#000000, link=#000000, vlink=#000000). Alternatively, he or she might choose a funky color for a background and then three more funky colors for text, links, and visited links. Either way, users have no way of knowing what is a hyperlink and what isn't. Often designers get bored and change these colors, even for different pages on the same site.

Here's a concrete example of how graphic design stupidity can cost the site owner money. I ordered an Internet cable modem from MediaOne, the cable TV monopoly in Cambridge, Massachusetts. It turned out to be only $10 a month extra for cable TV, so I asked for that also. The folks who installed everything did not leave me a channel card, so if a friend of mine said, "Let's watch *Beavis and Butthead* on MTV," we had no way of knowing which channel to type into the TV remote. "No problem," I said confidently. "I'll just print one out from the MediaOne Web site." MediaOne

had just paid the huge bucks to a fancy New York Web design firm for a complete site makeover, so naturally it was slow and painful to navigate to the channel lineup page. But we got there eventually and printed the document to my home HP LaserJet. The page was blank because the graphic *artistes* had chosen white text on a blue background. Netscape Navigator prepared a file for the printer with white text on a white background. So I called MediaOne (they paid for the call to their toll-free number) and they paid someone to grab a channel card (that they'd previously paid to have printed) and stick it into an envelope (which they paid for) and stamp the envelope and mail it to me.

Frames are probably the worst Netscape innovation yet. A graphic designer who has no idea what size or shape screen you have is blithely chopping it up. Screen space is any user's most precious resource, and frames give the publisher the tools to waste most of it with ads, navigation "aids," and other items extraneous to the documents that users click on. What's worse, with Netscape Navigator 2.0, when the user clicked on the Back button to undo his last mouse click, Navigator would undo hundreds of mouse clicks and pop the user out of the framed site altogether. Newer Web browsers handle frames a little more gracefully, but none of them handle scrolling as well as NCSA Mosaic did in 1993. In the old days, any Web site that brought up scroll bars could be scrolled down with a press of the space bar. With frames, even if there is only one scroll bar on screen, the space key does nothing until you click the mouse in the subwindow that owns the scroll bar.

I'm not saying that there isn't a place in this world for pretty Web sites. Or even that frames cannot sometimes be useful. However, the prettiness and utility of frames must be weighed against the cold shock of unfamiliar user interface that greets the user. This comparison is very seldom done and that's a shame.

JAVA AND SHOCKWAVE—THE BLINK TAG WRIT LARGE

A *Fortune 500* company executive told me not to be deceived by his company's lack of Web presence. "We're going to have a great site soon. Customers will be able to see products before their retail launch and upload audio comments on each item. We'll have Java applets and Shockwave animations."

"I'm glad to hear that your company is so profitable," I responded. "I guess since you're able to hire 50 tech support people for your Web site, then you must be raking in the bucks."

"What do you mean, 50 tech support people?!" he asked.

"If people can't get a plug-in to work on their Windows 3.1 machine or can't figure out how to record from a microphone on their Windows 95, then I'm sure you must have a plan for dealing with all the support emails that they'll be sending to your webmaster," I said.

"Uh, well, I guess we have to think about that," he mumbled as he wandered off.

Before you spend money on animation, Java, or authoring content for a plug-in, think about whether you could buy the online rights to an interesting book on your Web site's subject. Remember that AltaVista doesn't recognize images or Java applets or graphic design. It only indexes text. So that online book is going to pull a tremendous number of people into your site.

Maybe you have infinite money and can buy the book plus a raft of multimedia authors. It still might be worth remembering what brought users to the Web in the first place: control and depth. Software like Java and Shockwave enables you to lead users around by the nose. Flash them a graphic here, play them a sound there, roll the credits, and so on. But is that really why they came to your site? If they want to be passive, how come they aren't watching TV or going to a lecture?

This may seem like an obvious point, but I mention it because I've seen so many tools to convert PowerPoint presentations into Web sites. The whole point of a ViewGraph-based presentation is that you have a room full of people, all of whose thoughts have to be herded in a common direction by the speaker. Ideas are condensed to the barest bones because there is such limited time and space available and because the speaker is going to embroider them. The whole point of the Web is that

each reader finds his own path through a site. There is unlimited time and space for topics in which the reader has a burning interest.

A Java applet can make a good site great in the following situations:

- You need a richer user interface than you can get with HTML forms.

- You need to respond to user input without network delays—mouse movements, for example.

- You need to give the user real-time updates.

RICHER USER INTERFACE

A richer user interface is always harder to learn. Your readers don't *want* to learn how to use new programs. They already learned how to use a Web browser and probably also word processing, spreadsheet, and drawing programs. However, you *can* come up with a Java applet that delivers such great benefits that people will invest in learning your user interface.

Suppose I'm doing a mundane camera ownership survey. If the user owns a point-and-shoot camera, it doesn't make sense to ask which accessory lenses and flashes he owns. However, if he says, "I have a Nikon 8008," then I'd like to present a list of Nikon flash model numbers as options. I can do this now by essentially asking one question per HTML form. The user says, "I own an SLR (single-lens reflex)," then submits that form, "I own a Nikon" then submits that form, "I own an 8008" then submits that form, and my server finally generates the appropriate accessory flash form.

With a Java applet, the user's choice on the P&S/SLR menu will affect the choices available on the camera brand menu, which in turn will affect the choices available on the camera model menu. Is this better? It will take longer to download. Not only do you have to send the user the Java byte codes, but also all the text that you have in your database of camera models, only a small portion of which will ever be presented. On the plus side, the user can work in another window while the applet is downloading and, once loaded, the applet is much more responsive than a succession of forms.

Don't get *too* excited by the possibility of offering a rich custom user interface with Java. Adobe Photoshop has a beautiful user interface, but it took Adobe hundreds of person-years to perfect it. It takes Adobe hundreds of person-years to test each new version. It costs Adobe millions of dollars to write documentation and prepare tutorials. It takes users hours to learn how to use the program. You don't have a huge staff of programmers to concentrate on a single application. You don't have a full-time quality assurance staff. You don't have a budget for writing documentation and tutorials. Even if you did have all of those things, your users don't have extra hours to spend learning how to use the Web site that you build. Either they are experienced Web users and they want something that works like other sites or they are naive users who want their effort in learning to use Netscape and your site to pay off when they visit other sites.

REAL-TIME RESPONSE

Some of the user interface devices on a computer are just not well suited to the stateless request-response HTTP protocol. Even a continuous network connection might not be good enough, unless the Web server and Web client are physically close to each other. Examples of user interface devices that require real-time response are the mouse, the tablet, and the joystick.

You would not want to use a drawing tool that needed to go out to the network to add a line. An HTML forms-based game might be fun for your brain, but it probably won't have the visceral excitement of Doom. Anything remotely like a video game requires code executing on the user's local processor.

Note:
There actually is a Doom-like game implemented as a Java applet: Frag Island. You can play it at *http://fragisland .fragzone.se /fraggame.html*.

REAL-TIME UPDATES

Obvious candidates for Java include stock tickers, newsfeeds, and chat systems. The user can launch an applet that spends the whole day connected to a quote or headline server and then scrolls text around the screen. Though obvious, these are applications where Java isn't essential. The information provider could just as easily have written a "client-pull" HTML document by adding the following element to the HEAD:

```
<META HTTP-EQUIV=REFRESH CONTENT="60; URL=update.cgi">
```

The user's browser will fetch "update.cgi" 60 seconds after grabbing the page with this element.

I've been working for a few years with some folks from Boston Children's Hospital. We started back in 1994 by writing a Web interface to the hospital's 60 GB

Oracle database. As soon as browsers started to support Java applets, my collaborators got the idea to broadcast real-time waveforms from the intensive care unit out to physicians over the Internet. You can play with this at *http://www.emrs.org*.

Oh, yes, it will crash the user's browser

> *Java on the client doesn't work, and we at Netscape have done an about-turn on client-side Java in recent months.*
>
> —Marc Andreessen, VP Products at Netscape
> (Quoted in a trade journal, July 1998)

Java is often promoted as a safe and reliable language. Unfortunately, since those safe and reliable Java applets run on top of the unreliable substrate of Java Virtual Machine + Java window system, it is inevitable that your Java applet will eventually crash the user's browser. Plug-ins have similar drawbacks. You should read Chapter 10, Sites That Are Really Programs, and think about whether you can instead do everything with programs that run on your server.

WHY GRAPHIC DESIGNERS JUST DON'T GET IT

Most of what I've said in this chapter goes against conventional wisdom as observed on big corporate sites and in books on Web page design. My theory is that graphic designers get interfaces so wrong because they never figured out that they aren't building CD-ROMs. With a CD-ROM, you can control the user's access to the content. Borrow a copy of David Siegel's *Creating Killer Web Sites* (1997, Hayden Books) and note that he urges you to have an "entry tunnel" of three pages with useless, slow-to-load GIFs on them. Then there should be an "exit tunnel" with three more full-page GIFs. In between, there are a handful of "content" pages that constitute the site, per se.

Siegel is making some implicit assumptions: that there are no users with text-only browsers; that users have a fast enough Net connection that they won't have to wait 45 seconds before getting to the content of a site; that there are no users who've turned off auto image loading; that there is some obvious place to put these tunnels on a site with thousands of pages. Even if all of those things are true, if the internal pages do indeed contain any content, AltaVista will roar through and wreck everything. People aren't going to enter the site by typing "http://www.greedy.com" and then let themselves be led around by the nose *by you.* They will find the site by using a search engine and typing a query string that is of interest *to them.* The search engine will cough up a list of URLs that it thinks are of interest *to them.* AltaVista does not think a Dave Siegel "entry tunnel" is "killer." In fact, it might not even bother to index a page that is just one GIF.

AltaVista is going to send a user directly to the URL on your server that has the text closest to the user's query string. AltaVista doesn't care that your $125 an hour graphic designer thought this URL should be one-third of a frame. AltaVista doesn't care that the links to your home page and related articles are in another subwindow.

If you intend to get radical by putting actual content on your Web server, then it is probably a good idea to make each URL stand on its own. Making a URL stand on its own has implications for site navigation design. Each document will need a link to the page's author, the service home page, and the next page in a sequence if the document is part of a linear work. Remember, the Web is not there so that publishers can impose what they think is cool on readers. Each reader has his own view of the Web. Maybe that view is returned by a search engine in response to a query string. Maybe that view is links from a friend's home page. Maybe that view is a link from a personalization service that sweeps the Internet every night to find links and stories that fit the reader's interest profile.

Our task as Web publishers is to produce works that will fit seamlessly, not into the Web as we see it, but into the many Webs that our readers see.

AN INFORMATION DESIGNER WHO GOT IT

Everything important about Web design is on pages 146 to 149 of Edward Tufte's *Visual Explanations: Images and Quantities, Evidence and Narrative* (1997, Graphics Press). Here are Tufte's points:

- The screen should contain information, not navigation or administration icons. The information should become the interface: clicking on a word that is itself informational should take you to a screen with more detailed information.

- Give users broad, flat overviews of the information (tables of contents), rather than forcing them through sequential screens of choices.

- Organize your data according to expected user interest, rather than mimicking the internal structure of your organization (see Example 4 at page 9 of Chapter 1, Envisioning a Site that Won't Be Featured at suck.com).

- Why use icons for navigation when words are clearer and take up less screen space?

What is truly impressive is that Tufte wasn't even writing about the Web. He was explaining his design for a guide kiosk at Washington's National Gallery. Moreover, because the pages on which he articulates these ideas happen to be mostly given over to illustrations of kiosk screens, Tufte actually gets these fundamental ideas across in less than two pages of text.

MY PERSONAL HERO

A friend of mine was called in to design a Web site for a multibillion dollar company. The new president had called everyone responsible for the old site into a conference room. He plugged in a laptop with a 14.4 K modem and handed the Web group leader a stopwatch.

"Time how long it takes to download the home page."

63 seconds.

"Now time how long it takes to get the first results back from a search."

90 seconds.

"What do you guys plan to do about this?" asked the president.

"Uh, well, we could get a faster server," responded the Web expert.

"Great. Thanks. You're all fired."

My friend was specifically asked by the president to do a site with no animation and no Java. The focus would be entirely on a fast search of a server-side database.

MULTIPAGE DESIGN AND FLOW

Most of this chapter has been about the design of individual pages; most of this book is about the design of multipage Web applications. The bad design of a single page will offend a user; the bad design of the page-to-page flow of a site will defeat a user.

Are there general design principles that can be applied to different kinds of Web applications? I've found two.

One of the things that users love about the Web is the way in which computation is *discretized.* A desktop application is generally a complex miasma in which the state of the project is only partially visible. Despite software vendors having added multiple-level Undo commands to many popular desktop programs, the state of those programs remains opaque to users.

The first general principle is **Don't break the browser's Go menu.** Users should be able to go forward and back at any time in their session with a site. For example, consider the following flow of pages:

- choose a book
- enter shipping address
- enter credit card number
- confirm
- thank-you

A user who notices a typo in the shipping address on the confirm page should be able to return to the shipping address entry form with either the Go menu or the Back button, correct the address, and proceed from there. It would be nice if the credit card entry form was defaulted by the server with any previously entered credit card data, but this is not as essential as making sure that arbitrarily moving back and forth did not result in an error. This idea sounds simple but it can be difficult to implement, especially as publishers' ambitions become grander, as more session state is kept by the server, and as publishers start using JavaScript.

The second general principle is **Have users pick the object first and then the verb**. For example, consider the customer service area of an ecommerce site. Assume that Jane Consumer has already identified herself to the server. The merchant can show Jane a list of all the items that she has ever purchased. Jane clicks on an item (**picking the object**) and gets a page with a list of choices, such as "return for refund" or "exchange." Jane clicks on "exchange" (**picking the verb**) and gets a page with instructions on how to schedule a pickup of the unwanted item and pages offering replacement goods.

How original is this principle? It is lifted straight from the Apple Macintosh circa 1984 and is explicated clearly in *Macintosh Human Interface Guidelines* (Apple Computer, Inc., 1993; Addison-Wesley). Originality is valorized in modern creative culture, but it was not a value for medieval authors and it does not help users. The Macintosh was enormously popular to begin with, and then Microsoft went on to monopolize the desktop with a copy of the Macintosh. Web publishers can be sure that the vast majority of their users will be intimately familiar with the "pick the object then the verb" style of interface. Sticking with a familiar user interface cuts down on user time and confusion at a site.

What happens when publishers ignore these guidelines?

```
Date: Wed, 5 Aug 1998 23:20:33 -0400 (EDT)
From: Garrett Wollman <wollman@khavrinen.lcs.mit.edu>
To: philg@MIT.EDU
Subject: Another bad Web user interface example
```

```
I thought it was a really great idea when BankBoston replaced their
clunky modem-only terminal-based home banking system with one that works
over the Internet.  Not only is the user interface painfully slow
(downloading images that are different for every page over a 33.6 modem
and an encrypted connection), but it totally disregards the perfectly
good user interface built into my browser.  In particular, if you try to
actually navigate anywhere and then do something, you get this:
```

```
    Error Description 2300004 - Screen Error
```

You only need to click once on your selection. Please do not
double-click, use the buttons on your browser, or open a second
window while logged on to BankBoston. You can use the
buttons on the screen or Short Cut to move around the system
easily.

Oops!

What's worse, once you get it into this sort of a state, it is totally
unable to unwedge itself, and going back to the login screen gives only
the helpful message:

Error Description 1501002 - Invalid Card Number

This Card Number is currently logged on. Please make sure
you have logged off the system and try again.

Um, hello?!

The only way to communicate with them is through the feedback function,
which I can't use because their system won't talk to me. (Of course,
the whole thing is run under NT, judging by the file names. I think I
should probably be very concerned about that.)

Eventually, I was able to "log in" again, and got to the 'feedback'
section to send them a message. I spent about ten minutes composing
my diatribe, hit the "images" button to figure out which inline
image was hiding the "send" function, and then hit it. It comes
back with another error message -- the date I had given it did not fit
its simple-minded notions of what a date should look like, so it gave
me another error message. Of course, I didn't want to lose my
carefully composed diatribe, so I hit Meta-Back to get back to the
form. (I then added another paragraph about what kind of idiot would
give users a blank text field to enter a date without any indication
that the simple-minded program would only accept one form.) You can
of course guess what happened: I changed the format of the date to the
one it wanted, hit "send", and it gave me the original error message
again. Oops... better find something to waste ten minutes doing until
it times out again!

All in all, it took me a good hour to finally send my message, and I
never did manage to pay my bills.

Note:
According to the
July 27, 1997 issue
of *PC Week,*
BankBoston's
Web service was
developed by Sapient,
a consulting firm,
using virtually the
entire panopoly
of technologies
panned in the later
chapters of this
book: WebObjects,
Windows NT, and a
C++ and CORBA
middleware layer.

Summary

Here's what you might have learned in this chapter:

- Learning basic HTML shouldn't take more than a few minutes.

- The more HTML you know, the uglier and harder it is likely to be to use your site.

- HTML is not powerful enough to express the most interesting structural characteristics of your documents.

- XML is powerful enough to represent structure, but each XML document is really one record in a database.

- You may want to keep your content in a database management system of some kind instead, and generate HTML and XML pages programmatically.

- If you have a limited budget, spend it on content that search engines can index, rather than flash.

- Don't forget that using Java applets or plug-ins will get you into the business of educating and supporting users.

- Because a search engine can send users to any document at your site, every document on your site should have navigation links to the rest of your content.

MORE

- *HTML: The Definitive Guide* (Musciano and Kennedy, 1997; O'Reilly).

- If you work with a painfully creative designer at a big, rich company (I'm not mentioning any names here, Carrie, so as not to embarrass you), then you'll need to read *JavaScript: The Definitive Guide* (Flanagan, 1998; O'Reilly) in order to implement her user interface ideas.

- Stick Figure Death Theatre (*http://www.sfdt.com*) is a rare example of animated GIFs used effectively.

- If you're forced to work with people who think good design has something to do with "looking cool," then hit them over the head with Edward Tufte's books: *The Visual Display of Quantitative Information* (reprint edition 1992, Graphic Press), *Envisioning Information* (1990, Graphic Press), and *Visual Explanations: Images and Quantities, Evidence and Narrative* (1997, Graphic Press).

- Read *Macintosh Human Interface Guidelines* (Apple Computer, Inc., 1993; Addison-Wesley) to develop an appreciation for careful thinking about multistep interfaces.

- Learn to program XML in 21 years by periodically checking *http://www.w3.org/XML/* and *http://www.software.ibm.com/xml/* to see if anyone has done anything useful with the language.

6

Adding
Images to
Your Site

After a chapter with sections urging publishers to eschew graphics, why a chapter urging that publishers gear up to distribute thousands of photographs? *Independence Day.*

The book by Richard Ford, about a long, uneventful weekend in the life of Frank Bascombe, a divorced real estate salesman in Haddam, New Jersey, won the Pulitzer Prize for Literature:

> *Unmarried men in their forties, if we don't subside entirely into the landscape, often lose important credibility and can even attract unwholesome attention in a small, conservative community. And in Haddam, in my new circumstances, I felt I was perhaps becoming the personage I least wanted to be and, in the years since my divorce, had feared being: the suspicious bachelor, the man whose life has no mystery, the graying, slightly jowly, slightly too tanned and trim middle-ager, driving around town in a cheesy '58 Chevy ragtop polished to a squeak, always alone on balmy summer nights, wearing a faded yellow polo shirt and green suntans, elbow over the window top, listening to progressive jazz, while smiling and pretending to have everything under control, when in fact there was nothing to control.*

The script of *Independence Day*, the movie, in which aliens blow up the White House, wasn't quite as well crafted. Yet more people went to see the movie than read the book.

People like pictures.

This chapter documents a method for building an image library and presenting it to each Web user in the best way for that particular person.

Note:
People like movies even better than pictures, but, for most publishers, they are unrealistically expensive to produce and, for most users in 1998, they are unrealistically slow to download.

151

IMAGES ON THE WEB CAN LOOK BETTER THAN ON A MAGAZINE PAGE

Computer monitors don't have the resolution of photographic prints, but they can display a wide range of tones. If you take care with your images, you may be able to present the user with the experience of viewing a jewel-like photographic slide.

High-quality black-and-white photographic prints have a contrast range of about 100 to 1. That is, the most reflective portion of a print (whitest highlight) reflects 100 times more light than the darkest portion (blackest shadow). The ideal surface for reflecting a lot of light would be extremely glossy and smooth. The ideal surface for reflecting very little light would be something like felt.

It is not currently possible to make one sheet of paper that has amazingly reflective areas and amazingly absorptive areas. Magazine pages are generally much worse than photographic paper in this regard. Highlights are not very white and shadows are not very black, resulting in a contrast ratio of about 20 to 1.

Slides have several times the contrast range of a print. That's because they work by blocking the transmission of light. If the slide is very clear, the light source comes through almost undimmed. In portions of the slide that are nearly black, the light

source is obscured. Photographers always suffer heartbreak when they print their slides onto paper because it seems that so much shadow and highlight detail is lost. Ansel Adams devoted his whole career to refining the Zone System, a careful way of mapping the brightness range in a natural scene (as much as 10,000 to 1) into the 100 to 1 brightness range available in photographic paper.

Computer monitors are closer to slides than prints in their ability to represent contrast. Shadows correspond to portions of the monitor where the phosphors are turned off. Consequently, any light that comes from these areas is just room light reflected off the glass face of the monitor. You would think that the contrast ratio from a computer monitor would be 256 to 1, since display cards present 256 levels of intensity to the software. However, monitors don't respond linearly to increased voltage. Contrast ratios between 100 to 1 and 170 to 1 are therefore more typical.

Most Web publishers never take advantage of the monitor's ability to represent a wide range of tones. Rather than starting with the original slide or negative, they slap a photo down on a flatbed scanner. A photographic negative can only hold a tiny portion of the tonal range present in the original scene. A proof print from that negative has even less tonal range. So it is unsurprising that the digital image resulting from these scanned prints is flat and uninspiring.

START BY THINKING ABOUT BUILDING AN IMAGE LIBRARY

Rather than throwing together digital images on a per-project basis, a publisher is best off thinking in terms of building a digital image library. A successful image library has the following properties:

- You obtain high-quality digital representations of each image.

- Once the negative or slide is scanned, you never have to go back to the original.

- You can quickly find an image.

Obtaining a high-quality scan isn't so difficult. You must go back to whatever was in the camera, that is, the original negative or slide. You should not scan from a dupe slide. You should not scan from a print. The scan should be made in a dust-free room or you will spend the rest of your life retouching in Photoshop. Though resolution is the most often mentioned scanner specification, it is not nearly as important as the maximum density that can be scanned. You want a scanner that can see deep into shadows, especially with slides.

Never going back to the original slide or negative again means never. If a print magazine requests a high-resolution image to promote your site, you should be able to deliver a 2,000 × 3,000 pixel scan without having to dig up the slide again. If there is a fire at your facility and all of your slides burn up, you should have a digital backup stored elsewhere that is sufficient for all your future needs.

Quick retrieval means that if a user says, "I like the picture of the tiger in Heather Has Two Mommies" (*http://photo.net/zoo*), you can quickly find the high-resolution digital file.

USING KODAK PHOTOCD TO MANAGE YOUR IMAGE LIBRARY

Kodak PhotoCD is a scanning standard that kills three birds with one, er, CD. Every image on a CD is available in five resolutions, the highest of which is 2,000 × 3,000. Kodak will tell you that you can make photographic-quality prints up to 20 × 30 inches in size from the scans. Scans are made from original negatives or slides in dust-controlled environments inside photo labs. The newest generation (1996) of PhotoCD scanners can read *reasonably* deeply into slide film shadows. If you want more shadow detail and an additional 4,000 × 6,000 scan, you can get a Pro PhotoCD made.

Rather than taking up 5 MB of hard disk space, which you might be tempted to scavenge when you think a Web project has been completed, a PhotoCD scan permanently resides on a CD-ROM. That means you will always have the scan available if an unanticipated need arises. If a magazine publisher decides that it must have an image, you can email the full .pcd file.

Quickly locating an image on PhotoCD is facilitated by Kodak's provision of index prints. You can work through a few hundred images per minute by looking over the index prints attached to each CD-ROM.

What does all of this cost? About $1 to $3 for a standard scan from a 35-mm original, about $15 for a Pro scan from a medium format or 4 × 5-inch original. When you consider that you are getting 500 MB of media with each PhotoCD, the scanning per se is free (in other words, it is cheaper to have a PhotoCD made than to buy a hard disk capable of storing that much data).

See *http://photo.net/photo/labs.html* for my current favorite PhotoCD vendors.

Delivering your library to the Web

Users are not going to thank you if you present a 5 MB .pcd Image Pac file straight from the PhotoCD. For starters, it would take 12 minutes to download with a 56K modem. And then when they were all done, they wouldn't be able to view it because Web browsers don't understand Kodak PhotoCD format. There are two ways to reduce the size, and therefore downloading time, of digital image files. The first is to cut down the resolution; rather than offer 2,000 × 3,000 pixels (many more pixels than are displayable on current monitors), offer the 256 × 384 pixel size from the PhotoCD. Each pixel requires three bytes (one for red, one for green, and one for blue) and hence the file size reduction is from 18 MB down to 294 KB. The JPEG image compression system throws out information in a photographic picture that, in theory, your eye won't miss. Typical scenes can be compressed 10 to 1 before visually objectionable *artifacts* appear. That results in a file size of 29 KB, downloadable by a 28.8 K modem user in about 10 seconds.

Suppose that a publisher has a high-resolution digital image in a large uncompressed file. How do they make this image available to Web users?

What most commercial publishers do is manually produce a single JPEG that will fit nicely on the same page as the text, on a small monitor. This is usually about 180×250 pixels in size. The user gets a little graphical relief from plain text, but can't extract much information from the photo unless it is a very simple image.

A slightly more sophisticated approach is to produce two JPEGs. Place the smaller, thumbnail photo inline on the page and make it a hyperlink to the larger JPEG. This is what I used to do back in 1994, but it upset me right from the start that there was no effective way to caption the image. I also didn't like the fact that the user only got to choose from two sizes unless I uglified my pages by adding a second hyperlink to a "huge" JPEG.

In the "Road to Hell Is Paved with Good Intentions" department, technologists began to offer interactive systems. The server would store a high-resolution image and deliver to users the resolution, quality, and cropping that they requested, thus making optimum use of scarce Internet bandwidth. The Hewlett-Packard OpenPix tools, available from *http://image.hp.com,* are the best-developed example of this idea. Figure 6-1 shows a Java applet available at *http://photo.net/photo/flashpix-reference -images.html.* This applet features my photo of John Belushi's grave in Martha's Vineyard, Massachusetts.

The user can pan, zoom, and get to any pixel of this 72-megabyte image without ever having to download the entire 72 MB file. Technology doesn't get better than this . . . or does it? Do your readers want a user's manual off to the side of every image? Or a toolbar at the bottom? Do they want to have to learn to use an applet just so they can surf your site? Does this way of exploring images not make the pleasant activity of Web browsing a little too much like the hard work of using Adobe Photoshop?

Think about the user interface of the "small linked to large" system from the user's perspective. The publisher shows you a small picture. If you want a bigger view, you click on it. This is fundamentally the correct user interface, but it is a shame that clicking on an image doesn't also result in the display of a caption, of technical details behind the photograph, of options for yet larger sizes.

What readers really want is for a thumbnail to be a link to an HTML page showing the caption, technical details, a large JPEG, and links to still-larger JPEGs and interactive OpenPix sessions. This will involve a lot of work unless the publisher has automated production from PhotoCD through to the Web directories (more on that below), but the users get the best possible interface . . . or do they?

- **shift click** on the image to zoom in,
- **control click** to zoom out,
- **click and drag** to pan.

Figure 6-1: Devoted fans leave beer bottles and other items at a little fenced-in shrine in the Chilmark cemetery, Martha's Vineyard, Massachusetts. Web users can explore this 72-MB image file with the HP OpenPix Java applet at *http://photo.net/photo/flashpix-reference-images.html*.

What can my server infer from the user's action in clicking on a thumbnail? That he wants to see a 512×768 pixel JPEG? What if he has a really big monitor? A really small monitor? A really slow Internet connection? A really fast Internet connection? What if technology evolves and things like OpenPix get rolled into all the browsers? What if he has previously told me what he wants?

Most of the thumbnails on my site are now linked to computer programs. Since I run AOLserver, these are written in the AOLserver Tcl API, but they could just as easily be Perl CGI scripts or ASP pages. The programs first check the Magic Cookie headers on requests for larger images. If the user has previously said, "I'm a nerd with a $1,600 \times 1,200$ pixel monitor and a fast connection, please always give me $1,000 \times 1,500$ pixel JPEGs by default," then my program sees the cookie and generates an HTML page with a large JPEG on it, plus the caption and tech details (if available). If there is no cookie, the program has a reasonable default (in 1999, it is to serve an HTML page with a 512×768 pixel JPEG, captions, and links) plus a "click here to personalize this site" option.

CREATING JPEGS FROM PHOTOCD IMAGE PACS

Before plunging into a description of scripts that convert 100 images at a time, let's talk about what steps are necessary to convert an individual image.

Using Photoshop

Though it is time-consuming, the highest quality way to produce a JPEG from a PhotoCD Image Pac is with Adobe Photoshop. Here's the procedure that I think results in the best conversion:

1. Open the image pac file on the PhotoCD (typically something like G:\Photo_cd\Images\Img0001.pcd) from the File menu in Adobe Photoshop.

2. Remove the "PhotoCD haze." Start with the Levels command to see a histogram of the intensities in the image. Note that there is probably nothing at either the full white or full black ends of the spectrum. Try pushing the Auto Levels button. If the results are too radical, undo it and manually slide the white point a bit to the left and the black point a bit to the right. (Compare Figures 6-2 and 6-3.)

3. Edit and crop as desired. A WACOM drawing tablet makes it much easier to do fine touch-up work or realize artistic ambitions with Photoshop.

Figure 6-2: Straight off the PhotoCD. Note the warm purple sunset colors. What a dedicated photographer I must have been to stay out with a tripod until after sunset and then hike back to the car in the dark.

4. If you want to add a black border, change the background color to black and use the Canvas Size command to increase the canvas to 102 percent in width and height.

5. When you are satisfied with your image, save it as a Photoshop native format file using the Save As command.

6. Use the Unsharp Mask filter once with the following settings:

Image	base/16	base/4	base	base*4	base*16
Resolution	128 × 192	256 × 384	512 × 768	1024 × 1536	2K × 3K
Amount	100	100	100	100	100
Radius	0.25	0.5	1.0	2.0	4.0
Threshold	2	2	2	2	2

Be prepared to undo and change the settings if the result isn't what you want. Unsharp Mask finds edges between areas of color and increases the contrast along the edge. The Amount setting controls the strength of the filter. I usually stick to numbers between 60 percent and 140 percent.

Radius controls how many pixels in from the color edge are affected (so you need higher numbers for bigger images). Threshold controls how different the colors on opposing sides of an edge have to be before the filter goes to work. You need a higher threshold for noisy images or ones with subtle color shifts that you want left unsharpened.

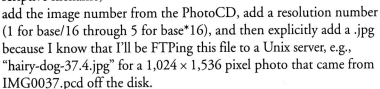

Figure 6-3:
After Auto Levels. A snapshot taken at midday! This is how I remember the scene and how the picture looks when printed by a pro lab.

7. Use the Save a Copy command to write your image out as JPEG, medium quality. I usually pick a descriptive filename, add the image number from the PhotoCD, add a resolution number (1 for base/16 through 5 for base*16), and then explicitly add a .jpg because I know that I'll be FTPing this file to a Unix server, e.g., "hairy-dog-37.4.jpg" for a 1,024 × 1,536 pixel photo that came from IMG0037.pcd off the disk.

8. Use the Revert command to reload the unsharpened Photoshop format file from disk.

9. Use the Image Size command to shrink the picture to a standard PhotoCD size, then use Unsharp Mask again.

10. Save the small image as JPEG, low or medium quality. I use the same filename as in Step 8, but with a different resolution number, for example, "hairy-dog-37.2.jpg" if the image was resized to 256 × 384.

One of the rationales behind this approach is that you never sharpen twice and that sharpening is always the very last image processing step. That's why an intermediate Photoshop native format file is necessary.

Batch processing

Instead of working with one image at a time, it is worth thinking about using a program that will take hundreds of images and, for each one, produce three sizes of JPEG, a FlashPix-format file, and a Web server script that will generate HTML pages on the fly with captions (see Figure 6-4). A simple way to start is by writing a flat file for each PhotoCD containing captions for each image on the disk. From this file, it is easy to write a program to automatically produce all the necessary Web content to implement the "user choice" scheme described above.

Here's the format for the description file:

```
line 1: spec for which resolutions to convert
line 2: on which resolution images to write copyright notice | notice
line 3: apply sharpening? (scanning blurs images)
line 4: add black borders (nice for negatives)
line 5: URL stub (where on the server will this image reside?)
lines 6-N: one line/image, formatted as the example below
<number on disk>|<target file name>|<which_resolutions>|<caption>|
  <tech details>|<alt>|<tutorial info>
```

and an example from one of my own disks:

```
101100
001111|copyright 1993 philg@mit.edu
sharpen:yes
borders:yes
url_stub:/photo/pcd1765/
2|bearfight||Brooks Falls, Katmai National Park|Nikon 8008, 300/2.8 AF
  lens (used in MF mode), FOBA ballhead, tripod, Kodak Ektar 25 film
3|montreal-flower||In Montreal's Botanical Gardens|Nikon 8008,
  60/2.8 macro lens, Fuji Velvia
4|montreal-olympic-stadium||Montreal's Olympic Stadium|Nikon 8008,
  20/2.8?, Fuji Velvia
```

The first line says, "By default, for each image, convert the first, third, and fourth resolutions from the PhotoCD file." The second line says, "On the third, fourth, fifth, and sixth resolutions, add 'copyright 1993 philg@mit.edu' to the bottom right corner of the JPEG." The next few lines specify that "all images from this disk will be sharpened and surrounded by black borders. The files will reside in the /photo/pcd1765/ directory from my server root."

The first image that I say I want converted is actually number 2 on the disk (see photo on the facing page). I want the JPEG files to contain the word bearfight. The next field is empty (||) because I'm satisfied with conversions to the default resolutions (1, 3, and 4). The caption comes next and, finally, some technical information behind the photo (most publishers wouldn't care about this, but remember that I publish photography tutorials in addition to travelogues).

What do I get for all of this? Most valuably, *http://photo.net/photo/pcd1765 /index-fpx.html.* Here's a fragment of the HTML from that undifferentiated list of all the photos on the disk:

```
<a href="/photo/pcd1765/bearfight-2.tcl">
    <img HEIGHT=134 WIDTH=196 src= "/photo/pcd1765/bearfight-2.1.jpg"
         ALT="Brooks Falls, Katmai National Park">
</a>
```

Note that this linked thumbnail can be cut and pasted into a document anywhere else on my Web server because the IMG and HREF are both to absolute URLs (beginning with a forward slash). In fact, I don't cut and paste. I've programmed my text editor (Emacs) with a new command, so that I can just type 1765 and then 2 and the editor finds the reference and inserts it into a document. Once I've written all the captions, it takes me only about an hour to add 100 images from a single PhotoCD to HTML documents dispersed around my server.

There are a couple of things to note about the .tcl script to which the thumbnail points. First, it runs inside the AOLserver process, rather than as a separately forked CGI script. This is more efficient by at least a factor of 10 than starting up a Perl script, or whatever. Since the script executes only when a user clicks on a thumbnail, the efficiency probably doesn't matter, unless you have an unusually popular site on an unusually wimpy server. Still, I like to conserve my computer's power for image processing and running Oracle.

The second point is about software engineering and is hard to illustrate without showing the source code for the Tcl script:

```
set the_whole_page \
    [philg_img_target $conn \
        "/photo/pcd1765/" \
        "IMG0002.fpx" \
        "bearfight-2" \
        "784" "536" \
        "copyright 1993 philg@mit.edu" \
        "Brooks Falls, Katmai National Park" \
        "Nikon 8008, 300/2.8 AF lens (used in MF mode), FOBA ballhead,
          tripod, Kodak Ektar 25 film" \
        "" ]
ns_return $conn 200 text/html $the_whole_page
```

Yes, the whole thing is basically just a single procedure call to philg_img_target, defined serverwide. Suppose Web standards evolve so that there is a way for the server to tell a client to what color space standards an image was calibrated. By changing this single procedure, I can make sure that all of the thousands of images on my site are sent out with a "I was scanned in the Kodak PhotoCD color space" tag. My photos will then be rendered on users' monitors with the correct tones (right now they come out way too dark on most Windows and Unix machines and a bit too light on the average Macintosh). All of the personalization code that sets and reads magic cookies is also encapsulated in philg_img_target (the source code for which is available at *http://photo.net/wtr/thebook/philg_img_target.txt*).

How does this all happen? The image conversions from PhotoCD to JPEG are done with ImageMagick. You can find precompiled binaries for most Unix variants and also Windows 95/NT at *http://www.wizards.dupont.com/cristy/ImageMagick.html.* Here's what a typical ImageMagick command (to make a thumbnail JPEG) looks like:

```
convert -interlace NONE -sharpen 50 -border 2x2 \
-comment 'copyright Philip Greenspun' \
'/cdrom/PHOTO_CD/IMAGES/IMG0013.PCD;1[1]' bear-salmon-13.1.jpg
```

Note that this is all a single shell command. I've used a bunch of optional image processing flags before the "from-file name." Because I don't like progressive JPEGs (see Alternatives to the JPEG Format at page 168), the default from ImageMagick, I invoke "-interlace NONE". Any kind of scanning introduces some fuzziness into the image, so I ask ImageMagick to sharpen a bit with "-sharpen 50". I want a two-pixel border all around, so I use "border 2×2". I could choose the color, but the default will be black. Finally, ImageMagick lets me add a comment to the JPEG file. Anyone who opens the JPEG with a standard text editor like Emacs will be able to see that it is "copyright Philip Greenspun" (conceivably other programs might display this information, but Photoshop doesn't seem to, on either the Macintosh or Windows). See *http://photo.net/wtr/thebook/imagemagick.html* for a complete list of options.

The from-file name, "/cdrom/PHOTO_CD/IMAGES/IMG0013.PCD;1[1]", is mostly dictated by the directory structure on a PhotoCD. However, the final "[1]" tells ImageMagick to grab the 128 × 192 pixel thumbnail out of the Image Pac (Base/16 size in Kodak parlance). The to-file name, "bear-salmon-13.1.jpg", includes the image number (13) from the original PhotoCD to make it easier for a human to find the entire Image Pac if requested.

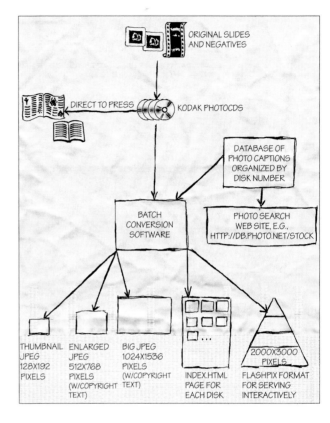

Figure 6-4:
A schema for batch processing images for the Web.

ImageMagick is convenient, but typing 300 commands like the above for each PhotoCD would get tedious. You know that an MIT woman really loves you when she offers to spare you the horrors of writing Perl. Just grab *http://photo.net/wtr/thebook/pcd-to-jpg-and-fpx.txt* if you want to use the Perl script that my girlfriend wrote as an expression of her love for me. Of course, no romance is one sunny Perl-filled day after another. When she delivered the code, I complained about the lack of data abstraction and told her that she needed to reread *Structure and Interpretation of Computer Programs* (Abelson and Sussman, 1997; MIT Press), the textbook for freshman computer science at MIT. I also asked her to rename helper procedures that returned Boolean values with "_p" (predicate) suffixes. She replied, "People will laugh at you for being an old Lisp programmer clinging pathetically to the 1960s," and then dumped me.

With a minimum of mechanical labor, I managed to get thousands of images online, in three sizes of JPEG and a 2000 × 3000 pixel FlashPix. What was my reward? Hundreds of email messages from people asking where they could find a picture of a Golden Retriever or a waterfall. Once again, MIT friends and Perl came through for me. Jin Choi spent 15 minutes writing a Perl script to grab up all my captions from the flat files into one big list. I then stuffed the list into an Illustra relational database table:

```
create table philg_photo_cds (
    photocd_id              varchar(20) not null primary key,
    -- bit vectors done with ASCII 0 and 1; probably convert this to
    -- Oracle 8 abstract data type
    jpeg_resolutions        char(6),
    -- on which resolutions to write copyright label
    copyright_resolutions   char(6),
    copyright_label         varchar(100),
    add_borders_p           char(1) check (add_borders_p in ('t','f')),
    sharpen_p               char(1) check (sharpen_p in ('t','f')),
    -- how this will be published
    url_stub                varchar(100)   -- e.g., 'pcd3735/'
);

create table philg_photos (
    photo_id                integer not null primary key,
    photocd_id              varchar(20) not null references philg_photo_cds,
    cd_image_number         integer,
    -- will be null unless photocd_id is set
    filename_stub           varchar(100),
    -- we may append frame number or cd image number
    caption                 varchar(4000),
    tech_details            varchar(4000)
)

-- build a full-text index using the PLS extension to Illustra
create index philg_photos_pls_index on philg_photos using pls
( filename_stub, caption, tech_details );
```

After an hour or two of programming, I was able to let users do full-text searches through my image filenames, captions, and tech details from *http://db.photo.net/stock/*. Try it out right now with

- "Golden Retriever"

- "waterfall"

- "70-200" (the images I've noted as taken with my Canon 70-200/2.8L zoom lens)

Is this a great system or what? Let's consider what happens if I make a mistake in spelling a word in a filename. To correct the mistake, I have to change the description.text file. Then I must either rerun the conversion script over the entire PhotoCD or manually change the filenames of three JPEGs (plus all of the HTML documents that reference the thumbnail). I have to rename the .tcl script that corresponds to the image and also update a row in the relational database table that sits behind the stock photo index system.

Perhaps it would be better to keep the image information in just one place: the relational database (RDBMS). Then we can drive the image conversion and .tcl file production from there. If we were willing to make the serving of plain old images dependent on the RDBMS being up and running, then we could just have HTML files reference photos according to their ID in the database and dispense with the static .tcl files.

Once we're running this as a database service, wouldn't it make more sense to let other people use it? If many photographers are using the same RDBMS server, then a fifth grader doing a report on Paris could search for "Eiffel Tower" and find all the photographers who had images of that monument and were willing to share it. It could also be useful for professional photographers who wanted to collaborate around images with their clients.

Coincidentally, such a collaborative database has been one of my back-burner projects for about three years. I think I might have it done by July 1999, though. Check *http:// photo.net/photo/*.

ORGANIZING JPEGS ON YOUR WEB SERVER

If you're not going to go the full RDBMS-backed route, you need to think about where to put JPEG files on your Web server. When I got my first PhotoCDs back for *Travels with Samantha,* I dumped all of the image files into the same directory as the .html files. That was stupid.

A few months after my site went up, magazines starting asking for high-resolution digital files corresponding to, say, *http://photo.net/samantha/bear-fight.jpg*. I wanted to send them the original .pcd file from the PhotoCD, but the URL told me nothing about which of my dozens of PhotoCDs held the Image Pac. When I'd use an image from *Travels with Samantha* in another service, such as *photo.net,* I'd have to use a cross-reference.

After a couple years of this, I hit upon the following system:

■ Keep a separate directory for each PhotoCD with a name like "pcd1253", where the "1253" corresponds to the last four digits of the Kodak serial number, printed prominently on the index print that comes with the disk and less prominently around the CD-ROM's spindle hole.

■ If you manipulate images from this disk, put them in a subdirectory like "pcd1253/manipulated-images".

- Make all of your references from HTML files absolute paths to the server root, for example,

```
<IMG SRC="/photo/pcd1253/pink-lady-and-dogs-8.1.jpg">
```

- Keep an index page for each PCD that contains absolute links to each image, each one ready to be cut and pasted into another HTML file and work properly.

ADDING IMAGES TO YOUR WEB PAGES

An image-rich HTML document need not take any longer to load than an image-free document. In 1994, Netscape extended the HTML element IMG with WIDTH and HEIGHT attributes. If set, they tell modern browsers how big an image will be once loaded. That way the browser is able to lay out the complete text of an HTML document before *any* of the images have loaded. Here's an example for a thumbnail:

```
<IMG SRC="/photo/pcd1253/pink-lady-and-dogs-8-sm.jpg" WIDTH=192 HEIGHT=128>
```

Note that if the image isn't exactly 128×192, the browser will crudely resize it to fit, potentially resulting in a fuzzy or blocky picture. Publishers who don't use automated production techniques such as those described above oftentimes find that they are lacking the desired size of digital image. They think to themselves, "I know that I want it to be 200×300 pixels, so I'll just put in WIDTH=300 HEIGHT=200 tags." Here's the result, an email message from a friend and my response:

```
I have just been through [a part of his site], which was completed six
months ago. It is beginning to erode. The images are fading. Something
is wrong with the server, or somewhere down the pipe.  I am very
worried that everything I'm doing has the possibility of fading. The
images look weakened, diluted, and on the Mac, they look shamefully
weak, like there's some complete idiot behind the site. None of us are
idiots, and I may have been very inexperienced at the beginning of
this web site, but I've been working with digital images since 1990
and I've never known of this happening before.

Something has to be done soon about this.
```

```
I notice in that you're using WIDTH and HEIGHT tags in Netscape to
rescale your images, e.g., on
```

```
http://.. [*** URL omitted to preserve my friendship ***]
```

```
do a "Page Info" in Netscape and you'll see that it is "455x288 (scaled
from 504x319)".
```

Unless you're using my batch conversion script or Web/db application, it is probably best to leave the WIDTH and HEIGHT blank. When you're all done with the page, run WWWis (originally wwwimagesize), a Perl program that grinds over an .html file, grabs all of the GIF and JPEG files to see how big they are, then writes out a new copy of the .html file with WIDTH and HEIGHT attributes for each IMG. The program is free and available from *http://www.tardis.ed.ac.uk/~ark/wwwis/*.

Other attributes potentially worth adding to your HTML tags are the following:

- "hspace=5 vspace=5." These will tell the browser to leave five pixels of white space around the image.

- "border=0." If the IMG is a hyperlink to a larger JPEG, it will be surrounded by a blue border. If you think this blue border is ugly, then you can set border=0 to turn it off. Personally I leave the border because it serves as a user interface cue.

- "align=left." This lets text flow around the right edge of the IMG.

ALTERNATIVES TO THE JPEG FORMAT

Standard JPEGs are not always the best format. If you are publishing line drawings or other very simple graphics with large areas of a single color, then a GIF can be sharper and smaller (see my comparison of GIF and JPEG sizes at *http://photo.net /wtr/img-format/*).

I personally don't like interlaced GIFs or progressive JPEGs (which only work with Netscape 2.0 and higher). The theory behind these formats is that the user can at least look at a fuzzy full-size proxy for the image while all the bits are loading. In practice, the user is *forced* to look at a fuzzy full-size proxy for the image while all the bits are loading. Is it done? Well, it looks kind of fuzzy. Oh wait, the top of the image seems to be getting a little more detail. Maybe it is done now. It is still kind of fuzzy, though. Maybe Greenspun wasn't using a tripod. Oh wait, it seems to be clearing up now....

A standard GIF or JPEG is generally swept into its frame as the bits load. The user can ignore the whole image until it has loaded in its final form, then take a good close look. He never has to wonder whether more bits are yet to come.

The most serious problem with JPEG files is that they aren't stored in any kind of standard color space. So if you edit them to look good on a Macintosh monitor (gamma-corrected), they might look horrible on someone's PC or Unix machine (typically not gamma-corrected). PhotoCD Image Pacs are always produced in a calibrated color space, thus preserving your investment in an image library against the day when the Web standards finally enable a publisher to specify a gamma along with an image. It is also possible to obtain FlashPix-format scans in a calibrated color space.

Note:
One of my favorite photo labs, Portland Photographics, deals with gamma in a very interesting way at *http:// www.portphoto.com*. I've written a bit more myself on the subject at *http:// photo.net/photo /fixing-gamma.html*.

ALTERNATIVES TO PHOTOCD

If you have a negative or slide larger than 4" × 5" in size and/or very dense, you will want to get a drum scan at a service bureau. Drum scanners use photomultiplier tubes that can read much higher densities than the CCD scanners used by Kodak for the Picture Imaging Workstation. Unfortunately, they are also expensive and slow, so it costs at least $75 to have a high-resolution drum scan made.

If you're in a hurry to get a handful of images from slides or negatives onto the Web, you may wish to use a desktop film scanner. The most interesting recent practical innovations in desktop scanners recently are systems that look at a piece of film from different angles and try to figure out what is a dust particle or scratch and what is part of the camera-formed image. An example of this technology is Digital ICE, incorporated in the Nikon Super Coolscan 2000.

ALTERNATIVES TO FILM

What if we lived in a world where lots of folks had desktop publishing software but nobody had word processors? That's kind of where we are today (1999) with digital imaging. Adobe Photoshop and similar packages are on many desktops, but generally getting an image into digital form requires a painful scanning step.

Current digital cameras are a mess both in terms of quality and ergonomics. Consumer products engineers tend not to innovate, and the imaging pipelines of products you can buy in 1999 are therefore largely derived from video cameras, where resolution of more than 640 × 480 pixels isn't useful. The goal for most companies is a high-quality camera with 1,000 × 1,000 pixel resolution. One million pixels is the number at which most people will accept a small print as "photographic quality." Note that there are many factors affecting image quality other than resolution. In some ways, a digital camera could produce better quality than a film-based camera because you can have purer whites under artificial lighting, greater dynamic range, and higher sensitivity (so you aren't forced to use on-camera flash).

If you need to get to the Web quickly and don't ever expect to want a wall-sized enlargement, you can probably find a good digital camera in March 1999 for $600.

However, in the long run you might not want a still camera at all. The Canon XL-1 DV camcorder makes 30 digital still images per second that are about as good as you get from cheaper digital "cameras." So you can wait until after you get home to decide whether to present video or still pictures. For accounts of my struggles in transferring digital video to hard disk, see *http://photo.net /wtr/streaming-video.html.* The short answer: Buy a Miro-brand board; don't buy a DPS-brand board.

Let me indulge in some punditry here. When digital cameras become widespread, people are going to need much more disk storage. That's because there is virtually no operating system support for migrating little-used data out to tape, even if the average person had a tape drive. The best Japanese digital still cameras will be made by Sony and Canon because they have such great experience in engineering video cameras. The best consumer-priced cameras overall, though, will come from Hewlett-Packard. Why? HP has better engineers to sweat the analogue and digital signal processing details of the imaging pipeline, and they have much more taste in user interface than the Japanese companies.

Once digital cameras become ubiquitous, you should figure out ways for users to contribute images to your site. Anywhere that users contribute text is an opportunity for you to let them contribute pictures, as well.

DIGITAL WATERMARKING

It is technologically feasible to hide a pattern of bits into an image and subsequently test for the presence or absence of this pattern. This process is called digital watermarking. It works by very slightly changing the color or intensity of individual pixels. In theory, the presence of the watermark need not visibly degrade image quality.

Here are two common uses of watermarking:

- tagging an image with "This image was taken by Joe Photographer"

- tagging an image with "This image was taken by Joe Photographer and downloaded by Jane User on August 6, 1998" (requires software to process images on the fly and also that Jane User identify herself to the server before downloading the image)

In theory, watermarking will make it more difficult for someone to misappropriate an image and use it without permission or payment. In practice, there are some minor problems:

- Unless it is so strong as to be visually objectionable, the watermark may be unrecoverable after a few JPEG decompressions and recompressions, as might be typical if an unauthorized user were adapting the image for some other use.

- There is no single standard watermarking system. Thus, an honest person who wished to check whether or not an image was watermarked would have no way to do so. They would have to download software from 20 different vendors and check a particular image with all those programs.

The most serious problem with watermarking is that it is unclear how it helps an individual photographer. The watermark might help alert a photographer to the theft of an image. However, if the user is in another country, it may not be practical to enforce ownership.

MY PERSONAL APPROACH TO COPYRIGHT

For my first couple of years of publishing on the Web, I got very huffy about copyright infringement. I entertained dark thoughts of litigation when I saw one of my photos, without credit or payment, filling the space between ads in *Forbes* or *Interactive Week*. I didn't spend days behind a tripod waiting for the perfect moment so that people could use my work to promote their ugly commercial ventures.

But realistically, litigation in the United States isn't for middle-class people. I couldn't afford to hire a team of lawyers to chase down the miscreants, and I didn't want to spend my life filing lawsuits myself. I decided to focus my energy on creating new works and not lose sleep over piracy of the old ones.

Then one of my readers emailed me a Web page with an uncredited usage of one of my bear photographs from *Travels with Samantha:*

Yes, the IRS does try to intimidate and bully you. And they publicly crucify some public figure each year (Willie Nelson, Leona Helmsley, Darryl Strawberry, Pete Rose, etc.) who has been caught with allegedly "fudged" returns. But, as you will learn, there is NO LAW, anywhere, that mandates you file a tax return!... For $88-$1000, you could purchase assistance in How To STOP Paying Federal Income Tax—LEGALLY!

This wasn't exactly what I had in mind when I set up my site, so I sent the company some email requesting that they remove the picture. The response was frustrating, but I was open-mouthed in admiration of its creativity:

```
Our programmer says that he has never seen your book, and that the
picture came from a site that listed lots of pix (both gif & jpg)
which were presented as available for download by anyone! At this
point we are not interested in getting into a tussle with you, but the
question is now open whether the picture is original with you or you
took the picture from the same source. We'll need some coroberation to
verify your claim to the picture before we go any farther.

Dana Ewell, CEO
!SOLUTIONS! Group
```

I still didn't have enough money to hire a team of lawyers to "put the genie back in the bottle," but I thought I could use my assets: (1) my site is more interesting than average; (2) my site is more stable and, because it is so old, better indexed than average. Every time another publisher used one of my 4,000 online images with a hyperlinked credit, I might earn a new reader. Did their site suck? So much the better. The user wouldn't be likely to press the Back button once he or she arrived at my site through the "photo courtesy Philip Greenspun" link. Of course, my site is noncommercial, so extra readers don't bring me any cash, but I do like the idea that my work is broadly exposed to people who might not find it otherwise. That took care of the good-faith users. Could I use my site's stability and presence in Web indices to deal with the bad-faith users?

It hit me all at once: an online Hall of Shame. I'd send noncrediting users a single email message. If they didn't mend their ways, I'd put their names in my Hall of Shame for their grandchildren to find. I figure that anyone reduced to stealing pictures is probably not creative enough to build a high Net profile, so a search for their name wouldn't result in too many documents, one of which would surely be my Hall of Shame. What if the infringer were to retaliate by putting up a page saying "Philip Greenspun beats his Samoyed"? Nobody would ever find it because an AltaVista search for "Philip Greenspun" returns too many documents. Try it right now; then try "Shawn Bonnough" for comparison, making sure to include the string quotes in both queries.

A practical-minded person might argue that my system doesn't get me any cash or stop any infringement. A technology futurist might argue that one of the micro-payment schemes from the 1960s is going to be set up Real Soon Now. Both of these people are right, I guess, but I won't be sorry if what seems to be the evolving custom on the Internet solidifies into law: Send email asking for permission to republish, be scrupulous about crediting authors, and prepare to be vilified if you flout these rules.

Would that be the best possible system? Maybe not, but it has to be much more efficient for society than a bunch of corporations hiring lawyers to sling mud at each other in court. Under my system, we can enjoy seeing our work (with credit) on other folks' sites, vent our spleens at midnight by adding to a Web page of transgressors, and then move on to new productive activities.

SUMMARY

Here is what you might have learned in this chapter:

- Photographs are valuable content, as distinct from graphics, which are generally a waste of your money and the user's downloading time.

- Always scan from an original negative or slide, never from a print.

- Think seriously about the fact that you are building an image library and whether the Kodak PhotoCD system can help you.

- Build a structured database of information about your images that you can use for automatic conversion to JPEG format, filenaming, and captioned HTML code generation.

- Use WIDTH and HEIGHT tags in your IMGs so that the text on pages with inline images doesn't take longer to load.

- Stopping other people from using your creative work probably won't increase your ability to sell that creative work and will cost a tremendous amount of time and money; it is usually better to build a hall of shame and devote yourself to creating new works.

MORE

- *http://photo.net/photo/* contains everything else that I know about taking pictures.

- For thinking about how traditional photography tackles the problem of compressing scene contrast down to the capabilities of negatives, slides, and prints, read Ansel Adams's *The Negative* (reprinted 1995, Little Brown) and *The Print* (reprinted 1995, Little Brown). Another great book about the technical aspects of photography is *Basic Photographic Materials and Processes* (Stroebel, 1990; Focal Press).

- Read "Using Kodak Photo CD Technology for Preservation and Access: A Guide for Librarians, Archivists, and Curators" by Anne Kenney and Oya Rieger (1998), available at *http://www.library.cornell.edu/preservation /kodak/cover.htm*.

- Digital watermarking is covered with a few survey articles in the July 1998 issue of *Communications of the ACM*. Given that ACM is the leading professional computer science organization, claims to be "devoted to the exchange of information, ideas, and discoveries," and did not pay for any of the articles in this journal, you might expect to find this content on their Web site. However, ACM was one of the last academic groups to wake up to the Internet and, when they finally did, all they could think to do was sell, sell, sell. As of August 1998, an enthusiast in an African village who wished to learn some computer science could download articles at a cost of $10 per article.

7

**Publicizing
Your Site
(without
Irritating
Everyone
on the Net)**

A good way to publicize your site is to buy a 60-second commercial during the Super Bowl. A black screen with your URL in white should get the message out. Your users will scribble down the URL on the cover of *Parade* magazine and then check it later. Suppose, however, that a six-pack of Budweiser should be spilled on that copy of *Parade*. Your URL is lost to the user unless he roots around in the Web directories and search engines. Web directories are manually maintained listings of sites, organized by category. If your Super Bowl spot was clear that you are selling beads, then the user might find *http://www.yahoo.com/Business_and _Economy/Companies/Hobbies/Beading/* and follow a link from there to your server. More likely, though, he'll just go into a search engine and type "beads". This chapter is about making sure that your site is at the top of the list computed by the search engine.

SEARCH ENGINES

This section explains how search services are built, how search engine sites sell advertising, how a publisher can determine the number of users who came to a site via a search engine (and what those people were searching for), how to improve a site's chances of being selected by a search engine in response to a query string, and how to make sure that dynamically served content isn't inadvertently hidden from search engines.

How search engines look to the user

The search engine's job is to produce a private view of the World Wide Web where links are sorted by relevance to a user's current interest. Users typing "history of Soho London" would expect to get a page of links to pages detailing the history of this neighborhood. The search engine user will bypass "entry tunnels" and bloated cover page GIFs and go right to the most relevant content anywhere on a Web server. That's the theory, anyway.

How search engines work

All the search engines have three components (Figure 7-1). Component 1 grabs all the Web pages that it can find. Component 2 builds a huge full-text index of those grabbed pages. Component 3 waits for user queries and serves lists of pages that match those queries. Your Web server deals with component 1 of the public search engines. When you are surfing *altavista.digital.com* or *www.webcrawler.com,* you are talking to component 3 of those search engines.

Component 1: The crawler (or how to get listed by a search engine)

Each search engine's crawler keeps a database of known URLs. When the time comes to rebuild the index, the crawler grabs every URL in this database to see if there are any changes or new links. It follows the new links, indexes the documents retrieved, and eventually will recursively follow links from those new documents.

If your site is linked from an indexed site, you do not have to take any action to get indexed. For example, Brian Pinkerton's original WebCrawler knew about the MIT Artificial Intelligence Laboratory home page (*http://www.ai.mit.edu*), grabbed a list of Lab employees linked from the page, then followed a link from there to my personal home page (*http://photo.net/philg/*). As soon as I finished *Travels with Samantha,* I linked to it from my home page. WebCrawler eventually discovered the new link, followed it, and then followed the links to individual chapters. The full text of my book was indexed without my ever being aware of WebCrawler's action.

The Web is getting larger (320 million pages as of December 1997) and the search engine crawlers have a tough time keeping up. It might be six months before a crawler revisits your page to see if anything has changed, though the more aggressive ones try to do it once every six weeks. If you are impatient to get your site indexed or you have recently changed a lot of content, or nobody is linking to you, it is worth using the "add my URL" forms on the search engine sites. The specific URLs that you enter will be available to querying users within a few days.

Component 2: The full-text indexer

Here's a word-frequency histogram for the first sentence of *Anna Karenina*:

Word	Frequency
all	1
another	1
but	1
each	1
families	1
family	1
happy	1
in	1
is	1
its	1
one	1
own	1
resemble	1
unhappy	2
way	1

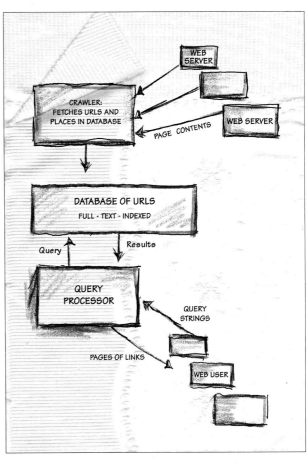

Figure 7-1: A generic Web search engine. Note that these are logical components and might all be running on one physical computer.

You might think that this sentence makes better literature as "All happy families resemble one another, but each unhappy family is unhappy in its own way," but the computer finds it more useful in this form.

After the crude histogram is made, it is typically adjusted for the prevalence of words in standard English. So, for example, the appearance of "resemble" is more interesting to the engine than "happy" because "resemble" occurs less frequently in standard English. Very common words such as "is" are thrown away altogether.

Component 3: User query processor

The query processor is the public face of a search engine. When the query machine gets a search string, such as "platinum mines in New Zealand", the "in" and probably the "New" are thrown away. The engine delivers articles that have the most occurrences of "platinum" and "Zealand". Suppose that "Zealand" is a rarer word than "platinum". Then a Web page with one occurrence of "Zealand" is favored over one with one occurrence of "platinum". A Web page with one occurrence of each word is preferred to an article where only one of those words shows up. This is a standard text retrieval algorithm in use since the early 1980s.

For relatively stupid indexer/query processor pairs, this is where the sorting stops. Smarter engines, however, use some further knowledge about the Web. For example, they know that

- whatever is wrapped in the <TITLE> element is the most interesting part of the document

- pages with the requested query words, plus "home" or "homepage" are the very best matches of all. So, in response to a "Travels with Samantha" query, smart engines will list the "Travels with Samantha home page" above any of the 17 chapters.

- an initial headline (enclosed in an <h1> or similar tag) is more important than the rest of the document. So a Web page where the query words appear in a headline is preferred over one where they appear in the footer.

How to stand tall in the search engines

A good way to measure the thoroughness of the corruption of the Internet is to type a query like "most reliable car" into the search engines and look at the banner ads in the results pages:

- AltaVista

- Infoseek

- WebCrawler

- Metacrawler

- HotBot

- Lycos

Do you think it is a coincidence that the banner ad above the search results is always for a car-related Web site (see Figure 7-2)? People are buying words. Yes, words. For thousands of dollars per month. Publishers pay the big bucks, and every time a user queries for "car" or "home" or "money", a relevant banner ad is served up.

If you can't afford to buy words, you will just have to earn exposure in the search engines the honest way: content.

Search engines take an even dimmer view of graphics than I do. You might have paid $25,000 for a flashing GIF or a Java animation. AltaVista does not care. It won't even download the ugly thing. You might have thought that lots of little GIFs with pretty text were better than plain old ASCII, but AltaVista doesn't think so. Search engines don't do OCR on GIFs to figure out what words are formed by the pixels. So if you've invested a sufficient amount in graphic design, your page won't be indexed at all.

What you want is text, text, text.

The more text on your site, the more words and therefore the greater chance that you'll have a combination of words for which users are searching. If you want readers to find you in the search engines, it's much better to spend $20,000 licensing the full text of a bunch of out-of-print books than on a graphical makeover of your site.

Advertising

Does advertising on the Web work? If what you're advertising is another Web site, the answer seems to be yes. Buying words on the search engines seems to be a good value. At a cost of about $5,000 a week, one of my consulting clients pumped its site up very quickly from 100,000 to 300,000 hits per day by buying words.

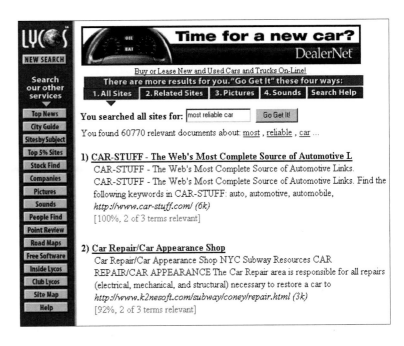

Figure 7-2: The result of typing "most reliable car" into *http://www.lycos.com*. It is not a coincidence that a banner ad for a car-related site was served along with the search results.

How much does advertising cost? Web publishers seem to be able to charge between one and ten cents per impression (showing the banner ad to a user) and over a dollar per clickthrough (when a user actually clicks on the banner).

Note that the analysis of the amazon.com referral system in Chapter 2 (the money chapter) reveals that a publisher might be able to acquire clickthroughs at a much lower cost by operating a similar referral scheme than by purchasing banner ads.

If you have a worthwhile not-for-profit site, advertising need not cost anything. Most commercial publishers have unsold banner ad space and they don't like to redesign their pages to serve documents without advertising. Environmental Defense Fund was able to get quite a few banner ad impressions to promote *www.scorecard.org*. The ads said, "Type in your zip code and we'll tell you who is polluting your town," and even had a little zip code entry form that would take users directly to a community page. Publishers are able to set some of their advertising rates as a function of the clickthrough rate on their site overall. They thus welcomed the ads for Scorecard because the clickthrough rate is as high as 3 percent (versus an industry average closer to 1 percent). If the ads had been ineffective and would therefore have reduced a publisher's sitewide average clickthrough rate, they would have been pulled, however much the publisher might have liked Scorecard.

How many users are you getting from search engines?

Often the user's browser will tell your Web server the URL from which the user clicked to your site. If you have a reasonably modern Web server program, it can log this *referer header* (yes, "referer" is misspelled in the HTTP standard).

Sometimes the referer URL will contain the query string. The very first time I ran a referer report on a server log was on a commercial site. I was all set to email it to "the suits upstairs" when I looked a little more closely at one line of the report. We were giving away "Cosmo Hunk calendars" where each month there was a picture of Fabio or someone. A WebCrawler user had grabbed this page and the referer header gave us some real insight into his interests:

Note:
I put this example
in the manuscript
of my first book on
Web stuff. Read
*http://photo.net
/wtr/dead-trees
/story.html*
to find out how it
went over with my
publisher at the time.

```
http://www.webcrawler.com/cgi-bin/WebQuery?searchText=hunks+with
   +big+dicks&maxHits=25
```

I decided not to use this particular report to demonstrate my powerful new logging system to the senior executives of my client, a $3 billion publisher.

Sometimes a user talks to the search engine via HTTP POST instead of GET. That makes the referer header much less interesting.

```
www-aa0.proxy.aol.com - - [01/Jan/1997:18:57:21 -0500]
"GET /photo/nudes.html HTTP/1.0" 304 0
http://webcrawler.com/cgi-bin/WebQuery
"Mozilla/2.0 (Compatible; AOL-IWENG 3.0; Win16)"
```

We know that this user is an America Online user because he is coming to my site from an AOL proxy server. We know that he is at least mildly naughty because his WebCrawler search has come up with *http://photo.net/photo/nudes.html* as an interesting URL for him. The user-agent header at the end supposedly tells us that he is using Netscape Navigator (Mozilla) 2.0. If we look a little more carefully, the "compatible" indicates in fact that he is in fact using some other browser that has been programmed to fraudulently advertise itself as Netscape. Publishers back in 1995 wrote scripts to look for the string "Mozilla/2". Those users would be served an "enhanced with frames" site. Presumably the "AOL-IWENG 3.0" browser in use here is frames-compatible and the false advertising as Netscape 2.0 is its way of saying so.

Here's an AltaVista user:

```
modem22.truman.edu - - [01/Jan/1997:23:41:08 -0500]
"GET /photo/body-paint.html HTTP/1.0" 200 7667
http://www.altavista.digital.com/cgi-bin/query?pg=q&what=web&fmt=.&q
   =body+painting+-auto+-automobile+-repair
"Mozilla/3.01 (Win95; I; 16bit)"
```

This user is more advanced. He's not using AOL. He's making a direct connection from his machine at Truman State University (Missouri). At first glance, it appears that he's had a problem with his car because he is searching for "body painting auto automobile repair". Won't he be surprised that AltaVista sent him to the rather naughty *http://photo.net/photo/body-paint.html*? Actually he won't be. I showed this to my friend Jin, and he said, "Look at the little minuses in front of *auto, automobile,* and *repair.* He was looking for documents that contained *body* and *painting* but not any of the auto repair words."

Sometimes the Web really does work like it should:

```
245.st-louis-011.mo.dial-access.att.net - - [01/Jan/1997:20:50:31 -0500]
"GET /cr/maps/ HTTP/1.0" 302 361
http://www-att.lycos.com/cgi-bin/pursuit?cat=lycos&query
   =Costa+Rica%2Bmap&matchmode=or
"Mozilla/2.02E (Win95; U)"
```

This fellow, apparently an ATT Worldnet user, wanted a map of Costa Rica and found it at *http://photo.net/cr/maps/*.

The bottom line is that if you have a content-rich site, you should be getting approximately 50 percent of your users from search engines.

Improving your pages' chances honestly (and dishonestly)

If you want to take the time to add META elements to the HEAD of your HTML documents, then most search engines will try to learn from them. If you have some extra keywords that you think describe your content, but that don't fit into the article or don't get enough prominence in the user-visible text, just add

```
<META name="keywords" content="making money fast greed">
```

to your page (remember that it is only legal within the <HEAD> of the document). People who do this tend to repeat the words over and over,

```
<META name="keywords" content="making money fast greed money
money money money money money money money fast fast fast greed">
```

which presumably does increase relevance—and therefore prominence—on badly programmed search engines. Eventually, the search engine programmers are going to get tired of seeing the sleaziest sites given the most prominence, though, and will only index each keyword once (AltaVista currently records 0, 1, and "2 or more" occurrences of a word, so "money money" and "money money money" are indistinguishable).

Also keep in mind that although information in META elements is never displayed on a page, all of your users will have to wait for these META tags to download. So you don't really want to put 50,000 bytes of text in the keywords tag (AltaVista in any case will only index the first 1,024 bytes).

A potentially more useful META tag is "description":

```
<META name="description" content="Journal for sophisticated
Web publishers, specializing in RDBMS-backed sites.">
```

Normally a search engine will condense the textual content of your site into something resembling a description. Perhaps it will take the first 25 words and serve that up along with the title. This becomes especially problematic if you have a graphics-heavy site with no content at all. If the first few sentences of a page aren't what you'd like people to see when a search engine offers it up as an option, then include a description META tag on that page.

And now the dishonest part

That's all how it is supposed to work. Of course, people immediately started to subvert the system by adding keyword tags like "nude photos of supermodels" to their boring computer science research papers and sleazy get-rich-quick schemes.

A more clever approach to getting extra hits is reprogramming your Web server. The server first determines if a request is being made by a robot by looking at the user-agent header or matching the hostname against *.webcrawler.com, *.altavista.digital.com, *.lycos.com, etcetera. If the client is a robot, then the server

delivers content calculated to match queries. Otherwise, on the assumption that the request is coming from a real person, the server redirects the client to a page of your choice.

You've made the Web a less user-friendly place, but you've got more hits. Not that I *personally* would ever sink so low as to program a Web server to deliver

> "A hot tub full of free nude supermodels. After all these years of thinking about money, money, money, that's what you thought you'd be coming home to. You made money fast by informing on your neighbor who was consuming child pornography and who had built a shocking collection of photos of beautiful women having sex with dogs and horses. Then you invested your money wisely in stocks, bonds, and mutual funds. You dumped your Macintosh software and bought an IBM PC running Microsoft Windows 95 (before switching to Windows NT)."

to search engines and then one of my own pages that I was anxious to hype to human surfers. But my, uh, friend did it. You can find his source code at *http:// photo.net/wtr/thebook/search-engine-bait.txt.*

What did my, uh, friend learn? Let's look at his server log:

```
macroint.com - - [06/Apr/1998:13:02:30 -0400]
"GET /car-buying.html HTTP/1.0" 302 335
http://www.altavista.digital.com/cgi-bin/query?pg=q&stq=30&what=web&kl=XX
  &q=%2B%22sex+with+dogs%22+-Re%3A&next.x=26&next.y=7
"Mozilla/4.04 [en] (Win95; U ;Nav)"
```

It is heartening to learn that the MBAs at Macro International, a $50 million management consulting firm, are right up to date and using Windows 95 with Netscape 4.0. However, I'm not sure that I want to see the products of the company on whose behalf they are researching "sex with dogs".

Hiding your content from search engines (intentionally)

Sometimes you don't want search engines to find your stuff. Here are some possible scenarios:

- You have a mirror of *http://photo.net/samantha/* at *http://euro.photo.net/samantha/,* a computer in Finland. You don't want people searching in Infoseek to find the Finland mirror.

- You have a draft version of a document whose URL you've distributed to a few friends. Some of them have linked to it from their home pages, despite your instructions to keep the URL private. Their home pages are known to the search engines, so the search engines will find your document before it is ready.

- You have an area where users can click to request standardized searches through a changing database. Each search requires 20 minutes of crunching by your server. You don't want robots initiating searches.

WebCrawler was the first robot on the Web. The folks who've taken it over from Brian Pinkerton maintain a robots page that gives information about how Web robots work at *http://info.webcrawler.com/mak/projects/robots/robots.html.*

This page links to the Standard for Web Exclusion, which is a protocol for communication between Web publishers and Web crawlers. You the publisher put a file on your site, accessible at /robots.txt, with instructions for robots. Here's an example that addresses the mirror site problem given above. I created a file at *http://euro.photo.net/robots.txt* containing the following:

```
User-agent: *
Disallow: /samantha
Disallow: /philg
Disallow: /cr
Disallow: /nz
```

```
Disallow: /webtravel
Disallow: /bp
Disallow: /~philg
Disallow: /zoo
Disallow: /photo
Disallow: /summer94
```

The User-agent line specifies for which robots the injunctions are intended. Each Disallow asks a robot not to look in a particular directory. Nothing requires a robot to observe these injunctions, but the standard seems to have been adopted by all the major indices nonetheless.

Remember that putting something in robots.txt is a very bad way to keep a document confidential. If I wanted to find ibm.com's secret Web content, I might very well start by requesting *http://www.ibm.com/robots.txt*. If you can be sure that nobody will link to you, you can keep a Web directory reasonably private merely by refraining from creating any internal links. Of course, if it is truly confidential information, then you will probably want to password-restrict the directory.

Hiding your content from search engines (by mistake)

If you hire Joe MBA to "proactively leverage your Web publishing paradigm into the next generation model," you can be pretty sure he will come up with the following brilliant idea: Require registration. As soon as you require users to register, you can give much more detailed information about them to your advertisers.

Unfortunately, if half of your readers have been coming from search engines, you'll only have half as many readers. AltaVista is not going to log into your site. Lycos is not going to fill out your demographics form. WebCrawler does not know what its username and password are supposed to be on www.greedy.com.

Depending on how flexible your Web server's programming facilities are, you can play some tricks with serving all of your content to search engine crawlers but hiding it from users who are accurately reporting their browser type and version.

I don't have an MBA, yet I managed to hide a tremendous amount of my content from the search engines by stupidity in a different direction. I built a question-and-answer forum for *http://photo.net/photo/*. Because I'm not completely stupid, all the postings were stored in a relational database. I used the AOLServer with its brilliant

TCL API to get the data out of the database and onto the Web. The cleanest way to develop software in this API is to create files named foobar.tcl among one's document tree. The URLs end up looking like *http://db.photo.net/bboard/fetch-msg.tcl ?msg_id=000037.*

So far, so good.

AltaVista comes along and says, "Look at that question mark. Look at the strange .tcl extension. This looks like a CGI script to me. I'm going to be nice and not follow this link, even though there is no robots.txt file to discourage me."

Then WebCrawler says the same thing.

Then Lycos.

I have achieved oblivion.

Then I had a notion that I developed into a concept and finally programmed into an idea: Write another AOLServer TCL program that presents all the messages from URLs that look like static files, such as /fetch-msg-000037.html, and point the search engines to a huge page of links like that. The text of the Q&A forum postings will get indexed out of these pseudostatic files, and yet I can retain the user pages with their *.tcl URLs. I could have converted the user pages to *.html URLs, but then it would have been more tedious to make changes to the software (see my discussion of why the AOLserver *.tcl URLs are so good in the chapters on Web programming (see Chapters 10 and 15); see *http://photo.net/wtr/thebook/bboard-for-search-engines.txt* for the source code).

WEB DIRECTORIES

It was easy in the old days. In 1994 there was just Yahoo. Yahoo was the original Web directory, reasonably well built and well maintained by David Filo and Jerry Yang, electrical engineering graduate students at Stanford. You'd submit your site to Yahoo and NCSA What's New and wait for traffic and links to develop organically.

By 1995, there was Yahoo, along with a bunch of pathetic wannabe imitation directories. There were too many entries in NCSA What's New for anyone to bother reading them, so NCSA shut down the page.

By 1997, some of the pathetic wannabes had become so bloated with money and staff that they actually had pretty reasonable directories. In this competition they were aided by Yahoo's apparent inability to write a Perl script to grind over their database and flush all the obsolete links.

If you are unwilling to figure out who is running all of the directories these days, then it is probably worthwhile to use a service that submits your site information to the directories for you. Here are a couple:

- Submit-it! (*http://www.submit-it.com*)
- Postmaster (*http://www.netcreations.com/postmaster/*)

Don't obsess over getting listed in every possible directory. In the long run the search engines will be much more important sources of users than the directories. Furthermore, it is much easier as a publisher to work with the search engines. They visit your site periodically and notice if things have changed.

How about the *New York Times* and CNN?

One of my neighbors writes for the *New York Times.* Am I better off buying a banner ad on Yahoo or hiring a chef, maid, and dog groomer to lure her to my house so that I can ply her with champagne and stories about my Web services? The first time *http://www.webho.com/WealthClock* was mentioned in the *Times* (both print and online editions), the reporter called me up eagerly to ask if there were a lot of extra users that day. I brought the access log into Emacs to scan the referer headers, then replied, "Yes, there are quite a few extra today, but five times as many are coming from some online magazine in Finland as from CyberTimes." In February 1998, the *Times* featured *http://www.arsdigita.com/remindme/,* the free birthday reminder service I built with some friends. We picked up about 700 extra users from that one article.

Television and radio? Various pages of mine have been featured on TV, radio, and cable (CNN). But the server logs weren't noticeably larger than usual (90 MB per day; between 400,000 and 500,000 hits).

What does work? When Netscape put *http://www.webho.com/WealthClock* on its What's New list, linked from a button right at the top of every browser, the page picked up two extra users per second.

Final tip

Reorganize your file system after you're listed in all the Web directories, after folks at other sites have linked to articles on your server, and after search engines have discovered your site. That way, users will be sure to get "404 Not Found" messages after finding your site in Yahoo or WebCrawler.

SUMMARY

Here's what you should have learned in this chapter:

- About half of your users will come from search engines.

- The more text you have on your site, the more likely users are to find your site.

- Users who come from search engines will arrive at arbitrary interior pages, so it is important that you always have links back to the top levels of your documents.

- Web directories and search engines will contain all kinds of links to your interior pages, so think carefully before changing any filenames on your server.

If you are smart about managing your profile in the search engines and Web directories, you'll have so much traffic that your server will melt, unless you carefully read the next chapter on how to choose server hardware and software.

MORE

- Steve Lawrence and Lee Giles are the source for the often quoted "320 million pages on the Web" figure. You can find background and their latest estimates at *http://www.neci.nj.nec.com/homepages/lawrence/websize.html.*

- It isn't Tolstoy, but *The AltaVista Search Revolution* (Ray, 1998; Osborne) provides an interesting look at how search engines work and how Web services are developed.

8

So You Want to Run
Your Own Server

At the risk of alienating my nerd readers, let me take a paragraph to explain why you need a Web server. Suppose that you have developed the world's most appealing Web site. It is a collection of .html files on your laptop computer and viewing it in Netscape is delightful. This won't do other folks on the Internet much good, though. You need to transfer those files to a computer that is permanently attached to the Internet. That computer, known as a *Web server*, needs to run a program, also conveniently known as a *Web server*, that waits for readers (clients) to request a page. When a request comes in, the Web server program digs around in the computer's file system and delivers the requested page back to the client over the Internet. Only at this point do you have a *public* Web site.

There are three levels at which you can take responsibility for your public Web site:

- You are a user of a remote machine.

- You are the owner/administrator of a machine inside someone else's network.

- You are the owner/administrator of a machine inside your own network.

BEING A USER ON A REMOTE MACHINE

If your Web site is on a remote machine that someone else administers, your only responsibility is periodically transferring your files there. As soon as the remote server is behaving the way you want it to, you can walk away until it is time to update your site. You can go away on vacation for two months at a stretch. If you need expensive software, such as a relational database, you can simply shop for a site-hosting service that includes use of that software as part of a package.

Most Internet service providers (ISPs), including universities, will give customers a free Web site on one of their servers. You won't be able to do anything fancy with relational databases (unless you use the services at *http://www.greenspun.com*).

You will have a URL that includes the ISP's domain name, such as *http://members .aol.com/netspringr/* or *http://www.mit.edu/people/thomascl*. If you are using a commercial ISP, they will usually be willing to sell you "domain-level service" for $50 to $100 a month. So now, instead of advertising http://members.aol.com /greenspun/ as your public site, you advertise http://www.greenspun.com. Instead of lovetochat@aol.com, you can publish an email address of philip@greenspun.com.

Domain-level service gives you a certain degree of freedom from your ISP. Suppose you're a graduate student in computer science at Stanford. Your URL is http://www.stanford.edu/~realnerd/ and your email address is realnerd@ cs.stanford.edu. Then Bill Gates asks Stanford, "What's the very least amount of money I can give you and get the CS building named after me?" It turns out that the price of self-respect in Palo Alto is $6 million, less than half a day's interest on Bill's fortune and less than what a medium-sized company might spend on computer hardware to support its firmwide database. So after five years of working on ways to make beautiful, reliable, innovative software, your new office is in the Gates Computer Science Building. The administration encourages you to use Windows 3.1.

You respond by reading Olin Shiver's Graduate Student's Guide to Automatic Weapons (*http://www.ai.mit.edu/people/shivers/autoweapons.html*), but like most academic results these days, his solutions appear to be untested and out of date. You find what you need on the Marine Corps Web site (*http://www.hqmc.usmc.mil /factfile.nsf/AVE?openview&count=3000*): the M2 machine gun, 50 caliber, 4-mile range, and 550 rounds per minute. Sadly, the gun control liberals have managed to infringe on your constitutional right to bear arms. With your history of mental illness, you won't be able to get a machine gun permit. Fortunately for liberty, there is a civilian semiautomatic version of the M2 available from *http://www.valkyriearms .com/m2.htm*. Once delivered, your M2 works just as advertised and you manage to create a bunch of new tenure-track openings at Stanford. Unfortunately, you're forced to change your ISP from stanford.edu to bighouse.gov. Your old URL and email address won't work. You could send everyone email asking them to change their links from http://www.stanford.edu/~realnerd to http://www.bighouse.gov/~realnerd and to record your new email address as realnerd@bighouse.gov. But wouldn't it have been nicer if you'd advertised http://www.realnerd.com to begin with? Then all of the links to your site that you'd carefully nurtured over the years would still work.

Even if you have your own domain, there are some potential downsides to having it parked on someone else's physical computer. You are entirely at the mercy of the system administrators of the remote machine. If email for your domain isn't being forwarded, you can't have your own Unix wizard fix the problem or go digging around yourself—you have to wait for people who might not have the same priorities that you do. If you are building a sophisticated relational database–backed site, you might not have convenient access to your data because you aren't allowed shell access to the remote machine, only the ability to FTP and HTTP PUT files.

YOUR MACHINE/THEIR NETWORK

If you are the owner of a Web-serving computer inside someone else's network, then you have total freedom to make changes to your configuration and software. You'll have root password and shell access and therefore can use the machine for software development or other experiments. Whoever is hosting your box is responsible for network connectivity. If packets aren't getting to your machine, they'll probably notice and do something about it. You don't have to pay the $2,500 per month cost of a T1 line yourself.

The downside to running your own box is that you have to carefully watch over your computer and Web server program. Nobody else will care about whether your computer is serving pages. You'll have to carry a pager and sign up for a service like Uptime (*http://uptime.arsdigita.com/uptime/*) that will email you and beep you when your server is unreachable. You won't be able to go on vacation unless you find someone who understands your computer and the Web server configuration to watch it. Unless you are using free software, you may have to pay shockingly high licensing fees. Internet service providers charge between $250 a month and $4,000 a month for physical hosting, depending on who supplies the hardware, how much system administration the ISP performs, and how much bandwidth your site consumes.

The people who do this usually call the service *co-location.* The most highly automated company in this business is *http://above.net.* They run a terminal concentrator in reverse, so you can telnet into one of their boxes and then connect to the serial port on the back of your Unix box, just as though you were at the machine's console. For the Windows NT crowd, above.net has a device whereby you can visit a Web page and power-cycle your machine to bring it back up. If all else fails, they have technicians in their facilities 24×7. They have redundant connectivity directly to MAE-East and MAE-West and private peering with most backbone operators. Above.net seems to pride themselves on their huge bank of batteries and backup natural gas generator. I thought this was overkill, but five days after I flew a server from Cambridge to above.net, we had a late night at MIT:

```
From: William Wohlfarth <wpwohlfa@PLANT.MIT.EDU>
Subject: Power Outage August 7, 1997
Date: Fri, 8 Aug 1997 07:39:43 -0400

At approximately 5:35 pm on August 7, 1997 a manhole explosion in the
Kendall Sq area caused Cambridge Electric to lose Kendall Station. MIT
lost all power and the gas turbine tripped. Power was fully restored
at 7 pm.

At approximately 7:05 pm, a second manhole explosion,caused 1
fatality, and injuries to 4 other Cambridge Electric utilitymen,
including a Cambridge Policeman. Putnam Station was also tripped and
MIT lost all power again.
```

```
At approximately 10:30 pm, MIT had power restored to all buildings
within our distribution system. Several East campus ( E28, E32, E42,
E56, E60, NE43)and North/Northwest buildings( N42, N51/52, N57, NW10,
NW12, NW14, NW15, NW17, NW20, NW21, NW22, NW30, NW61, NW62, W11, WW15)
which are fed directly from Cambridge Electric, were restored by
Cambridge Electric personal.

Cambridge Electric is still sorting out the chain of events. At last
discussions with them, a total of 3 manhole explosions had taken
place. Additional information will be posted when available.
```

I've worked with above.net since August 1997 and they've proven to be extremely reliable and competent. Above.net takes a very strong "we do power, IP connectivity, and monitoring; you do the rest" position. Exodus Communications (*http://www .exodus.net*) is an alternative, offering a broader range of services; for instance, they will run a packet-filtering router or firewall for you or help with system and database administration. I've been a user of machines parked at Exodus since mid-1997 and can't really recall a time when I lost an Emacs or ssh connection to a box inside Exodus.

YOUR MACHINE/YOUR NETWORK

If you are the owner of a machine inside your own network, then you can sit right down at the console of your Web server and do software development or poke through the database. This can be a substantial convenience if you are running an RDBMS-backed Web site and there is no obvious way to have development and production sites. If you are already paying for a high-speed network connection to your desktop, then the marginal cost of hosting a server this way may be zero, a fact that was not lost on university students throughout the early years of the Web. The downside is that you have all of the responsibilities and hassles of owning a server physically inside someone else's network, plus all of the responsibilities and hassles of keeping the network up.

MY PERSONAL CHOICE

Which hosting option did I choose for my personal Web site? The last one, of course. At MIT we don't let random commercial losers host our Web sites. We've had a hardwired network since the 1960s, so of course we always do things at the highest level of professionalism. In fact, during the "papal visit" (when Bill Gates came to speak), the director of our lab took particular care to note that MIT was "the home of the Web."

He probably hadn't read this problem report that I had sent to some folks with whom I share a Web server:

1) Saturday, July 13, 1996, 6:30 am: we had a 2-second power glitch
2) we do not have an uninterruptible power supply for Martigny
   [HP Unix file server for a cluster of user machines] so it crashed
3) we do not have an uninterruptible power supply for Swissnet
   [swissnet.ai.mit.edu, our Web server at the time,
   an antique HP Unix workstation] so it crashed
4) there is something we never figured out about Swissnet so
   that it doesn't boot properly after a power interruption
5) Saturday, 4 pm: I went down to the 3rd floor and manually
   instructed Swissnet to boot from its root disk, thus ending
   almost 10 hours of off-the-Web time
6) Somewhere along the line, Tobler [one of the user machines
   managed from Martigny] tried to reboot. Because it couldn't
   get to Martigny, it booted from a locally attached disk.
   This disk was the old Swissnet root disk [we'd hooked it up
   to Tobler after upgrading from HP-UX 9.x to 10.10 because we
   thought we might need some files from it]. Tobler consequently
   advertised itself as "18.23.0.16" [Swissnet's IP address].
7) Saturday, 10:30 pm: Radole [the main router for the MIT
   Laboratory for Computer Science] saw that there were two
   computers advertising themselves as 18.23.0.16 and apparently
   decided to stop routing to the physical Swissnet on the 3rd floor
8) Sunday, 4 pm: I arrive at work to a phone message from Brian:
   "Swissnet's routing is hosed". I reboot the machine. No
   improvement. I page George Rabatin [LCS network administrator
   and the Radole guru].
9) Sunday, 5 pm: George figures out that the problem is
   Tobler's false advertising. We turn Tobler off.
10) Sunday, 9 pm: George has manually purged all the caches on
    Radole and I've rebooted Swissnet but still no routing.
11) Sunday, 11 pm: George Rabatin declares a "network emergency"
    with the main MIT Net administrators so that they can probe
    the Building 24 FDDI router [FDDI is the 100 Mbit/second token
    ring that serves the entire MIT campus.]
12) Sunday, midnight: One of the MIT guys manually flushed the
    ARP cache on the FDDI router and Swissnet instantly came
    back into existence. Given that Tobler wasn't on the same
    subnet and that Radole supposedly stopped doing proxy ARP
    around seven months ago, it is a mystery to me how this
    router could have had an ARP entry (mapping IP address to
    physical Ethernet hardware address) for Faux Swissnet.
    But it apparently did. So we're back on the Web.
Good news: We saved $500 by not buying two uninterruptible power
supplies. We found out that George Rabatin is a hero.
Bad news: We probably denied services to about 5000 users over 34
hours. We burned up about 20 person-hours of various folks' time
on a Sunday trying to fix a problem that we created.

That's how professionals do things....

Choosing a Computer

Computers are the tools of the devil. It is as simple as that. There is no monotheism strong enough that it cannot be shaken by Unix or any Microsoft product. The devil is real. He lives inside C programs.

Hardware engineers have done such a brilliant job over the last 40 years that nobody notices that, in the world of commercial software, the clocks all stopped in 1957. Society can build a processor for $50 capable of executing 200 million instructions per second. Marvelous. With computers this powerful, the amazing thing is that anyone still has to go into work at all. Perhaps part of the explanation for this apparent contradiction is that, during its short life, the $50 chip will consume $10,000 of system administration time.

Everything that I've learned about computers at MIT I have boiled down into three principles:

- Unix: You think it won't work, but if you find the right wizard, he can make it work.

- Macintosh: You think it will work, but it won't.

- PC/Windows: You think it won't work, and it won't.

In theory, a Macintosh or Windows 95 machine could function as a low-volume Web server for static files. However, since those operating systems lack multiprocessing and memory protection, you'd have to dedicate an entire machine to this task. Finally, you'd never be able to do anything interesting with a Mac- or Win95-hosted site because relational database management systems such as Oracle require a multitasking operating system.

Most people buying a server computer make a choice between Unix and Windows NT. These operating systems offer important 1960s innovations like multiprocessing and protection among processes. Certainly the first thing to do is figure out which operating system supports the Web server and database management software that you want to use. If the software that appeals to you runs on both operating systems, then make your selection based on which computer you, your friends, and your coworkers know how to administer. If that doesn't result in a conclusion, then read the rest of this section.

Unix

Buying a Unix machine guarantees you a descent into hell. It starts when you plug the computer in and it won't boot. Yes, they really did sell you a $10,000 computer with an unformatted disk drive. There is only one operating system in the world that will run on your new computer, but the vendor didn't bother to install it. That's how you are going to spend your next couple of nights. You'll be asked dozens of questions about disk partitioning and file system journaling that you couldn't possibly answer. Don't worry, though, because Unix vendors have huge documentation departments to help you. Unfortunately, your computer shipped without any documentation. And, although the marketing department has been talking about how their company is God's gift to the Internet, the rest of the company still hasn't jacked into this World Wide Cybernet thing. Thus you won't find the documentation on the Web.

So you decide to save some trees and order a documentation CD-ROM. You plug it into your nearest Macintosh or PC and... nothing happens. That's right, the documentation CD-ROM isn't usable unless you have a completely working Unix computer made by the same company.

A week later, you've gotten the machine to boot and you call over to your Web developer: "Set up the Web server." But it turns out that he can't use the machine. Everything in Unix is configured by editing obscure incantations in text files. Virtually all competent Unix users edit text in a program called Emacs, probably the best text editor ever built. It is so good that the author, Richard Stallman, won a MacArthur genius fellowship. It is also free. But that doesn't mean that it meets the standards of Unix vendors. No, the weeklong installation process has left you only with vi, an editor that hardly anyone worth hiring knows how to use (even the guy who wrote vi now uses Emacs).

So you download the Emacs source code over the Internet and try to compile it. Good luck. Your computer didn't come with a compiler. The most popular C compiler for Unix is gcc, another free program from Richard Stallman. But it would have been too much trouble for the vendor to burn that onto their software CD-ROM, so you don't have it.

At this point, you are in serious enough trouble that you have to hire a $175-per-hour consultant just to make your computer function. Two days and $4,000 later, your computer is finally set up the way a naive person would assume that it must have shipped from the factory.

That's what setting up a Unix box is like. If it sounds horribly painful, rest assured that it is. The reason that anyone is willing to buy these computers is that they are usually administered in clusters of 100 machines. The time to administer 1,000 Unix boxes is about the same as the time to administer one, and therefore the administrative cost per machine isn't ruinous. This will be cold comfort to you if you have only the one Web server, though.

There is an upside to all of this. The operating system configuration resides in hundreds of strangely formatted text files. During the week you spent setting up Unix, you cursed this feature. But once your system is working, it will continue working forever. As long as you don't go into Emacs and edit any of those configuration files, there is no reason to believe that your Unix server won't function correctly. It isn't like the Macintosh or Windows worlds where things get silently corrupted and the computer stops working.

Which brand of Unix box?

Hewlett-Packard makes the fastest and most reliable Unix computers. You would think that Unix would be impossible to support because different sites have completely different configurations. Nonetheless, I've found that the HP support people can usually telnet into my machines and fix problems (usually ones that I've created) over the network. If you call them at 1:00 A.M., you'll be working with an engineer in Australia. If you call at 4:00 A.M., you'll be working with their staff in England.

The most popular commercial Unix and therefore the one for which the most packaged software is available is SPARC/Solaris from Sun Microsystems. I personally am not a big fan of Sun hardware. It has historically been slow. Sun hardware also can be unreliable, which isn't so bad except that Sun contracts out most of its hardware service. So a hardware failure results in a clueless boardswapper being dispatched from the phone company. "Iz video card," said one of these guys in a heavy Russian accent. "I have seen ziz before." (It was the power supply. The pizza box machine went on to log six more catastrophic failures in four months.)

Sun software is a different story. Solaris is fundamentally a very high-quality operating system. And it works great for my friend Noah Friedman, Netscape's Unix toolsmith and one of the authors of GNU Emacs. But my Unix knowledge is measured in the milliFriedmans. If it is 3:00 A.M. and I've got a misbehaving Solaris box, I'm stuck. I've never gotten any useful answers from Sun support. At this point, it would never even occur to me to call them. Does that mean I won't use Solaris? No. In fact, I have two SPARC/Solaris servers that I rely on to some extent. However, I can only do this because I'm friends with Noah and I'm partners in arsdigita.com with two recent MIT grads who were rebuilding Unix kernels in their cradles. So I know that my box will be up and running as long as I can reach any one of those three guys. The bottom line is that Solaris is fine if you employ or are a monster Unix wizard. However, in those cases you'd probably be running Linux, the most popular free Unix, instead.

The traditional appeal of Linux is cheap hardware + free software (with source code). For me, though, the most impressive thing about Linux is the installation process. You can download Linux off the Net for nothing. But if you pay $50 to a company like Red Hat (*www.redhat.com*) for a CD-ROM, you work through a few menus and then your PC will be running

- Unix

- Emacs, Perl, Tcl, gcc, the X Window System, ImageMagick, and all the other software that you would have paid a consultant $50,000 to install on your Digital, HP, or Sun box

- the Apache Web server

- an NFS server to deliver files to other Unix machines

- a Windows-protocol file server to deliver files to Windows machines

- an Appleshare file and print server to deliver files to Macintoshes

and all of this out of several CPUs simultaneously, if you recompile the kernel to do symmetric multiprocessing.

Running a free Unix on a PC entails a different philosophy than buying hardware and software from the same company. You are abandoning the fantasy that there is a single company out there who will support you if only you give them enough money. You or someone you hire will take a little more responsibility for fixing bugs. You have the source code, after all. If you want support, you have to make an intelligent decision about who can best provide it (note that *www.redhat.com* offers support contracts and hence comes closest to offering the traditional Unix vendor relationship).

PC hardware is so much cheaper than workstation hardware that for the price of one regular Unix workstation you will probably be able to buy two complete PC systems, one of which you can use as a hot backup. Keep in mind that 99 percent of PC hardware is garbage. A friend of mine was a small-time Internet service provider. He was running BSDI, a not-quite-free Unix, on a bunch of PC clones. A hard disk was generating errors. He reloaded from backup tape. He still got errors. It turned out that his SCSI controller had gone bad some weeks before. It had corrupted both the hard disk and the backup tapes. He lost all of his data. He lost all of his clients' data.

> **Lesson 1:** You are less likely to lose with a SCSI controller designed by a real engineer in the Hewlett-Packard Unix workstation division than you are with one thrown in on a $49 sound card.

> **Lesson 2:** Mirrored disks on separate SCSI chains. Period.

I'm afraid to run Linux because I don't think that I understand enough about PC hardware to put together anything as reliable as my HP-UX servers. My old server was one of a cluster of more than 100 HP workstations that we got at MIT

for research and education. I don't remember ever seeing one suffer a hardware failure. Certainly none of the ones that I used ever failed, despite the fact that I once dropped my six-year-old pizza box server off a desk onto the machine-room floor.

I'm reluctant to run Linux because it will divorce me from the HP support center, which has saved me dozens of hours of frustration (and my users quite a few hours of downtime).

A final rock to throw at Linux is that, because the source code is available, there are lots of people constantly figuring out how to break into Linux systems. Most of the Linux boxes at MIT have been cracked, for example. Someone usually comes up with a security patch within a few hours or days of an attack, but Linux sysadmins have to be vigilant about keeping the operating system up to date if they don't want their machines knocked over.

Note:
Linux is not the only free Unix. Hotmail and Yahoo run on FreeBSD (*www.freebsd.org*).

Running your Unix system

First, you should give some thought to security. Unix systems out of the box are not especially secure. This is partly because of how they are used. People log in over the network, partly because of where they are typically located—exposed to the wide Internet rather than behind a corporate firewall—and partly because of the wide

206

range of services that a typical Unix box offers remote machines. Running a firewall that really protects requires a lot of effort and expertise. Also, it reduces overall system reliability, since both the Web server and the firewall machine need to be up and running before anyone can get a page.

If you can't or don't want to put your Unix server behind a firewall, you should at least close the obvious security holes. Traditional Internet services like telnet and ftp transmit user passwords in the clear. So anyone listening to network packets (e.g., from a compromised Linux box on the same wire), will be able to then log into your computer. So turn off the telnet daemon. Don't let anyone log in except via ssh or some other encrypted system. Turn off the ftp daemon. Make shell users use scp (a counterpart to ssh) to grab files from other systems. Install AOLserver and use its FTP module to let graphic designers and such transfer files to you. If someone sniffs a packet during this kind of FTP session, he will then be able to overwrite content on a portion of your Web directory, but he won't be able to log into the machine and make your life hell.

Partly for reasons of security and partly for reasons of convenience, I install post.office from *http://www.software.com* instead of using sendmail, the bundled-with-Unix mailer that is almost impossible to configure (the "sendmail in a nutshell" handbook from O'Reilly is 950 pages long; post.office takes 20 minutes to download, install, and configure). See my review of post.office at *http://photo.net/wtr /post-office.html.*

At the end of the day, it is impossible to have a bulletproof system. Install Tripwire so that you can tell when your machine has been compromised (free software available from *http://www.cs.purdue.edu/coast/coast-tools.html*). Make sure that your backup tapes are complete and verified. My favorite backup software by far is HP Omniback II. It is available for a huge list of Unices, also works on Windows NT, can back up Win95 desktop systems from a central server, and understands relational databases down to the tablespace level.

If your system isn't as fast as you'd like, it is very unlikely you'll be able to understand it without some kind of diagnostic tools. My favorite is GlancePlus, an HP product that is available for most brands of Unix, including Solaris. Partly because it is graphical and partly because it has some built-in knowledge, GlancePlus is much easier to use than the tools recommended in most sysadmin books.

Speaking of sysadmin books, my most current recommendations are in *http:// photo.net/wtr/bookshelf.html.*

Unix inspiration

I'll leave you with an anecdote from my last book about my old desktop Hewlett-Packard 715/80 Unix workstation. Let's see how long it had been up:

```
orchid.lcs.mit.edu 33: uptime
 11:30pm  up 53 days, 10:28,  5 users,  load average: 0.10, 0.07, 0.06
```

Yes, that's 53 days, 10 hours, and 28 minutes. It was running a relational database management system. It was serving 10 hits per second to the Web from an AOLserver process listening on four different IP addresses. It was running the X Window system so that I could use it from my home computer just as easily as if I'd been on the MIT campus. Although this was an old computer and not nearly as powerful as a Pentium Pro that a child might find under a Christmas tree, it was doing all of this while working only about one-tenth of the time. That's what a load average of 0.10 means.

Windows NT

Windows NT crashed.
I am the Blue Screen of Death.
No one hears your screams.
       —Peter Rothman (in *www.salonmagazine.com*
          haiku error message contest)

When I was a kid I didn't like the taste of Coca-Cola. After I'd been exposed to 100,000 TV commercials and billboards for Coke, I decided that it was the best drink in the world. Just opening a can made me feel young, good-looking, athletic, surrounded by gorgeous blondes.

Windows NT is sort of like that. At first glance, it looks like a copy of Unix (which in turn was a copy of operating systems from the 1960s) with a copy of the Macintosh user interface (which in turn was based on systems developed at Xerox PARC in the 1970s). I didn't think much more about it.

Eventually, the Microsoft PR mill convinced me that Windows NT was the greatest computer innovation ever. Bill Gates had not only invented window systems and easy-to-use computers, but also multitasking, protection among processes, and networking. It would be like Unix without the obscurity.

I told all of my friends how they were losers for running Unix. They should switch to NT. It was the future. That was more or less my constant refrain until one pivotal event changed my life: I actually tried to use NT.

Having once watched three MIT wizards each spend 10 hours installing a sound card in a PC, I was in no mood to play with clones. I got myself an Intel-inside and Intel-outside, genuine, Intel-brand PC. I reformatted the hard drive with NT File System (NTFS) and installed WinNT Server. The machine booted smoothly, but running any program triggered Macintosh emulation mode: You move the mouse but nothing happens on the screen.

I spent two weeks trying to figure out why the user interface was crashing, reinstalling NT several times. I enlisted the help of a professional NT administrator. He tried eight different combinations of file systems but none of them worked.

What I learned: Do not buy a computer that isn't "NT certified." In fact, don't buy one unless the vendor has already installed the version of NT that you intend to use. I've had pretty good luck with an HP Vectra system that came preinstalled with NT 4.0.

NT Success Story 1: I downloaded some fax software from Microsoft. It was never able to talk to my modem or send a fax. But it did consume 20 percent of the machine's CPU and 30 MB of virtual memory. The standard system monitoring tools that come with NT make it almost impossible to figure out what is killing one's machine.

NT Success Story 2: I bought an HP LaserJet 5M printer for my house, so that I could be the first one on my block with a duplexing printer. It took me five seconds to get my Macintosh to print to it. It took me five minutes to get all of the Unix boxes at MIT to print to it. It took me five hours to get my Windows NT computer to recognize this printer, even though both were on the same Ethernet wire. As part of my five-hour saga, I had to download a 4-MB program from the HP Web site. Four megabytes. That's larger than any operating system for any computer sold in the 1970s. Mainframes in the 1970s could run entire airlines with less than 4 MB of code.

NT Success Story 3: I was having trouble installing Internet Explorer 4.0. I called Microsoft tech support. They suggested that my registry might be out of sync with what was actually on the hard disk. "Just reinstall the operating system from CD-ROM. That won't affect your application programs or user data. They will still be on the disk. But the new registry won't contain information about how to find any of them. So you'll have to reinstall all the apps that you use. Then you should be able to install IE4."

Yeah, thanks....

Unix versus NT

Here is a chart that summarizes what I know:

	Unix	NT
Easy to maintain remotely	Yes	No
Consultants	Cheap and smart	Expensive and stupid
Price of software	Free or expensive	Cheap
Reliability	High	Medium
Support	Depends on vendor; sometimes excellent	Reinstall the OS
Price of hardware	Cheap with Linux, FreeBSD, Solaris X86; otherwise expensive	Cheap

If this table doesn't help, then you might want to see if Microsoft Corporation itself has managed to get NT to work. In 1997, Microsoft acquired Hotmail and put their best technical folks on the task of converting the service from Unix/Apache to NT/IIS. You can monitor their progress from any Unix shell:

```
bash-2.01$ telnet www.hotmail.com 80
Trying...
Connected to www.hotmail.com.
Escape character is '^]'.
HEAD / HTTP/1.0

HTTP/1.1 200 OK
Date: Sun, 28 Jun 1998 04:14:00 GMT
Server: Apache/1.2.1
```

Looks like they are still running Unix.

Most of the people I know who are facile with both NT and Unix have eventually taken down their NT Web servers and gone back to Unix. The WebCrawler's comprehensive statistics, gathered as it indexes the Web, confirm my anecdotal evidence: As of January 1997, Unix sits behind 84 percent of the world's Web sites; NT sits behind 7 percent.

It turns out that, once you get to a certain level of traffic, you want your Web server in a closet right up against the routers that carry bits out of your building. You might think that the user interface of Unix sucks. But, thanks to the X Windows standard, it doesn't get any worse if you stay in your comfortable office or cozy house and drive your Web server remotely. Any program that you can run on the console, you can run from halfway around the world. Most sysadmins don't even go up to the physical machine to reboot their Unix boxes.

Unless you are a lot smarter than anyone I know, you will need consultants. You're buying into a user community when you buy into an operating system. A big part of the Unix user community consists of the smartest and poorest paid people in the world: science and engineering graduate students. Moreover, these people are accustomed to helping each other over the Net, usually for no money. When I'm running a Unix program at a commercial site and want an enhancement, I send the author email asking if he'll make the changes for $200 or so. Since most such requests come from users at universities who can't offer any money, this kind of proposal is invariably greeted with delight. When I'm confronted with a useless Unix box that doesn't have Emacs on it, I get the client to hire one of my friends to install it. He telnets in and lets the compiler run while he's answering his email in another window.

By contrast, anyone who has learned to install Microsoft Word on a Windows NT machine is suddenly a $150-an-hour consultant. Unless you count nerdy high school kids, there is no pool of cheap expertise for NT. And because NT boxes are tough to drive remotely, a wizard at another location can't help you out without disturbing his daily routine.

There is no technical reason why it couldn't have been the other way around, but it isn't. A true Windows NT wizard is making $175,000 a year maintaining a financial firm's servers; he isn't going to want to bother with your Web server.

Software licensing can be much more expensive with Unix. True, much of the best and most critical software is free. Furthermore, Web server programs and relational database management systems seem to be two areas in which Unix and NT prices are the same. But if you intend to purchase a lot of commercial software for your Web server, it is probably worth checking vendor price lists first to make sure that you couldn't pay for the entire NT machine with the Unix/NT license fee spread.

Unix wizards love to tell horror stories about Unix in general and Solaris in particular. That's usually because the best of them were accustomed to the superior operating systems of the 1960s and 70s that Unix replaced. But the fact remains that Windows NT is less reliable than Unix and has more memory leaks. In the

Microsoft culture, it is amazing when a computer stays up and running for more than one day, so nobody complains if it takes two months to make Oracle work or if the NT server has to be rebooted once a week.

Support can be much better with Unix. The whole idea of the Apple and Microsoft support 800 number doesn't make any sense in an Internet age. Why are you talking into a telephone telling someone what text is appearing on your screen? Your computers are both on the Internet and capable of exchanging data at perhaps 500,000 bps. I'm not so sure about the other Unix vendors, but I know from personal experience that Hewlett-Packard has figured this out. Plus, you actually get better support when you dial in at 4:00 A.M., because the kind of people willing to take a tech support job in England are much more able than the kind of people willing to take a tech support job in California. Keep in mind that support does not *have* to be much better with Unix. As noted earlier, I've personally never gotten any useful assistance from the official Sun support apparatus.

That's about as much as I can say. I don't think that there is a universal truth for making the NT/Unix choice, other than my original one: Computers are tools of the Devil. I learned that from a tenured professor in computer science at MIT. I think he is still trying to get his Macintosh to stop crashing.

Final hardware selection note

Whatever server computer you buy, make sure that you get an uninterruptible power supply and mirrored disks. You should not go offline because of a power glitch. You should not go offline because of a disk failure.

HOW MUCH CAPACITY?

The typical Web site saga goes as follows:

1. Publisher spends $500,000 developing a site.

2. Site attracts 50 users a day.

3. Publisher spends $100,000 on promotion.

4. Site gets hyperlinked from cnn.com, resulting in five new users a second.

5. All the new users are greeted with a "server not responding" error message.

Do you size for your usual traffic or for "the big day"? If you have a static Web site, then it is easy to size for the big day. A pizza-box Unix machine running an efficient threaded server program won't start slowing down until requests reach the two-million-a-day mark. If you're on your own T1 line, you'll find that two million hits a day for 7-KB files (typical size for a small JPEG image) will just fill it up. If you're hosted at a co-location facility, any extra network demand will be easily absorbed (above.net transfers more than 1 Gbit per second on a regular basis; Exodus was sending about 500 Mbits per second outbound on June 25, 1998).

What if you have a database-backed site? If you're doing an SQL query for every page load, don't count on getting more than 500,000 hits a day out of a cheap computer. Even 500,000 a day is too much if your RDBMS installation is regularly going out to disk to answer user queries. In other words, if you are going to support 10 to 20 SQL queries per second, you must have enough RAM to hold your entire data set and must configure your RDBMS to use that RAM. You must also be using a Web/DB integration tool like AOLserver that does not spawn new processes or database connections for each user request.

One of the darker days of my life was April 15, 1998. My consulting company, ArsDigita, had built a site for Environmental Defense Fund, *www.scorecard.org*. At midnight, my partner Jin and I started building up an Oracle 8 installation on ArsDigita's Sun Ultra 2 at AboveNet. We transferred a 750-MB database and the associated AOLserver Tcl scripts from our development server, then brought up the live site. At 6:00 A.M., I went to bed, waking up every 30 minutes to run into the bathroom and throw up. In the abstract, it is tough to say whether food poisoning or system/database administration is less pleasant. But after comparing them side by side, I can say with confidence that food poisoning makes even Microsoft products look pretty good.

While I was hurling, EDF was sending out 10,000 press releases. These resulted in ABC TV covering the site and telling viewers to come to abcnews.com and click through to *http://www.scorecard.org*. They did. About 40 of them per second. We might have been able to handle the traffic, except that our machine had only 256 MB of RAM and the Scorecard data set was 750 MB. Oracle was hitting the disk drives about 15 percent of the time. I had configured AOLserver to spawn up to six connections to Oracle. When a query in any connection would wait for data from disk, it would block for a few seconds and cause 100 new requests to stack up. In order to keep the machine from melting, I reconfigured AOLserver to allow no more than 30 total threads and deliver an "I'm busy" page to everyone else.

Fortunately, a couple of days earlier, I had ordered an extra GB of RAM for the machine because I was worried that people might otherwise find page loading of the graphics version of the site rather slow. But I was in Boston and our server was in San Jose. I emailed my friend Rochelle and asked her if she'd mind stopping by above.net on her way home from work and stuffing the RAM into our Sun box. Why Rochelle? Girls you knew in college aren't usually good for much in the Unix world unless "college" happens to have been MIT. In addition to being an MIT grad, she is an engineer at Hal Computer, where they make SPARC clones that run twice as fast as comparably priced Sun machines. I figured that if she could design a machine that boots Solaris from the Sun CD-ROM, then she was probably qualified to add a few SIMMs.

After a few minutes of downtime, Rochelle got some lavender roses and Oracle got 750 MB of the new RAM as a buffer cache:

```
SELECT name, value
FROM v$sysstat
WHERE name IN ('db block gets', 'consistent gets','physical reads');


NAME                          VALUE
--------------------          ---------
db block gets                    320936
consistent gets                12360355
physical reads                    25150
```

In the 12 hours since Oracle had started up, it had tried 12 million times to get blocks of data from the database. Only 25,000 of those attempts resulted in physical reads from the computer's hard disk drives; in other words, we hit the memory cache 99.8 percent of the time. I had prepared to spend hours sifting through queries and entering special hints for the Oracle optimizer, but in fact Oracle 8 turned out to be smart enough to use all the memory efficiently on its own.

We upped AOLserver's maximum threads and number of simultaneous Oracle connections, and the machine was happily processing 20 queries per second, as expected. Service degraded a bit when 30 to 40 requests a second would arrive, but AOLserver managed to queue the requests so that everyone got pages in what seemed like a reasonable amount of time. In fact, even under the heaviest load, the RAM-enhanced site was faster than the average static site on the Internet.

What if we had been linked from abcnews.com, cnn.com, netscape.com, and yahoo.com all on the same day? Our little Sun Ultra would have been destroyed and all the users would have been denied service. Should we plan for that day by ordering an eight-CPU HP Unix box? Yes and no. A computer that can serve a DB-backed site to a significant portion of the Internet will cost at least $500,000, plus $40,000 a year for maintenance. Most ISPs host each high-traffic Web site on a dedicated Unix box. This makes it easy to give customers shell logins and custom email configurations. Because the ISP would go broke buying a $500,000 computer for each customer, it also means that any time one of those customers is featured in the news, its particular (wimpy) Unix box will collapse, while all the other customers' boxes are 90 percent idle.

What's our solution? At ArsDigita we try to run relatively large Unix boxes and give each customer a slice. The machine is 75 percent idle most of the time, leaving enough overhead for any one customer's site to have its day of glory.

SERVER SOFTWARE

Once you have bought a Web server *computer,* you need to pick a Web server *program.* The server program listens for network connections and then delivers files in response to users' requests. These are the most important factors in choosing a program:

- quality of application programming interface (API)
- tools for connecting to relational database management systems (RDBMS)
- support and source code availability
- availability of shrinkwrapped plug-in software packages
- speed

Each of these factors needs to be elaborated upon.

API

Unless your publishing ambition is limited to serving static files, you will eventually need to write some programs for your Web site. It is quite possible that you'll need to have a little bit of custom software executing every time a user requests any file. Any Web server program can invoke a common gateway interface (CGI) script. However, CGI scripts impose a tremendous load on the server computer (see Chapter 10 on server-side programming). Furthermore, an all-CGI site is less straightforward for authors to maintain and for search engines to search than a collection of HTML files.

A Web server API makes it possible for you to customize the behavior of a Web server program without having to write a Web server program from scratch. In the early days of the Web, all the server programs were free. You would get the source code. If you wanted the program to work differently, you'd edit the source code and recompile the server. Assuming you were adept at reading other people's source code, this worked great until the next version of the server came along. Suppose the authors of NCSA HTTPD 1.4 decided to organize the program differently than the authors of NCSA HTTPD 1.3. If you wanted to take advantage of the features of the new version, you'd have to find a way to edit the source code of the new version to add your customizations.

An API is an abstraction barrier between your code and the core Web server program. The authors of the Web server program are saying, "Here are a bunch of hooks into our code. We guarantee and document that they will work a certain way. We reserve the right to change the core program, but we will endeavor to preserve the behavior of the API call. If we can't, then we'll tell you in the release notes that we broke an old API call."

An API is especially critical for commercial Web server programs for which the vendor does not release the source code. Here are some typical API calls from the AOLserver documentation (*http://www.aolserver.com*):

ns_user exists *user* returns 1 (one) if the specified *user* exists and 0 (zero) if it does not
ns_sendmail *to from subject body* sends a mail message

The authors of AOLserver aren't going to give you their source code and they aren't going to tell you how they implement the user/password database for URL access control. But they give you a bunch of functions like ns_user exists that let you query the database. If they redo the implementation of the user/password database in the next release of the software, then they will redo their implementation of ns_user so that you won't have to change your code. The ns_sendmail API call not only shields you from changes by AOLserver programmers, it also allows you not to think about how sending email works on various computers. Whether you are running AOLserver on Windows NT, HP Unix, or Linux, your extensions will send email after a user submits a form or requests a particular page.

Aside from having a rich set of functions, a good API has a rapid development environment and a safe language. The most common API is for the C programming language. Unfortunately, C is probably the least suitable tool for Web development. Web sites are by their very nature experimental and must evolve. C programs like Microsoft Word remain unreliable, despite hundreds of programmer-years of development and thousands of person-years of testing. A small error in a C subroutine that you might write to serve a single Web page could corrupt memory critical to

the operation of the entire Web server and crash all of your site's Web services. On operating systems without interprocess protection, such as Windows 95 or the Macintosh, the same error could crash the entire computer.

Even if you were some kind of circus freak programmer and were able to consistently write bug-free code, C would still be the wrong language because it has to be compiled. Making a small change in a Web page might involve dragging out the C compiler and then restarting the Web server program, so that it would load the newly compiled version of your API extension.

By the time a Web server gets to version 2.0 or 3.0, the authors have usually figured that C doesn't make sense and have compiled in an interpreter for Tcl, Java byte codes, or JavaScript.

I have some standard questions that I ask Web tool vendors to probe the flexibility of their API:

- The president of my client, a large publisher, is going before Congress at 2:00 P.M. tomorrow to testify about what her company is doing to protect children from seeing indecent content. She wants to be able to say, "We are writing a PICS header on every one of our pages that says 'parental discretion advised'." The site has 40,000 pages, some of them static HTML, some CGI scripts, some API scripts. How much code is required to add a PICS output header to each request?

- I've learned that AltaVista hasn't been indexing our dynamically served content because it doesn't look like static .html URLs. How much code is required to program the server to deliver a tree of dynamically generated .html URLs to search engines?

AOLserver has one of the best and most flexible APIs. The answer to both scenarios is a few lines of Tcl code. Apache gives you the source code, so the answer is some C programming; a wizard could do it in a day. But the truly expensive and allegedly powerful "application servers" and Web publishing systems usually will require you to rewrite every page on your site.

RDBMS connectivity

You've chosen to publish on the Web because you want to support collaboration among users and customize content based on each individual user's preferences and history. You see your Web site as a lattice of dazzling little rubies of information. The Unix or Windows NT file system, though, only understands burlap sacks full of sod. As you'll find out when you read the chapters on building database-backed Web sites (Chapters 11–13 and 15), there aren't too many interesting things that you can implement competently on top of a standard file system. Sooner or later, you'll break down and install a relational database management system (RDBMS).

You'll want a Web server that can talk to this RDBMS. All Web servers can invoke CGI scripts that in turn can open connections to an RDBMS, execute a query, and return the results formatted as an HTML page. However, some Web servers offer built-in RDBMS connectivity. The same project can be accomplished with much cleaner and simpler programs and with a tenth of the server resources.

Support and source code availability

Most computer programs that you can buy in the 1990s are copies of systems developed in the 1960s. Consider the development of a WYSIWYG word processor. A designer could sit down in 1985 and look at 10 existing what-you-see-is-what-you-get word processors: Xerox PARC experiments from 1975, MacWrite, workstation-based systems for documentation professionals (e.g., Interleaf). He would not only have access to the running programs, but also to user feedback. By 1986, the designer hands off the list of required features to some programmers. By 1987, the new word processor ships. If enough of the users demand more sophisticated features, the designers and programmers can go back to Interleaf or Frame and see how those features were implemented. Support consists of users saying "it crashes when I do x" and the vendor writing this information down and replying "then don't do x." By 1989, the next release of the word processor is ready. The "new" features lifted from Interleaf are in place and "doing x" no longer crashes the program.

Does this same development cycle work well for Web server programs? Although the basic activity of transporting bits around the Internet has been going on for three decades, there was no Web at Xerox PARC in 1975. There is no one designer who can anticipate even a fraction of user needs. Web publishers cannot wait years for new features or bug fixes.

An important feature for a Web server is source code availability. If worst comes to worst, you can always get a wizard programmer to extend the server or fix a bug. Vendor indifference cannot shut down your Web site. That doesn't mean you should ignore commercial servers that are only available as binaries. They may offer features that let you build a sophisticated site in a fraction of the time it would take with a more basic public domain server.

If you can't get source code, then you must carefully consider the quality of the support. What is the culture of the vendor like? Do they think, "We know a lot more than our users, and every couple of years we'll hand them our latest brilliant innovation" or "We have a lot to learn from our users and will humbly work to meet their needs"? A good vendor knows that even a whole company full of Web wizards can't come up with all the good ideas. They expect to get most of their good ideas from working with ambitious customers. They expect to deliver patched binaries to customers who find bugs. They expect to make a customer problem their own and keep working until the customer is online with his publishing idea.

Availability of shrinkwrap plug-ins

Are your ideas banal? Is your Web site like everyone else's? If so, you're a good candidate for shrinkwrapped software. In a field changing as rapidly as Web publishing, packaged software usually doesn't make anyone's life easier. Sometimes a $500 program is helpful, but the grand $50,000 package ends up being a straitjacket because the authors didn't anticipate the sorts of sites that you'd want to build.

Still, as the Web matures, enough commonality among Web sites will be discovered by software vendors to make shrinkwrapped software useful. An example of a common need is "I just got a credit card from a consumer and I want to bill it before returning a confirmation page to him." Often these packages can be implemented as CGI scripts suitable for use with any Web server. Sometimes, however, it is necessary to add software to the API of your Web server. If you are using a Web server that is popular among people who are publishing similar sites, then you are more likely to be able to buy shrinkwrapped software that fits into your API.

Speed

It is so easy now to get a high-efficiency server program that I initially thought this point wasn't worth mentioning. In ancient times, the Web server forked a new process every time a user requested a page, graphic, or other file. The second generation of Web servers pre-forked a big pool of processes (e.g., 64 of them) and let each one handle a user. The server computer's operating system ensured that each process got a fair share of the computer's resources. A computer running a pre-forking server could handle at least three times the load. The latest generation of Web server programs uses a single process with internal threads. This has resulted in another tripling of performance.

It is possible to throw away 90 percent of your computer's resources by choosing the wrong Web server program. Traffic is so low at most sites and computer hardware so cheap that this doesn't become a problem until the big day when the site gets listed on the Netscape site's What's New page. In the summer of 1996, that was good for several extra users every second at Bill Gates' Personal Wealth Clock (*http://www.webho.com/WealthClock*). I'm glad now that in the back of my mind I had been thinking about efficiency.

Given these criteria, let's evaluate the three Web server programs that are sensible choices for a modern Web site (see Chapter 13, Interfacing a Relational Database to the Web, for a few notes on why the rest of the field was excluded).

AOLserver

America Online is gradually converting its services from proprietary protocols to HTTP. When you have 11 million users, life begins at 50 million hits/day/service, and you don't have too much patience for bogus "scalable application server" products. Back in 1995, a small company in Santa Barbara called Navisoft was making the most interesting Web server program. America Online bought the whole company just so that they could use the product inhouse. They changed the name of the program to AOLserver, dropped the Windows NT version (AOL is a Unix shop), and cut the price of the program from $5,000 to $0.

AOLserver has a rich and comprehensive set of API calls. Some of the more interesting ones are the following:

- `ns_sendmail` (sends email)
- `ns_httpget` (grabs a Web page from another server)
- `ns_schedule_daily` (specifies a procedure to be run once a day)

These kinds of API calls let you write sophisticated Web/e-mail/database systems that are completely portable among different versions of Unix.

These are accessible from C and, more interestingly, from the Tcl interpreter that they've compiled into the server. I have written thousands of Tcl procedures to extend the AOLserver and have never managed to crash the server from Tcl. There are several ways of developing Tcl software for the AOLserver, but the one with the quickest development cycle is to use *.tcl URLs or *.adp pages.

A file with a .tcl extension anywhere among the .html pages will be sourced by the Tcl interpreter. So you have URLs like "/bboard/fetch-msg.tcl". If asking for the page results in an error, you know exactly where in the Unix file system to look for the program. After editing the program and saving it in the file system, the next time a browser asks for "/bboard/fetch-msg.tcl" the new version is sourced. You get all of the software maintenance advantages of interpreted CGI scripts without the CGI overhead.

What the in-house AOL developers like the most are their .adp pages. These work like Microsoft Active Server Pages. A standard HTML document is a legal .adp page, but you can make it dynamic by adding little bits of Tcl code inside special tags.

AOLserver also includes Java Servlet and ATG Dynamo modules.

Though AOLserver shines in the API department, its longest suit is its RDBMS connectivity. The server can hold open pools of connections to multiple relational database management systems. Your C or Tcl API program can ask for an already open connection to an RDBMS. If none is available, the thread will wait until one

is, then the AOLserver will hand your program the requested connection, into which you can pipe SQL. This architecture improves Web/RDBMS throughput by at least a factor of ten over the standard CGI approach.

Source code availability is the weakest point for AOLserver. Though free, AOLserver is a commercial product and AOL won't give out the source code. The documentation and the API are superb, so I've never actually wanted the source code for any reason in building nearly 100 sites. Still, there is no telling what kinds of interesting plug-ins would have been written if AOLserver source code had been distributed freely.

Though the AOLserver developer team has been diligent in fixing bugs, support is strictly third party. If you can't figure it out from their four-volume documentation set or from the developer mailing list, then you'll have to buy a support contract (check *http://www.aolserver.com* for the currently authorized vendors).

Availability of shrinkwrapped software for the AOLserver is very poor. AOLserver is being run by only about 20,000 sites, and most of the people who run it are capable of writing their own back-end systems. They aren't going to pay $50,000 for a program to serve advertising banners when they can write a few pages of Tcl code to do the same thing more reliably. Of course, AOLserver can run packages of CGI scripts or Java Servlets as well as any other Web server, so you can still install important packages like local full-text search engines.

AOLserver 1.0 was the first of the threaded Web server programs and is therefore right up there with the fastest products on the market. AOLserver 2.3 has all the latest performance-enhancing tricks and they are all configurable. One that is hard to explain is single-thread serving of static pages. This means that AOLserver is scheduling how bytes are served to multiple users rather than letting the operating system do it.

An obvious performance enhancer is optional in-memory caching of static files. If there are 47 GIFs on your home page that every user requests, AOLserver won't keep fetching them from the Unix file system. You can also use AOLserver to cache Tcl-generated pages or page fragments. This can be a huge savings if the Tcl page executes an expensive RDBMS query.

The bottom line is that you can probably serve five million static and cached Tcl hits a day from a modest Unix box with AOLserver. I haven't really tested this myself, though, because my most popular static site is *http://photo.net/photo/* and it is running on a mid-range HP Unix K460 server. At 500,000 hits per day, AOLserver takes up about 1 to 3 percent of the machine, according to the HP GlancePlus performance monitoring package.

My favorite AOLserver story starts in the seventh-floor lounge of the MIT Artificial Intelligence Laboratory. I was asking Robert Thau, primary author of the Apache server program, why the Netscape 1.1 server was so slow. He said, "Oh, that's because those guys don't understand Unix. They're actually using the `read` system call to read files." Everyone in the room laughed, except me. "What? What's wrong with that?" I asked. He replied, "Everyone knows you can't use `read`; you have to use memory-mapped I/O."

I knew that the NaviSoft guys were about to release a new version, so I thought I'd give the naifs in Santa Barbara the benefit of some hardcore MIT engineering knowledge. I told them the story and asked them what NaviServer, as it was then called, did. They replied, "NaviServer uses memory-mapped file I/O on single-processor machines, but automatically configures itself to use operating system `read` on multi-CPU machines so as to reduce shared memory contention."

Ah.

One final note about AOLserver: If you want to exploit its Tcl API and RDBMS connectivity without any sysadmin or dbadmin hassles, then you can pay about $200 a month for a virtual server in someone else's cluster. You get your own domain name, your own database, and redundant T1 or T3 connectivity. ISPs providing this service include Primehost (*www.primehost.com*), AM Computers (*http://am.net*), and a German outfit (*http://www.carpe.net*).

Apache

Proceeding alphabetically, we arrive at the most popular Web server, Apache, which is running behind roughly half the world's Web sites. Apache seems to be used for the very simplest and the very most complex Web sites. The simple users just want a free server for static files. The complex users basically need a custom Web server, but don't want to start programming from scratch.

The Apache API reflects this dimorphism. The simple users aren't expected to touch it. The complex users are expected to be C programming wizards. So the API is flexible, but doesn't present a very high-level substrate on which to build.

Support for Apache is as good as your wallet is deep. You download the software free from *http://www.apache.org* and then buy support separately from the person or company of your choice. Because the source code is freely available, there are thousands of people worldwide who are at least somewhat familiar with Apache's innards.

Big companies that like to spend big dollars on trivial shrinkwrapped software generally don't trust free software. Hence, I haven't seen too many simple hacks packaged on CD-ROM for the Apache API. However, there are lots of interesting freeware modules, including some popular ones that let you

- embed a Perl or Python interpreter in the server and thus avoid CGI overhead

- do user authentication from an RDBMS

- add SSL support (encrypted sessions)

- run Java Servlets

- throttle back the usage on a per-user basis (very useful for ISPs)

- run FastCGI scripts

- add a server-parsed scripting language (PHP)

See *modules.apache.org* for a current list.

Apache is a pre-forking server and is therefore reasonably fast. Bottom line: Owners of most Web sites have decided that a source code–available server is the right one for them; Apache is the best and most popular of the source code–available server programs.

Microsoft IIS/ASP

For people who are enslaved to Windows NT, Internet Information Server (IIS) isn't a bad choice. Active Server Pages (ASP) has the right architecture for Web service development. There is a reasonably gentle slope from plain-old HTML to full-out custom program. ASP provides high-performance connectivity to relational databases.

Support and source code availability are IIS's weak point. You don't get the source code, and if something goes wrong, you'll be reminded of this comment from a reader:

> It is easy to become a qualified system administrator for NT because 99 percent of all NT problems can be solved using the same technique: "reinstall the (what for lack of strong ethics we call) Operating System, reinstall the applications...."

Virtually everyone selling shrinkwrapped software for Web services offers a version for IIS, including Microsoft with its Site Server package.

IIS is more than fast enough for serving static files.

CONNECTIVITY

An eight-headed DEC Alpha with 4 GB of RAM in your living room is an impressive personal Web server, but not if it has to talk to the rest of the Internet through a 28.8 K modem. You need some kind of high-speed Internet connection. If you aren't going to be like me and park your server at above.net or exodus.net, then you need to think about higher-speed connectivity to your premises.

ISDN

Integrated Services Digital Network (ISDN) is a 128 K point-to-point connection from the phone company. It is the bare minimum bandwidth that you need to run any kind of Web server, though most publishers would be far better off

co-locating a Unix box in a T1-connected network somewhere and remotely maintaining it.

If you decide to take the ISDN plunge for your home or business in order to manage that co-located Web server, try to get one vendor to take responsibility for the entire connection. Otherwise, your position will be the following: You want packets to go from the back of your Macintosh into the Net. If the packets are getting stalled, it could be a malfunctioning or misconfigured BitSURFR, in which case you need to call Motorola tech support (yeah, right). It could be the line, in which case you should call your local telephone company. It could be your Internet service provider, in which case you should pray.

With three organizations pointing fingers at each other and saying it's the other guys' fault, it is amazing to me that anyone has ever gotten ISDN to work. I finally got mine to work by scrapping the Motorola BitSURFR and getting an Ascend Pipeline 50 router, the product recommended by my ISP (an inhouse MIT organization). They wanted me to get an Ascend 50 so that they could configure it properly and I would just have to take it home and it would work.

It didn't.

I called Ascend tech support and waited two minutes on hold before being connected to Jerome. He dialed into one of my ISDN channels and poked around inside the Pipeline 50. Then he said, "Your subnet mask is wrong for the range of IP addresses that they've given you. I fixed it." I noted that my Macintosh was complaining that another computer on the same wire was claiming that same IP address. "Oh, you've got Proxy ARP turned on," Jerome said. "I've turned it off. Everything should work now."

It didn't.

It turns out that MIT bought its big ISDN concentrator from Ascend, as well. So I had Jerome connect into that and poke around. "They've set the subnet mask incorrectly for you there, as well."

The only thing that could have darkened my day at this point was the bill. ISDN was designed in the 1970s to provide efficient, reasonably low-cost, point-to-point digital communication across the continent. You really cared to whom you were connected and would be willing to pay a big price for that service.

Now people just want to use ISDN for Internet access. They don't really care to whom they are connected. In fact, having to choose an ISP is an annoyance and they would probably much rather the phone company took the bits and routed them into the Net. However, due to regulatory restrictions and corporate inertia, all the Regional Bell Operating Companies (RBOCs) haven't caught up to this.

Most of the RBOCs charge you per minute if you are using your ISDN line to call across town with a data connection. An example of a forward thinking RBOC is Pacific Bell. They will provide you with a complete package: ISP service, modem, and line. For this you pay $75 per month. If you use the line between 8:00 A.M. and 5:00 P.M. Monday through Friday, you pay one cent per minute. So if you left your line connected continuously, you'd pay an extra $120 per month. By contrast, assuming you could ever get three vendors in Massachusetts to work together, the same pattern of usage would cost you 1.6 cents a minute times 24 hours times 60 minutes times 30 days equals... about $700 a month! If you want to call a little farther or, God forbid, your line is billed at business rates, you could be paying a lot more. One guy in my lab at MIT got a bill from NYNEX for $2,700 one month. NYNEX will be naming its next building after him, I guess.

A more common approach is to defraud the phone company by programming your equipment to originate all calls with a voice header. It looks to the phone company like you've made a voice call to another ISDN telephone and are chatting away. But your ISP has in fact programmed the "modem bank" to answer all calls, whether they have voice or data headers. You end up getting 56 K instead of 64 K per channel, but you only pay the voice tariff, for which there is usually a flat monthly rate.

The reaction to this common practice varies among the RBOCs. The good ones say, "We really ought to provide flat-rate ISDN data for customers. In fact, we really ought to just give them Internet service before they all desert us for the cable TV companies." A more common attitude is "We're never going to do flat-rate ISDN because the customers are tying up our switches and capacity and it is costing us, and we'd really like to disallow flat-rate voice, too, so that the analog modem crowd doesn't clutter our switches."

Your first T1

If you want to join the club of Real Internet Studs, then at a minimum you need a T1 line. This is typically a 1.5-Mbps dedicated connection to somebody's backbone network. You generally get the physical wire from the local telephone monopoly and they hook it up to the Internet service provider of your choice. The cost varies by region. In the San Francisco Bay Area, you can get a whole package from Pac Bell, including the wire plus the Internet packet routing, for $800. More typical is a $2,000-a-month package from a "Tier 1" vendor like ANS, MCI, or Sprint.

I think it is risky to rely on anyone other than a Tier 1 network for T1 service. It is especially risky to route your T1 through a local ISP, who in turn has T1 service from a backbone operator. Your local ISP may not manage its network competently. They may sell T1 service to 50 other companies and funnel you all up to Sprint through one T1 line.

You'll have to be serving about 500,000 hits a day before you max out a T1 line (or be serving 50 simultaneous real-time audio streams). When that happy day arrives, you can always get a 45-Mbps T3 line for about $50,000 a month.

Cable modems and ADSL

The cable network is almost ideal topologically for providing cheap Internet. There is one wire serving 100 or 200 houses. Upstream from this there is a tree of wires and video amplifiers. The cable company can say, "We declare the wire going to your house to be a Class C subnet." Then they put a cable modem in your house that takes Ethernet packets from the back of your computer and broadcasts them into an unused cable channel. Finally, the cable company just needs to put an Internet router upstream at every point where there is a video amp. These routers will pull the Internet packets out of the unused cable channels and send them into one of the usual Internet backbones.

If all of the folks on your block started running pornographic Web servers on their NT boxes, then you'd have a bit of a bandwidth crunch because you are sharing a 10 Mbps channel with 100 other houses. But there is no reason the cable company couldn't split off some fraction of those houses onto another Ethernet in another unused video channel.

My personal IP-over-cable experience has been with MediaOne in Cambridge, Massachusetts. I get 1.5 Mbps down and 300 Kbps up for $40 a month, unlimited access. The price includes some traditional ISP services like POP mail, a News server, and a simple Web site on one of MediaOne's boxes. The main limitation is that you only get one IP address and it is dynamically assigned via DHCP. A dynamic IP address is problematic for computer nerds who might need to configure a firewall somewhere else on the Internet to "be open to 18.43.0.156". The single-IP address limitation is a real problem if you have a small home network with a few computers and a laser printer. Most of my friends get around this by running "IP masquerading" software on a Linux machine. If the only reason you'd be getting a Linux machine is to

run this software, you might want to consider getting a Cayman Systems 2e-500h router/hub from *www.cayman.com*. It costs about $1,000 (August 1998) and does the same job as the Linux box, while taking up little more space than a standard eight-port hub. Setup time is about 30 minutes.

If you don't trust your cable company, don't give up on the local phone company. In their more candid moments and incarnations, phone companies more or less concede that ISDN sucks. Their attempt to keep you from pulling the plug on them and letting your cable monopoly supply all of your communications needs is Asymmetrical Digital Subscriber Line (ADSL).

Telephony uses 1 percent of the bandwidth available in the twisted copper pair that runs from the central phone office to your house (the local loop). ISDN uses about 10 percent of that bandwidth. With technology similar to that in a 28.8 K modem, ADSL uses 100 percent of the local loop bandwidth, enough to deliver 6 Mbps to your home or business. There are only a handful of Web sites on today's Internet capable of maxing out an ADSL line. The price will certainly be very low because the service was primarily designed to deliver video streams to consumers, in competition with video rental stores and pay-per-view cable.

As a Web publisher, your main question about ADSL will be what happens to the packets. There is no reason the phone company couldn't build a traditional hierarchical data network to sit in their central offices next to their point-to-point network. Then they could sell you low-cost, one-vendor Internet access and their cost would be comparable to that of the cable companies. Some of the RBOCs, however, are afflicted with the brain-damaged notion that people want to choose their router hardware and their ISP. So you'll have to buy an ADSL line from your RBOC and then also cut a deal with ANS, MCI, or Sprint to carry your packets into the Net.

The big picture

Processing power per dollar has been growing exponentially since the 1950s. In 1980, a home computer was lucky to execute 50,000 instructions per second and a fast modem was 2,400 bps. In 1997, a home computer could do 200 million instructions per second, but it communicated through a 28.8 K modem. We got a 4,000-fold improvement in processing power, but only a tenfold improvement in communication speed.

The price of bandwidth is going to start falling at an exponential rate. Our challenge as Web publishers is to figure out ways to use up all that bandwidth.

SUMMARY

- There are a bunch of layers that go into making a Web service work. You have to decide where your expertise lies and therefore which of these layers you ought to manage and which to outsource.

- Until Microsoft is able to get Windows NT to work at its own sites (e.g., hotmail.com), it is probably safest to rely on a Unix server.

- The most important factors in choosing a Web server program are the quality of its API, its ability to connect to a relational database management system, and whether or not the source code is available.

- Bandwidth is cheap and getting rapidly cheaper, notably because of cable modems. Don't make too many decisions based on the assumption that users will be connecting at 28.8 K.

MORE

- For an overview of one proven method of keeping Web services up and running, see the ArsDigita Server Architecture (*http://photo.net/wtr /arsdigita-server-architecture.html*).

- To understand computer networks, start with *TCP/IP Illustrated, Volume 1* (Stevens, 1994; Addison-Wesley), one of the best books on any engineering subject.

- To understand processors and systems, read *Computer Organization and Design* (Patterson and Hennessy, second edition 1998; Morgan Kaufmann), *Computer Architecture: A Quantitative Approach* (Hennessy and Patterson, second edition 1996; Morgan Kaufmann), and *Computer Architecture: Concepts and Evolution* (Blaauw and Brooks, 1997; Addison-Wesley). These are the standard textbooks in the field, written by people whose ideas have been built into every modern computer (e.g., Hennessy and Patterson were prime forces behind reduced instruction set computers [RISC]).

- To understand Windows NT, read *Inside Windows NT* (Solomon, 1998; Microsoft Press).

- *UNIX Power Tools* (Peek et al., 1997; O'Reilly) is a very useful introduction to using Unix.

- *http://www.cs.purdue.edu/coast/* and *http://www.cert.org* are good places to start learning about computer security. Dan Farmer, author of the SATAN security checker/cracker, found in 1996 that 60 percent of Internet servers could be easily compromised (see *http://www.trouble.org/survey/*).

9
User
Tracking

This chapter discusses what we can infer from monitoring user activity on the Web, how to use that information to personalize a user's Web experience, and whether it wouldn't be better to push some of the responsibility for personalization onto the client.

LEARNING FROM SERVER LOGS

What do you want to know? Figure that out and then affirmatively devise a logging strategy. If your goal is to fill up your hard disk, any Web server program will do that quite nicely with its default logs. However, this information might not be what you want or need.

Here are some examples of starting points:

- I want to know how many users requested nonexistent files and where they got the URLs.

- I want to know how many people are looking at Chapter 3 of *http://photo.net/samantha/*.

- I want to know how long the average reader of Chapter 3 spends before moving on to Chapter 4.

- I sold a banner ad to Sally's Sad Saab Shop. I want to know how many people clicked on the banner and went over to her site.

- I want to know the age, sex, and zip code of every person who visited my site, so that I can prepare a brochure for advertisers.

Let's take these one at a time.

"I want to know how many users requested nonexistent files and where they got the bad URLs."

Web server programs are configured by default to log every access by writing a line into a file system file. Here is an example, broken up into multiple lines for readability:

```
ip248.providence.ri.pub-ip.psi.net - - [28/Jan/1997:12:35:54 -0500]
"GET /sammantha/travels-withsammantha.html HTTP/1.0"
404 170
  -
"Mozilla/3.0 (Macintosh; I; 68K)"
```

The first field is the name of the client machine. It looks like someone connected to the Internet via PSI in Providence, Rhode Island. My Web server program, AOLserver, has written the date and time of the connection and then the request line that the user's browser sent: "GET /sammantha/travels-withsammantha.html HTTP/1.0". This says, "Get me the file named /sammantha/travels-withsammantha.html and return it to me via the HTTP/1.0 protocol." This is close to /samantha/travels-with-samantha.html, but not close enough for the Unix file system, which tells AOLserver that it can't find the file. AOLserver returns a "404 File Not Found" message to the user. We see the 404 status code in the log file and then the number of bytes sent (170). The dash after the 170 normally contains the value of the "referer header" (yes, it is misspelled in the standard), indicating the page from which the user clicked. In this case that field is empty, meaning either that the user has typed in the URL directly from "Open Location" or that the user's browser did not supply a referer header. I instructed AOLserver to log the user-agent header, so I know that this person is using Netscape (Mozilla) 3.0 on the Macintosh. Netscape 3.0 definitely does supply the referer header. So unless I can drive down to Providence and teach this user how to spell, we're both out of luck.

Note: The pixels were barely dry on the above sentence before I got some email pointing me to Alexei Kosut's mod_speling module for Apache that attempts to correct user spelling/capitalization errors and redirects appropriately. The existence of this module is a testament to the value of free software.

Moving on to the next 404:

```
hd07-097.compuserve.com - - [28/Jan/1997:12:42:53 -0500]
"GET /philg/photo/canon-70-200.html HTTP/1.0" 404 170
   http://www.cmpsolv.com/photozone/easy.htm
"Mozilla/2.0 (compatible; MSIE 2.1; Windows 3.1)"
```

Here's a user from CompuServe. This person is asking for my review of the Canon EOS 70-200/2.8L lens (a delicious $1,500 piece of glass) and gets the same 404 and 170 bytes. But this user's referer header was "http://www.cmpsolv.com/photozone

"/easy.htm". There is a link from this page to a nonexistent file on my server. Does that mean that the photozone folks at cmpsolv.com are losers? No, it means I'm a loser.

I didn't think carefully enough about my file system organization. The file used to be at /philg/photo/canon-70-200.html, but then I created a canon subdirectory and moved this review into it. So now a correct request would be for */philg/photo /canon/canon-70-200.html.*

What should I do about this? I could try to find the maintainers of photozone and send them an email message asking them to update their link to me. Creating extra work for them because of my incompetence—that seems like a nice way to pay them back for doing me a favor by linking to me in the first place. Alternatively, I could reconfigure my AOLserver to redirect requests for the old filename to the new file. I have already installed quite a few of these redirects, a testament to my inability to learn from experience. Finally, I could be relatively user-unfriendly and put an HTML file at the old location saying "please click to the new location." That's not really any less trouble than installing the redirect, though, so there wouldn't be much point to doing it, unless I was using someone else's Web server on which I wasn't able to install redirects.

An interesting side note about this server log entry is the user-agent header "Mozilla/2.0 (compatible; MSIE 2.1; Windows 3.1)". The first part says, "I'm Netscape 2.0." The second part says, "I'm Microsoft Internet Explorer 2.1." In 1995, Web publishers with too much time and money programmed their services to deliver a frames-based site to Netscape 2.0 Achievers and a nonframes site to other browsers. The CGI or API scripts made the decision of which site to display based on whether the user-agent header contained the string "Mozilla/2". Microsoft, anxious that its users not be denied the wondrous user interface experience of frames, programmed Internet Explorer to pretend to be Netscape 2.0 so that publishers wouldn't have to rewrite their code.

"I want to know how many people are looking at Chapter 3 of http://photo.net/samantha/."

My answer here could be adapted from an article in *Duh* magazine: Search the server log for "GET /samantha/samantha-III.html". Here's a typical log entry:

```
1d20-147.compuserve.com - - [30/Jan/1997:18:28:50 -0500]
"GET /samantha/samantha-III.html HTTP/1.0" 200 17298
http://www-swiss.ai.mit.edu/samantha/samantha-II.html
"Mozilla/2.01E-CIS (Win16; I)"
```

The hostname tells us that this person is a CompuServe user. The document requested was Chapter 3 and it was successfully delivered (status code of 200; 17,298 bytes served). The referer header is "samantha-II.html", meaning that this reader

was reading Chapter 2 and then clicked on "next chapter". Finally, we learn that the reader is running Netscape 2.01 on a Windows 3.1 box.

What are the subtleties here? First, the user might be coming through a caching proxy server. America Online, for example, doesn't let most of its users talk directly to your Web server. Why not? For starters, AOL Classic doesn't use Internet protocols, so their users don't necessarily have software that understands TCP/IP or HTTP. Even if their users had Internet software, AOL has only a limited connection to the rest of the world. When 100 of their users request the same page, say, *http://www.playboy.com,* at around the same time, AOL would rather that only one copy of the page be dragged through their Internet pipe, so all of their users talk first to the proxy server. If the proxy has downloaded the page from the Internet recently, the cached copy is delivered to the AOL user. If there is no copy in the cache, the proxy server requests the page from *Playboy*'s server and finally passes it on to the AOL customer.

A lot of companies require proxy connections for reasons of security. This was already an issue in pre-Java days, but Java provides the simplest illustration of the security problem. A badly implemented Java-enhanced browser will permit an applet to read files on a user's computer and surreptitiously upload them to a foreign Web server. At most companies, the user's computer has the authority to read files from all over the internal company network. So one downloaded Java applet could potentially export all of a company's private data. On the other hand, if the company uses a firewall to force proxy connections, it can enforce a "no Java applet" policy. Computers with access to private information are never talking directly to foreign computers. Internal computers talk to the proxy server and the proxy server talks to foreign computers. If the foreign computer manages to attack the proxy server, that may interfere with Web browsing for employees, but it won't compromise any internal data, since the proxy server is outside of the company's private network.

Company security proxies distort Web server stats just as badly as AOL's private protocol-Internet bridge proxies. In my server's early days, there was one computer at Digital that downloaded about 250 .html files a day. I thought, "Wow, this guy at DEC must be my biggest fan; I really must find out whose machine this is." I eventually did find out. The computer was not sitting on a bored engineer's desktop; it was the proxy server for the entire corporation.

If proxy servers result in statistical understatements of traffic, user behavior can result in overstatements. Suppose a user with a flaky connection is trying to read Chapter 3 of *Travels with Samantha* and 2 of the 18 inline images don't load properly. The user clicks Reload in hopes of getting a fully illustrated page, adding 19 spurious hits to the server log (1 for the .html file and 18 for the images).

These statistical inaccuracies troubled me until I realized, "Hey, I'm not launching the Space Shuttle here." On average, more downloads equals more readers. The number of people reading Chapter 3 is pretty well correlated with the number of "GET /samantha/samantha-III.html" requests. I'll just collect that number and be happy.

If you aren't that easygoing, what can you do to get more accurate data? See the next section.

"I want to know how long the average reader of Chapter 3 spends before moving on to Chapter 4."

I remember when my Web site was new, back in the winter of 1993–94. Every day or two, I'd load the whole HTTPD access log into Emacs and lovingly read through the latest lines, inferring from the host name which of my friends it was, tracing users' paths through *Travels with Samantha*. I could see that Michael at Stanford downloaded Chapter 3, requested an enlarged version of the Gopher Prairie Motel image two minutes later, then waited four more minutes before requesting Chapter 4. I would infer from this that Michael spent six minutes reading Chapter 3.

Lately, my server gets 25 hits a second during peak hours. Emacs on my HP K460 is happy to display a 100 MB log file, so there is no reason why volume per se should keep me from doing "visual thread analysis." A big problem, though, is that these hits are coming from dozens of simultaneous users whose threads are

intertwined. Worse yet, I don't see the readable host names that I've printed in this book. A Web server gets only IP addresses, which are 32-bit integers. You have to explicitly do a "reverse Domain Name System (DNS)" lookup to turn an IP address into a readable name, for example, "129.34.139.30" turns into "ibm.com". Reverse DNS consumes network and CPU resources and can lead to the server process hanging. So I turned it off and now my brain is completely unable to untangle the threads and figure out which users are getting which files in what sequence.

One approach to tracking an individual reader's surfing is to reprogram your Web server to issue a magic cookie to every user of your site. Every time a user requests a page, your server will check to see if a cookie header has been sent by his browser. If not, your server program will generate a unique ID and return the requested page with a Set-Cookie header. The next time the user's browser requests a page from your server, it will set the cookie header so that your server program can log "user with browser ID #478132 requested /samantha/samantha-III.html".

This gives you a very accurate count of the number of users on your Web site, and it is easy to write a program to grind over the server log and print out actual user click streams.

Problems with this approach? Not all browsers support the Netscape Magic Cookie protocol (introduced with Netscape 1.0; see *http://photo.net/wtr/* for a link to the spec). Some users set their browsers to warn them before setting cookies. Some users or companies set their browsers to reject all cookies. If they reject the cookie that you try to set, their browser will never give it back to your server program. So you keep issuing cookies to users unable or unwilling to accept them. If such a user requests 50 documents from your server, casually implemented reporting software will see him as 50 distinct users requesting one document each.

"I sold a banner ad to Sally's Sad Saab Shop. I want to know how many people clicked on the banner and went over to her site."

The number of clickthroughs is information that is contained only in Sally's server log. She can grind through her server log and look for people who requested "/index.html" with a referer header of "http://yoursite.com/page-with-banner-ad.html". Suppose your arrangement with Sally is that she pays you 10 cents per clickthrough. And further suppose that she has been hanging around with Internet entrepreneurs and has absorbed their philosophy. Here's how your monthly conversation would go:

You: How many clickthroughs last month, Sally?

Sally: Seven.

You: Are you sure? I had 28,000 hits on the page with the banner ad.

Sally: I'm sure. We're sending you a check for 70 cents.

You: Can I see your server logs?

Sally: Those are proprietary!

You: I think something may be wrong with your reporting software; I'd like to check.

Sally [*sotto voce to her sysadmin*]: How long will it take to write a Perl script to strip out all but seven of the referrals from this loser's site? An hour? Okay.

Sally [*to you*]: I'll put the log on my anonymous FTP site in about an hour.

Of course, Sally doesn't have to be evil-minded to deny you this information or deliver it in a corrupted form. Her ISP may be running an ancient Web server program that doesn't log referer headers. Some of your readers may be using browsers that don't supply referer headers. Sally may lack the competence to analyze her server log in any way.

What you need to do is stop linking directly to Sally. Link instead to a click-through server that will immediately redirect the user to Sally's site but keep a thread alive to log the clickthrough. If you have a low-tech site, your clickthrough script could dump an entry to a file. Alternatively, have the thread establish a connection to a relational database and record the clickthrough there.

What if you have a really low-tech site? You are hosted by an ISP that doesn't know how to spell "relational database." Fill out a form on my clickthrough server and establish a realm for your site. My server will log clickthroughs and prepare reports for you. Figure 9-1 maps out the system architecture.

In addition to being the author of the clickthrough server software, I also use the software to collect statistics on my personal site (*http://clickthrough.photo.net /click/by-foreign-url-aggregate.tcl?realm=philg&minimum=10*). Here's a portion of one of my report pages, heavily edited for brevity:

- *http://cayman.com.ky* (from *webtravel/cayman.html*): 1,939

- *http://elsa.photo.net* (from *philg/index.html*): 3,807

- *http://elsa.photo.net* (from *photo/portraits.html*): 684

- *http://image.hp.com* (from *philg/humor/bill-gates-fpx.html*): 2,876

- *http://image.hp.com* (from *photo/color-printers.html*): 801

- *http://image.hp.com* (from *photo/index.html*): 6,062

- *http://image.hp.com* (from *photo/personalize-thumbnail-targets.tcl*): 224

- *http://image.hp.com* (from *photo/publishing-flashpix.html*): 1,413

- *http://image.hp.com* (from *photo/travel/new-mexico.html*): 656

- . . .

- *http://mitpress.mit.edu* (from *wtr/index.html*): 104

- *http://nz.com/webnz/flying_kiwi/* (from *nz/iwannago.html*): 184

- *http://nz.com/webnz/flying_kiwi/* (from *nz/nz-mtn-bike.html*): 424

- *http://nz.com/webnz/flying_kiwi/* (from *nz/wellington-to-milford.html*): 508

- *http://photoarts.com/banning /gallery/evans.html* (from *photo/walker -evans.html*): 300

- *http://photomosaic.com* (from *philg/humor/bill-gates-fpx.html*): 3,252

- *http://www.above.net* (from *wtr/above.net.html*): 68

- *http://www.above.net* (from *wtr/servers.html*): 384

- *http://www.above.net/* (from *photo/upgrade-report.html*): 279

- *http://www.acura.com/* (from *philg/cars/nsx.html*): 1,764

- *http://www.adiweb.com/* (from *italy/index.html*): 516

- *http://www.adiweb.com/* (from *photo/credits.html*): 47

- *http://www.adiweb.com/* (from *photo/labs.html*): 1,913

- *http://www.adiweb.com/* (from *photo/speed-graphic.html*): 244

- . . . a bunch more items for ADI, which does PhotoCD scanning . . .

- *http://www.alitalia.it/english/* (from *italy/index.html*): 58

- *http://www.alitalia.it/english/* (from *italy/transporation.html*): 40

- *http://www.audioadvisor.com/* (from *materialism/stereo.html*): 110

- *http://www.bhphotovideo.com/* (from *photo/where-to-buy.html*): 46,697

- . . . a bunch more items for B&H Photo, a big camera retailer in New York . . .

- *http://www.bostonphoto.com/* (from *photo/labs.html*): 2,982

- *http://www.bostonphoto.com/* (from *photo/travel/foliage.html*): 1,658

- . . . a bunch more links to Boston Photo, my favorite local lab . . .

- *http://www.canon.com/* (from *photo/canon/canon-reviews.html*): 5,023

- *http://www.cool.co.cr/crexped.html* (from *cr/central-valley.html*): 2,027

- *http://www.cool.co.cr/crexped.html* (from *cr/tour-operators.html*): 1,979

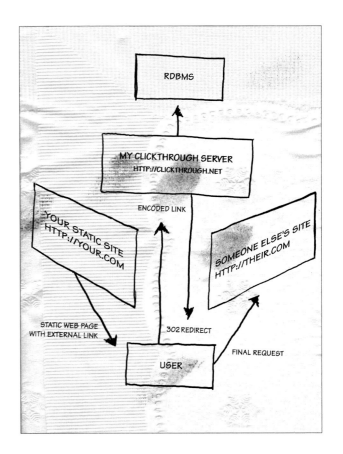

Figure 9-1: My clickthrough monitoring service (*http://clickthrough.net /click/*) allows low-tech Web publishers to measure traffic going from their site to other sites. This can be useful if you are selling banner ads. Instead of linking directly to http://their.com, you link to http://clickthrough.net /your?send_to= http://their.com. A user clicking through will first make a request of my clickthrough server. The request is logged in a relational database and then an HTTP 302 redirect is returned to the user's browser, causing it finally to make a request to http://their.com.

- ... a bunch more links to tour operator Costa Rica Expeditions, from my Costa Rica travel site ...

- *http://www.cuisinart.com/* (from *materialism/kitchen.html*): 135

- *http://www.dacorappl.com/* (from *materialism/kitchen.html*): 469

- *http://www.dtpdirect.com* (from *wtr/scanners.html*): 597

- *http://www.fujifilm.co.jp/usa/aps/smartcity/f-better.html* (from *photo/aps.html*): 2,383

- *http://www.goodnet.com/~rmnsx* (from *philg/cars/nsx.html*): 2,168

- *http://www.hasselblad.com/* (from *photo/rollei-6008.html*): 412

- *http://www.hp.com/peripherals/pc_photography/photo_printer.html* (from *photo/color-printers.html*): 1,122

- *http://www.ibiscycles.com/* (from *materialism/bikes.html*): 102

- *http://www.keh.com/* (from *photo/where-to-buy.html*): 8,945

- *http://www.klt.co.jp/nikon/* (from *photo/nikon/nikon-reviews.html*): 6,006

- *http://www.kodak.com:80/ciHome/APS /APS.shtml* (from *photo/aps.html*): 2,919

- *http://www.meworkshops.com/* (from *photo/workshops/*): 1,321

- *http://www.moon.com/* (from *cr/moon/index.html*): 1,531

- *http://www.mpex.com/* (from *photo/where-to-buy.html*): 4,597

- *http://www.novanet.co.cr/milvia /index.html* (from *cr/milvia.html*): 444

- *http://www.portphoto.com* (from *photo/labs.html*): 3,007

- *http://www.portphoto.com* (from *samantha/gift-shop.html*): 475

- *http://www.sfworkshop.com/* (from *photo/workshops/*): 950

- *http://www.software.com* (from *wtr/post-office.html*): 198

- *http://www.soundlab-speakers.com* (from *materialism/stereo.html*): 116

- *http://www.thephotolab.com* (from *photo/publishing-flashpix.html*): 392

- *http://www.thermador.com/* (from *materialism/kitchen.html*): 531

- *http://www.vanguard.com/* (from *materialism/money.html*): 196

- *http://www.wweb.com/cayman* (from *webtravel/cayman.html*): 286

- *http://www.zzyzxworld.com/* (from *photo/labs.html*): 1,246

Take a look at the first line. It shows that 1,939 people clicked from my Cayman Islands photo essay to *http://cayman.com.ky/*, a commercial site. Cruise down to the "*http://www.bhphotovideo.com/* (from *photo/where-to-buy.html*): 46,697" entry. That means 46,697 people were referred to *http://www.bhphotovideo.com/* from my photo.net magazine's "where to buy" page. Forty-six thousand is getting to be an interesting number. What if we click on it?

- 1998-04-13: 195
- 1998-04-12: 111
- 1998-04-11: 116
- 1998-04-10: 129
- 1998-04-09: 148
- 1998-04-08: 158
- 1998-04-07: 145
- 1998-04-06: 153
- . . .

Hmmm . . . 150 people a day, people who were reading my reviews of cameras in *http://photo.net/photo/* then decided to click on "where to buy," and then decided to click on my link to B&H Photo's home page. I've always liked B&H Photo, but my evil twin wonders how much another camera shop would pay us to make just a few changes to the text of *http://photo.net/photo/where-to-buy.html*.

Anyway, not to bore you too thoroughly by walking you statically through a dynamic site, but it seems like a good time to show off the advantages of using an RDMBS for this. The clickthrough server can slice and dice the reports in all kinds of interesting ways. Suppose I want to lump together all referrals from my personal site to B&H Photo, regardless of from which page they originated. Click:

- 1998-04-13: 207
- 1998-04-12: 119
- 1998-04-11: 127
- 1998-04-10: 137
- 1998-04-09: 155
- 1998-04-08: 168
- 1998-04-07: 154
- . . .

What about that day when there were 207 clickthroughs? Where did they come from? Oh, "207" seems to be a hyperlink. Let me click on it:

- from *photo/edscott/spectsel.htm*: 3
- from *photo/labs.html*: 3
- from *photo/nikon/n90s.html*: 6
- from *photo/where-to-buy.html*: 195

Hmmm... This "where to buy" page seems to be crushing the other pages on my site in terms of clickthroughs to foreign sites. Can I see a report of all the clickthroughs from this page to others?

- 1998-04-13: 248
- 1998-04-12: 141
- 1998-04-11: 156
- 1998-04-10: 172
- 1998-04-09: 175
- 1998-04-08: 199
- 1998-04-07: 188

What about April 13, 1998? Where did those 248 clickthroughs go?

- to *http://www.bhphotovideo.com/*: 195
- to *http://www.keh.com/*: 35
- to *http://www.mpex.com/*: 18

Oooh! I'm in RDBMS heaven now. And all I had to do was

1. fill out a Web form to establish a realm on the clickthrough server.
2. replace things like "http://www.bhphotovideo.com" with things like "http://clickthrough.photo.net/ct/philg/photo/where-to-buy.html?send_to =http://www.bhphotovideo.com/" in my static .html files.

If you want to get reports like this for your own Web site, just visit *http://photo.net/philg/services.html* to get started.

"I want to know the age, sex, and zip code of every person who visited my site, so that I can prepare a brochure for advertisers."

The traditional answer to this request is, "All you can get is the IP address; HTTP is an anonymous peer-to-peer protocol." Then Netscape came out with the Magic Cookie protocol in 1994. It looked pretty innocent to me. The server gives me a cookie. My browser gives it back to the server. Now I can have a shopping basket. My friends all said, "This is the end of privacy on the Internet, Greenspun, and you're a pinhead if you can't figure out why."

So I thought about it for a while. Then I added some code to my clickthrough server.

Suppose I add an invisible GIF to my photo.net page:

```
<img width=1 height=1 border=0
  src="http://clickthrough.photo.net/blank/philg/photo/index.html">
```

This is a coded reference to my clickthrough server. The first part of the URL, "blank", tells the clickthrough server to deliver a one-pixel blank GIF. The second part, "philg", says "this is for the philg realm, whose base URL is http://photo.net/". The last part is a URL stub that specifies where on the philg server this blank GIF is appearing.

This is a somewhat confusing way to use the Web that is only possible with programs like AOLserver that allow a publisher to register a whole range of URLs, such as those starting with "blank", to be passed to a program. So this reference looks like it is grabbing a static .html page, but actually it is running a Tcl script that ultimately returns a GIF.

If *http://photo.net/photo/index.html* is the first page that Joe User has ever requested with one of these GIFs from clickthrough.photo.net, his browser won't offer a cookie to clickthrough.photo.net. My program sees the cookieless request and says, "Ah, new user, let's issue him a new browser_id and log this request with his IP address and user-agent header." If Joe is the sixth user that clickthrough.photo.net has ever seen, my Tcl program then issues a

```
Set-Cookie: ClickthroughNet=6; path=/; expires=Fri, 01-Jan-2010 01:00:00 GMT
```

This output header tells Joe's browser to return the string "ClickthroughNet=6" in a cookie header every time it requests any URL from clickthrough.photo.net (that's the "path=/" part). This cookie would normally expire when Joe terminated his browser session. However, I'd really like to track Joe for a while, so I explicitly set the expiration date to January 1, 2010. I could have made it last longer, but I figured that by 2010 Joe will have abandoned all of his quaint notions about privacy and will be submitting his name, address, home phone number, and VISA card number with every HTTP GET.

Every time Joe comes back to *http://photo.net/photo/,* his browser will see the IMG reference to the clickthrough server again. Normally, his browser would say, "Oh, that's a GIF that I cached two days ago, so I won't bother to rerequest it." However, I wrote my program to include a "`Pragma: no-cache`" header before the blank GIF. This instructs proxy servers and browser programs not to cache the reference. They aren't required to obey this instruction, but most do.

On his next visit to photo.net, Joe's browser will request the blank GIF again. This time, though, his browser will include a cookie header with his browser ID, so my clickthrough server can just return the blank GIF and then keep a thread alive to log the access.

Now I can ask questions like "What are all the times that the Netscape with browser_id 6 requested tagged pages from my server?" and "What percentage of users return to *http://photo.net/photo/* more than twice a week?"

To make life a little more interesting, suppose I add a little bit of code to *http://www.webho.com/WealthClock* (Bill Gates' Personal Wealth Clock):

```
<img width=1 height=1 border=0 src="http://clickthrough.photo.net
  /blank/webho/WealthClock">
```

Note that www.webho.com is a different server from photo.net. If photo.net had issued Joe User's browser a cookie, his browser would not offer that cookie up to www.webho.com. But photo.net did not issue Joe a cookie; *clickthrough*.photo.net did. And that is the same server being referenced by the inline IMG on the Wealth Clock. So my clickthrough server will be apprised of the access, as shown in Figure 9-2.

Finally, I added an extra few lines of code to my clickthrough stats collector. *If* there was a browser_id *and* detailed logging was enabled, *then* also write a log entry for the clickthrough.

After all of this evil work is done, what do we get?

```
Realm where originally logged: philg
original IP address: 18.23.10.101
browser used initially: Mozilla/3.01 (WinNT; I)
email address: CLICK STREAM
1997-01-30 01:44:36 Page View: philg/photo/index.html
1997-01-30 01:46:11 Page View: philg/photo/where-to-buy.html
1997-01-30 01:46:17 Clickthrough from text ref:
  philg/photo/where-to-buy.html to http://www.bhphotovideo.com/
1997-01-30 02:30:46 Page View: webho/WealthClock
1997-01-31 13:13:17 Page View: webho/WealthClock
1997-02-01 08:04:15 Page View: philg/photo/index.html
1997-02-01 18:33:17 Page View: philg/photo/index.html
1997-02-03 12:46:18 Page View: philg/photo/where-to-buy.html
1997-02-03 14:53:56 Page View: webho/WealthClock
```

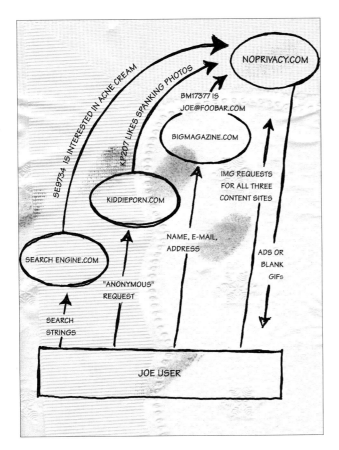

Figure 9-2: Magic cookies mean the end of privacy on the Internet. Suppose that three publishers cooperate and agree to serve all of their banner ads from http://noprivacy.com. When Joe User visits search-engine.com and types in "acne cream", the page comes back with an IMG referencing noprivacy.com. Joe's browser will automatically visit noprivacy.com and ask for "the GIF for SE9734". If this is Joe's first time using any of these three cooperating services, noprivacy.com will issue a Set-Cookie header to Joe's browser. Meanwhile, search-engine.com sends a message to noprivacy.com saying "SE9734 was a request for acne cream pages". The "acne cream" string gets stored in noprivacy.com's database along with "browser_id 7586". When Joe visits bigmagazine.com, he is forced to register and give his name, email address, snailmail address, and credit card number. There are no ads in bigmagazine.com. They have too much integrity for that. So they include in their pages an IMG referencing a blank GIF at noprivacy.com. Joe's browser requests "the blank GIF for BM17377" and, because it is talking to noprivacy.com, the site that issued the Set-Cookie header, the browser includes a cookie header saying "I'm browser_id 7586". When all is said and done, the noprivacy.com folks know Joe User's name, his interests, and the fact that he has downloaded six spanking JPEGs from kiddieporn.com.

We know that this guy was originally logged at 18.23.10.101 (my old home computer) and that he is using Netscape 3.01 on Windows NT. We don't yet know his email address, but only because he hasn't yet visited a guestbook page served by clickthrough.photo.net.

Then there is the click stream. We know that he downloaded the photo.net home page at 1:44 A.M. on January 30, 1997. Two minutes later, he downloaded the "where to buy" page. Six seconds later, he clicked through to B&H Photo. Forty-five minutes later, he showed up on another server (the webho realm) viewing the Wealth Clock. The next day at 1:30 P.M., this guy checks the Wealth Clock again. On February 1, 1997, he visits photo.net at 8:04 A.M. and then again at 6:33 P.M. He's back on the "where to buy" page on February 3. Two hours after that, he's checking the Wealth Clock once more . . . .

If I get enough Web sites to cooperate in using one clickthrough server and even one of those sites requires registration, offers a contest, or does anything else where users type in names and email addresses, it is only a matter of time before I can

associate browser_id 6 with "philg@ mit.edu; Philip Greenspun; 5 Irving Terrace, Cambridge, MA 02138."

Of course, I don't have to use this information for evil. I can use it to offer users a page of "new documents since your last visit." Suppose someone comes to the photo.net home page for the fourth time. I find that she has looked at my travel page but not read *Travels with Samantha*. I probably ought to serve her a banner that says, "You might like *Travels with Samantha;* click *here* to read it."

Does all this sound too futuristic and sinister to be really happening? Have a look at your browser's cookies file. With Netscape Navigator, you'll find this as "cookies.txt" in the directory where you installed it. With Internet Explorer, you can find one file/cookie by doing View → Options → Advanced → View (Temporary) Files. See if there is an entry that looks like this:

```
ad.doubleclick.net    FALSE    /
    FALSE    942191940    IAF    248bf21
```

Then go to *http://www.doubleclick.net/* and see the long list of companies (including AltaVista) that are sharing this ad server so that your activity can be tracked. Of course, Double Click assures everyone that your privacy is assured.

Case studies conclusions

Here are the conclusions that we can draw from these case studies:

- Web users have no privacy and haven't had any ever since late 1994 when the Netscape Magic Cookie protocol came out.

- Vital information for most Web publishers, such as number of click-throughs, is unobtainable from standard server logs and traditional linking practices.

- With a little bit of RDBMS programming or a visit to *http://photo.net/philg/services.html,* you're on your way to collecting the infor-mation you need.

LET'S BACK UP FOR A MINUTE

Suppose that the preceding talk about clickthroughs and cookies has overloaded your brain. You don't want to spend the rest of your life programming Tcl and SQL. You don't even want to come to *http://photo.net/philg/services.html* and fill out a form to use Greenspun's clickthrough.net server. You just want to analyze the server logs that you've already got.

Is that worth doing?

Well, sure. As discussed in the first case above, you certainly want to find out which of your URLs are coughing up errors. If you have hundreds of thousands of hits per day, casual inspection of your logs isn't going to reveal the 404 File Not Found errors that make users miserable. This is especially true if your Web server program logs errors and successful hits into the same file.

You can also use the logs to refine content. My very first log summary revealed that half of my visitors were just looking at the slide show for *Travels with Samantha*. Did that mean they thought my writing sucked? Well, maybe, but it actually looked like my talents as a hypertext designer were lame. The slide show was the very first link on the page. Users had to scroll way down past a bunch of photos to get to the Chapter 1 link. I reshuffled the links and traffic on the slide show fell to 10 percent.

You can also discover "hidden sites." You might have read Dave Siegel's book and spent $20,000 designing http://yourdomain.com/entry-tunnel.html. But somehow, the rest of the world has discovered http://yourdomain.com/old-text-site.html and is linking directly to that. You're getting 300 requests a day for the old page, whose information is badly organized and out of date. That makes it a hidden site. You'd ceased spending any time or money maintaining it because you thought there weren't any users. You probably want either to bring the site up to date or add a redirect to your server to bounce these guys to the new URL.

Finally, once your site gets sufficiently popular, you will probably turn off hostname lookup. Attempting to look up every IP address (e.g., turning 18.30.0.217 into lilac.lcs.mit.edu) is slow and sometimes causes odd server hangs. Anyway, after you turn lookup off, your log will be filled up with just plain IP addresses. You can use a separate machine to do the lookups offline, and at least figure out whether your users are foreign, domestic, internal, or what.

ENTER THE LOG ANALYZER

The first piece of Web "technology" that publishers acquire is the Web server program. The second piece is often a log analyzer program. Venture capitalists demonstrated their keen grasp of technology futures by funding at least a dozen companies to write and sell commercial log analyzer programs. This might have been a great strategy if the information of importance to Web publishers was present in the server log to begin with. Or if a bunch of more reliable freeware programs wasn't available. Or if companies like Netscape hadn't bundled log analyzers into their Web server programs.

Anyway, be thankful that you don't have money invested in any of these venture funds and that you have plenty of log analyzer programs from which to choose. These programs can be categorized along two dimensions:

- availability of source code
- whether standalone or substrate-based

Whether or not the source code is available is extremely important in a new field like Web publishing. As with Web server programs, software authors can't anticipate your needs or the evolution of Web standards. If you don't have the source code, you are probably going to be screwed in the long run. Generally, the free public domain packages come with source code and the commercial packages don't.

A substrate-based log analyzer makes use of a well-known and proven system to do storage management, and sometimes more. Examples of popular substrates for log analyzers are Perl and relational databases. A standalone log analyzer is one that tries to do everything by itself. Usually these programs are written in primitive programming languages like C and do storage management in an ad hoc manner. This leads to complex source code that you might not want to tangle with and, with some commercial products, crashes on logs of moderate size.

Unix shell tools

If you just want some rough numbers, you don't need to bother with log analyzers. Standard Unix shell commands, most of which are now available on Windows machines as well, will tell you a lot.

Note:
If you've forgotten your Unix commands, pick up *Unix Power Tools* (Peek, 1997; O'Reilly).

On my personal Web site, AOLserver rolls the log file every night at midnight. So the access log for Sunday, April 26th is called "philg.log.98-04-27-00:00":

```
> ls -l
-rw-r--r--   1 nsadmin  arsdigit 135288672 Apr 27 00:00 philg.log.98-04-27-00:00
```

My experience tells me that 135 MB is probably about 700,000 hits. If I want more precision, I can use the Unix word count facility:

```
> wc -l philg.log.98-04-27-00:00
 714855 philg.log.98-04-27-00:00
```

Okay, it was 714,855 hits. What's the relative browser population?

```
> grep -c 'Mozilla/1' philg.log.98-04-27-00:00
4349
> grep -c 'Mozilla/2' philg.log.98-04-27-00:00
209128
> grep -c 'Mozilla/3' philg.log.98-04-27-00:00
130199
> grep -c 'Mozilla/4' philg.log.98-04-27-00:00
350763
```

Looks like Netscape 2 and 4 are the leaders. Oops, but let's recall that Microsoft pretends that MSIE is actually Netscape.

```
> grep -c 'MSIE' philg.log.98-04-27-00:00
366247
```

Wow! 366,247 out of 714,855 hits were from Internet Explorer. Time to short Netscape stock.

What about my content?

```
> grep -c 'GET /wtr/' philg.log.98-04-27-00:00
2736
```

There aren't really any images underneath my Web Tools Review pages, so it looks as though there were 2,736 page loads. Remember that this log file is from a Sunday, when sane folks aren't working, so we'd expect traffic for nerd content like this to be lower than on weekdays.

What about my programming mistakes, identified by the server delivering a page with a status code of 500?

```
> grep '" 500 ' philg.log.98-04-27-00:00
207.212.238.29 - - [26/Apr/1998:03:31:16 -0400] "POST /photo/tutorial/focal
  -length.tcl HTTP/1.0" 500 359 http://photo.net/photo/nikon/nikon
  -reviews.html "Mozilla/3.01 (Win95; I; 16bit)"
```

My lens focal length calculator wasn't gracefully handling situations in which users left fields blank.

What about my publishing mistakes, identified by the server delivering pages with a status code of 404 (Not Found)?

```
> grep '" 404 ' philg.log.98-04-27-00:00
204.94.209.1 - - [26/Apr/1998:02:56:55 -0400] "GET /photo/nikon/comparison
    -chart HTTP/1.0" 404 537 http://www.zaiko.kyushu-u.ac.jp/~walter
    /nikon.html#slr "Mozilla/4.04C-SGI [en] (X11; I; IRIX 6.2 IP22)"
207.170.89.121 - - [26/Apr/1998:22:20:28 -0400] "GET /photo/what-camera
    -should-I-bu HTTP/1.0" 404 537 http://www.productweb.com/c/index.cfm?U1
    =216406052&CategoryID=948&CategoryName=Cameras%2C%2035mm&guidesOn
    =1&PageName=948.4.1 "Mozilla/4.04 [en] (Win95; I)"
```

Shell tools can almost always answer your questions, but they're a very cumbersome way of discovering patterns for which you weren't looking.

My first log analyzer: wwwstat

My first experiments were with wwwstat, an ancient public-domain Perl script, available for download and editing from *http://www.ics.uci.edu/WebSoft/wwwstat/*.

I found that it didn't work very well on my personal site, for the following reasons:

- There are at least three URLs to get to many of my pages: *http:// photo.net/~philg/samantha/travels-with-samantha.html* was what I used initially. In spring 1994, I discovered the index.html religion, so *http:// photo.net/~philg/samantha/* is another gateway to the same page. Then I got a little symlink-happy and made *http://photo.net/samantha/* work. But I also made *http://photo.net/philg/samantha/* work, too. So there are six URLs for the same file. They are all reported separately by wwwstat and there was no easy way to group them together. I think the latest version is beginning to have grouping capabilities.

- wwwstat doesn't count distinct hosts like a lot of other tools. In the era of proxy servers, counting distinct hosts is a mighty crude way to gauge the number of users, but it is better than nothing.

- wwwstat doesn't understand the extra information that modern Web servers log, such as browser and referer. These extra items don't interfere with wwwstat, but you don't get a "90% using Netscape" report either.

- wwwstat had no built-in facility for doing hostname lookup, though it now does.

On the plus side, I was able to feed wwwstat 50-MB and larger log files without once seeing it fail. There is a companion tool called gwstat that makes pretty graphs from the wwwstat output. It is free, but you have to be something of a Unix wizard to make it work.

Note: There are a lot of public domain tools newer than wwwstat listed in *http://www.yahoo.com/Computers_and _Internet /Software/Internet/World_Wide_Web/Servers /Log_Analysis_Tools/*. A lot of wizards seem to like analog (referenced from Yahoo), which is what we use at photo.net.

My second log analyzer: WebReporter

WebReporter was a standalone commercial product, written in C and sold by Open-Market, Inc. It took me two solid days of reading the manual and playing around with a small log file to figure out how to tell WebReporter 1.0 what I wanted. For a brief time, I was in love with the program. It would let me lump certain URLs together and print nice reports saying "Travels with Samantha cover page." I fell out of love when I realized:

- If you wanted cumulative reports, you'd have to freeze your groups when you started accumulating data. That made WebReporter a great tool for sites where files are never added, subtracted, or moved. Yeah.

- It crashed trying to show ASCII histograms of activity from a puny log file (just an hour or two's worth of data for a popular site).

When I complained about the crashes, OpenMarket said, "Oh, yes, we might have a fix for that in the next release. Just wait four months." So I waited and let some friends at a commercial site beta-test the new release. "How do you like it?" I asked. They responded quickly, "It crashes."

My experience with WebReporter has made me wary of standalone commercial products in general. Cumulative log data might be important to me. Do I want to store it in a proprietary format accessible only to a C program for which I do not have source code? What guarantee do I have that the people who made the program will keep it up to date? Or even stay in business?

Shortly after these reservations took root in my mind, the WebReporter product disappeared from the OpenMarket Web site. On April 19, 1998, I checked the company's profile over at *quote.yahoo.com*. They had a book value of $1.40 a share (99 cents in cash) but had lost $1.98 a share in the preceding 12 months. Without a cash infusion, they'd be bankrupt in six to nine months if losses continued (and my friend Bruce, one of the best engineers with whom I've worked, had tried without success to get the latest version of their flagship LiveCommerce program to work).

Maybe it would be wise to give cumulative data a more stable footing.

RELATIONAL DATABASE–BACKED TOOLS

What are the characteristics of our problem anyway? Here are some obvious ones:

- We need to maintain a data set over many years.

- We can't know now what kinds of queries we're going to want to do into this data set later.

- We may end up with many gigabytes of data.

- We don't trust one vendor to serve all of our needs. We can't afford to lose access to our data if an application code vendor folds.

Do these sound like the problems that IBM thought they were solving in the early 1970s with the relational model? Call me an SQL whore, but it seems apparent that the correct tool is a relational database management system.

So brilliant and original was my thinking on this subject that the net.Genesis guys (*www.netgenesis.com*) apparently had the idea a couple of years earlier. They make a product called net.Analysis that purports to stuff server logs into a (bundled) Informix RDBMS in real-time.

This could be the best of all possible worlds. You do not surrender control of your data. With a database-backed system, the data model is exposed. If you want to do a custom query or the monolithic program crashes, you don't have to wait four months for the new version. Just go into a standard database client and type your query. Any of these little Web companies might fold or decide that they've got better things to do than write log analyzers, but Oracle, Informix, and Sybase will be around. Furthermore, SQL is standard enough that you can always dump your data out of Brand O into Brand I, or vice versa.

More important, if you decide to get a little more ambitious and start logging clickthroughs or sessions, you can use the same RDBMS installation and do SQL JOINs on the vanilla server log tables and the tables from your more sophisticated logs.

Caveats? Maintaining a relational database is not such a thrill, though using it for batch inserts isn't too stressful. If you don't want the responsibility of keeping the RDBMS up 24 × 7, then you can have your Web server log to a file as usual and insert the data into your RDBMS in batches.

If you do decide to go for real-time logging, be a little bit thoughtful about how many inserts per second your RDBMS can handle. I maintain some RDBMS benchmarks at *http://photo.net/wtr,* but the bottom line is that you should start to worry if you need to log more than 10 hits per second on a standard Unix box with one disk.

OBJECT DATABASE–BACKED TOOLS

If you care about massive aggregates of data, the relational database is a great tool. But if you want to "chase pointers" and follow the actions of a particular user, an RDBMS is extremely inefficient. If you can't fit all of your log data into RAM, then it will become spectacularly inefficient. RAM is cheap, so why is this a problem?

Suppose I want to know something simple like "How long after downloading foo.html does it take the average IP address to request bar.html?" This requires the RDBMS to JOIN a table with itself. If you have 500,000 hits a day, then this is a self-JOIN on a 500,000-row table. Ouch! As discussed in Chaper 12, Database Management Systems, this might result in the database looking at 500,000 × 500,000 pairs of rows (250 *billion* pairs).

Suppose I want to study how long it takes people with MediaOne cable modems (*.mediaone.net hostnames) to read all of *Travels with Samantha* compared to folks at America Online, or the propensity for the AOL users to give up on us, presumably because their slow connections make it unpleasant to download 300 JPEGs. If I've cookied all of these users and told AOLserver to log the cookie header, it will be easy to find the threads. However, if I want to give each user up to two months to read the book, I need to keep and grind through two months of server logs. My personal site generates 100 MB of log files a day, so it looks like I'll need about 6 GB of RAM.

Suppose I'm a crass commercial publisher and get paid per clickthrough. I've bought my own banner ads on Yahoo and America Online. Is a user who came in via America Online more likely to find his way to my ad-bearing pages? To click through? If so, I should probably limit my own ad buying to AOL or demand a lower price from Yahoo. If my site is a popular million-hit-per-day site, that's about 200 MB of logs a day. I probably bought ads for a month, so again I'll need to look at buying 6 GB of RAM just for server log analysis.

Could it be time to break out of the "when all you've got is a hammer, everything looks like a nail" mentality? The RDBMS solves so many problems, and hardcore computing users are so heavily invested in it, that typing up a little SQL query is second nature. If that query is taking a few hours to return a result, though, it might be time to consider using an object database as a substrate.

That's precisely what Andromedia (*http://www.andromedia.com*) did. They built a very interesting system called ARIA that logs Web site activity into an Object Design object database. The first nice thing about ARIA is that it uses a standard, popular,

Note:
Secure in the knowledge that this chapter will seem laughable 10 years from now when standard cellular telephones come with 6 GB of RAM, I'd better note that computers in 1998 were generally only capable of addressing a maximum of 4 GB of RAM, which would cost about $20,000.

well-tested, old object database management system (ObjectStore). If Andromedia tanks, you can still write a C, Java, Lisp, or Perl program to run whatever queries you want against your old data. The second nice thing about ARIA is that it has the potential to be minimally invasive. Although it is possible to tightly integrate it with your Web server program, you can run ARIA separately as a network packet snooper. If there is a bug in ARIA or the ObjectStore system gets wedged, your Web services will be unaffected. A third nice thing is that ObjectStore can be much easier to manage than a relational database management system.

Does this mean ARIA is the perfect tool? My biggest complaint with it is that I've already sold my site's soul to a relational database. All of my user personalization data are stored in RDBMS tables. My Web server program has a bunch of built-in convenient ways of getting to data in every important implement of the RDBMS. If I want to customize a user's experience based on his click-stream history, I have to find a way to (1) periodically transfer summary data from ObjectStore into the RDBMS or (2) simultaneously talk to an RDBMS and ObjectStore (or the Java Beans that Andromedia makes available). I think I could work around both of these issues with a few weeks of programming, but my site isn't commercial so I haven't put aside the time to do it.

We've discussed how to track the user. Now let's think about how to use the data collected to help the user.

PERSONALIZATION

My favorite course to teach at MIT is 6.041, a probability class designed by Al Drake, one of the fully-human human beings who never seems to get past tenure committees these days. Drake taught the course for decades and wrote the text *Fundamentals of Applied Probability Theory,* which offers the clearest explanation of statistics that I've seen.

Each week in 6.041, we meet with students in small groups. I make them go up to the blackboard and work through problems that they haven't seen before. Partly the idea is to see how they think and offer corrections. Partly the idea is to prepare them to give engineering presentations and communicate their ideas. The student at the board isn't really supposed to solve the problem, just coordinate hints from other students at the conference table.

One day I gave a problem to a quiet midwestern girl named Anne. She studied it for a moment, walked over to the board, and gave a five-minute presentation on how to solve it, mentioning all of the interesting pedagogical points of the problem and writing down every step of the solution in neat handwriting. Her impromptu talk was better prepared than any lecture I'd ever given in the class.

Anne and I were chatting one day before class.

"What did you do on Sunday?" she asked.

"Oh, I don't know. Ate. Brushed the dog. Watched *The Simpsons*. And you?" I replied.

"My housemates and I decided to have a hacking party. We do this every month or so. Since we have a network of PCs running Unix at home, it is easy to get lots of people programming together. We couldn't decide what to build, so I said, 'Well, we all like science fiction novels. So let's build a system where we type in the names of the books that we like and a rating. Then the system can grind over the database and figure out what books to suggest.'"

"And?"

"It took us the whole afternoon, but we got it to the point where it would notice that I liked Books A, B, and C but hadn't read Book D, which other people who liked A, B, and C had liked. So that was suggested for me. We also got it to notice if you and I had opposite tastes and suppress your recommendations."

This was back in 1994. Anne and her friends had, in one afternoon, completed virtually the entire annual research agenda of at least two MIT professors (neither in my department, I'm relieved to note).

The first lesson to be drawn from this example is that Anne is a genius. The second is that an afternoon hack, even by a genius, isn't enough to solve the personalization problem. Yet, if you cut through the crust of hype that surrounds any of the expensive Web server personalization software "solutions," all that you find underneath is Anne's afternoon hack.

What's wrong with Anne's system? First, it imposes a heavy burden of logging in and rating on users. Given that we're going to lose our privacy and have an unfeeling computer system know everything about our innermost thoughts and tastes, can't it at least be a painless process?

Suppose we did get everyone in the world to subscribe to Anne's system and tirelessly rate every Usenet posting, every Web site, every musical composition, every movie, every book. Does this help Joe User make the choices that matter? If Joe types in that he likes the *Waldstein* sonata, probably Anne's software can tell him that he wouldn't like the Pat Boone cover of AC/DC's *It's a Long Way to the Top (If You Wanna Rock and Roll)*. But will it help him pick among Beethoven's other 31 piano sonatas? Is it meaningful to rate Beethoven's sonatas on a linear scale: *Pastoral* good, *Appassionata* great, *Moonlight* somewhere in between?

Suppose Joe User's taste changes over time? Consider that old French saying: "If you're not a liberal when you're young, then you have no heart; if you're not a conservative when you're old, then you have no mind." Perhaps he liked Guy de Maupassant and Charles Dickens when he was foolish and young, but now that he's old he's come to see the supreme truth of Ayn Rand. Joe doesn't want Anne's system recommending a bunch of sissy books about people helping each other when he could be reading about a perfect society where rich people rent rather than loan their cars to friends.

That's no big deal. We'll just expire the ratings after 10 years. But what if Joe's taste changes over the course of a few days? Last week, Joe was content to sit through four hours of *Hamlet*. This week Joe has had to go back to his Dodge dealer four times to get the rattling plastic pieces on the interior stuck back to the metal; he needs a comedy.

Reader ratings: A big mistake?

Why do we ask readers to explicitly rate content? Each American is being watched by so many computers so much of the time that if we have to ask a person what he or she likes, then that only reveals the weakness of our imagination and technology.

Ken Phillips, a professor at New York University, has been thinking about these issues since the late 1970s when he set up a massive computer network for Citibank. He asked me what I thought AT&T's most valuable asset was. I tried to estimate the cost of undersea cables versus the fiberlinks that crisscross the continent. Ken laughed.

"AT&T gives you long distance service, so they know which companies you call and how long you spend on the phone with each one. AT&T gives you a credit card, so they know what you buy. AT&T owns Cellular One so, if you have a cell phone, they know where you drive and where you walk. By combining these data, AT&T can go to a travel agency and say, 'For $100 each, we can give you the names of people who drive by your office every day, who've called airline 800 numbers more than three times in the last month, who have not called any other travel agencies, and who have spent more than $10,000 on travel in the last year.'"

Ken is a lot smarter than I am.

As discussed above, Web publishers and marketeers are trying to do some of this with persistent magic cookies issued by central ad delivery/tracking services. However, these systems are extremely crude compared to traditional direct marketing databases.

Compare the relevancy of the junk snailmail that you receive to that of the spam email cluttering your inbox. Your behavior on the Web is much more consistently logged than your behavior in real life. Why then is your Internet profile so much less accurate? Partly because Web data are fragmented. Information about which files you've downloaded is scattered among many different sites' server logs. But mostly because publishers don't know what to do with their data. Server-side junkware and Web site marketeers are invariably expert at telling a story about all the wonderful data that they can collect. Occasionally, they actually do collect and store these data. However, once data go into the big user tracking table, they seldom come back out.

Before considering smarter server-side approaches, let's ask ourselves if the server is the right place to be doing personalization.

Client-side personalization

Suppose that the U.S. government adopts my proposal to free themselves of the Microsoft Monopoly and run Linux (see *http://photo.net/philg/humor/bill-gates.html*). Then consider the case of Jane Civil Servant, who telecommutes from her home office and is currently taking a break to browse the Web from her desktop Linux

box. If publishers added semantic tags to their sites (see Chapter 5 on HTML), her Web browser could warn her that the software whose blurbs she was investigating weren't available for Linux. Her desktop machine knows not only which Web pages she has downloaded, but also how long she has spent viewing each one. It knows which Web pages she has deemed important enough to save to her local disk. Her desktop machine knows that she's sent a bunch of email today to friends asking for tips on places to visit in California. It can listen to her phone line and figure out that she has called 10 numbers in California today. You'd think that her desktop machine could put all of this together to say, "Jane, you should probably check out *http://photo.net/ca/*. I also note that you've been typing at the keyboard on this machine for an average of 11 hours every day for the last two weeks. You ought to relax tonight. I notice from your calendar program that you don't have any appointments. I notice from your Quicken database that you don't have any money, so you probably shouldn't be going to the theater. I notice that *Naked Gun* is on cable tonight. I don't see any payments in your Quicken database to a cable TV vendor, so I assume you aren't a Cable Achiever. I remember seeing some email from your friend David two months ago containing the words 'invite' and 'cable TV,' so I assume that David has cable.

I see from watching your phone line's incoming caller line ID that he has called you twice in the last week from his home phone, so I assume he is in town. Call him up and invite yourself over."

We trust our desktop computers with our email. We trust them with our credit card numbers. We trust them to monitor our phone calls. We trust our desktop computers with financial and tax data. We can program our desktop computers to release or withhold information without relying on publishers' privacy notices. If publishers would stop trying to be clever behind our backs, most of us would be happy to give them personal information of our choosing. Publishers could spend a few weeks sitting down to come up with a standard for the exchange of personalization information. Netscape would add a Profile Upload feature to Navigator 6.0. Then a magazine wouldn't have to go out and join an ad banner network to find out what we like; they could just provide a button on their site and we'd push it to upload our profiles. This would be useful for more mundane transactions, as well. For example, instead of each publisher spending $150,000 developing a shopping basket system and order form, publishers could just put an "upload purchase authorization and shipping address" button on their sites. We'd type our credit card numbers and mailing addresses just once into our browsers' Options menus, rather than 1,000 times into various publishers' forms.

The foregoing is not meant as an argument against mobile computing, by the way. Nor is it meant to vitiate the argument presented in Chapter 1 (suck.com) that progress in computing won't occur until we move away from desktop-centric applications. People who are heavily dependent on mobile computing can simply designate a single hardwired computer as their personalization proxy, more or less like the Internet Fish that Brian LaMacchia built back in 1995 (see *www.farcaster.com*). To quote the source, these are "semiautonomous, persistent information brokers; users deploy individual IFish to gather and refine information related to a particular topic. An IFish will initiate research, continue to discover new sources of information, and keep tabs on new developments in that topic. As part of the information-gathering process, the user interacts with his IFish to find out what it has learned, answer questions it has posed, and make suggestions for guidance." As far as a Web publisher is concerned, a proxy such as an Internet Fish looks exactly the same as a desktop client.

Publishers can help client-side systems by adding semantic tags to their content, as discussed in Chapter 5 (HTML), where it is also noted with dismay that publishers can't currently do the right thing. There is no agreed upon language for tagging the semantics of Web documents. Against the day that the XML folks make real progress, publishers can be ready by keeping content in a more structured, more semantically meaningful form than HTML, namely, *a database.*

Quiet server-side personalization

It is possible to do server-side personalization without harassing users. The crux of success in this area is a good data model. Most sites would probably want to start with the basic data model set forth in Chapter 3, Scalable Systems for Online Communities:

- Keep track of which users have looked at which pieces of content.

- Keep track of how users came into the site and which external links they are selecting (clickthroughs).

- Keep track of which advertisers' banner ads have been served to each user and whether or not they were clicked on.

- Keep track of whether particular users fall into sitewide classes.

- If the site has an ecommerce component, keep track of what purchases a user has made.

Amazon.com is a good example of quiet server-side personalization. They keep track of what you've bought. They keep track of what everyone else has bought. They compute "people who bought X also bought Y, so you might want it too."

What would *www.adobe.com* look like if we added quiet server-side personalization? As of August 1998, the home page offers a choice of paths into the content. A reader can choose by language, by product, or by verb (e.g., "download" or "discuss"). Consider the case of Yoshito Morita, who, from the same browser, does the following:

1. selects the Japanese version of the site

2. buys a copy of Photoshop 5.0 for the Macintosh

3. downloads a patch for Photoshop 5.0 for the Macintosh

4. downloads trial versions of PageMill and SiteMill for the Macintosh

At this point, without ever having asked Yoshito any explicit questions, Adobe's server-side software should be able to infer that Yoshito prefers Japanese to English, is a Macintosh user, and is a Web publisher. The next time Yoshito comes to the server from his cookied browser, www.adobe.com should adjust itself to serve pages in Japanese, suppress products that only run on Unix or Windows, and give greater prominence to tips on Web publishing. When a new release of Photoshop becomes available, the most prominent item on www.adobe.com should read, "Welcome back, Yoshito, did you know that you can upgrade to Photoshop 6.0?"

There should be two links following this question. The "I'd like to buy an upgrade now" link would take Yoshito to an order form. The "I already upgraded" link would take Yoshito to a form to register his new purchase (and do the market research of asking where he bought it).

SUMMARY

Here's what you should have learned from reading this chapter:

- You can collect a metric buttload of data about user activity on your site without too much effort.

- You have to think and work if you want to collect data that are truly more interesting than what a 10-year-old could get from his home Web server and a freeware stats package.

- You can use free software and services from *http://photo.net/wtr/* to do a lot of the fancy tricks that well-funded Web publishers use.

- A good data model will yield important dividends for personalization.

MORE

- If you want to sleep at night with a clear conscience, make sure that you visit *www.eff.org* before applying any of the user tracking techniques described above.

- If you want to sleep at night knowing that your database can handle the logging requirements imposed on it by your server, read *The Benchmark Handbook for Database and Transaction Processing Systems* (Jim Gray, second edition 1993; Morgan Kaufmann). Note that this book explains what is meant by the TPC-C figures that are often advertised by software and hardware vendors.

- We distribute some free open-source software for managing log analysis: ArsDigita Reporte (*http://www.arsdigita.com/free-tools/reporte.html*).

10

Sites that Are Really
Programs

The classic (circa 1993) Web site comprises static .html files in a Unix file system. This kind of site is effective for one-way noncollaborative publishing of material that seldom changes.

You needn't turn your Web site into a program just because the body of material that you are publishing is changing. Sites like *http://www.yahoo.com,* for example, are sets of static files that are periodically generated by programs grinding through a dynamic database. With this sort of arrangement, the site inevitably lags behind the database, but you can handle millions of hits a day without a major investment in computer hardware, custom software, or thought.

If you want to make a collaborative site, however, then at least some of your Web pages will have to be computer programs. Pages that process user submissions have to add user-supplied data to your Web server's disk. Pages that display user submissions have to look through a database on your server before delivering the relevant contributions.

Even if you want to publish completely static, noncollaborative material, at least one portion of your site will require server-side programming: the search engine. To provide a full-text search over your material, your server must be able to take a query string from the user, compare it to the files on the disk, and then return a page of links to relevant documents.

This chapter discusses the options available to Web publishers who need to write program-backed pages. Here are the steps:

1. Decide whether you're building a dynamic document or a program with a Web interface.

2. Choose a computer language.

3. Choose a program invocation mechanism.

4. Choose a Web server program to support the first three choices.

STEP 1: DOCUMENT OR PROGRAM?

A *document* is typically edited or updated over a period of days. Changes in one portion of a document don't have far-reaching implications for other portions. A *computer program* is typically versioned, debugged, and tested over a period of months.

Every interesting Web site has some characteristics of both a document and a computer program. There is thus no correct answer to the question, "Is your site a hypertext document with bits of computation or a computer program with bits of static text?" However, the tools that make it easy for a team of experts to develop a computer program will get in the way if your site is fundamentally a document. Conversely, the tools that make it convenient to edit a document can lead to sloppy and error-filled computer programs.

Server-side programming systems that take the document model to its logical extreme are AOLserver Dynamic Pages (ADP) and Microsoft Active Server Pages (ASP). A vanilla HTML file is a legal ADP or ASP document. If you want to add some computation, you weave in little computer language fragments, surrounded by <% ... %>. If you want to fix a typo or a programming bug, you edit the .adp or .asp file and hit reload in your Web browser to see the new version. Almost always, the connection is direct and immediate between the URL where the problem was observed and the file on the server that you must edit. You don't have to understand much of the document's structure to fix a bug.

At the other end of the document/program spectrum are various *application servers* that require you to program in C or Java. HTML text is inevitably buried inside these programs. Fixing a typo requires editing the program, compiling the program, and reloading the compiled code into the Web or application server. If there is a problem with a URL, fixing it might require reading and editing dozens of program files and understanding most of the program's overall structure.

With the right tools and programmer resources, you can build a jewel-like software system to sit behind a Web site. But ask yourself whether the entire service isn't likely to be redesigned after six months and if, realistically, your site isn't going to be thrown together hastily by overworked programmers. If so, perhaps it will be best to look for the tightest development cycle.

STEP 2: CHOOSE A COMPUTER LANGUAGE

People usually choose a computer language according to how well it supports management of complexity. Much of the complexity in a Web site, however, is in the number of URLs and how they interact—for example, how many form-variable arguments get passed from one page to another. So the system structure is very similar, regardless of the computer language employed.

Consider these aspects:

- support for complex data types
- safety
- development time
- library

You would think that picking a Web site development language would be trivial. Obviously, the best languages are safe and incorporate powerful object systems. So let's do everything in Common Lisp or Java. Common Lisp can run interpreted as well as compiled, which makes it a more efficient language for developers. So Common Lisp should be the obvious winner of the Web server language wars. Yet nobody uses Common Lisp for server-side scripting. Is that because Java-the-hype-king has crushed it? No. In fact, to a first approximation, nobody uses Java for server-side scripting. Almost everyone is using simple interpreted languages such as Perl, Tcl, or Visual Basic.

How could a lame scripting language like Tcl possibly compete with Lisp? At some level, the only data type available in Tcl is a string. Well, guess what? The only data type that you can write to a Netscape browser is a string. And all the information from the Oracle relational database management system on which you are relying comes back to you as strings. So maybe it doesn't matter whether your scripting language has an enfeebled type system.

Are these languages really the best? My computer science friends would shoot me for saying that Tcl is as good as Common Lisp and better than Java. But it turns out to be almost true. Tcl is better than Java because Tcl doesn't have to be compiled. Tcl can be better than Lisp because string manipulation is simpler. For example, in Tcl

```
"posted by $email on $posting_date."
```

will generate a string from the fragments of static ASCII above plus the contents of the variables $email and $posting_date. These were presumably recently pulled from a relational database. The result might look something like

```
"posted by philg@mit.edu on February 15, 1998."
```

In Common Lisp, you'd have

```
(concatenate 'string "posted by " email " on " posting-date ".")
```

which uses a fabulously general mechanism for concatenating sequences. concatenate can work on sequences of ASCII characters (strings) or sequences of TCP packets or sequences of three-dimensional arrays or sequences of double-precision complex numbers. Sequences can either be lists (fast to modify) or vectors (fast to retrieve).

This kind of flexibility, which Java apes, is wonderful, except that Web programmers are concatenating strings 99.99 percent of the time and Tcl's syntactic shortcuts make code easier to read and more reliable.

What's my prediction for the powerful language that will sit behind the Web sites of the future?

HTML.

HTML? But didn't we spend a whole chapter talking about how deficient it was even as a formatting language? How can HTML function as a server-side programming language?

Server-parsed HTML

In the beginning, there was server-parsed HTML. You added an HTML comment to a file, as, for example,

```
<!--#include FILE="/web/author-info.txt" -->
```

and then reloaded the file in a browser.

Nothing changed. Anything surrounded by "<!--" and "-->" is an HTML comment. The browser ignores it.

Your intent, though, was to have the Web server notice this command and replace the comment with the contents of the file /web/author-info.txt. To do that, you have to change the filename of this URL to have an .shtml extension. Now the server knows that you are actually programming in an extended version of HTML.

The AOLserver takes this one step further. To the list of standard SHTML commands, they've added the #nstcl command:

```
<!--#nstcl script=
  "ns_httpget "http://cirrus.sprl.umich.edu/wxnet/fcst/boston.txt" -->
```

which lets a basically static HTML page use the ns_httpget Tcl API function to go out on the Internet, from the server, and grab *http://cirrus.sprl.umich.edu /wxnet/fcst/boston.txt* before returning the page to the user. The contents of *http:// cirrus.sprl.umich.edu/wxnet/fcst/boston.txt* are included in place of the comment tag.

This is a great system because a big Web publisher can have its programmers develop a library of custom Tcl functions that its content authors simply call from server-parsed HTML files. That makes it easy to enforce style conventions company-wide. For example,

```
<!--#nstcl script="webco_captioned_photo samoyed.jpg
  {This is a Samoyed}" -->
```

might turn into

```
<h3>
<img src="samoyed.jpg"
     alt="This is a Samoyed">
This is a Samoyed
</h3>
```

until the day that the Webco art director decides that HTML tables would be a better way to present these images. So a programmer redefines the procedure webco_captioned_photo and the next time they are served, thousands of image references instead turn into

```
<table>
<tr>
  <td><img src="samoyed.jpg"
           alt="This is a Samoyed">
  <td>This is a Samoyed
</tr>
</table>
```

HTML as a programming language

As long as we're programming our server, why not define a new language, "Webco HTML?" Any file with a .whtml extension will be interpreted as a Webco HTML program, and the result, presumably standard HTML, will be served to the requesting users. Webco HTML has the same syntax as standard HTML, just more tags. Here's the captioned photo example:

```
<CAPTIONED-PHOTO "samoyed.jpg" "This is a Samoyed">
```

Just like the Tcl function, this Webco HTML function takes two arguments, an image file name and a caption string. And just like the Tcl function, it produces HTML tags that will be recognized by standard browsers. I think it is cleaner than the "include a Tcl function call" .shtml example, because the content producers don't have to switch back and forth between HTML syntax and Tcl syntax.

How far can we go with this? Pretty far. The best of the enriched HTMLs is Meta-HTML (*http://www.metahtml.com*). Meta-HTML is fundamentally a macro expansion language. We'd define our captioned-photo tag thusly:

```
<define-tag captioned-photo image-url text>
  <h3>
    <img src="<get-var image-url>" alt="<get-var text>"> <br>
    <get-var text>
  </h3>
</define-tag>
```

Now that we are using a real programming language, though, we'd probably not stop there. Suppose that Webco has decided that it wants to be on the leading edge as far as image format goes. So it publishes images in three formats: GIF, JPEG, and progressive JPEG. Webco is an old company, so every image is available as a GIF, but only some are available as JPEG and even fewer as progressive JPEG. Here's what we'd really like captioned photo to do:

1. Change the function to take just the filename as an argument, with no extension; for example, "foobar" instead of "foobar.jpg".

2. Look at the client's user-agent header.

3. If the user-agent is Mozilla 1, then look in the file system for foobar.jpg and reference it if it exists (otherwise reference foobar.gif).

4. If the user-agent is Mozilla 2, then look in the file system for foobar-prog.jpg (progressive JPEG) and reference it; otherwise look for foobar.jpg; otherwise reference foobar.gif.

This is straightforward in Meta-HTML:

```
<define-function captioned-photo stem caption>
  ;;; If the user-agent is Netscape, try using a JPEG format file
  <when <match <get-var env::http_user_agent> "Mozilla">>
    ;;; this is Netscape
    <when <match <get-var env::http_user_agent> "Mozilla/[2345]">>
      ;;; this is Netscape version 2, 3, 4, or 5(!)
      <if <get-file-properties
          <get-var mhtml::document-root>/<get-var stem>-prog.jpg>
        ;;; we found the progressive JPEG in the Unix file system
        <set-var file-to-reference = <get-var stem>-prog.jpg>>
    </when>
    ;;; If we haven't defined FILE-TO-REFERENCE yet,
    ;;; try the simpler JPEG format next.
    <when <not <get-var file-to-reference>>>
      <if <get-file-properties
          <get-var mhtml::document-root>/<get-var stem>.jpg>
        <set-var file-to-reference = <get-var stem>.jpg>>
    </when>
  </when>
  ;;; If FILE-TO-REFERENCE wasn't defined above, default to GIF file
  <when <not <get-var file-to-reference>>>
    <set-var file-to-reference <get-var stem>.gif>
  </when>
  ;;; here's the result of this function call, four lines of HTML
  <h3>
  <img src="<get-var file-to-reference>" alt="<get-var caption>">
  <br>
  <get-var caption>
  </h3>
</define-function>
```

This example only scratches the surface of Meta-HTML's capabilities. The language includes many of the powerful constructs such as session variables that you find in Netscape's LiveWire system. However, for my taste, Meta-HTML is much cleaner and better implemented than the LiveWire stuff. Universal Access offers a "pro" version of Meta-HTML, compiled with the OpenLink ODBC libraries, so that it can talk efficiently to any relational database (even from Linux!).

Is the whole world going to adopt this wonderful language? Meta-HTML does seem to have a lot going for it. The language and first implementation were developed by Brian Fox and Henry Minsky, two hard-core MIT computer science grads. Universal Access is giving away their source code (under a standard GNU-type license) for both a standalone Meta-HTML Web server and a CGI interpreter that

Note:
If you want to try out a brilliant Meta-HTML site, visit my friend Neil's postcard system at *http://www.yobaby.com/photo4u/*.

277

you can use with any Web server. They distribute precompiled binaries for popular computers. They offer support contracts for $500 a year. If you don't like Universal Access support, you can hire the C programmer of your choice to maintain and extend their software. Minsky and Fox have put the language into the public domain. If you don't like any of the Universal Access stuff, you can write your own interpreter for Meta-HTML, using their source code as a model.

Trouble in paradise

The biggest problem with extended HTML is that it is not HTML. The suite of tools that you're using to work with HTML may not work with whatever HTML extensions you've adopted. For example, suppose that you are using the `CAPTIONED-PHOTO` tag throughout your content. You hire a writer to update some of your pages. He downloads them in Netscape Navigator, at which time your server converts them into standard HTML `TABLE`, `TR`, and `TD` tags. He edits the document in Netscape Composer and uses HTTP PUT or FTP to place it back on the server. At this point, all the `CAPTIONED-PHOTO` tags have been lost and with them your insurance against changes in the HTML standard.

So if someone offers you even a minor variation on HTML, ask him what tools he's developed and how the new language will fit into all of your production processes.

Step 3: Choose a Program Invocation Mechanism

What happens after the user requests a dynamic page? How does the server know that a program needs to be called and what does it have to do to run that program?

The oldest and most common mechanism for program invocation via the Web is the common gateway interface (CGI). The CGI standard is an abstraction barrier that dictates what a program should expect from the Web server, for example, user form input, and how the program must return characters to the Web server program for them eventually to be written back to the Web user. If you write a program with the CGI standard in mind, it will work with any Web server program. You can move your site from NCSA HTTPD 1.3 to Netscape Communications 1.1 to AOLserver 2.1 and all of your CGI scripts will still work. You can give your programs away to other webmasters who aren't running the same server program. Of course, if you wrote your CGI program in C and compiled it for an HP Unix box, it isn't going to run so great on a Windows NT machine.

Oops.

We've just discovered why most CGI scripts are written in Perl, Tcl, or some other interpreted computer language. The systems administrator can install the Perl or Tcl interpreter once, and then Web site developers on that machine can easily run any script that they download from another site.

Fixing a bug in an interpreted CGI script is easy. A message shows up in the error log when a user accesses http://yourserver.nerdu.edu/bboard/subject-lines.pl. If your Web server document root is at /web (my personal favorite location), then you know to edit the file /web/bboard/subject-lines.pl. After you've found the bug and written the file back to the disk, the next time the page is accessed, the new version of the subject-lines Perl script will be interpreted.

For concreteness, let's summarize Unix CGI:

- The server stuffs a bunch of information into Unix "environment variables," the name of the host that made the request, for example.

- Form-variable values get to the script via an environment variable (if a GET) or via *standard-in* (if a POST).

- The server binds *standard-out* effectively to the client's screen, so that the CGI script thinks it is writing straight to the user.

- The first thing the CGI script must write is a *content-type* header that tells the client what sort of data to expect (HTML, plain text, a GIF, a JPEG, and so on).

Here's an example program:

```
#!/usr/contrib/bin/perl
# the first line in a Unix shell script says where to find the
# interpreter. If you don't know where perl lives on your system, type
# "which perl", "type perl", or "whereis perl" at any shell
# and put the result after the #!
print "Content-type: text/html\n\n";
# now we have printed a header (plus two newlines) indicating that the
# document will be HTML; whatever else we write to standard output will
# show up on the user's screen
print "<h3>Hello World</h3>";
```

Note:
This example program will print "Hello World" as a level-three headline. If you want to get more sophisticated, read some online tutorials, *The CGI/ Perl Cookbook* (Patchett and Wright, 1997; Wiley) or *CGI Programming on the World Wide Web* (Gundavaram, 1996; O'Reilly).

It is that easy to write Perl CGI scripts and get server independence, a tight software development cycle, and ease of distribution to other sites. With that in mind, you might ask how many of my thousands of dynamic Web pages use this program invocation mechanism. The answer? One. It was written by Architext and it looks up user query strings in the site's local full-text index. Why don't I have more?

Reason 1: My Unix box does not like to fork 500,000 times a day. Every time a CGI script is run, the Web server computer has to start a new process (fork). Think about how long it takes to start a program on a Macintosh or Windows NT machine. It is a thousand times faster to indent a paragraph in an already running word processor than it is to fire up that word processor to view even a one-paragraph document. I don't want my users to wait for this and I don't want to buy a 64-processor HP Unix X-class server.

Reason 2: My RDBMS does not like to be opened and closed 500,000 times a day. Anytime that I add collaboration to my site, user data are going into and out of a relational database management system (RDBMS). The RDBMS is implemented as a server that waits for requests for connections from client programs (see Chapter 13, Interfacing a Relational Database to the Web). IBM, Oracle, Sybase, and Informix have been working for two decades to make the RDBMS fast once a connection is established. Until the Web came along, however, nobody cared too much about how long it took to open a connection. With the Web came the CGI script, a program that runs for only a fraction of a second. In its brief life, it must establish a connection to the RDBMS, get the results of a query, and then close the connection. Users would get their data in about one-tenth the time if their requests could be handled by an already connected RDBMS client.

Enter the server application programming interface (API). As I discussed in Chapter 8, So You Want to Run Your Own Server, most Web server programs allow you to supplement their behavior with extra software that you write. This software will run inside the Web server's process, saving the overhead of forking CGI scripts. Because the Web server program generally will run for at least 24 hours, it becomes the natural candidate to be the RDBMS client.

All Web server APIs allow you to specify, "If the user makes a request for a URL that starts with /foo/bar/, then run Program X". The really good Web server APIs allow you to request program invocation before or after pages are delivered. For example, you ought to be able to say, "When the user makes a request for any HTML file, run Program Y first and don't serve the file if Program Y says it is unhappy". Or, "After the user has been served any file from the /car-reviews directory, run Program Z" (presumably Program Z performs some kind of logging).

Step 4: Choose a Web Server Program to Support the First Three Choices

Remember the steps:

1. Decide whether you're building a dynamic document or a program with a Web interface.

2. Choose a computer language.

3. Choose a program invocation mechanism.

4. Choose a Web server program to support the first three choices.

You've made the first three choices. Now you have to look around for Web server software that will support them. If you've settled on CGI as a program invocation mechanism, then it won't really matter which server you use (server independence being the main point of CGI, after all). If you want to use a server's API, then you need to find a server program that supports the language and development style that you've chosen in steps 1 and 2.

Example 1: Redirect

When my friend Brian and I were young and stupid, we installed the NCSA 1.3 Web server program on our research group's file server, martigny.ai.mit.edu. We didn't bother to make an alias for the machine like www.brian-and-philip.org, so the URLs we distributed looked like *http://martigny.ai.mit.edu/samantha/*.

Sometime in mid-1994 the researchers depending on Martigny, whose load average had soared from 0.2 to 3.5, decided that a 100,000-hit-per-day Web site was something that might very nicely be hosted elsewhere. It was easy enough to find a neglected HP Unix box, which we called swissnet.ai.mit.edu. And we sort of learned our lesson and did not distribute this new name in the URL, but rather aliases: www-swiss.ai.mit.edu for research publications of our group (known as "Switzerland" for obscure reasons); webtravel.org for my travel stuff; photo.net for my photo stuff; pgp.ai.mit.edu for Brian's public key server; samantha.rules-the.net for fun.

But what were we to do with all the hardwired links out there to martigny.ai.mit.edu? We left NCSA 1.3 loaded on Martigny but changed the configuration files, so that a request for "http://martigny.ai.mit.edu/foo/bar.html" would result in a 302 redirect being returned to the user's browser, so that it would instead fetch "http://www-swiss.ai.mit.edu/foo/bar.html".

Two years later, in August 1996, someone upgraded Martigny from HP-UX 9 to HP-UX 10. Nobody bothered to install a Web server on the machine. People began to tell me, "I searched for you on the Web but your server has been down since last Thursday." Eventually, I figured out that the search engines were still sending people to Martigny, a machine that was in no danger of ever responding to a Web request, since it no longer ran any program listening to port 80.

Rather than try to dig up a copy of NCSA 1.3, I decided it was time to get some experience with Apache, the world's most popular Web server. I couldn't get the 1.2 beta sources to compile. So I said, "This free software stuff is for the birds; I need the heavy-duty iron." I installed the 80-MB Netscape Enterprise Server and sat down with the frames- and JavaScript-heavy administration server. After 15 minutes, I'd configured the port 80 server to redirect. There was only one problem: It didn't work.

I spent a day going back and forth with Netscape tech support. "Yes, the Enterprise server definitely could do this. Probably it wasn't configured properly. Could you email us the obj.conf file? Hmmm . . . it appears that your obj.conf file is correctly specifying the redirect. There seems to be a bug in the server program. You can work around this by defining custom error message .html files with Refresh: tags so that users will get popped over to the new server if they are running a Netscape browser."

I pointed out that this would redirect everyone to the Swissnet server root, where-as I wanted /foo/bar.html on Martigny to redirect to /foo/bar.html on Swissnet.

"Oh."

They never got back to me.

I finally installed AOLserver, which doesn't have a neat redirect facility, but I figured that the Tcl API was flexible enough that I could make the server do what I wanted.

First, I had to tell AOLserver to feed all requests to my Tcl procedure, instead of looking around in the file system:

```
ns_register_proc GET / martigny_redirect
```

This is a Tcl function call. The function being called is named ns_register_proc. Any function that begins with ns_ is part of the NaviServer Tcl API (NaviServer was the name of the program before AOL bought NaviSoft in 1995). ns_register_proc takes three arguments: method, URL, and procname. In this case, I'm saying that HTTP GETs for the URL "/" (and below) are to be handled by the Tcl procedure martigny_redirect as follows:

```
proc martigny_redirect {} {
    append url_on_swissnet "http://www-swiss.ai.mit.edu" [ns_conn url]
    ns_returnredirect $url_on_swissnet
}
```

This is a Tcl procedure definition, which has the form "proc procedure-name arguments body". Since martigny_redirect takes no arguments, there is a "{ }" after the procedure name. When martigny_redirect is invoked, it first computes the full URL of the corresponding file on Swissnet. The meat of this computation is a call to the API procedure ns_conn asking for the URL that was part of the request line.

With the full URL computed, martigny_redirect's second body line calls the API procedure ns_returnredirect. This writes back to the connection a set of 302 redirect headers instructing the browser to rerequest the file, this time from *http://www-swiss.ai.mit.edu.*

Here's what I learned from this experience:

- Hugely hyped popular commercial software may not be able to perform even the simplest task.

- Commercial software support is of little value in the Web business.

- You want to have the source code, and you want to have a flexible, safe, easy-to-use API.

Example 2: Customizing access

Some friends of mine at MIT Press wanted to sell subscriptions to electronic journals, either to institutions or to individuals. They also wanted portions of the journals to be freely available. In the case of an institutional subscriber, the server needed to recognize that the client came from a range of authorized IP addresses; for example, any computer whose IP address starts with "36." is at Stanford, so if they've paid for a sitewide subscription, don't demand username or password from individuals. For individuals, they decided to start by simply distributing the same username/password pair to all the subscribers. All of the information about who was authorized had to come from their relational database. It turned out that this set of constraints was too complex for the standard permissions module that comes with AOLserver, if only because it uses its own little Unix-files–based database. Fortunately, the AOLserver API provides for program invocation prior to page service via a mechanism called *filters*. After 20 minutes we came up with the following program:

```
# tell AOLserver to watch for PDF file requests under the /ejournal
# directory if we don't add additional ns_register_filter commands,
# all the other files will be available to everyone
```

```
ns_register_filter preauth GET /ejournal/*.pdf ejournal_check_auth

proc ejournal_check_auth {args why} {
    # all the parameters we might want to change
    set user "open"
    set passwd "sesame"
    # on the real-life server, these are pulled from a relational database
    # but here for an example, let's just set it to MIT and Stanford
    set allowed_ip_ranges [list "18.*" "36.*"]

    foreach pattern $allowed_ip_ranges {
        if { [string match $pattern [ns_conn peeraddr> } {
            # a paying customer; the file will be sent
            return "filter_ok"
        }
    }

    # not coming from a special IP address, let's check the
    # username and password headers that came with the request
    if { [ns_conn authuser] == $user && [ns_conn authpassword] == $passwd
} {
        # they are an authorized user; the file will be sent
        return "filter_ok"
    }

    # not a good IP address, no headers, hammer them with a 401 demand
    ns_set put [ns_conn outputheaders] WWW-Authenticate "Basic realm=\"MIT
        Press:Restricted\""
    ns_returnfile 401 text/html
        "[ns_info pageroot]ejournal/please-subscribe.html"

    # stop AOLserver from handling the request by returning a special code
    return "filter_return"
}
```

Example 3: Aid to evaluating your accomplishments (randomizing a page)

For me grad school is fun, just like playing Tetris all night is fun. In the morning you realize that it was sort of enjoyable, but it didn't get you anywhere and it left you very, very tired.

—Michael Booth's comment on my Women in Computing page
(http://photo.net/philg/careers/acm-women-in-computing.html)

Computer science graduate students earn a monthly stipend that wouldn't hire a good Web/DB programmer for an afternoon. If you've been reading Albert Camus lately ("It is a kind of spiritual snobbery to think one can be happy without money"), then you'd expect this to lead to occasional depression. For these depressed souls, I published *Career Guide for Engineers and Scientists* (*http://photo.net /philg/careers.html*).

I thought that starving graduate students forgoing six years of income would be cheered to read the National Science Foundation report that "Median real earnings remained essentially flat for all major non-academic science and engineering occupations from 1979–1989. This trend was not mirrored among the overall work force where median income for all employed persons with a bachelor's degree or higher rose 27.5 percent from 1979–1989 (to a median salary of $28,000)."

I even did custom photography for the page (see Figure 10-1).

But I didn't think I'd really be able to get under the skin of America's best and brightest young computer scientists until Eve Andersson (the brilliant Caltech Pi Goddess) and I released *Aid to Evaluating Your Accomplishments* (see Figure 10-2).

Achievement Gallery

Portraits of people who are putting their advanced training to good use.

Aid to Evaluating Your Accomplishments

part of Career Guide for Engineers and Scientists

Compare yourself to these four ordinary people who were selected at random:

Judean Carpenter Jesus of Nazareth

Told young women he was God and they believed him.

(more)

Science Fiction Author L. Ron Hubbard

Created the religion of Scientology in 1950. 1998 membership: more than one million.

(more)

Encyclopedia Americana staff writer Norbert Wiener

Received Ph.D. from Harvard at age 18, subsequently founded field of communication science/cybernetics.

(more)

Polish Student Marya Sklodowska

Received Nobel Prize in Physics (1903) and in Chemistry (1911), under the name "Marie Curie". She was the first woman to win a Nobel prize.

(more)

Figure 10-1 (top): From *Career Guide for Engineers and Scientists* at *http:// photo.net/philg/careers.html.*

Figure 10-2 (bottom): Another feature of *Career Guide for Engineers and Scientists* at *http://photo.net/ philg/careers.html.*

Here's the source code:

```
# a helper procedure to pick N items randomly from a list
# note that it uses tail-recursion, importing a little bit
# of the clean Scheme philosophy into the ugly world of Tcl

proc choose_n_random {choices_list n_to_choose chosen_list} {
    if { $n_to_choose == 0 } {
        return $chosen_list
    } else {
        set chosen_index [randomRange [llength $choices_list>
        set new_chosen_list [lappend chosen_list
          [lindex $choices_list $chosen_index>
        set new_n_to_choose [expr $n_to_choose - 1]
        set new_choices_list
          [lreplace $choices_list $chosen_index $chosen_index]
        return [choose_n_random $new_choices_list
          $new_n_to_choose $new_chosen_list]
    }
}

# we encapsulate the printing of an individual person so that
# one day we can easily change the design of the page (we display
# four people at once and putting this in a procedure keeps us from
# having to edit the same code four times).

proc one_person {person} {
    set name [lindex $person 0]
    set title [lindex $person 1]
    set achievement [lindex $person 2]
    return "<h4>$title $name</h4>\n $achievement <br><br> <center>
        (<a href=\"http://altavista.digital.com/cgi-bin/
        query?pg=q&what=web&fmt=&q=[ns_urlencode $name]\">more</a>)
        </center>\n"
}

# we return HTTP headers to the client

ReturnHeaders

# we return as much of the page as we can before figuring out which four
# people we're going to display; this way if we were going to query a
# relational database (potentially taking 1/2 second), the user would
# have something on screen to read
```

```
ns_write "<html>
<head>
<title>Aid to Evaluating Your Accomplishments</title>
</head>

<body bgcolor=#ffffff text=#000000>
<h2>Aid to Evaluating Your Accomplishments</h2>

part of <a href=\"/philg/careers.html\">Career Guide for Engineers and
Scientists</a>

<hr>

Compare yourself to these four ordinary people who were selected at
random:

<br>
<br>
"

# each person is name, title, accomplishment(s)

set einstein [list "A. Einstein" "Patent Office Clerk" \
                "Formulated Theory of Relativity."]

set mill [list "John Stuart Mill" "English Youth" \
              "Was able to read Greek and Latin at age 3."]

set mozart [list "W. A. Mozart" "Viennese Pauper" \
              "Composed his first opera, <i>La finta
              semplice</i>, at the age of 12."]

set jesus [list "Jesus of Nazareth" "Judean Carpenter" \
              "Told young women he was God and they believed him."]

set stevens [list "Wallace Stevens" "Hartford Connecticut Insurance
  Executive"
                "Won Pulitzer Prize for Poetry in 1954; best known for
                \"Thirteen Ways of Looking at a Blackbird\"."]

# ... there are a bunch more in the real live script

set average_folks [list $einstein $mill $mozart $jesus]

# we call our choose_n_random procedure, note that we give it an empty
# list to kick off the tail-recursion

set four_average_folks [choose_n_random $average_folks 4 [list>
```

```
ns_write "<table cellpadding=20>
<tr>
<td valign=top>
[one_person [lindex $four_average_folks 0]]
</td>
<td valign=top>
[one_person [lindex $four_average_folks 1]]
</td>
</tr>
<tr>
<td valign=top>
[one_person [lindex $four_average_folks 2]]
</td>
<td valign=top>
[one_person [lindex $four_average_folks 3]]
</td>
</tr>
</table>
"

# note how in the big block of static HTML below, we're forced to
# put backslashes in front of the string quotes.  This is annoying
# and we wouldn't have to do it if we'd implemented this using
# AOLserver Dynamic Pages (where the text is HTML by default,
# Tcl code by exception).

ns_write "

<p>

Programmed by <a href=\"http://www.ugcs.caltech.edu/~eveander/\">Eve
Astrid Andersson</a> and <a href=\"/philg/\">Philip Greenspun</a> in
<a href=\"/wtr/servers.html#naviserver\">AOLserver Tcl</a>.  If you're
a nerd, you might find <a href=\"four-random-people.txt\">the source
code</a> useful.

<P>

Original Inspiration: <cite>How to Make Yourself Miserable</cite>, by
Dan Greenburg

<hr>
<a href=\"/philg/\"><address>philg@mit.edu</address></a>
</body>
</html>
"
```

Example 4:
Focal length calculator
(taking data from users)

Back in the 1960s, an IBM engineer had a good idea. Build a smart terminal that could download a form from a mainframe computer. The form would have reserved fields for display only, input fields where the user could type, and blinking fields. After the user had filled out all the input fields, the data would be submitted to the mainframe and acknowledged or rejected if there were any mistakes. This method of interaction was rather frustrating and disorienting for users, but made efficient use of the mainframe's precious CPU time. This was the "3270" terminal, and hundreds of thousands were sold 20 years ago, mostly to big insurance companies and the like.

The forms user interface model fell into the shade after 1984 when the Macintosh "user drives" pulldown menu system was introduced. However, HTML forms as classically conceived work exactly like the good old 3270. Here's an example that is firmly in the 3270 mold, taken from the lens chapter of my photography tutorial textbook (*http://photo.net/photo/tutorial/lens.html*). The basic idea is to help people figure out what size lens they will need to buy or rent in order to make a particular image. They fill in a form with distance to subject and the height of their subject (see Figure 10-3). The server then tells them what focal length lens they need for a 35-mm camera.

Exactly how long a lens do you need?

How far away is your subject? [   ] (in feet)

How high is the object you want to fill the frame? [   ] (in feet)

[Submit Query]

Figure 10-3: Exactly how long a lens do you need?

Here's the HTML source for the form:

```
<form method=post action=focal-length.tcl>
How far away is your subject?
<input type=text name=distance_in_feet size=7>  (in feet)
<p>
How high is the object you want to fill the frame?
<input type=text name=subject_size_in_feet size=7>  (in feet)
<p>

<input type=submit>
</form>
```

Here's the AOLserver Tcl program that processes the user input:

```
set_form_variables

# distance_in_feet, subject_size_in_feet are the args from the form
# they are now set in Tcl local variables thanks to the magic
# utility function call above
# let's do a little IBM mainframe-style error-checking here

if { ![info exists distance_in_feet] || [string compare $distance_in_feet\
        ""] == 0 } {
    ns_return 200 text/plain "Please fill in the \"distance to subject\"
        field"
    # stop the execution of this script
    return
}

if { ![info exists subject_size_in_feet] || [string compare\
        $subject_size_in_feet ""] == 0 } {
    ns_return 200 text/plain "Please fill in the \"subject size\" field"
    # stop the execution of this script
    return
}

# we presume that subject is to fill a 1.5 inch long-dimension of a
# 35mm negative

# ahhh... the joys of arithmetic in Tcl, a quality language so
# much cleaner than Lisp

set distance_in_inches [expr $distance_in_feet * 12]
set subject_size_in_inches [expr $subject_size_in_feet * 12]

set magnification [expr 1.5 / $subject_size_in_inches]
```

```
set lens_focal_length_inches [expr $distance_in_inches /
    ((1/$magnification) + 1)]

set lens_focal_length_mm [expr round($lens_focal_length_inches * 25.4)]

# now we return a page to the user, one big string into which we let Tcl
# interpolate some variable values

ns_return $conn 200 text/html "<html>
<head>
<title>You need $lens_focal_length_mm mm </title>
</head>

<body bgcolor=#ffffff text=#000000>
<table>
<tr>
<td>
<a href=\"/photo/pcd0952 /boston-marathon-46.tcl\"><img HEIGHT=198
WIDTH=132 src=\"/photo/pcd0952/boston-marathon-46.1.jpg\"
ALT=\"100th Anniversary Boston Marathon (1996).\"></a>
<td>

<h2>$lens_focal_length_mm millimeters</h2>

will do the job on a Nikon or Canon or similar 35mm camera

<P>

(according to the <a href=\"/photo/tutorial/lens.html\">photo.net lens
tutorial</a> calculator)

</tr>
</table>

<hr>

Here are the raw numbers:

<ul>
<li>distance to your subject:  $distance_in_feet feet ($distance_in_inches
    inches)
<li>long dimension of your subject:  $subject_size_in_feet feet
    ($subject_size_in_inches inches)
<li>magnification:  $magnification
<li>lens size required:  $lens_focal_length_inches inches
    ($lens_focal_length_mm mm)

</ul>
```

Assumptions: You are using a standard 35mm frame (24x36mm) whose long dimension is about 1.5 inches. You are holding the camera in portrait mode so that your subject is filling the long side of the frame. You are supposed to measure subject distance from the optical midpoint of the lens, which for a normal lens is roughly at the physical midpoint.

```
<P>

Source of formula:
<a href=\"/photo/dead-trees/professional-photoguide.html\">
Kodak Professional Photoguide</a>
<br>
Source of serverside programming knowledge:  Chapter 9 of
<a href=\"http://photo.net/wtr/dead-trees/\">How to be a Web Whore Just
Like Me</a>
<br>
Time required to write this program:  15 minutes.
<br>
Proof that philg is a nerd:  <a href=\"focal-length.txt\">view the source
code</a>
<br>

What this is not: a slow Java program that will crash everyone's browser
(except those behind corporate firewalls that block all Java applets)

<br>

Another thing this is not:  a CGI program that will make my poor old Unix
box fork

<br>

Yet another thing this is not: a JavaScript program that you'd think
would be the right thing, but then on the other hand it wouldn't work with
some browsers and the last thing that I need is email from confused users

<h3>Bored?  Try again</h3>

<form method=post action=focal-length.tcl>
How far away is your subject?
<input type=text name=distance_in_feet size=7 value=\"$distance_in_feet\">
(in feet)
<p>
How high is the object you want to fill the frame?
<input type=text name=subject_size_in_feet size=7
value=\"$subject_size_in_feet\">  (in feet)

<p>
```

```
<input type=submit>

</form>

<h3>European?  Macro-oriented?</h3>

<form method=post action=focal-length-mm.tcl>
How far away is your subject?
<input type=text name=distance_in_mm size=7>  (in millimeters)
<p>
How high is the object you want to fill the frame?
<input type=text name=subject_size_in_mm size=7>  (in millimeters)

<p>

<input type=submit>

</form>

<hr>
<a href=\"/philg/\"><address>philg@mit.edu</address></a>
</body>
</html>"
```

Example 5: Bill Gates' personal wealth clock (taking data from foreign servers)

Academic computer scientists are the smartest people in the world. There are an average of 800 applications for every job. And every one of those applicants has a Ph.D. Anyone who has triumphed over 799 Ph.D.s in a meritocratic selection process can be pretty sure that he or she is a genius. Publishing is the most important thing in academics. Distributing one's brilliant ideas to the adoring masses. The top computer science universities have all been connected by the Internet or ARPAnet since 1970. A researcher at MIT in 1975 could send a technical paper to all of his or her interested colleagues in a matter of minutes. With this kind of heritage, it is natural that the preferred publishing medium of 1990s computer science academics is . . . dead trees.

Yes, dead trees.

If you aren't in a refereed journal or conference, you aren't going to get tenure. You can't expect to achieve quality without peer review. And peer review isn't just a positive feedback mechanism to enshrine mediocrity. It keeps uninteresting papers from distracting serious thinkers at important conferences. For example, there was this guy in a physics lab in Switzerland, Tim Berners-Lee. And he wrote a paper about distributing hypertext documents over the Internet. Something he called

"the Web." Fortunately for the integrity of academia, this paper was rejected from conferences where people were discussing truly serious hypertext systems.

Anyway, with foresight like this, it is only natural that academics like to throw stones at successful unworthies in the commercial arena. IBM and its mainframe customers provided fat targets for many years. True, IBM research labs had made many fundamental advances in computer science, but it seemed to take at least 10 years for these advances to filter into products. What kinds of losers would sell and buy software technology that was a decade behind the state of the art?

Then Bill Gates came along with technology that was 30 years behind the state of the art. And even *more* people were buying it. IBM was a faceless impediment to progress, but Bill Gates gave bloated monopoly a name, a face, and a smell. And he didn't have a research lab cranking out innovations. And every nongeek friend who opened a newspaper would ask, "If you are such a computer genius, why aren't you rich like this Gates fellow?"

Naturally, I maintained a substantial "Why Bill Gates is Richer than You" section on my site, but it didn't come into its own until the day my friend Brian showed me that the U.S. Bureau of the Census had put up a real-time population clock at *http://www.census.gov/cgi-bin/popclock*. There had been stock quote servers on the Web almost since day one. How hard could it be to write a program that would reach out into the Web and grab the Microsoft stock price and the population, then do the math to come up with what you see at *http://www.webho.com/WealthClock* (see Figure 10-4).

This program was easy to write because the AOLserver Tcl API contains the ns_httpget procedure. Having my server grab a page from the Census Bureau is as easy as

```
ns_httpget "http://www.census.gov/cgi-bin/popclock"
```

Tcl the language made life easy because of its built-in regular expression matcher. The Census Bureau and the Security APL stock quote folks did not intend for their pages to be machine-parsable. Yet I don't need a long program to pull the numbers that I want out of a page designed for reading by humans.

Tcl the language made life hard because of its deficient arithmetic. Some computer languages (e.g., Pascal) are strongly typed. You have to decide when you write the program whether a variable will be a floating-point number, a complex number, or a string. Lisp is weakly typed. You can write a mathematical algorithm with hundreds of variables and never specify their types. If the input is a bunch of integers, the output will be integers and rational numbers (ratios of integers). If the input is a complex double-precision floating-point number, then the output will be complex double-precision. The type is determined at run-time. I like to call Tcl "whimsically" typed. The type of a variable is never really determined. It can be a number or a string. It depends on the context. If you are looking for a pattern, "29" is a string. If you are adding it to another number, "29" is a decimal number. But "029" is an octal number, so trying to add it to another number results in an error.

Anyway, here is the code. Look at the comments.

Figure 10-4: "Bill Gates is just smarter than everyone else," Mike Maples, an executive vice president of Microsoft, says. *The New Yorker*, January 10, 1994.

```
# this function turns "99 1/8" into "99.125"
proc wealth_RawQuoteToDecimal {raw_quote} {
    if { [regexp {(.*) (.*)} $raw_quote match whole fraction] } {
# there was a space
if { [regexp {(.*)/(.*)} $fraction match num denom] } {
    # there was a "/"
    set extra [expr double($num) / $denom]
    return [expr $whole + $extra]
}
# we couldn't parse the fraction
```

```
      return $whole
         } else {
     # we couldn't find a space, assume integer
     return $raw_quote
         }
 }
 ###
 #    done defining helpers, here's the meat of the page
 ###
 # grab the stock quote and stuff it into QUOTE_HTML
 set quote_html [ns_httpget "http://qs.secapl.com/cgi-bin/qs?ticks=MSFT"]

 # regexp into the returned page to get the raw_quote out
 regexp {Last Traded at</a></td><td align=right><strong>([^A-z]*)</strong>} \
        $quote_html match raw_quote

 # convert whole number + fraction, e.g., "99 1/8" into decimal,
 # e.g., "99.125"
 set msft_stock_price [wealth_RawQuoteToDecimal $raw_quote]
 set population_html [ns_httpget "http://www.census.gov/cgi-bin/popclock"]

 # we have to find the population in the HTML and then split it up
 # by taking out the commas
 regexp {<H1>[^0-9]*([0-9]+),([0-9]+),([0-9]+).*</H1>} \
        $population_html match millions thousands units

 # we have to trim the leading zeros because Tcl has such a
 # brain damaged model of numbers and thinks "039" is octal
 # this is when you kick yourself for not using Common Lisp
 set trimmed_millions [string trimleft $millions 0]
 set trimmed_thousands [string trimleft $thousands 0]
 set trimmed_units [string trimleft $units 0]

 # then we add them back together for computation
 set population [expr ($trimmed_millions * 1000000) + \
                      ($trimmed_thousands * 1000) + \
                      $trimmed_units]

 # and reassemble them in a string for display
 set pretty_population "$millions,$thousands,$units"

 # Tcl is NOT Lisp and therefore if the stock price and shares are
 # both integers, you get silent overflow (because the result is too
 # large to represent in a 32 bit integer) and Bill Gates comes out as a
 # pauper (< $1 billion). We hammer the problem by converting to double
 # precision floating point right here.
 #
 # (Were we using Common Lisp, the result of multiplying two big 32-bit
 # integers would be a "big num", an integer represented with multiple
```

```
# words of memory; Common Lisp programs perform arithmetic correctly.
# The time taken to compute a result may change when you move from a
# 32-bit to a 64-bit computer but the result itself won't change.)
set gates_shares_pre_split [expr double(141159990)]
set gates_shares [expr $gates_shares_pre_split * 2]
set gates_wealth [expr $gates_shares * $msft_stock_price]
set gates_wealth_billions \
    [string trim [format "%10.6f" [expr $gates_wealth / 1.0e9>]]
set personal_share [expr $gates_wealth / $population]
set pretty_date [exec /usr/local/bin/date]

# we're done figuring, now let's return a page to the user
ns_return 200 text/html "<html>
<head>
<title>Bill Gates Personal Wealth Clock</title>
</head>
<body text=#000000 bgcolor=#ffffff>
<h2>Bill Gates Personal Wealth Clock</h2>
just a small portion of
<a href=\"http://www-swiss.ai.mit.edu/philg/humor/bill-gates.html\">
Why Bill Gates is Richer than You</a>
by <a href=\"http://www-swiss.ai.mit.edu/philg/\">Philip Greenspun</a>
<hr>
<center>
<br>
<br>
<table>
<tr><th colspan=2 align=center>$pretty_date</th></tr>
<tr><td>Microsoft Stock Price:
    <td align=right> \$$msft_stock_price
<tr><td>Bill Gates's Wealth:
    <td align=right> \$$gates_wealth_billions billion
<tr><td>U.S. Population:
    <td align=right> $pretty_population
<tr><td><font size=+1><b>Your Personal Contribution:</b></font>
    <td align=right>  <font size=+1><b>\$$personal_share</font></b>
</table>
<p>
<blockquote>
"If you want to know what God thinks about money, just look at the
 people He gives it to.\" <br> -- Old Irish Saying
</blockquote>
</center>
<hr>
<a href=\"http://photo.net/philg/\"><address>philg@mit.edu</address>
</a>
</body>
</html>
"
```

So is this the real code that sits behind *http://www.webho.com/WealthClock?* Actually, no. You'll find the real source code linked from the above URL.

Why the differences? I was concerned that, if it became popular, the Wealth Clock might impose an unreasonable load on the subsidiary sites. It seemed like bad netiquette for me to write a program that would hammer the Census Bureau and Security APL several times a second for the same data. It also seemed to me that users shouldn't have to wait for the two subsidiary pages to be fetched if they didn't need up-to-the-minute data.

So I wrote a general-purpose caching facility that can cache the results of any Tcl function call as a Tcl global variable. This means that the result is stored in the AOLserver's virtual memory space and can be accessed much faster than even a static file. Users who want a real-time answer can demand one with an extra mouse click. The calculation performed for them then updates the cache for casual users.

Does this sound like overengineering? It didn't seem that way when Netscape put the Wealth Clock on their What's New page for two weeks (summer 1996). The URL was getting two hits per second. Per *second.* And all of those users got an instant response. The extra load on my Web server was not noticeable. Meanwhile, all the other sites on Netscape's list were unusably slow. Popularity had killed them.

Here are the lessons that I learned from this example:

- Powerful APIs lead to innovative Web sites; I probably never would have gotten around to writing the Wealth Clock if it hadn't been for the `ns_httpget` call.

- Hard-core performance engineering pays off; Web sites can catch on fast— you heard it here first.

- You want to get your site linked from one of the Netscape Navigator buttons.

Example 6: AOLserver Dynamic Pages

As long as we're on the subject of Bill Gates, it is worth demonstrating the syntax and style that his company inspired with its Active Server Pages. The folks at America Online fell in love with this idea, but not with the reliability of NT or IIS. Thus, they added a similar facility to AOLserver called AOLserver Dynamic Pages (ADP), which I used to build the WimpyPoint system, described in Chapter 1, Envisioning a Site that Won't Be Featured at suck.com.

See Figure 10-5 for the WimpyPoint page that offers public presentations to casual surfers. The idea is that someone will come to the site, look for the name of the author, then click down to find the presentation of interest.

Here's the ADP source code:

```
<% wimpy_header "Choose Author" %>

<h2>Choose an Author</h2>

in <a href="/"><%=[wimpy_system_name]%></a>

<hr>

Here's a list of users who have public presentations:

<ul>

<%

set db [ns_db gethandle]
set selection [ns_db select $db "select distinct u.user_id, u.last_name,
    u.first_names, u.email from wimpy_users u,
    wimpy_presentation_ownership wpo, wimpy_presentations wp
where u.user_id = wpo.user_id
and wpo.presentation_id = wp.presentation_id
and wp.public_p = 't'
order by upper(u.last_name), upper(u.first_names)"]

while { [ns_db getrow $db $selection] } {
    set_variables_after_query
    ns_puts "<li><a href=\"user-top.adp?user_id=$user_id\">$last_name,
        $first_names ($email)</a>\n"
}

%>

</ul>

Or you can do a full-text search through all the slides:

<form method=GET action="search.adp">
Query String:  <input type=text name=query_string size=50>
<input type=submit value="Submit">
</form>

<% wimpy_footer %>
```

Choose an Author

in WimpyPoint

You can do a full-text search through all the slides:

Query String: [   ] [Submit]

Or ask for a list of new presentations.

Or browse from this list of users who have created presentations (number of slides created shown in parantheses):

- Boyd, Daniel, boyd@way.com (15)
- Dolicki, Branimir, bdolicki@tel.hr (5)
- Greenspun, Philip, philg@mit.edu (149)
- Kraemer, Edwin, ekraemer@ics.uci.edu (6)
- Lehrer, Barney, lehrer@imex.com (7)
- Menon, Krish, krish@netrox.net (6)
- Parker, Lindon, Lindon@twomoon.com.au (8)
- Reed, Dale, dfreed@nwu.edu (5)
- spann, john, spann.john@hq.navy.mil (19)
- Trajano, Robert, robert_trajano@stratagene.com (6)
- Yen, Joseph, jyen@us.oracle.com (5)

Figure 10-5: Selecting presentations by author at WimpyPoint.

Note that I'm allowed to use arbitrary HTML, including string quotes, at the top level of the file. Note further that there are two escapes to the ADP evaluator. The basic escape is <%, which will execute a bunch of Tcl code for effect. If the Tcl code wants to write some bytes to the browser, it has to call ns_puts. The second escape sequence is <%=, which will execute a bunch of Tcl code and then write the result to the browser. Generally, I use the <%= style when I want to do something simple, such as including the system name that I grab from the Tcl procedure wimpy_system_name. I use the <% style when I want to execute a sequence of Tcl procedures to query the database.

Example 7: Active Server Pages

I haven't personally written any Microsoft Active Server Pages. Fortunately, Microsoft set up NT/IIS/ASP such that if you were curious to see the source code behind *http://foobar.com/yow.asp,* you had only to type "http://foobar.com/yow.asp." (note the trailing period) into your Netscape and the foreign server would deliver the source code right to your desktop. This was a great convenience for people trying to learn ASP; however, it presented something of a security problem for Web publishers, because they would often have their database or system administration passwords in the source code. It seems that Microsoft's intention was not to make public all of its customers' source code, and hence they eventually released a security patch to change this behavior. However, a few months later, people learned that requesting

302

"http://foobar.com/yow.asp::$DATA" (note the trailing ":$DATA") would also get them the source code.

Anyway, thanks to Microsoft's sloppiness, in just a couple of hours of surfing one night in July 1998, I managed to accumulate a nice collection of ASP examples at *http://photo.net/wtr/thebook/aspharvest/*. Note that I did my surfing some time after the bug had become common knowledge, yet companies such as Digital, Arthur Andersen, and banks had not patched their servers.

I find firewall.asp amusing because it is Digital's advertisement for their network security products. Similarly I like the fact that GAP Instrument Corp. took the trouble to warn users that

```
You have reached a computer system providing United States government
information. Unauthorized access is prohibited by Public Law 99-474,
(The Computer Fraud and Abuse Act of 1986) and can result in
administrative, disciplinary or criminal proceedings.
```

(the very first link from *http://net.gap.net* and all the other pages on their Web sites), yet had left their ASP pages wide open.

CompuServe gives us a nice simple example with Conf.asp. The goal of the script is first to figure out whether the person browsing is a CompuServe member or not, and then serve one of two entirely separate HTML pages. An if statement is thus opened inside one <% %> and closed in another:

```
<!--#INCLUDE VIRTUAL="/Forums/member.inc"-->
<% if member = 1 then %>
<HTML>
<HEAD>
<TITLE>TW Crime Forum</TITLE>
</HEAD>
<BODY BGCOLOR=#FFFFFF>

... ** a page for nonmembers *** ..

</BODY>
</HTML>

<BR><I>We Update the Forum Directory Weekly.  The directory was last
updated: Thursday, January 08, 1998</I>
...
</BODY>
</HTML>

<% else %>
```

```
<HTML>
<HEAD>
<TITLE>TW Crime Forum</TITLE>
</HEAD>
<BODY BGCOLOR=#FFFFFF>

... ** a page for nonmembers ***

</BODY>
</HTML>
<%End If%>
```

An interesting thing to note about this page is that CompuServe hasn't run their HTML through a syntax checker, which would no doubt have complained about the stuff after the `</HTML>` (I've highlighted the extraneous text in cyan, above).

Let's move on to some DB-backed pages.

The folks who built Fulton Bank's site (*www.fulton.com*) are very enthusiastic about Microsoft:

> *The hottest technology to hit the Internet which is actually useable now is Active Server Page scripting. This has given us a number of advantages over the ancient art of CGI. . . . Intranets and Extranets where the variety of user machine platforms, processors, etc. are an issue ASP can play in nicely.*
> — *http://coolnew.xspot.com/what_we_use.asp*

Let's see how ASP works for them in */aspharvest/process_product.asp*, a script that takes a query string and tries to find banking products that match this query string.

```
<% affcode = 1057 %>

<HTML>
<HEAD>
<TITLE>Fulton Bank</TITLE>
</HEAD>
<BODY BGCOLOR="#FFFFFF">

<BLOCKQUOTE>
<TABLE WIDTH=370 ALIGN="middle">
<TR>
<TD>
<BR>
<IMG SRC="images/header_products.gif"><BR>
<BR>
<BR>
```

304

```
<%
   Set Conn=Server.CreateObject("ADODB.Connection")
   Conn.Open "FultonAffiliates"

   SQL = "SELECT *
FROM products
WHERE productname
LIKE '%" & Request.Form("product") & "%'
AND affiliate = '" & affcode & "'"

   Set RS = Conn.Execute(SQL)
%>

<TABLE>

<% if RS.EOF then %>
<TR><TD>Sorry No Products Found</TD></TR>
<% end if %>

<% DO UNTIL RS.EOF %>
<TR>
<TD VALIGN="top"><IMG SRC="images/diamond3.gif"></TD>
<TD>
<A HREF="<% = RS("url") %>"><FONT COLOR="blue">
<% = RS("productname") %></FONT></A><BR>
<% = RS("shortdesc") %><BR>
<BR> <BR>
</TD>
</TR>
<% RS.MoveNext %>
<% LOOP %>
</TABLE></BLOCKQUOTE>
</TD>
</TR>
</TABLE>
<% rs.close
   conn.close
%>
<!--#include file="footer.asp"-->
</BODY>
</HTML>
```

This is some pretty clean code. The programmers have encapsulated the database password in their ODBC connection configuration. Also, rather than just bury the magic number "1057" in the code, they set affcode to it as the very first line of the program. Finally, they've parked the page footer in a centralized footer.asp file that gets included by all of their scripts.

What you should have learned from this section is that, if you're going to use Microsoft server tools, you shouldn't take any programming shortcuts, leave the database or Administrator password in the code, or put any naughty words into comments. When the next NT/IIS/ASP bug is discovered and your source code becomes public, you want people to admire your work!

Note: If you're thinking that ASP sounds like a better-than-average idea from Microsoft, you won't be surprised to learn that it wasn't their idea. They dipped into some of their desktop monopoly profits to acquire the small company that developed ASP. As I wrote this, I tried to surf over to *http://www.microsoft.com/iis/* to see if they credit the programmers who developed ASP, but the Microsoft server farm was taking 45 seconds to deliver each page, so I gave up.

SUMMARY

Server-side programming is straightforward and can be done in almost any computer language, including extended versions of HTML itself. However, making the wrong technology decisions can result in a site that requires ten times the computer hardware to support. Bad programming can also result in a site that becomes unusable as soon as you've gotten precious publicity. Finally, the most expensive asset you are developing on your Web server is content. It is worth thinking about whether your server-side programming language helps you get the most out of your investment in content.

MORE

- *Structure and Interpretation of Computer Programs* (Abelson and Sussman, 1996; MIT Press) is the book that we use at MIT to teach people how to program. Even if you're already an experienced programmer, the book can be inspiring and useful for the vocabulary it introduces.

- If you want to write some basic Web scripts that will work on most Web servers, you'll probably benefit from reading *The CGI/Perl Cookbook* (Patchett and Wright, 1997; Wiley).

- To get started with AOLserver and Tcl, the online documentation at *www.aolserver.com* is useful. My favorite Tcl book is *Practical Programming in Tcl and Tk* (Welch, 1997; Prentice Hall), though really you need to read only the first 80 pages (the rest covers user interface programming with Tk, an irrelevant consideration for server-side programming). An experienced programmer will need about two hours to learn Tcl.

- *Professional Active Server Pages* (Homer et al., 1997; Wrox Press) is the Microsoft book that everyone seems to like.

- For my thoughts on Java in general, grab *http://photo.net/wtr/dead-trees/53008.htm.*

- For my thoughts on Java as a server-side programming language, read *http://photo.net/wtr/application-servers.html.*

11

Sites that Are Really Databases

A rmed with knowledge from the last chapter, a publisher might be tempted to rush into writing a big pile of server-side programs. It is worth stepping back from the technology for one chapter, however. First, we want to think about how technology works to achieve a publishing objective. Second, we want to see to what extent a Web publishing problem can be thought of as a database problem. Why? If we can think of our Web application as a database application, we can attack it with the database management software that industry has carefully developed since 1960.

Web applications that replace desktop applications, such as the WimpyPoint system (*wimpy.arsdigita.com*), are natural candidates for database management software. What about public sites? Let's revisit the four categories presented in Chapter 2, The World's Grubbiest Club: Internet Entrepeneurs:

1. **Sites that provide traditional information.** This is the type of site that requires the least imagination but also the most capital investment. Find bodies of information that consumers in the 1980s bought offline and sell them online. This includes movies/videos/television, newspapers, magazines, weather reports, and stock market information. Revenue comes from advertising, links to sites that do retail transactions and give you a kickback, and occasionally subscriptions.

2. **Sites that provide collaboratively created information.** This is information that was virtually impossible to collect before the Internet. A dead-trees example would be the *Consumer Reports* annual survey of automobile reliability. They collect information from their readers via mail-in forms, collate the results, and publish them once a year. The Internet makes this kind of activity less costly for the provider and gives the user much more immediate and in-depth information. Revenue comes from the same sources as in Category 1, but production expenses are lower.

3. **Sites that provide a service via a server-side program.** An example of this would be providing a wedding planning program. The user tells you how much he or she wants to spend, when and where the wedding is, who is invited, and so on. Your program then figures a detailed budget, develops an invitation list, and maintains gift and thank-you lists. You are then in a position to sell an ad to the Four Seasons Hotel that will be delivered to couples getting married on June 25, who live less than 100 miles away, are inviting fewer than 80 guests, and have budgeted more than $17,000.

4. **Sites that define a standard enabling a consumer to seamlessly query multiple databases.** For example, car dealers have computers managing their inventory, but such data are imprisoned on the dealers' computers and are unavailable to consumers in a convenient manner. Suppose you define a standard that allows the inventory computers inside car dealerships to download their current selection of cars, colors, and prices. You get the car dealers to agree to provide their information to you. Then your site becomes a place where a consumer can say, "I want a new dark green Dodge Grand Caravan with air conditioning and antilock brakes that's for sale within 60 miles of zip code 02176." From your query to the dealers' multiple databases, your user can get a list of all the cars available that match the criteria, and can then jump right to the relevant dealer's Web site.

If you are trying to get rich and famous under category 1, providing traditional information on the Web, then your site doesn't really start out as a database except in a degenerate way. But if you implement all of the collaboration and personalization systems that most publishers eventually want, a growing percentage of your site will look like a database.

Categories 2 through 4 are really databases disguised as Web servers. Information is collected in small, structured chunks from a variety of simultaneous sources. It is distributed in response to queries that cannot be anticipated when the data are stored. You might not be an Oracle Achiever. You might not know how to spell "SQL." But if your site falls into categories 2 through 4 above, you are running a database.

As long as you are running a database, you might as well do it right. Building a database-backed Web site requires a hard part that is heavy on the thinking and an easy part that is heavy on the implementation. Before you start building, though, you need a publishing idea. Let's suppose that you want to build a mailing list system for your site. You want users to be able to add and remove themselves. You need their email addresses and you want their real names. You want to be the only one who can view the list and the only one who can send mail to the list.

THE HARD PART

We have to take our publishing idea (the mailing list) and apply three standard steps:

1. Develop a data model. What information are you going to store and how will you represent it?

2. Develop a collection of legal transactions on that model, e.g., inserts and updates.

3. Come up with a set of Web forms that let the user build up to one of those transactions.

Step 1: The data model

You've decided to store email addresses and real names. If you are a Defense-Department–funded artificial intelligence researcher, you might spend a few years studying this "knowledge representation" problem. Otherwise, you'd probably budget two variable-length ASCII strings, one for email address and one for name.

This is the step at which you decide whether or not you are going to allow two entries with the same email address, whether you're going to assign some kind of guaranteed unique key to each entry, and whether to also store the time and date of the entry. When I built a system like this for myself, I decided that there wasn't any point in having two entries with the same email address, so the email address could serve as the key. I also chose not to record the time and date of the entry.

Step 2: Legal transactions

Users have to be able to add themselves to the list, so one legal transaction is the insertion of a name/email pair into the database. Users should also be able to remove themselves. In the system I built, the email address is the database key, so the removal transaction is "delete the entry for joe@bigcompany.com". To simplify the user interface, I decided against having any update transactions. If a user changed his name or email address, he could just remove the old entry and make a new one.

Step 3: Mapping transactions onto Web forms

The only way that users can interact with your database is via the Web, so you have to come up with ways for them to formulate legal transactions using HTML forms. If the transaction is complicated and early choices change the possibilities for subsequent choices, you may need a series of forms. In the case of this mailing list system, you probably can get away with two forms. The entry form has email and name TEXT inputs. The removal form has only an email TEXT input.

That's it. You've done the hard part.

THE EASY PART

You have only one thing left to do: Write a couple of programs that parse the HTML forms and turn them into actual database transactions.

Note that it is only during the easy part that you have to think about the particular technologies you are using on your server. The user has no way of knowing whether you are running the latest release of Oracle or whether all the form submissions actually turn into email to someone who manually updates a regular file. The site will still work the same as far as the user is concerned.

In practice, you will probably be using some kind of relational database (see the next chapter on DBMSs). So your programs will be turning HTML form submissions into SQL and results from the database back into HTML. It is important to choose the best brand of database management system and the best Web connectivity tools for that system, but your site will not live or die by the choice. If you make the wrong choices, you will work harder at writing your programs and might have to buy a computer ten times larger than an efficiently constructed site would need. But whether a site is worth using or not depends mostly on the data model, transactions, and form design.

Prototyping the site, my theory

You're building a database. You're modeling data from the real world. You're going to have to write computer programs in a formal language. You have to design a user interface for that computer program. If you had an MBA then your natural first step would be . . . hire a graphic designer. After all, this computer stuff is confusing. Databases frighten you. What you really need is something that will look good at your next meeting. Graphic designers make pages that look good. You can always hire a programmer later to actually make the forms work.

The server logs of these MBAs would be a lot fatter if graphic design were the same thing as user interface design. You are building a program. The user interface happens to be Web pages. The links among the pages are part of the user interface. Whoever puts in those links has to understand whether the server can actually answer the query and, if so, how much crunching will be required.

Here's my theory on how to develop a database-backed Web site:

1. Publisher/editor decides what service he wants to offer, e.g., "automatic survey of camera reliability for readers of photo.net".

2. Programmer builds prototype with text-only user interface.

3. Publisher/editor critiques prototype.

4. Programmer refines user interface.

5. Graphic designer comes in to add graphics/layout, but without changing user interface.

Prototyping the site, the reality

I was asked to "make a classified ad system using a relational database that looks and works like this set of static HTML files we've put together." They had a category for each ad, but decided that it "looked cleaner" to make full-text search the only option on the cover page. I tried to explain about the decades of information retrieval literature that demonstrated just how bad users were at formulating full-text queries. Full-text search was mainly useful when you weren't able to categorize. Since we had a big list of categories, why not make those primary and offer the full-text search as an alternative?

"We like the look."

Then I explained that full text search was slow. The database could cough up all the ads in a category in about 1/20th of a second, but full-text search chewed up close to a full second of time on a $120,000 computer. And, by the way, we'd have to do the query twice. Once to fill the space between <NOFRAMES> tags for the Netscape 1.1 crowd. And then again for the subwindows for users with frames-capable browsers. The same expensive query, twice!

"We like frames."

DO I NEED A COLLEGE EDUCATION TO UNDERSTAND YOUR SYSTEM?

The next few chapters are going to get a little bit formal and technical. If you have been ingesting your daily quota of Web technology hype, then you know that anyone can build a dynamic site without ever having to learn a programming language. Just fill out some forms, make a few strokes with your mouse, and presto: DB-backed Web site. The $50,000 may seem steep, but not when you compare it to the cost of a computer science education at Stanford.

If you can buy a $500 or $5,000 or $50,000 product, why bang your head against the wall trying to get through the next two chapters? Because there is no magic bullet. All the glossy brochures and PR budgets in the world can't disguise the fact that nobody has solved the automatic programming problem. There is no program that can take an English description of what you want done and turn that into software.

The fact that technology doesn't work is no bar to success in the marketplace, though, and tools that purport to automate programming have been selling well for decades. The worst of these tools simply don't work. You'd have been better off using EDSAC machine code. (The Electronic Delay Storage Automatic Computer was a vacuum-tube machine built in 1949, the first computer in which the program instructions were stored in memory along with the data.) The best of these tools are sort of like Lotus 1-2-3.

If your problem is very simple, it is much easier to code it up in a spreadsheet than it is to write a program from scratch. The spreadsheet generates the user interface.

You just enter some rules for how cells relate to each other; the spreadsheet figures out in which order to perform the computations.

After a while, though, you become dissatisfied with your program. It looks and feels, well, like a spreadsheet. Rather than ask the user to just look at the row headings and type the data into the correct cells, you'd like a little series of interview dialog boxes. When the user gets through filling them all out, your little program will stuff the spreadsheet appropriately.

Only now do you find that the spreadsheet macro language will not let you do two or three of the things that you desperately need to do. Furthermore, documentation of what the language can and can't do is scant, so you spend days looking for clever ways to accomplish your objective. Finally, you give up and start from scratch with a standard programming language.

Why don't customers wise up?

After three decades of shelling out for magic programming bullets that fail, you'd think that corporate managers would wise up. Yet these products proliferate. Hope seems to spring eternal in the breasts of MBAs.

My personal theory requires a little bit of history. Grizzled old hackers tell of going into insurance companies in the 1960s. The typical computer cost at least $500,000 and held data of great value. When Cromwell & Jeeves Insurance needed custom software, they didn't say, "Maybe we can save a few centimes by hiring a team of guys in India." They hired the best programmers they could find from MIT and didn't balk at paying $10,000 for a week of hard work. Back in those days, $10,000 was enough to hire a manager for a whole year, a fact not lost on managers who found it increasingly irksome.

Managers control companies, and hence policies that irk managers tend to be curtailed. Nowadays, companies have large programming staffs earning, in real dollars, one-third of what good programmers earned in the 1960s. When even that seems excessive, work is contracted out to code factories in India. Balance has been restored. Managers are once again earning three to ten times what their technical staff earn. The only problem with this arrangement is that most of today's working programmers don't know how to program.

Companies turn over projects to their horde of cubicle-dwelling C-programming drones and then are surprised when, two years later, they find only a tangled useless mess of bugs and a bill for $3 million. This does not lead companies to reflect on the fact that all the smart people in their college class went to medical, law, or business school. Instead, they embark on a quest for tools that will make programming simpler. Consider the case of Judy CIO, who is flying off to meet with the executives at Junkware Systems. Judy will book her airplane ticket using a reliable reservation system programmed by highly paid wizards in the 1960s. There is no middleware in an airline reservation system. There is no Microsoft software. There is no code written by C drones. Just one big IBM mainframe.

Judy changes planes in the new Denver airport. She could reflect on the fact that the airport opened a couple of years late because the horde of C programmers couldn't make the computerized baggage handling system work (it was eventually scrapped). She could reflect on the fact that the air traffic controllers up in the tower are still using software from the 1960s because the FAA can't get their new pile of C code to work—billions of dollars, 15 years, and acres of cubicles stuffed with $50,000-per-year programmers wasn't good for much besides a lot of memory allocation bugs. She could compare the high programmer salaries of the past and their still-working software to the low programmer salaries of the present and their comprehensive collection of bloated, bug-ridden, ready-any-year-now systems. However, these kinds of reflections aren't very productive for a forward looking CIO, and Judy uses her time at the airport to catch up on what passes for literature among MBAs: *The Road Ahead* and *Dollar Signs: An Astrological Guide to Personal Finance*.

Note: I'm not making up that last title. Here's the synopsis from Amazon.com: "Financial astrology is used by many prominent investment houses to analyze and predict markets. Now, Yvonne Morabito, Penthouse's "Cosmic Cashflow" columnist and a guest correspondent on financial astrology on CNBC, shows how anyone can use financial astrology to achieve greater success with this quick-reference guide." I don't believe in astrology myself. However, I think that's because I'm a Libra and Libras are always skeptical.

Judy CIO rushes from her last flight segment into the Junkware Systems demo room, where their $100,000-per-year marketing staff will explain why the Junkware 2000 system, programmed by Junkware's cubicle drones, will enable her cubicle drones to write software ten times faster and more reliably. Judy rushes to take notes on this exciting product, but becomes flustered when Windows 95 on her laptop crashes. Not to worry, Judy, the Macintosh OS running the Junkware Systems LCD projector also crashed . . . .

Is there a better way?

There *is* a better way: Learn to program (or hire someone who already knows how). The Junkware 2000 systems of the world might save you a few keystrokes here and there, but they don't attack the fundamental difficulty of correctly executing the three hard steps of designing a DB-backed Web site. Here they are again:

1. Develop a data model. What information are you going to store and how will you represent it?

2. Develop a collection of legal transactions on that model, e.g., inserts and updates.

3. Come up with a set of Web forms that let the user build up to one of those transactions.

Throughout these steps, the difficulty is never the putatively arcane syntax of SQL or HTML, both of which can be learned in a few days. The difficulty is thinking sufficiently formally about all the system requirements that you can boil them down to table and column definitions. The difficulty is in understanding the implications of adding and removing information from tables. The difficulty is in coming up with a user interface sufficiently perspicuous that a busy and unmotivated user won't get stuck halfway through a transaction. If you are capable of that kind of formal thinking, you ought to be able to type

```
create table mailing_list (
        email           varchar(100),
        name            varchar(100)
);
```

If you despair of understanding the profound mysteries of the preceding SQL statement, Junkware 2000 is for you. Maybe the program will interview you and learn that you want a two-column table, the first column of which should be called "email" and store a string, the second of which should be called "name" and also store a string. Then Junkware 2000 will crank out the above SQL code.

Fantastic!

But Junkware 2000 can't know that your organization will need to produce a Web page from this table sorted by last name. That means that you really need to store first and last names in separate columns. Junkware 2000 can't know that your application programs will fail if there are two entries with the same email address. Somewhere during the data modeling process, you have to be thoughtful enough to tell SQL or Junkware 2000 to constrain the email column to be unique.

Just say no to middleware

As we enter the 21st century we find that rifle marksmanship has been largely lost in the military establishments of the world. The notion that technology can supplant incompetence is upon us in all sorts of endeavors, including that of shooting.
—Jeff Cooper in *The Art of the Rifle* (1997, Paladin Press)

Any interesting Web/RDBMS problem can be solved using just the standard software shipped with the RDBMS. If you can't solve it with those tools, you can't solve it with any tool, no matter how glitzy and turnkey. The critical element is not the tools, it is the programmer.

I wrote my first database-backed Web site in 1994 using Oraperl CGI scripts. Kevin Stock sat down for about two weeks and linked Perl 4 with the Oracle C libraries, adding about five new Perl functions in the process. He christened the new version "Oraperl" and distributed the source code for free.

In terms of maintainability, clarity of code, software development cycle, and overall Web server performance and reliability, Oraperl CGI scripts are better than any of the purpose-built Web/RDBMS tools that I have used, with the exception of AOLserver and Meta-HTML. Would I cry if I had to give up the brilliantly designed AOLserver and go back to Oraperl and NCSA HTTPD 1.3? Not really. Using AOLserver probably only cuts 10 percent of the development time out of a big DB-heavy project. It gives me about a tenfold improvement in server throughput over a CGI-based approach, but AOLserver can't think and write software for me.

Would I cry if I had to use the latest and greatest hyped tools? Absolutely. Oraperl, AOLserver, and Meta-HTML let me change a script in Emacs (standard Unix text editor) and the new version is immediately live on the Web. The total solution of Netscape LiveWire would force me to recompile my application to test any change, slowing my development effort. If I were to shell out $70,000 for the complete Informix Universal Server and Informix's award-winning Web Blade, I wouldn't be able to use Emacs anymore to write my code. I'd be using Netscape Navigator as a text editor for a programming language even more obscure and less powerful than Perl. My pages would deadlock each other. I'd be thrust into a hell of system administration trying to figure out what was wrong.

A substantial portion of your investment in Web site programming can be wasted if you choose a middleware approach. Depending on SQL, C, Java, Lisp, Perl, or Tcl isn't dangerous. These languages have been around for years and exist in free and commercial versions for a wide variety of computer systems. But if your Web site is programmed in a sui generis language—let's call it Middle Webbish—that can only be parsed by a commercial product that is only available for one kind of computer, you're in trouble. What if the company that sold you Middle Webbish is crushed by Microsoft? You don't have the source code for the Middle Webbish parser, so you can't even hire a programmer to maintain your Web site. What if Middle Webbish fails to catch on and you're the only customer left? Your vendor isn't going to invest much in extending and porting Middle Webbish. Again, since you don't have the source code for the parser, you can't hire a programmer to extend and port Middle Webbish yourself.

Occasionally a product is sufficiently good and sufficiently stable and sufficiently likely to last that it is worth the dependency risk. But don't take that risk simply because you are afraid to think and program. Afraid or not, you will eventually have to think and program.

SUMMARY

This chapter was intended to inspire you to read the next two. Should I have failed to inspire a contempt of lucre in Chapter 2, it is worth reiterating that the most profitable sites on the Web are really databases. Furthermore, even if your own site loses money, once you've absorbed the lessons of the next two chapters, you can pull in $1,250 per day as a Web/RDBMS programmer.

I hope that you'll steel yourself against the marketing assaults of junkware/middleware vendors by remembering that all the hard stuff is independent of specific technology and product choices. The next three chapters aren't all that technical. If you read them carefully, you won't turn into one of those people who are afraid to program and therefore go running into the arms of junkware peddlers.

If you already have an MBA and despair of learning how to do anything productive, then at least I hope that you've learned from this chapter that you should work with the programmer and user interface designer to build the site that fits your publishing model before bringing in a graphic designer to make it pretty. I hope I've also reminded you that we don't need the FBI to figure out why most modern software doesn't work.

If none of the above seems inspiring, I'll close with a quote from *The Magic Mountain*, possibly the most boring book ever written (writing a high-quality computer book like this naturally gives me license to criticize winners of the Nobel Prize for Literature). Thomas Mann clearly knew just how dull these 700 pages would seem to an audience spoiled by the twentieth century because he wrote in the foreword:

> *We shall tell it at length, thoroughly, in detail—for when did a narrative seem too long or too short by reason of the actual time or space it took up? We do not fear being called meticulous, inclining as we do to the view that only the exhaustive can be truly interesting.*

MORE

- *The Mythical Man-Month* (Brooks, 1995; Addison-Wesley) is the all time classic work on software engineering and why it is so expensive and prone to delays. Brooks's primary mine of information is the System 360 project at IBM in the 1960s, which gave us the modern mainframe.

- *Code Complete* (McConnell, 1993; Microsoft Press) and *Rapid Development: Taming Wild Software Schedules* (McConnell, 1996; Microsoft Press) document the 1990s equivalents to the IBM 360 project.

12

Database Management Systems

W hen you build an information system, of which a Web site is one example, you have to decide how much responsibility for data management your new custom software will take and how much you leave to packaged software and the operating system. This chapter explains what kind of packaged data management software is available, covering files, flat-file database management systems, relational database management systems (RDBMSs), object-relational database management systems, and object databases. Because RDBMS is the most popular technology, I cover it in the most depth and include a brief tutorial on SQL.

WHAT'S WRONG WITH A FILE SYSTEM (AND ALSO WHAT'S RIGHT)

The file system that comes with your computer is a very primitive kind of database management system. Whether your computer came with the Unix file system, NTFS, or the Macintosh file system, the basic idea is the same. Data are kept in big unstructured, named clumps called *files*. The great thing about the file system is its invisibility. You probably didn't purchase it separately, you might not be aware of its existence, you won't have to run an ad in the newspaper for a file system administrator with five-plus years of experience, and it will pretty much work as advertised. All you need to do with a file system is back it up to tape every day or two.

Despite its unobtrusiveness, the file system on a Macintosh, Unix, or Windows machine is capable of storing any data that may be represented in digital form. For example, suppose that you are storing a mailing list in a file system file. If you accept the limitation that no email address or person's name can contain a newline character, you can store one entry per line. Then you could decide that no email address or name may contain a vertical bar. That lets you separate email address and name fields with the vertical bar character.

So far, everything is great. As long as you are careful never to try storing a newline or vertical bar, you can keep your data in this "flat file." Searching can be slow and expensive, though. What if you want to see if philg@mit.edu is on the mailing list? Your computer must read through the entire file to check.

Let's say that you write a program to process "insert new person" requests. It works by appending a line to the flat file with the new information. Suppose, however, that several users are simultaneously using your Web site. Two of them ask to be added to the mailing list at exactly the same time. Depending on how you wrote your program, the particular kind of file system that you have, and luck, you could get any of the following behaviors:

- Both inserts succeed.

- One of the inserts is lost.

- Information from the two inserts is mixed together so that both are corrupted.

In the last case, the programs you've written to use the data in the flat file may no longer work.

So what? Emacs may be ancient but it is still the best text editor in the world. You love using it, so you might as well spend your weekends and evenings manually fixing up your flat file databases with Emacs. Who needs concurrency control?

It all depends on what kind of stove you have.

Yes, that's right, your stove. Suppose that you buy a $268,500 condo in Harvard Square. You think to yourself, "Now my friends will really be impressed with me" and invite them over for brunch. Not because you like them but just to make them envious of your large lifestyle. Imagine your horror when all they can say is "What's this old range doing here? Don't you have a Viking stove?"

A *Viking stove*?!? They cost $5,000. The only way you are going to come up with this kind of cash is to join the growing ranks of online entrepreneurs. So you open an Internet bank. An experienced Perl script/flat file wizard by now, you confidently build a system in which all the checking account balances are stored in one file, `checking.text`, and all the savings balances are stored in another file, `savings.text`.

A few days later, an unlucky combination of events occurs. Joe User is transferring $10,000 from his savings to his checking account. Judy User is simultaneously depositing $5 into her savings account. One of your Perl scripts successfully writes the checking account flat file with Joe's new, $10,000 higher balance. It also writes the savings account file with Joe's new, $10,000 lower savings balance. However, the script that is processing Judy's deposit started at about the same time and began with the version of the savings file that had Joe's original balance. It eventually finishes and writes Judy's $5 higher balance, but also overwrites Joe's new lower balance with the old high balance. Where does that leave you? Ten thousand dollars poorer, cooking on an old GE range, and wishing you had concurrency control.

After a few months of programming and reading operating systems theory books from the 1960s that deal with mutual exclusion, you've solved your concurrency problems. Congratulations. However, like any good Internet entrepreneur, you're running this business out of your house and you're getting a little sleepy. So you heat up some coffee in the microwave and simultaneously toast a bagel in the toaster oven. The circuit breaker trips. This is the time when you are going to regret having bought that set of Calphalon pots to go with your Viking stove, rather than investing in an uninterruptible power supply for your server. You hear the sickening sound of disks spinning down. You scramble to get your server back up and don't really have time to look at the logs and notice that Joe User was back transferring $25,000 from savings to checking. What happened to Joe's transaction?

The good news for Joe is that your Perl script had just finished crediting his checking account with $25,000. The bad news for you is that it hadn't really gotten started on debiting his savings account. You're so busy preparing the public offering for your online business that you fail to notice the loss. But your underwriters eventually do and your plans to sell the bank to the public go down the toilet.

Where does that leave you? Cooking on an old GE range and wishing you'd left the implementation of transactions to professionals.

What do you need for transaction processing?

Data processing folks like to talk about the "ACID test" when deciding whether or not a database management system is adequate for handling transactions. An adequate system has the following properties:

Atomicity. Results of a transaction's execution are either all committed or all rolled back. All changes take effect or none do. For Joe User's money transfer, that means both his savings and checking balances are adjusted or neither are.

Consistency. The database is transformed from one valid state to another valid state. This defines a transaction as legal only if it obeys user-defined integrity constraints. Illegal transactions aren't allowed and, if an integrity constraint can't be satisfied, then the transaction is rolled back. For example, suppose that you define a rule that, after a transfer of more than $10,000 out of the country, a row is added to an audit table so that you can prepare a legally required report for the IRS. Perhaps for performance reasons that audit table is stored on a separate disk from the rest of the database. If the audit table's disk is offline and can't be written, the transaction is aborted.

Isolation. The results of a transaction are invisible to other transactions until the transaction is complete. For example, if you are running an accounting report at the same time that Joe is transferring money, the accounting report program will either see the balances before Joe transferred the money or after, but never the intermediate state where checking has been credited but savings not yet debited.

Durability. Once committed (completed), the results of a transaction are permanent and survive future system and media failures. If the airline reservation system computer gives you seat 22A and crashes a millisecond later, it won't have forgotten that you are sitting in 22A and also give it to someone else. Furthermore, if a programmer spills coffee into a disk drive, it will be possible to install a new disk and recover the transactions up to the coffee spill, showing that you had seat 22A.

That doesn't sound too tough to implement, does it? And, after all, one of the most refreshing things about the Web is how it encourages people without formal computer science backgrounds to program. So why not build your Internet bank on a transaction system implemented by an English major who has just discovered Perl?

Because you still need indexing.

Finding your data (and fast)

One facet of a database management system is processing inserts, updates, and deletes. This all has to do with putting information into the database. Sometimes it is also nice, though, to be able to get data out. And with popular sites getting 20 hits per second, it pays to be conscious of speed.

Flat files work okay if they are very small. A Perl script can read the whole file into memory in a split second and then look through it to pull out the information requested. But suppose that your online bank grows to have 250,000 accounts. A user types his account number into a Web page and asks for his most recent deposits. You've got a chronological financial transactions file with 25 million entries. Crunch,

crunch, crunch. Your server laboriously works through all 25 million to find the ones with an account number that matches the user's. While it is crunching, 25 other users come to the Web site and ask for the same information about their accounts.

You have two choices: Buy a 64-processor HP X-class server with 64 GB of RAM or build an index file. If you build an index file that maps account numbers to sequential transaction numbers, then your server won't have to search all 25 million records anymore. However, you have to modify all of your programs that insert, update, or delete from the database to also keep the index current.

This works great until two years later when a brand new MBA arrives from Harvard. She asks your English major cum Perl hacker for "a report of all customers who have more than $5,000 in checking or live in Oklahoma and have withdrawn more than $100 from savings in the last 17 days." It turns out that you didn't anticipate this query, so your indexing scheme doesn't speed things up. Your server has to grind through all the data over and over again.

ENTER THE RELATIONAL DATABASE

You are a Web publisher. On the cutting edge. You need the latest and greatest in computer technology. That's why you use, uh, Unix. Yeah. Anyway, even if your operating system harks back to the 1960s, you definitely can't live without the most modern database management system available. Maybe this guy E. F. Codd can help:

> *Future users of large data banks must be protected from having to know how the data is organized in the machine (the internal representation). . . . Activities of users at terminals and most application programs should remain unaffected when the internal representation of data is changed and even when some aspects of the external representation are changed. Changes in data representation will often be needed as a result of changes in query, update, and report traffic and natural growth in the types of stored information.*
>
> *Existing noninferential, formatted data systems provide users with tree-structured files or slightly more general network models of the data. In Section 1, inadequacies of these models are discussed. A model based on n-ary relations, a normal form for data base relations, and the concept of a universal data sublanguage are introduced. In Section 2, certain operations on relations (other than logical inference) are discussed and applied to the problems of redundancy and consistency in the user's model.*

Sounds pretty spiffy, doesn't it? Just like what you need. That's the abstract to "A Relational Model of Data for Large Shared Data Banks," a paper Codd wrote while working at IBM's San Jose research lab. It was published in the *Communications of the ACM* in June 1970.

Note:
Codd's paper is reprinted in *Readings in Database Systems* (Stonebraker and Hellerstein, 1998; Morgan Kaufmann).

Yes, that's right, 1970. What you need to do is move your Web site into the 70s with one of these newfangled relational database management systems (RDBMS). Actually, as Codd notes in his paper, most of the problems we've encountered so far in this chapter were solved in the 1960s by off-the-shelf mainframe software sold by IBM and the "seven dwarves" (as IBM's competitors were known). By the early 1960s, businesses had gotten tired of losing important transactions and manually uncorrupting databases. They began to think that their applications programmers shouldn't be implementing transactions and indexing on an ad hoc basis for each new project. Companies began to buy database management software from computer vendors like IBM. These products worked fairly well but resulted in brittle data models. If you got your data representation correct the first time and your business needs never changed, then a 1967-style hierarchical database was great. Unfortunately, if you put a system in place and subsequently needed new indices or a new data format, then you might have to rewrite all of your application programs.

From an application programmer's point of view, the biggest innovation in the relational database is that one uses a *declarative* query language, SQL (an acronym for Structured Query Language and pronounced "ess-cue-el" or "sequel"). Most computer languages are *procedural*. The programmer tells the computer what to do, step by step, specifying a procedure. In SQL, the programmer says, "I want data that meet the following criteria" and the RDBMS query planner figures out how to get it. There are two advantages to using a declarative language. The first is that the queries no longer depend on the data representation. The RDBMS is free to store data however it wants to. The second is increased software reliability. It is much harder to have "a little bug" in an SQL query than in a procedural program. Generally, it either describes the data that you want and works all the time or it completely fails in an obvious way.

Another benefit of declarative languages is that less sophisticated users are able to write useful programs. For example, many computing tasks that required professional programmers in the 1960s can be accomplished by nontechnical people with spreadsheets. In a spreadsheet, you don't tell the computer how to work out the numbers or in what sequence. You just *declare,* "This cell will be 1.5 times the value of that other cell over there."

RDBMSs can run very, very slowly. Depending on whether you are selling or buying computers, this may upset or delight you. Suppose that the system takes 30 seconds to return the data you asked for in your query. Does that mean you have a lot of data? That you need to add some indices? That the RDBMS query planner made some bad choices and needs some hints? Who knows? The RDBMS is an enormously complicated program that you didn't write and for which you don't have the source code. Each vendor has tracing and debugging tools that purport to help you, but the process is not simple. Good luck figuring out a different SQL incantation that will return the same set of data in less time. If you can't, call 1-800-USESUNX and ask them to send you a 16-processor Sun Enterprise 10000 with 32 GB of RAM. Alternatively, you can keep running the nonrelational software you used in the 1960s, which is what the airlines do for their reservations systems.

HOW DOES THIS RDBMS THING WORK?

Database researchers love to talk about relational algebra, n-tuples, normal form, and natural composition, while throwing around mathematical symbols. This patina of mathematical obscurity tends to distract your attention from their bad suits and boring personalities but is of no value if you just want to use a relational database management system.

In fact, this is all you need to know to be a Caveman Database Programmer: A relational database is a big spreadsheet that several people can update simultaneously.

Each *table* in the database is one spreadsheet. You tell the RDBMS how many columns each row has. For example, in our mailing list database, the table has two columns: name and email. Each entry in the database consists of one row in this table. An RDBMS is more restrictive than a spreadsheet in that all the data in one column must be of the same type, for example, integer, decimal, character string, or date. Another difference between a spreadsheet and an RDBMS is that the rows in

an RDBMS are not ordered. You can have a column named row_number and ask the RDBMS to return the rows ordered according to the data in this column, but the row numbering is not implicit, as it would be with Visicalc or its derivatives, such as Lotus 1-2-3 and Excel. If you do define a row_number column or some other unique identifier for rows in a table, it becomes possible for a row in another table to refer to that row by including the value of the unique ID.

Here's what some SQL looks like for the mailing list application:

```
create table mailing_list (
        email           varchar(100) not null primary key,
        name            varchar(100)
);
```

The table will be called mailing_list and will have two columns, both variable-length character strings. We've added a couple of integrity constraints on the email column. The not null will prevent any program from inserting a row where name is specified but email is not. After all, the whole point of the system is to send people email, so there isn't much value in having a name with no email address. The primary key tells the database that this column's value can be used to uniquely identify a row. That means that the system will reject an attempt to insert a row with the same email address as an existing row. This sounds like a nice feature, but it can have some unexpected performance implications. For example, every time anyone tries to insert a row into this table, the RDBMS will have to look at all the other rows in the table to make sure that there isn't already one with the same email address. For a really huge table, that could take minutes, but if you had also asked the RDBMS to create an index for mailing_list on email, then the check becomes almost instantaneous. However, the integrity constraint still slows you down because every update to the mailing_list table will also require an update to the index and therefore you'll be doing twice as many writes to the hard disk.

That is the joy and the agony of SQL. Inserting two innocuous-looking words can cost you a factor of 1,000 in performance. Then inserting a sentence (to create the index) can bring you back so that it is only a factor of two or three. (Note that many RDBMS implementations, including Oracle, automatically define an index on a column that is constrained to be unique.)

Anyway, now that we've executed the Data Definition Language "create table" statement, we can move on to *Data Manipulation Language:* an INSERT.

```
insert into mailing_list (name, email)
values ('Philip Greenspun','philg@mit.edu');
```

Note that we specify into which columns we are inserting. That way, if someone comes along later and does

```
alter table mailing_list add (phone_number varchar(20));
```

(the Oracle syntax for adding a column), our INSERT will still work. Note also that the string-quoting character in SQL is a single quote. Hey, it was the 70s. If you visit the newsgroup comp.databases right now, I'll bet that you can find someone asking, "How do I insert a string containing a single quote into an RDBMS?" Here's one I harvested from AltaVista just a few minutes ago:

```
demaagd@cs.hope.edu (David DeMaagd) wrote:

>hwo can I get around the fact that the ' is a reserved character in
>SQL Syntax?  I need to be able to select/insert fields that have
>apostrophes in them.  Can anyone help?

You can use two apostrophes '' and SQL will treat it as one.


=================================================================
Pete Nelson        | Programmers are almost as good at reading
weasel@ecis.com    | documentation as they are at writing it.
=================================================================
```

We'll take Pete Nelson's advice and double the single quote in "O'Grady":

```
insert into mailing_list (name, email)
values ('Michael O''Grady','ogrady@fastbuck.com');
```

Having created a table and inserted some data, at last we are ready to experience the awesome power of the SQL SELECT. Want your data back?

```
select * from mailing_list;
```

If you typed this query into a standard shellstyle RDBMS client program, for example Oracle's SQL*PLUS, you'd get... a horrible mess. That's because you told Oracle that the columns could be as wide as 100 characters (`varchar(100)`). Very seldomly will you need to store email addresses or names that are anywhere near as long as 100 characters. However, the solution to the "ugly report" problem is not to cut down on the maximum allowed length in the database. You don't want your system failing for people who happen to have exceptionally long names or email addresses. The solution is either to use a more intelligent tool for querying your database, such as AOLserver's ad hoc query forms or many Mac and PC DB client apps, or to give SQL*Plus some hints for preparing a report:

```
SQL column email format a25
SQL column name  format a25
SQL column phone_number format a12
SQL set feedback on
SQL select * from mailing_list;
```

EMAIL	NAME	PHONE_NUMBER
philg@mit.edu	Philip Greenspun	
ogrady@fastbuck.com	Michael O'Grady	

```
2 rows selected.
```

Note that there are no values in the `phone_number` column because we haven't set any. As soon as we do start to add phone numbers, we realize that our data model is inadequate. This is the Internet and Joe Typical User will have his pants hanging around his knees under the weight of a cell phone, beeper, and other personal communication accessories. One phone number column is clearly inadequate, and even `work_phone` and `home_phone` columns won't accommodate the wealth of information users might want to give us. The clean database-y way to do this is to remove our `phone_number` column from the `mailing_list` table and define a helper table just for the phone numbers. Removing or renaming a column turns out to be impossible in Oracle 8, so we

```
drop table mailing_list;
```

```
create table mailing_list (
        email           varchar(100) not null primary key,
        name            varchar(100)
);

create table phone_numbers (
        email           varchar(100) not null references mailing_list,
        number_type     varchar(15) check (number_type in
                            ('work','home','cell','beeper')),
        phone_number    varchar(20)
);
```

Note that in this table the email column is *not* a primary key. That's because we want to allow multiple rows with the same email address. If you are hanging around with a database nerd friend, you can say that there is a *relationship* between the rows in the phone_numbers table and the mailing_list table. In fact, you can say that it is a *many-to-one relation* because many rows in the phone_numbers table may correspond to only one row in the mailing_list table. If you spend enough time thinking about and talking about your database in these terms, two things will happen:

1. You'll get an A in an RDBMS course at a mediocre state university.

2. You'll pick up readers of *Psychology Today* who think you are sensitive and caring because you are always talking about relationships (see "Using the Internet to Pick up Babes and/or Hunks" at *http://photo.net/wtr/getting-dates.html* before following any of my dating advice).

Another item worth noting about our two-table data model is that we do not store the user's name in the phone_numbers table. That would be redundant with the mailing_list table and potentially self-redundant as well, if, for example, "robert.loser@fastbuck.com" says he is "Robert Loser" when he types in his work phone and then "Rob Loser" when he puts in his beeper number, and "Bob Lsr" when he puts in his cell phone number while typing on his laptop's cramped keyboard. A database nerd would say that this data model is consequently in "Third Normal Form." Everything in each row in each table depends only on the primary key and nothing is dependent on only part of the key. The primary key for the phone_numbers table is the combination of email and number_type. If you had the user's name in this table, it would depend on only the email portion of the key.

Anyway, enough database nerdism. Let's populate the phone_numbers table:

```
SQL insert into phone_numbers values
    ('ogrady@fastbuck.com','work','(800) 555-1212');

ORA-02291: integrity constraint (SCOTT.SYS_C001080) violated -
    parent key not found
```

Oops! When we dropped the `mailing_list` table, we lost all the rows. The `phone _numbers` table has a referential integrity constraint (`references mailing_list`) to make sure that we don't record email addresses for people whose names we don't know. We have to first insert the two users into `mailing_list`:

```
insert into mailing_list (name, email)
values ('Philip Greenspun','philg@mit.edu');
insert into mailing_list (name, email)
values ('Michael O''Grady','ogrady@fastbuck.com');

insert into phone_numbers values
     ('ogrady@fastbuck.com','work','(800) 555-1212');
insert into phone_numbers values
     ('ogrady@fastbuck.com','home','(617) 495-6000');
insert into phone_numbers values
     ('philg@mit.edu','work','(617) 253-8574');
insert into phone_numbers values
     ('ogrady@fastbuck.com','beper','(617) 222-3456');
```

Note that the last four INSERTs use an evil SQL shortcut and don't specify the columns into which we are inserting data. The system defaults to using all the columns in the order that they were defined. Except for prototyping and playing around, I don't recommend ever using this shortcut.

The first three INSERTs work fine, but what about the last one, where Mr. O'Grady misspelled "beeper"?

```
ORA-02290: check constraint (SCOTT.SYS_C001079) violated
```

We asked Oracle at table definition time to check (number_type in ('work', 'home', 'cell', 'beeper')) and it did. The database cannot be left in an inconsistent state.

Let's say we want all of our data out. Email, full name, phone numbers. The most obvious query to try is a JOIN.

```
SQL select * from mailing_list, phone_numbers;
```

EMAIL	NAME	EMAIL	TYPE	NUMBER
philg@mit.edu	Philip Greenspun	ogrady@fastbuck.	work	(800) 555-1212
ogrady@fastbuck.	Michael O'Grady	ogrady@fastbuck.	work	(800) 555-1212
philg@mit.edu	Philip Greenspun	ogrady@fastbuck.	home	(617) 495-6000
ogrady@fastbuck.	Michael O'Grady	ogrady@fastbuck.	home	(617) 495-6000
philg@mit.edu	Philip Greenspun	philg@mit.edu	work	(617) 253-8574
ogrady@fastbuck.	Michael O'Grady	philg@mit.edu	work	(617) 253-8574

```
6 rows selected.
```

Yow! What happened? There are only two rows in the `mailing_list` table and three in the `phone_numbers` table. Yet here we have six rows back. This is how joins work. They give you the *Cartesian product* of the two tables. Each row of one table is paired with all the rows of the other table, in turn. So if you join an N-row table with an M-row table, you get back a result with N*M rows. In real databases, N and M can be up in the millions, so it is worth being a little more specific as to which rows you want:

```
select *
from mailing_list, phone_numbers
where mailing_list.email = phone_numbers.email;
```

EMAIL	NAME	EMAIL	TYPE	NUMBER
ogrady@fastbuck.	Michael O'Grady	ogrady@fastbuck.	work	(800) 555-1212
ogrady@fastbuck.	Michael O'Grady	ogrady@fastbuck.	home	(617) 495-6000
philg@mit.edu	Philip Greenspun	philg@mit.edu	work	(617) 253-8574

```
3 rows selected.
```

Probably more like what you had in mind. Refining your SQL statements in this manner can sometimes be more exciting. For example, let's say that you want to get rid of Philip Greenspun's phone numbers, but aren't sure of the exact syntax.

```
SQL delete from phone_numbers;
```

```
3 rows deleted.
```

Oops. Yes, this does actually delete *all* the rows in the table. You probably wish you'd typed

```
delete from phone_numbers where email = 'philg@mit.edu';
```

but it is too late now. I guess there is one more SQL statement that is worth learning. Suppose that I move to Hollywood to realize my long-standing dream of becoming a major motion picture producer. Clearly a change of name is in order, though I'd be reluctant to give up the email address I've had since 1976. Here's the SQL:

```
SQL> update mailing_list set name = 'Phil-baby Greenspun'
where email = 'philg@mit.edu';
```

```
1 row updated.
```

```
SQL> select * from mailing_list;
```

EMAIL	NAME
philg@mit.edu	Phil-baby Greenspun
ogrady@fastbuck.com	Michael O'Grady

```
2 rows selected.
```

As with DELETE, I don't recommend playing around with UPDATE statements unless you have a WHERE clause at the end.

SQL THE HARD WAY

So you've gotten your pathetic Web site up and running and are proud of yourself for your wimpy little SELECTs. You had planned to live on the advertising revenue from your site, but find that $1.37 a month doesn't go very far in Manhattan. So you say, "At least I've become a database wizard; I can work in the financial industry." The next day, you're interviewing for that $200,000-a-year database hacking job at CitiCorp. Everything is going smoothly until they ask you how you'd investigate a performance problem with a "self-join with subquery." Self-join? Subquery? Maybe you have a little more to learn about RDBMS. Here's an example drawn from my real-life suffering.

My site would hand out a unique session key to every new user who arrived at the site. Since the keys were an ascending sequence of integers, I realized that I could keep track of how many users came to the site by simply inserting an audit row every day showing the value of the session key generator. Here's the history table I created:

```
create table history (
        sample_time     date,       -- when did the cookie have the value
        sample_value    integer
);
```

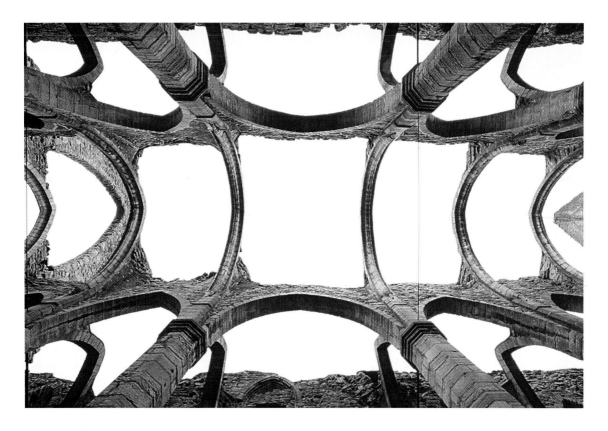

```
insert into history values
        (to_date('1998-03-01 23:59:00','YYYY-MM-DD HH24:MI:SS'),75000);
insert into history values
        (to_date('1998-03-02 23:59:00','YYYY-MM-DD HH24:MI:SS'),76000);
insert into history values
        (to_date('1998-03-03 23:59:00','YYYY-MM-DD HH24:MI:SS'),77000);
insert into history values
        (to_date('1998-03-04 23:59:00','YYYY-MM-DD HH24:MI:SS'),78000);

select * from history order by sample_time;

SAMPLE_TIM  SAMPLE_VALUE
----------  ------------
1998-03-01  75000
1998-03-02  76000
1998-03-03  77000
1998-03-04  78000
```

Note:
Oracle does not
implement ANSI SQL
date-time data types;
the DATE data type
is able to represent
time down to one-
second precision,
sort of like an ANSI
TIMESTAMP(0).

I knew that I had the information I needed and waited a few days to write the trivial AOLserver Tcl script to prepare a report page. It turns out to be easy to extract the rows of a table in order, as in the last SELECT above. However, it is impossible for a row to refer to "the last row in this SELECT". I could have written a Tcl procedure to walk through the rows in order, just setting things up on the first pass through the loop and then doing the appropriate subtraction for subsequent rows. However, Tcl doesn't have primitives for doing arithmetic on SQL date-time data types. If I'd been using Oracle, I could have written this in PL/SQL, a language with all the procedural expressiveness of Tcl, plus all the datatypes and functions of SQL. But I was using Illustra, so I had to resort to classical SQL techniques.

If the history table had N rows, I needed an interval table with N-1 rows. Each row would have the start time, end time, time interval, and cookie interval. Since I needed information from two different rows in the database, the most basic way to get it was with a JOIN. Since there was only one table, though, this would have to be a self-JOIN.

```
SQL select h1.sample_time, h2.sample_time
from history h1, history h2;

SAMPLE_TIM  SAMPLE_TIM
----------  ----------
1998-03-04  1998-03-04
1998-03-01  1998-03-04
1998-03-02  1998-03-04
1998-03-03  1998-03-04
1998-03-04  1998-03-01
1998-03-01  1998-03-01
1998-03-02  1998-03-01
1998-03-03  1998-03-01
1998-03-04  1998-03-02
1998-03-01  1998-03-02
1998-03-02  1998-03-02
1998-03-03  1998-03-02
1998-03-04  1998-03-03
1998-03-01  1998-03-03
1998-03-02  1998-03-03
1998-03-03  1998-03-03

16 rows selected.
```

A note about syntax is in order here. In an SQL FROM list, one can assign a correlation name to a table. In this case, I assign h1 and h2 to the two copies of history from which I am selecting. Then I can refer to h1.sample_time and get "the sample_time column from the first copy of the history table".

The main problem with this query, though, has nothing to do with syntax. It is the fact that I have 13 rows too many. Instead of N-1 rows, I specified the Cartesian product and got N × N rows. I've successfully done a self-join and gotten all the pairings I need, but now I must specify which pairings are legal.

```
select h1.sample_time as s1,
       h2.sample_time as s2
from history h1, history h2
where h2.sample_time > h1.sample_time;

S1          S2
----------  -----------
1998-03-01  1998-03-04
1998-03-02  1998-03-04
1998-03-03  1998-03-04
1998-03-01  1998-03-02
1998-03-01  1998-03-03
1998-03-02  1998-03-03

6 rows selected.
```

Note first that I've given correlation names to the columns as well, resulting in my report being labeled with s1 and s2 (in a database with a smarter SQL parser than Oracle's, we could also use these as shorthand in the WHERE clause). The critical change here is the WHERE clause, which states that we want only intervals where s2 is later than s1. That kills off 10 of the rows from the Cartesian product, but there are still three unwanted rows, the pairing of 1998-03-01 and 1998-03-04 being one of them. I only want the pairing of 1998-03-01 and 1998-03-02. I can specify that with a different WHERE clause:

```
select h1.sample_time as s1,
       h2.sample_time as s2
from history h1, history h2
where h2.sample_time = (select min(h3.sample_time)
                        from history h3
                        where h3.sample_time > h1.sample_time)
order by h1.sample_time;

S1         S2
---------  -----------
1998-03-01  1998-03-02
1998-03-02  1998-03-03
1998-03-03  1998-03-04

3 rows selected.
```

Note that I am now asking the database, for each of the six rows, to do a subquery:

```
select min(h3.sample_time)
from history h3
where h3.sample_time > h1.sample_time
```

This will scan the history table yet again to find the oldest sample that is still newer than s1. In the case of an unindexed history table, this query should probably take an amount of time proportional to the number of rows in the table cubed (N^3). If we'd done this procedurally, it would have taken time proportional to N*log(N) (the limiting factor being the sort for the ORDER BY clause). There are a couple of lessons to be learned here: (1) Sometimes declarative languages can be difficult to use and vastly less efficient than procedural languages and (2) It is good to have a fast database server.

When I knew I had the rows that I wanted, I added the trivial syntax to the SELECT list to subtract the times and cookie values:

```
select h1.sample_time as s1,
       h2.sample_time as s2,
       h2.sample_time - h1.sample_time as gap_time,
       h2.sample_value - h1.sample_value as gap_cookie
from history h1, history h2
where h2.sample_time = (select min(h3.sample_time)
                        from history h3
                        where h3.sample_time > h1.sample_time)
order by h1.sample_time;
```

S1	S2	GAP_TIME	GAP_COOKIE
1998-03-01	1998-03-02	1	1000
1998-03-02	1998-03-03	1	1000
1998-03-03	1998-03-04	1	1000

```
3 rows selected.
```

So before you apply for that $200,000-a-year database job, remember that formulating SQL queries can be an art and you'll need time and experience to get good at thinking declaratively.

BRAVE NEW WORLD

Training an African Grey parrot to function as an information systems manager can be very rewarding. The key sentence is "We're proactively leveraging our object-oriented client/server database to target customer service during reengineering." In the 1980s DB world, the applicable portion of this sentence was "client/server" (see the next chapter, Interfacing a Relational Database to the Web). In the Brave New World of database management systems, the key phrase is "object-oriented."

Object systems contribute to software reliability and compactness by allowing programmers to factor their code into chunks that are used as widely as possible. For

example, suppose that you are building a catalog Web site to sell magazines, videos, books, and CDs. It might be worth thinking about the data and functions that are common to all of these and encapsulating them in a product class. At the product level, you'd define characteristics such as `product_id`, `short_name`, and `description`. Then you'd define a magazine subclass that inherited all the behavior of product and added things like `issues_per_year`.

Programmers using modern computer languages like Smalltalk and Lisp have been doing this since the mid-1970s, but the idea has only recently caught on in the RDBMS world. Here are some table definitions for the Illustra system (these would also work with the Informix Universal Server):

```
create table products of new type product_t
(
        product_id              integer not null primary key,
        short_name              text not null,
        description             text
);
```

Then we define new types and tables that inherit from products:

```
create table magazines of new type magazine_t (
        issues                  integer not null,
        foreign_postage         decimal(7,2),
        canadian_postage        decimal(7,2)
)
under products;
create table videos of new type video_t (
        length_in_minutes       integer
)
under products;
```

Having defined our data model, we can load some data:

```
* insert into magazines (product_id,short_name,description,issues)
values (0,'Dissentary','The result of merging Dissent and Commentary',12);
* insert into videos (product_id,short_name,description,length_in_minutes)
values (1,'Sense and Sensibility','Chicks dig it',110);
* select * from products;
-------------------------------------------------
|product_id    |short_name           |description    |
-------------------------------------------------
|1             |Sense and Sensibility|Chicks dig it|
|0             |Dissentary           |The result o*|
-------------------------------------------------
```

Suppose that our pricing model is that magazines cost $1.50 an issue and videos cost 25 cents a minute. We want to hide these decisions from programs using the data:

```
create function find_price(product_t) returns numeric with (late)
as
return 5.50;
```

So a generic product will cost $5.50.

```
create function find_price(magazine_t) returns numeric
as
return $1.issues * 1.50;
create function find_price(video_t) returns numeric
as
return  $1.length_in_minutes * 0.25;
```

The appropriate version of the function find_price will be invoked, depending on the type of the row.

```
* select short_name, find_price(products) from products;
- - - - - - - - - - - - - - - - - - - - - - - - - - - - - - - - -
|short_name            |find_price      |
- - - - - - - - - - - - - - - - - - - - - - - - - - - - - - - - -
|Sense and Sensibility|           27.50|
|Dissentary           |           18.00|
- - - - - - - - - - - - - - - - - - - - - - - - - - - - - - - - -
```

This doesn't sound so impressive, but suppose you also wanted a function to prepare a special order code by concatenating product_id, price, and the first five characters of the title.

```
create function order_code(product_t) returns text
as
return $1.product_id::text ||
       '--' ||
       trim(leading from find_price($1)::text) ||
       '--' ||
       substring($1.short_name from 1 for 5);
* select order_code(products) from products;
- - - - - - - - - - - - - - - -
|order_code      |
- - - - - - - - - - - - - - - -
|1--27.50--Sense|
|0--18.00--Disse|
- - - - - - - - - - - - - - - -
```

This function, though trivial, is already plenty ugly. The fact that the find_price function dispatches according to the type of its argument allows a single order_code to be used for all products.

This Brave New World sounds great in DBMS vendor brochures, but the database folks have only recently gotten the object-oriented religion and they never met Dave Moon. Who is Dave Moon? One of the world's best programmers, a pioneer in modern object systems but, alas, not a patient man in his youth.

Moon was one of the chief architects of the MIT Lisp Machine, the world's easiest to program computer. It did things in 1978 that, if we are lucky, will be announced as innovations by Microsoft in the year 2005. A tiny company called Symbolics was spun out of MIT to commercialize the Lisp Machine and Moon was one of the founders. I was working there in 1984 when the company moved into a new building next to MIT. The facilities manager sent around some email telling people not to tape posters to their office walls because we'd be moving to bigger

quarters in a few years and didn't want the landlord to charge us for excessive wear. That night, the Foonly crashed. A Foonly was a clone of the PDP-10, a mainframe computer designed by Digital in the 1960s. MIT and Stanford people loved the PDP-10 but couldn't afford DEC's million dollar price tags. So there were these guys in a basement in California smoking dope and wirewrapping clones that were one-third the speed and one-twentieth the cost. Nobody ever figured out why they called the machines Foonlies.

Moon was a superb hardware engineer and nobody doubted that he would get the Foonly up and running. Still, people were a bit surprised when a huge steel cylinder came crashing through the machine room wall. The cause of the crash had been one of those washing machine–sized Control Data T-300 disk packs. The cylindrical missile had been the spindle holding together the bad 12-inch platters. Moon had hurled it through the wall after determining its guilt in the crime of the Foonly crash. I went back to my office and taped up a poster.

This story illustrates that great programmers are not necessarily patient. One of the things that drove them crazy about the object systems of the 1970s (Smalltalk, Lisp Machine Flavors) was that if you changed a class definition, the existing instances of that class did not get modified. You'd have to restart your program, maybe even reboot your computer if you changed your mind about how to represent something. You could lose 20 minutes or even more.

Thus, the object systems of the 1980s, Common Lisp Object System for example, were designed to touch up running instances of classes if the class definition changed.

Back in 1995, I was using Illustra and built myself a beautiful table hierarchy more or less like what I've described above. Six months later I needed to add a column to the products table. E. F. Codd understood back in 1970 that data models have to grow as business needs change. But the Illustra folks were so excited by their object extensions that they forgot. The system couldn't add a column to a table with dependent subclasses. "What should I do," I asked the support folks? "Dump the data out of all of your tables, drop all of them, rebuild them with the added column, then load all of your data back into your tables."

Uh, thanks...

I had high hopes for the merged Informix/Illustra system. A couple of years had passed since I'd pointed out that table inheritance was useless because of the brittleness of the resulting data models. So I figured surely they would have plugged this hole in the feature set. But it turned out that the new "solution to all of your problems" Informix Universal Server has the same limitation. I guess in the end, it is much easier to hype twenty-first century features than to actually sit down and implement features from two decades ago.

Note:
Oracle Release 8 is supposed to eventually have some of the object extensions pioneered by Illustra/Informix, but 8.0.x, which I've been using since September 1997, only allows you to define some simple compound data types and collections.

BRAVER NEW WORLD

If you really want to be on the cutting edge, you can use a bona fide object database, like Object Design's ObjectStore (*http://www.odi.com*). These persistently store the sorts of object and pointer structures that you create in a Smalltalk, Common Lisp, C++, or Java program. Chasing pointers and certain kinds of transactions can be 10 to 100 times faster than in a relational database. If you believed everything in the object database vendors' literature, then you'd be surprised that Larry Ellison still has $100 bills to fling to peasants as he roars past in his Acura NSX. The relational database management system should have been crushed long ago under the weight of this superior technology, introduced with tremendous hype in the mid-1980s.

After 10 years, the market for object database management systems is about $100 million a year, perhaps 1 percent the size of the relational database market. Why the fizzle? Object databases bring back some of the bad features of 1960s pre–relational database management systems. The programmer has to know a lot about the details of data storage. If you know the identities of the objects you're interested in, then the query is fast and simple. But it turns out that most database users don't care about object *identities;* they care about object *attributes*. Relational databases tend to be

faster and better at coughing up aggregations based on attributes. That said, I'm surprised that object databases aren't more popular. My personal theory is that the ascendance of C++ is responsible for the foundering of object databases. Anyone intelligent can quickly write a highly reliable program in Smalltalk or Common Lisp. But the world embraced C++, a language in which almost nobody has ever managed to write a reliable program. Corporations tend to be conservative about databases, among their most valuable assets. They never developed enough trustworthy C++ applications to make an object database worth buying, and hence they continued to program in SQL.

Java to some extent restores programmers to where they were in 1978 with their Xerox Smalltalk environment or MIT Lisp Machine. Since Java seems to have enough money behind it to catch on and object databases are very naturally suited to backing up Java programs, I predict an increase in object database popularity.

What to do with it all? User tracking and personalization is where I would start. This is a perfect example of when you care much more about an object's identity than you do about attributes. When user #4758 visits your site, you need to quickly scoop up all the data about user #4758. Has this user seen /articles/new-page.html or not? Has this user seen /ads/screaming-banner.gif or not? With an RDBMS, you'd be sifting through 100-MB tables to find all this stuff. Mind you, an RDBMS is very good at sifting through 100-MB tables, especially if they are properly indexed, but it will never be as good as an object database that doesn't have to sift through tables at all.

Note: Andromedia (*http://www .andromedia.com*) has developed a Web activity tracking system using ObjectStore as the back end.

Choosing an RDBMS Vendor

All the RDBMS vendors claim to understand exactly how a winning Web site should be built. You give them your money and they'll tell you what time it is on the Web. It all sounds plausible until you look at the slow, content-free Web sites they've built for themselves. None of the Web crawlers were built by any of the database vendors and,

so far as I know, none of the Web crawlers even use any software made by the RDBMS vendors. None of the database management system vendors have built popular Web server programs.

Don't choose an RDBMS on the basis of any claims about Web tools.

Does your choice really matter? After all, every RDBMS comes with a standard SQL front end. Actually the vendors' flavors of SQL are different enough that porting from one RDBMS to another is generally a nightmare. Plan to live with your choice for five or ten years.

Here are the factors that I think are important in choosing an RDBMS to sit behind a Web site:

1. cost/complexity to administer

2. lock management system

3. full-text indexing option

4. maximum length of VARCHAR data type

5. support

Cost/complexity to administer

If you install Oracle on your $500,000 Unix box and accept all the defaults, you'll find that the rollback segment is about 15 MB. That means that you can't do a transaction updating more than 15 MB of data at a time. That's right, on a computer with 200 GB of free disk space, you will find a transaction failing because Oracle won't by default just grab some more disk space.

Sloppy RDBMS administration is one of the most common causes of downtime at sophisticated sites. If you aren't sure that you'll have an experienced staff of database administrators to devote to your site, then you might want to consider whether an "Enterprise RDBMS" is really for you. There are databases, such as Solid, specifically engineered to require minimal administration.

Lock management system

Relational database management systems exist to support concurrent users. If you didn't have 100 people simultaneously updating information, you'd probably be better off with a Perl script than with a commercial RDBMS (i.e., 100 MB of someone else's C code).

All database management systems handle concurrency problems with locks. Before an executing statement can modify some data, it must grab a lock. While this lock is held, no other simultaneously executing SQL statement can update the same data. In order to prevent another user from reading half-updated data, while this lock is held, no simultaneously executing SQL statement can even *read* the data.

Readers must wait for writers to finish writing. Writers must wait for readers to finish reading.

This kind of system is simple to implement, works great in the research lab, and can be proven correct mathematically. The only problem with it? It doesn't work. Commercial implementations of this scheme (e.g., Illustra, Microsoft SQL Server 6.5) get confused and stuck when there are more than a handful of users.

With the Oracle RDBMS, *readers never wait for writers and writers never wait for readers.* If a SELECT starts reading at 9:01 and encounters a row that was updated

(by another session) at 9:02, Oracle reaches into a rollback segment and digs up the pre-update value for the SELECT (this preserves the Isolation requirement of the ACID test). A transaction does not need to take locks unless it is modifying a table and, even then, only takes locks on the specific rows that are to be modified.

This is the kind of RDBMS locking architecture that you want for a Web site.

Full-text indexing option

Suppose that a user says he wants to find out information on dogs. If you had a bunch of strings in the database, you'd have to search them with a query like

```
select * from magazines where description like '%dogs%';
```

This requires the RDBMS to read every row in the table, which is slow. Also, this won't turn up magazines whose description includes the word "dog." A full-text indexer builds a data structure (the index) on disk so that the RDBMS no longer has to scan the entire table to find rows containing a particular word or combination of words. The software is smart enough to be able to think in terms of word stems rather than words. So "running" and "run" or "dog" and "dogs" can be interchanged in queries. Full-text indexers are also generally able to score a user-entered

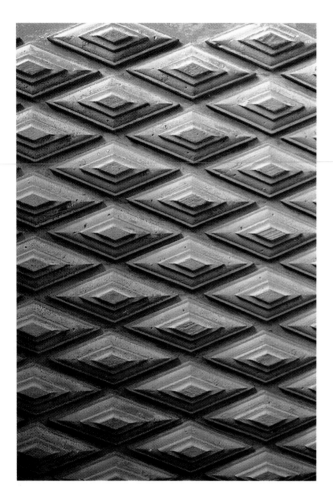

phrase against a database table of documents for relevance so that you can query for the most relevant matches.

Finally, the modern text search engines are very smart about how words relate. So they might deliver a document that did *not* contain the word "dog" but did contain "Golden Retriever." This makes services like classified ads, discussion forums, etcetera, much more useful to users.

Relational database management system vendors are gradually incorporating full-text indexing into their products. Sadly, there is no standard for querying using this index. Thus, if you figure out how to query Oracle 8.1 with ConText for "rows relating to 'running' or its synonyms", the SQL syntax will not be useful for asking the same question of Microsoft SQL Server 7.0 with its corresponding full-text indexing option.

My best experiences have been with the Illustra/PLS combination. I fed it 500 short classified ads for photography equipment, then asked, "What word is most related to Nikon?" The answer, according to Illustra/PLS: Nikkor (Nikon's brand name for lenses).

Maximum length of VARCHAR data type

You might naively expect a relational database management system to provide abstraction for data storage. After defining a column to hold a character string, you'd expect to be able to give the DBMS a ten-character string or a million-character string and have each one stored as efficiently as possible.

In practice, current commercial systems are very bad at storing unexpectedly long data; for example, Oracle only lets you have 4,000 characters in a VARCHAR. This is okay if you're building a corporate accounting system, but bad for a public Web site. You can't really be sure how long a user's classified ad or bulletin board posting is going to be. The SQL standard provides for a LONG data type to handle this kind of situation and modern database vendors often provide character large-objects (CLOBs). These types theoretically allow you to store arbitrarily large data. However, in practice there are so many restrictions on these columns that they aren't very useful.

For example, you can't use them in a SQL WHERE clause and thus the preceding "LIKE '%dogs%'" would be illegal. You can't build a standard index on a LONG column. You may also have a hard time getting strings into or out of LONG columns. The Oracle SQL parser only accepts string literals up to 4,000 characters in length; Informix lets you insert up to 32,000 characters. After that, both systems make you use special C API calls.

Currently, Solid seems to be the leader in this area. They let you keep up to 2 GB in a VARCHAR, though their SQL parser can only handle about 60,000 bytes in a string literal.

Informix does not do badly. They let you store 32,000 char-

acters in a VARCHAR and insert those 32,000 characters in a string literal. The Netscape browser won't let users put much more than that in a TEXTAREA, so it is nearly a perfect fit with the Web.

As noted above, Oracle 8 lets you have 4,000 characters in a VARCHAR. It turns out that this is enough for 99 percent of Web interactions, but not for that last 1 percent. photo.net is Oracle-backed and this limitation has been one of the most painful for me (see *http://photo.net/wtr/oracle-tips.html*).

A surprising number of RDBMSs have the ridiculously low limit of 255 characters, beyond which you're forced to use special SQL-unfriendly data types.

Caveat emptor.

PAYING AN RDBMS VENDOR

This is the part that hurts. The basic pricing strategy of database management system vendors is to hang the user up by his heels, see how much money falls out, take it all, and then ask for another $50,000 for "support." Ideally, they'd like to know how much your data are worth and how much profit you expect from making them available, and then extract all of that profit from you. In this respect, they behave like the classical price-discriminating profit-maximizing monopoly from Microeconomics 101.

Classically, an RDBMS license was priced per user. Big insurance companies with a thousand claims processors would pay more than small companies with five. The Web confused the RDBMS vendors. On the one hand, the server was accessible to anyone anywhere in the world. Thus, the fair arrangement would be a $64,000 per CPU, unlimited user license. On the other hand, not too many Web publishers actually had $64,000 per CPU lying around in their checking accounts. So the RDBMS vendors would settle for selling a five-user or eight-user license.

Microsoft started a refreshing trend toward charging the same price for everyone. You can go to their Web site and find a price for SQL Server: $1,400 for a five-user license. Microsoft explains clearly that if you are using it for the Internet, they want you to buy an Internet Connector for another $3,000 (prices on February 7, 1999).

Another vendor brave enough to expose its prices is Solid (*http://www.solidtech.com*). For a server behind a Web site, they want $500 for Linux, $1,000 for NT, and $2,000 for most Unices (though if you tell them that you're a reader of this book, they will knock the Unix price down to $1,000).

Note: If you want to learn about RDBMS, Solid is the best current choice. It is easy to install, easy to administer, and free on Linux.

PERFORMANCE

According to their sales staff, Informix has "by far the fastest and most scalable core database engine in the world." This has an oddly familiar ring to it if you've just heard the Oracle guy note that "everyone agrees that the Oracle core code is the world's fastest and most scalable on multiprocessor machines." And if you go to the Sybase Web site, you'll see that their "Sybase System 11 has proved to be the leader in performance across a wide variety of hardware platforms." I suspect that somebody is not telling the truth.

Be assured that any RDBMS product will be plenty slow. I had 70,000 rows of data to insert into Oracle 8. Each row contained six numbers. It turned out that the data wasn't in the most convenient format for importation, so I wrote a one-line Perl script to reformat it. It took less than one second to read all 70,000 rows, reformat them, and write them back to disk in one file. Then I started inserting them into an Oracle 8 table. It took about 20 minutes (60 rows per second). This despite the fact that the table wasn't indexed and therefore Oracle did not have to update multiple locations on the disk.

There are several ways to achieve high performance. One is to buy a huge multiprocessor computer with enough RAM to hold your entire data model at once. Unfortunately, unless you are using Solid Server or Microsoft SQL Server, your RDBMS vendor will probably give your bank account a reaming that it will not soon forget. The license fee will be four times as much for a four-CPU machine as for a one-CPU machine. When the basic fee is $60,000 to $100,000, multiplying by four can result in a truly staggering figure. Thus, it might be best to try to get hold of the fastest possible single-CPU computer.

If you are processing a lot of transactions, all those CPUs bristling with RAM won't help you. Your bottleneck will be disk spindle contention. The solution to this is to chant, "Oh, what a friend I have in Seagate." Disks are slow. Very slow. Literally almost one million times slower than the computer. Therefore, the computer spends a lot of time waiting for the disk(s). You can speed up SQL SELECTs simply by buying so much RAM that the entire database is in memory. However, the Durability requirement in the ACID test for transactions means that some record of a transaction will have to be written to a medium that won't be erased in the event of a power failure. If a disk can only do 100 seeks a second and you only have one disk, your RDBMS is going to be hard pressed to do more than about 100 updates a second.

The first thing you should do is mirror all of your disks. If you don't have the entire database in RAM, this speeds up SELECTs because the disk controller can read from whichever disk is closer to the desired track. The opposite effect can be achieved if you use "RAID level 5," where data is striped across multiple disks. Then the RDBMS has to wait for five disks to seek before it can cough up a few rows. Straight mirroring, or "RAID level 1," is what you want.

The next decision that you must make is How many disks? The *Oracle 8 DBA Handbook* (Loney, 1998; Osborne) recommends a 7×2 disk configuration as a minimum *compromise* for a machine doing nothing but database service. Their *solutions* start at 9×2 disks and go up to 22×2. The idea is to keep files that might be written in parallel on separate disks so that one can do 2,200 seeks a second instead of 100.

Here's the *Oracle 8 DBA Handbook*'s 17-disk (mirrored ×2) solution for avoiding spindle contention:

Disk	Contents
1	Oracle software
2	SYSTEM tablespace
3	RBS tablespace (rollback segment in case a transaction goes badly)
4	DATA tablespace
5	INDEXES tablespace (changing data requires changing indices; this allows those changes to proceed in parallel)
6	TEMP tablespace
7	TOOLS tablespace
8	Online Redo log 1, Control file 1 (these would be separated on a 22-disk machine)
9	Online Redo log 2, Control file 2
10	Online Redo log 3, Control file 3
11	Application Software
12	RBS_2
13	DATA_2 (tables that tend to be grabbed in parallel with those in DATA)
14	INDEXES_2
15	TEMP_USER
16	Archived redo log destination disk
17	Export dump file destination disk

Now that you have lots of disks, you finally have to be very thoughtful about how you lay your data out across them. "Enterprise" relational database management systems force you to think about where your data files should go. On a computer with one disk, this is merely annoying and keeps you from doing development; you'd probably get similar performance with a zero-administration RDBMS like Solid. But the flexibility is there in enterprise databases because you know which of your data areas tend to be accessed simultaneously and the computer doesn't. So if you do have a proper database server with a rack of disk drives, an intelligent manual layout can improve performance fivefold.

Don't forget to back up

Be afraid. Be very afraid. Standard Unix or Windows NT file system backups will not leave you with a consistent and therefore restoreable database on tape. Suppose that your RDBMS is storing your database in two separate Unix filesystem files, foo.db and bar.db. Each of these files is 200 MB in size. You start your backup program running and it writes the file foo.db to tape. As the backup is proceeding, a transaction comes in that requires changes to foo.db and bar.db. The RDBMS

makes those changes, but the ones to foo.db occur to a portion of the file that has already been written out to tape. Eventually, the backup program gets around to writing bar.db to tape and it writes the new version with the change. Your system administrator arrives at 9:00 A.M. and sends the tapes via courier to an offsite storage facility.

At noon, an ugly mob of users assembles outside your office, angered by your introduction of frames and failure to include WIDTH and HEIGHT tags on IMGs. You send one of your graphic designers out to explain how "cool" it looked when run off a local disk in a demo to the vice president. The mob stones him to death and then burns your server farm to the ground. You manage to pry your way out of the rubble with one of those indestructible HP Unix box keyboards. You manage to get the HP disaster support people to let you use their machines for a while and confidently load your backup tape. To your horror, the RDBMS chokes up blood following the restore. It turned out that there were linked data structures in foo.db and bar.db. Half of the data structures (the ones from foo.db) are the old pre-transaction version and half are the new post-transaction version (the ones from bar.db). One transaction occurring during your backup has resulted in a complete loss of availability for all of your data. Maybe you think that isn't the world's most robust RDBMS design, but there is

nothing in the SQL standard or manufacturer's documentation that says Oracle, Sybase, or Informix can't work this way.

Full mirroring keeps you from going offline due to media failure. But you still need snapshots of your database in case someone gets a little excited with a DELETE FROM statement or in the situation just described.

There are two ways to back up a relational database: offline and online. For an offline backup, you shut down the databases, thus preventing transactions from occurring. Most vendors would prefer that you use their utility to make a dump file of your offline database, but in practice it will suffice just to back up the Unix or NT file system files. Offline backup is typically used by insurance companies and other big database users who need to do transactions for only eight hours a day.

Each RDBMS vendor has an advertised way of doing online backups. It can be as simple as "call this function and we'll grind away for a couple of hours building you a dump file that contains a consistent database but minus all the transactions that occurred after you called the function." That's what the Illustra 2.4 documentation said. But when I tested it by restoring from the dump file, a table that had been the subject of ten transactions during the dump came out broken. The dump file was not consistent. It took a year of wrangling with tech support, the testing of about ten "fixed binaries", and a new major release of the software (3.2) before the online backups would restore into legal databases.

I've had better luck with the Oracle equivalent:

```
exp DBUSER/DBPASSWD file=/exportdest/foo.980210.dmp owner=DBUSER
    consistent=Y
```

(this exports all the tables owned by DBUSER, pulling old rows from a rollback segment if a table has undergone transactions since the dump started); but if you read *Oracle Performance Tuning* (Gurry and Corrigan, 1996; O'Reilly), you'll find some dark warnings that you *must* export periodically in order to flush out cases

where Oracle has corrupted its internal data structures. Another good reason to export is that periodically dropping all of your tables and importing them is a great way to defragment your data.

What if your database is too large to be exported to a disk and can't be taken offline? Here's a technique that I learned from the Oracle studs at Boston Children's Hospital:

- Break the mirror.

- Back up from the disks that are offline
  as far as the database is concerned.

- Reestablish the mirror.

What if one of the online disks fails during backup? Are transactions lost? No. The redo log is on a separate disk from the rest of the database. This increases performance in day-to-day operations and ensures that it is possible to recover transactions that occur when the mirror is broken, albeit with some offline time. Children's Hospital has held onto their 100 GB of data for quite a few years, so I guess the procedure works.

The lessons here are several. First, whatever your backup procedure, make sure you test it with periodic restores. Second, remember that at most companies the backup and maintenance of an RDBMS is done by a full-time staffer called "the DBA," short for database administrator. If the software worked as advertised, you could expect a few days of pain during the install and then periodic recurring pain to keep current with improved features. However, DBAs earn their moderately lavish salaries. No amount of marketing hype suffices to make a C program work as advertised. That goes for an RDBMS just as much as for a word processor. Coming to terms with bugs can be a full-time job at a large installation. Most often this means finding workarounds, since vendors are notoriously sluggish with fixes. Another full-time job is hunting down users who are doing queries that are taking 1,000 times longer than necessary because they forgot to build indices or don't know SQL very well. Children's Hospital has three full-time DBAs and they work hard.

If all of this sounds rather tedious just to ensure that your data are still around tomorrow, then you might be cheered by the knowledge that Oracle DBAs are always in high demand and start at $60,000 to $80,000 a year. When the Web bubble bursts and your friends who are "HTML programmers" are singing in the subway, you'll be kicking back at some huge financial services firm.

I'll close by quoting Perrin Harkins. A participant in the Web/DB question-and-answer forum (*http://db.photo.net/bboard/q-and-a.tcl?topic=web/db*) asked whether caching DB queries in Unix files would speed up his Web server. Here's Perrin's response:

```
Modern databases use buffering in RAM to speed up access to often
requested data. You don't have to do anything special to make this
happen, except tune your database well (which could take the rest
of your life).
```

SUMMARY

Here's what you should have learned from reading this chapter:

- You and your programmers will make mistakes implementing transaction processing systems. You are better off focusing your energies on the application and leaving indexing, transactions, and concurrency to a database management system.

- The most practical database management software for Web sites is a relational database management system with a full-text indexer. IBM's DB2, Informix Universal Server, and Oracle/ConText are the real contenders.

- If you can program a spreadsheet, you can program an RDBMS in SQL.

- RDBMSs are slow. Prepare to buy a big machine with a lot of disks.

- RDBMSs, though much more reliable than most user-written transaction processing code, are not nearly as reliable as a basic Unix system with a Web server pulling static files out a file system. Prepare to hire a half- or full-time database administrator. If you can't afford this, consider a zero-administration RDBMS such as Solid.

In the next chapter, we'll see how to best integrate an RDBMS with a Web server.

MORE

- *The Practical SQL Handbook* (Bowman, Emerson, Darnovsky, 1996; Addison-Wesley) is my favorite introductory SQL tutorial. If you want to see how the language is used in real installations, get *SQL for Smarties: Advanced SQL Programming* (Celko, 1995; Morgan Kaufmann).

- For some interesting history about the first relational database implementation, visit *http://www.mcjones.org/System_R/*.

- For a look under the hoods of a variety of database management systems, get *Readings in Database Systems* (Stonebraker and Hellerstein, 1998; Morgan Kaufmann).

- *Building an Object-Oriented Database System* will help you take off your RDBMS blinders as it describes the O_2 system.

- If you want to really drive an RDBMS, you'll need to read more than this chapter. I recommend a brace of database books at *http://photo.net/wtr /bookshelf.html*.

13

Interfacing a Relational
Database to the Web

366

Okay, you've got your RDBMS, 30 disk drives, and a computer connected to the Internet. It is time to start programming. Uh, but in what language? And what's the correct system architecture? And how do I get this database thing to respond to an HTTP request? Maybe we'd better take a step back and look at the overall system before we plunge into detailed software design.

How Does an RDBMS Talk to the Rest of the World?

Remember the African Grey parrot we trained in the last chapter? The one holding down a $250,000 information systems management position saying, "We're proactively leveraging our object-oriented client/server database to target customer service during reengineering"? The profound concept behind the client/server portion of this sentence is that the database *server* is a program that sits around waiting for another program, the database *client,* to request a connection. Once the connection is established, the client sends SQL queries to the server, which inspects the physical database and returns the matching data. These days, connections are generally made via TCP sockets, even if the two programs are running on the same computer. Figure 13-1 is a schematic.

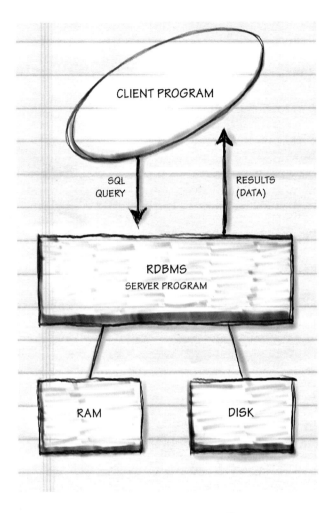

Figure 13-1:
The client/server architecture of a basic relational database management system.

Let's get a little more realistic and dirty. In a classical RDBMS, you have a daemon program that waits for requests from clients for new connections. For each client, the daemon spawns a server program. All the servers and the daemon cache data from disk and communicate locking information via a large block of shared RAM (often as much as 1 GB). The raison d'être of an RDBMS is that N clients can simultaneously access and update the tables. We could have an AOLserver database pool taking up six of the client positions, a programmer using a shelltype tool such as SQL*Plus as another, an administrator using Microsoft Access as another, and a legacy CGI script as the final client. The client processes could be running on

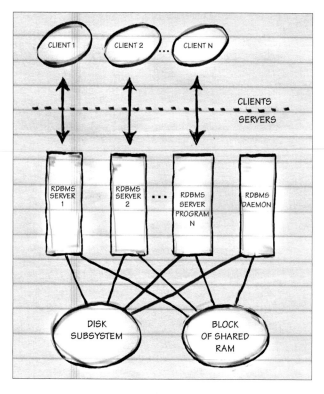

Figure 13-2:
A classical RDBMS
implementation.

three or four separate physical computers. The database server processes would all be running on one physical computer (this is why Macintoshes and Windows 95/98 machines, which lack multiprocessing capability, are not used as database servers). Figure 13-2 is a schematic.

Note that the schematic in Figure 13-2 is for a "classical" RDBMS. The trend is for database server programs to run as one operating system process with multiple kernel threads. This is an implementation detail, however, that doesn't affect the logical structure that you see in the schematic.

For a properly engineered RDBMS-backed Web site, the RDBMS *client* is the Web server program, (e.g., AOLserver). The user types something into a form on a *Web client* (e.g., Netscape Navigator) and that gets transmitted to the *Web server,* which has an already established connection to an *RDBMS server* (e.g., Oracle). The data then go back from the RDBMS server to the RDBMS client, the Web server, which sends them back to the Web client. See Figure 13-3 for a schematic.

Note that an essential element here is database connection pooling. The Web server program must open connections to the database and keep them open. When a server-side program needs to query the database, the Web server program finds a free database connection and hands it to the program.

Does this system sound complicated and slow? Well, yes it is, but not as slow as the ancient method of building RDBMS-backed Web sites (see Figure 13-4). In ancient times, people used CGI scripts. The user would click on the Submit button in his Web client (e.g., Netscape Navigator), causing the form to be transmitted to the Web server (e.g., NCSA 1.4). The Web server would fork off a CGI script, starting up a new operating system process. Modern computers are very fast, but think about how long it takes to start up a word processing program versus making a change to a document that is already open. Once running, the CGI program would immediately ask for a connection to the RDBMS, often resulting in the RDBMS forking off a server process to handle the new request for connection. The new RDBMS server process would ask for a username and password and authenticate the CGI script as a user. Only then would the SQL transmission and results delivery commence. A lot of sites are still running this way in 1998, but either they aren't popular or they feel unresponsive.

HOW TO MAKE REALLY FAST RDBMS-BACKED WEB SITES

The Web-server-as-database-client software architecture is the fastest currently popular Web site architecture. The Web server program maintains a pool of already open connections to one or more RDBMS systems. You write scripts that run inside the Web server program's process instead of as CGI processes. For each URL requested, you save:

- the cost of starting up a process ("forking" on a Unix system) for the CGI script

- the cost of starting up a new database server process (though Oracle 7 and imitators prefork server processes and many new RDBMS systems are threaded)

- the cost of establishing the connection to the database, including a TCP session and authentication (databases have their own accounts and passwords)

- the cost of tearing all of this down when it is time to return data to the user

The AOLserver guys realized this in 1994 and produced the first connection-pooling Web server program. In the intervening years, there have been surprisingly few imitators, but as of March 1998, there are a handful. See the product review sections later in this chapter for specific product recommendations.

If you are building a richly interactive site and want the ultimate in user responsiveness, client-side Java is the way to go. You can write a Java applet that, after a painful and slow initial download, starts running inside the user's Web client. The applet can make its own TCP connection back to the RDBMS, thus completely

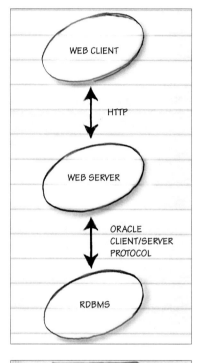

Figure 13-3:
A high-performance RDBMS-backed Web site configuration.

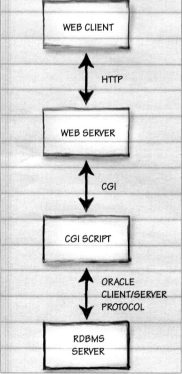

Figure 13-4:
An old-style RDBMS-backed Web site.

bypassing the Web server program. The problems with this approach include security, licensing, performance, and compatibility.

The client/server RDBMS abstraction barrier means that if you're going to allow a Java applet that you distribute to connect directly to your RDBMS, then in effect you're going to permit any program on any computer anywhere in the world to connect to your RDBMS. To deal with the security risk that this presents, you have to create a PUBLIC database user with a restricted set of privileges. Database privileges are specifiable on a set of actions, tables, and columns. It is not possible to restrict users to particular rows. So in a classified ad system, if the PUBLIC user has enough privileges to delete one row, then a malicious person could easily delete all the rows in the ads table.

The magnitude of the licensing problem raised by having Java applets connect directly to your RDBMS depends on the contract you have with your database management system vendor and the vendor's approach to holding you to that contract. Under the classical DB-backed Web site architecture, the Web server might have counted as one user, even if multiple people were connecting to the Web site simultaneously. Certainly, it would have *looked* like one user to fancy license manager programs, even if there was legal fine print saying that you have to pay for the multiplexing. Once you "upgrade to Java," each Java applet connecting to your RDBMS will definitely be seen by the license manager program as a distinct user. So you might have to pay tens of thousands of dollars extra, even though your users aren't really getting anything very different.

A standard RDBMS will fork a server process for each connected database client. Thus, if you have 400 people playing a game in which each user interacts with a Java applet connected to Oracle, your server will need enough RAM to support 400 Oracle server processes. It might be more efficient in terms of RAM and CPU to program the Java applets to talk to AOLserver Tcl scripts via HTTP and let AOLServer multiplex the database resource among its threads.

The last problem with a Java applet/RDBMS system is the most obvious: Users without Java-compatible browsers won't be able to use the system. Users with Java-compatible browsers behind corporate firewall proxies that block Java applet requests will not be able to use the system. Users with Java-compatible browsers who successfully obtain your applet may find their machine (Macintosh, Windows 95) or browser process (Windows NT, Unix) crashing.

CORBA: Middleware Meets Vaporware

A variant of the Java-connects-directly-to-the-RDBMS architecture is Java applets running an Object Request Broker (ORB) talking to a Common Object Request Broker Architecture (CORBA) server via the Internet Inter-ORB Protocol (IIOP). The user downloads a Java applet. The Java applet starts up an ORB. The ORB makes an IIOP request to get to your server machine's CORBA server program. The CORBA server requests an object from the server machine's ORB. The object, presumably some little program that you've written, is started up by the ORB and makes a connection to your RDBMS, and then starts streaming the data back to the client.

CORBA is the future. CORBA is backed by Netscape, Oracle, Sun, Hewlett-Packard, IBM, and 700 other companies (except Microsoft, of course). CORBA is so great, its proponents proudly proclaim it to be … "middleware":

> *The (ORB) is the middleware that establishes the client-server relationships between objects. Using an ORB, a client can transparently invoke a method on a server object, which can be on the same machine or across a network. The ORB intercepts the call and is responsible for finding an object that can implement the request, pass it the parameters, invoke its method, and return the results. The client does not have to be aware of where the object is located, its programming language, its operating system, or any other system aspects that are not part of an object's interface. In so doing, the ORB provides interoperability between applications on different machines in heterogeneous distributed environments and seamlessly interconnects multiple object systems.*
> *— http://www.omg.org*

The basic idea of CORBA is that every time you write a computer program you also write a description of the computer program's inputs and outputs. Modern business managers don't like to buy computer programs anymore, so we'll call the computer program an "object." Technology managers don't like powerful computer languages such as Common Lisp, so we'll write the description in a new language: Interface Definition Language (IDL).

Suppose that you've written an object (computer program) called `find_cheapest_flight_to_paris` and declared that it can take methods such as `quote_fare` with arguments of city name and departure date and `book_ticket` with the same arguments plus credit card number and passenger name.

Now a random computer program (object) out there in cyberspace can go hunting via ORBs for an object named `find_cheapest_flight_to_paris`. The foreign object will discover the program that you've written, ask for the legal methods and arguments, and start using your program to find the cheapest flights to Paris.

The second big CORBA idea is the ability to wrap services such as transaction management around arbitrary computer programs. As long as you've implemented all of your programs to the CORBA standard, you can just ask the Object Transaction Service (OTS) to make sure that a bunch of methods executed on a bunch of objects all happen or that none happen. You won't have to do everything inside the RDBMS anymore, just because you want to take advantage of its transaction system.

Complexity (or "It probably won't work")

Given the quality of the C code inside the Unix and Windows NT operating systems and the quality of the C code inside RDBMS products, it is sometimes a source of amazement to me that there is even a single working RDBMS-backed Web site on the Internet. What if these sites also had to depend on two ORBs being up and running? Netscape hasn't yet figured out how to make a browser that can run a simple Java animation without crashing, but we're supposed to trust the complicated Java ORB that they are putting into their latest browsers?

Actually, I'm being extremely unfair. I've never heard, for example, of a bug in a CORBA Concurrency Control Service, used to manage locks. Perhaps, though, that is because eight years after the CORBA standard was proposed, nobody has implemented a Concurrency Control Service. CORBA circa 1998 is a lot like an Arizona housing development circa 1950. The architect's model looks great. The model home is comfortable. You'll have water and sewage hookups real soon now.

What if it did work?

Assume, for the sake of argument, that all the CORBA middleware actually worked. Would it usher in a new dawn of reliable, high-performance software systems? Yes, I guess so, as long as your idea of new dawn dates back to the late 1970s.

Before the Great Microsoft Technology Winter, there were plenty of systems that functioned more or less like CORBA. Xerox Palo Alto Research Center produced SmallTalk and the InterLISP machines. MIT produced the Lisp Machine.

All of these operating systems/development environments supported powerful objects. The objects could discover each other. The objects could ask each other what kinds of methods they provided. Did that mean that my objects could invoke methods on your objects without human intervention?

No. Let's go back to our `find_cheapest_flight_to_paris` example. Suppose the foreign object is looking for `find_cheap_flight_to_paris`. It won't find your perfectly matching object because of the slight difference in naming. Or suppose the foreign object is looking for `find_cheapest_flight` and expects to provide the destination city in an argument to a method. Again, your object can't be used.

That was 1978, though. Isn't CORBA an advancement over Lisp and SmallTalk? Sure. CORBA solves the trivial problem of objects calling each other over computer networks rather than from within the same computer. But CORBA ignores the serious problem of semantic mismatches. My object doesn't get any help from CORBA in explaining to other objects that it knows something about airplane flights to Paris.

This is my personal theory for why CORBA has had so little practical impact during its eight-year life.

Aren't objects the way to go?

Maybe CORBA is nothing special, but wouldn't it be better to implement a Web service as a bunch of encapsulated objects with advertised methods and arguments? After all, object-oriented programming is a useful tool for building big systems.

The simple answer is that a Web service already is an encapsulated object with advertised methods and arguments. The methods are the legal URLs, "insert-msg.tcl" or "add-user.tcl" for example. The arguments to these methods are the form-variables in the pages that precede these URLs.

A more balanced answer is that a Web service is already an encapsulated object but that its methods and arguments are not very well advertised. We don't have a protocol whereby Server A can ask Server B to "please send me a list of all your legal

URLs and their arguments." Hence, CORBA may one day genuinely facilitate server-to-server communication. For the average site, though, it isn't clear whether the additional programming effort over slapping something together in AOLserver Tcl, Apache mod_perl, or Microsoft ASP is worth it. You might decide to completely redesign your Web service before CORBA becomes a reality.

In concluding this CORBA-for-Cavemen discussion, it is worth noting that the issues of securing your RDBMS are the same, whether you are using a classical HTTP-only Web service architecture or CORBA.

SECURITY

I hope that we have spent most of our time in this book thinking about how to design Web services that will be popular and valued by users. I hope that I've also conveyed some valuable lessons about achieving high performance and reliability. However, a responsive, reliable, and popular Web server that is delivering data inserted by your enemies isn't anything to email home about. So it is worth thinking about security occasionally. I haven't written anything substantial about securing a standard Windows NT or Unix server. I'm not an expert in this field, there are

plenty of good books on the subject, and ultimately it isn't possible to achieve perfect security, so you'd better have a good set of backup tapes. However, running any kind of RDBMS raises a bunch of new security issues that I *have* spent some time thinking about, so let's look at how Carrie Cracker can get into your database.

Before Carrie can have a data modeling language (INSERT, UPDATE, DELETE) party with your data, she has to

1. successfully connect to the IP address and port where the RDBMS is listening and,

2. once connected, present a username and password pair recognized by the RDBMS.

One of the easiest ways to prevent direct network connections to your RDBMS is to use a traditional RDBMS in a nontraditional manner. If you install Oracle 8, you have to spend a whole day reading SQL*Net manuals before you can think about setting up networking. The only programs that will be able to connect to your new Oracle server are programs running on the RDBMS server itself. This would be useless in an insurance company where clerks at a thousand desktops need to connect to Oracle. But for many Web sites, there is no reason why you can't run the database and Web server on the same box. The database will consume 95 percent of your resources. So if a computer is big enough to run Oracle, you can just add a tiny bit of CPU and memory and have a maximally reliable site (since you only have to keep one computer up and running).

Suppose that you must install SQL*Net to let folks inside your organization talk directly to Oracle, or that you're using a newer-style RDBMS (e.g., Solid) that is network-centric. By installing the RDBMS, you've opened a huge security hole: a program listening on a TCP port and happy to accept connections from anywhere on the Internet.

A remarkably incompetent publisher would be

- running the RDBMS on the same machine as the Web server, both binding to the same well-advertised IP address

- leaving the RDBMS to listen on the default port numbers
- leaving the RDBMS with well-known usernames and passwords (like "scott/tiger" for Oracle)

With a publisher running a configuration like this, to achieve step 1 (connecting to the RDBMS) Carrie need only use the same IP address as the Web site and the default port number as published in the RDBMS documentation. To achieve step 2, Carrie need only try a well-known username/password pair.

Is anyone out there on the Internet really this incompetent? Sure! I have done at least one consulting job for a company whose Web server had been set up and left like this for months. The ISP was extremely experienced with both the Web server program and the RDBMS being used. The ISP was charging my client thousands of dollars per month. Was this reasonably popular site assaulted by the legions of crackers one reads about in the dead-trees media? No. Nobody touched the data. The lesson: Don't spend your whole life worrying about security.

However, you'll probably sleep better if you spend at least a little time foiling Carrie Cracker. The easiest place to start is with the username/password pairs. You want to set these to something hard to guess. Unfortunately, these aren't super secure, because they often must be stored as clear text in CGI scripts or cron jobs that connect to the database. Then anyone who gets a Unix username/password pair can read the CGI scripts and collect the database password. On a site where the Web server itself is the database client, the Web server configuration files will usually contain the database password in clear text. This is only one file, so it is easy to give it meager permissions, but anyone who can become root on your Unix box can certainly read it.

A worthwhile parallel approach is to try to prevent Carrie from connecting to the RDBMS at all. You could just configure your RDBMS to listen on different ports from the default. Carrie can't get in anymore by just trying port 7599, because she saw the little "backed by Sybase" on your home page and knows that Sybase will probably be listening there. Carrie will have to sweep up and down the port numbers until your server responds. Maybe she'll get bored and try someone else's site.

A much more powerful approach is moving the database server behind a firewall. This is necessary mostly because RDBMSs have such lame security notions. For example, it should be possible to tell the RDBMS, "Only accept requests for TCP connections from the following IP addresses...". Every Web server program since 1992 has been capable of this. However, I'm not aware of any RDBMS vendor who has figured this out. They talk the Internet talk, but they walk the *intranet* walk.

Because Oracle, Informix, and Sybase forgot to add a few lines of code to their products, you'll be adding $10,000 to your budget and buying a firewall computer. This machine sits between the Internet and the database server. Assuming your Web server is outside the firewall, you program the firewall "not to let anyone make a TCP connection to port 7599 on the database server except 18.23.0.16" (your Web

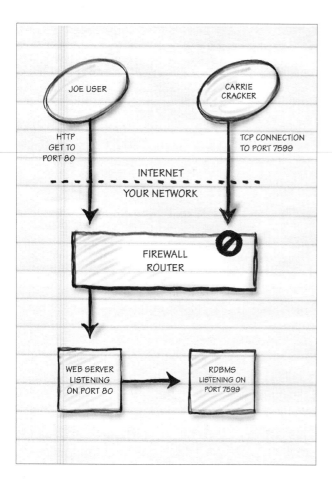

server). This works great until crackers compromise your Web server. Now they are root on the computer that the firewall has been programmed to let connect to the database server. So they can connect to the database.

Oops.

So you move your Web server inside the firewall, too. Then you program the firewall to allow *nobody* to connect to the database server for any reason. The only kind of TCP connection that will be allowed will be to port 80 on the Web server (that's the default port for HTTP). Now you're *reasonably* secure (see Figure 13-5).

WHAT DOES THIS STUFF LOOK LIKE?

Here's a typical AOLserver Tcl API DB-backed page. Tcl is a safe language and an incorrect Tcl program will not crash AOLserver or result in a denial of service to other users. This program reads through a table of email addresses and names and prints each one as a list item in an unnumbered list. If this is placed in a file named

Figure 13-5: You don't want Carrie Cracker connecting directly to your RDBMS.

"view.tcl" in the Greedy Corporation's Web server root directory, then it may be referenced at http://www.greedy.com/view.tcl.

```
# send basic text/html headers back to the client

ns_write "HTTP/1.0 200 OK
MIME-Version: 1.0
Content-Type: text/html

"

# write the top of the page
# note that we just put static HTML in a Tcl string and then
# call the AOLserver API function ns_write

ns_write "<head>
<title>Entire Mailing List</title>
</head>
```

```
<body>
<h2>Entire Mailing List</h2>
<hr>
<ul>
"

# get an open database from the AOLserver
# and set the ID of that connection to the local variable DB

set db [ns_db gethandle]

# open a database cursor bound to the local variable SELECTION
# we want to read all the columns (*) from the mailing_list table

set selection [ns_db select $db "select * from mailing_list
                                 order by upper(email)"]

# loop through the cursor, calling ns_db getrow to bind
# the Tcl local variable SELECTION to a set of values for
# each row; it will return 0 when there are no more rows
# in the cursor

while { [ns_db getrow $db $selection] } {
    # pull email and name out of SELECTION
    set email [ns_set get $selection email]
    set name [ns_set get $selection name]
    ns_write "<li><a href=\"mailto:$email\">$email</a> ($name)\n"
}

ns_write "</ul>
<hr>
<address><a href=\"mailto:philg@mit.edu\">philg@mit.edu</a></address>
</body>
"
```

Not exactly rocket science, was it? Still, there are some fine points here. One is that the program returns headers and the top portion of the page before asking AOLserver for a database connection or asking the database to do anything. This kind of construction ensures that users aren't staring at a blank Netscape window. A second fine point is that we wrap the email address in a MAILTO tag. Maybe no user will ever actually want to send email from this page, but at least nobody will say, "What a bunch of losers who don't know how to use MAILTO tags." Third, a microfine point is that there is an advertised author for this page. I've put my email address at the bottom, so that if it isn't working the user can tell me. Finally, even if there were a Tcl compiler, it wouldn't be able to check the correctness of this program. Tcl doesn't know anything about the database, so it doesn't know if the `mailing_list` table exists or what the names of the columns are. So you won't find typos until you test the page or a user follows a branch you didn't test (ouch!). The plus side of this is that a Tcl program is free to construct SQL queries on the fly. Because Tcl makes no attempt to test program correctness before execution, you can easily write a Tcl program that, for example, takes a `table_name` argument from a user and then puts it into a query.

Let's try something similar in Oracle Application Server. We're going to use PL/SQL, Oracle's vaguely ADA-inspired procedural language that runs inside the server process. It is a safe language and an incorrect PL/SQL program will usually not compile. If an incorrect program gets past the compiler, it will not run wild and crash Oracle unless there is a bug in the Oracle implementation of PL/SQL. This PL/SQL program is from a bulletin board system. It takes a message ID argument, fetches the corresponding message from a database table, and writes the content out in an HTML page. Note that in Oracle WebServer 2.0 there is a 1-to-1 mapping between PL/SQL function names and URLs. This one will be referenced via a URL of the following form:

```
http://www.greedy.com/public/owa/bbd_fetch_msg
```

Nobody ever said Oracle was pretty....

```
-- this is a definition that we feed directly to the database
-- in an SQL*PLUS session.  So the procedure definition is itself
-- an extended SQL statement.  The first line says I'm a Web page
-- that takes one argument, V_MSG_ID, which is a variable length
-- character string
create or replace procedure bbd_fetch_msg ( v_msg_id IN varchar2 )
AS
  -- here we must declare all the local variables
  -- the first declaration reaches into the database and
  -- makes the local variable bboard_record have
  -- the same type as a row from the bboard table
  bboard_record bboard%ROWTYPE;
  days_since_posted integer;
  age_string varchar2(100);
BEGIN
  -- we grab all the information we're going to need
  select * into bboard_record from bboard where msg_id = v_msg_id;
  -- we call the Oracle function "sysdate" just as we could
  -- in a regular SQL statement
  days_since_posted := sysdate - bboard_record.posting_time;
  -- here's something that you can't have in a declarative
  -- language like SQL...  an IF statement
  IF days_since_posted = 0 THEN
    age_string := 'today';
  ELSIF days_since_posted = 1 THEN
    age_string := 'yesterday';
  ELSE
    age_string := days_since_posted || ' days ago';
```

```
   END IF;
   -- this is the business end of the procedure.  We
   -- call the Oracle WebServer 2.0 API procedure htp.print
   -- note that the argument is a big long string produced
   -- by concatenating (using the "||" operator) static
   -- strings and then information from bboard_record
   htp.print('<html>
<head>
<title>' || bboard_record.one_line || '</title>
</head>
<body bgcolor=#ffffff text=#000000>
<h3>' || bboard_record.one_line || '</h3>
from ' || bboard_record.name || '
(<a href="mailto:' || bboard_record.email || '">'
 || bboard_record.email || '</a>)
<hr>
' || bboard_record.message || '
<hr>
(posted '|| age_string || ')
</body>
</html>');
END bbd_fetch_msg;
```

The first thing to note in this program is that we chose v_msg_id instead of the obvious msg_id as the procedure argument. If we'd used msg_id, then our database query would have been

```
select * into bboard_record from bboard where msg_id = msg_id;
```

which is pretty similar to

```
select * from bboard where msg_id = msg_id;
```

Does that look a little strange? It should. The WHERE clause is inoperative here because it is tautological. *Every* row in the table will have msg_id = msg_id so all the rows will be returned. This problem didn't arise in our AOLserver Tcl program because the Tcl was being read by the Tcl interpreter compiled into the AOLserver and the SQL was being interpreted by the RDBMS back end. With a PL/SQL program, the whole thing is executing in the RDBMS.

Another thing to note is that it would be tough to rewrite this procedure to deal with a multiplicity of database tables. Suppose you decided to have a separate table for each discussion group. So you had photo_35mm_bboard and photo_medium_format_bboard tables. Then you'd just add a v_table_name argument to the procedure. But what about these local variable declarations?

```
bboard_record bboard%ROWTYPE;
```

This says, "Set up the local variable bboard_record so that it can hold a row from the bboard table." No problem. You just replace the static bboard with the new argument

```
bboard_record v_table_name%ROWTYPE;
```

and voilà... you get a compiler error: "v_table_name could not be found in the database." All of the declarations have to be computable at compile time. The spirit of PL/SQL is to give the compiler enough information at procedure definition time so that you won't have any errors at run-time.

You're not in Kansas anymore and you're not Web scripting either. This is programming. You're declaring variables. You're using a compiler that will be all over you like a cheap suit if you type a variable name incorrectly. Any formally trained computer scientist should be in heaven. Well, yes and no. Strongly typed languages like ADA and Pascal result in more reliable code. This is great if you are building a complicated program like a fighter jet target tracking system. But when you're writing a Web page that more or less stands by itself, being forced to dot all the i's and cross all the t's can be an annoying hindrance. After all, since almost all the variables are going to be strings and you're just gluing them together, what's the point of declaring types?

I don't think it is worth getting religious over which is the better approach. For one thing, as discussed in Chapter 11, Sites that Are Really Databases, this is the easy part of building a relational database–backed Web site. You've developed your data model, defined your transactions, and designed your user interface. You're engaged in an almost mechanical translation process. For another, if you were running AOLserver with Oracle as the back-end database, you could have the best of both worlds by writing simple Tcl procedures that called PL/SQL functions. We would touch up the definition bbd_fetch_msg so that it was designed as a PL/SQL *function,* which can return a value, rather than as a procedure, which is called for effect. Then instead of htp.print, we'd simply RETURN the string. We could interface it to the Web with a five-line AOLserver Tcl function:

```
# grab the input and set it to Tcl local variable MSG_ID
set_form_variables

# get an open database connection from AOLserver
set db [ns_db gethandle]

# grab one row from the database.  Note that we're using the
# Oracle dummy table DUAL because we're only interested in the
# function value and not in any information from actual tables.
set selection [ns_db 1row $db "select bbd_fetch_msg('$msg_id') as
        moby_string from dual"]

# Since we told the ns_db API call that we only expected
# one row back, it put the row directly into the SELECTION
# variable and we don't have to call ns_db getrow
set moby_string [ns_set get selection moby_string]

# we call the AOLserver API call ns_return to
# say "status code 200; MIME type is text/html"
# and then send out the page
ns_return 200 text/html $moby_string
```

APPLICATION SERVERS

Application servers for Web publishing are generally systems that let you write database-backed Web pages in Java. The key selling points of these systems, which sell for as much as $35,000 per CPU, are increased reliability, performance, and speed of development.

Problem 1: Compilation

Java, because it must be compiled, is usually a bad choice of programming languages for Web services (see Chapter 10 on server-side programming). Thus, *an application server increases development time.*

Problem 2:
Java runs inside the DBMS now

If what you really want to do is write some Java code that talks to data in your database, you can execute Java right inside of your RDBMS (Oracle 8.1, Informix 9.x). Java executing inside the database server's process is always going to have faster access to table data than Java running as a client. In fact, at least with Oracle on a Unix box, you can bind port 80 to a program that will call a Java program running in the Oracle RDBMS. You don't even need a Web server, much less an application server. It is possible that you'll get higher performance and easier development by adding a thin-layer Web server like AOLserver or Microsoft's IIS/ASP, but certainly you can't get higher reliability by adding a bunch of extra programs and computers to a system that need only have relied on one program and one computer.

An application server reduces Web site speed and reliability.

Problem 3: Nonstandard API

Application servers encourage publishers to write Java code to nonstandard specifications. If you really want to build a Web site in Java, use the Java Servlet standard, so that you can run the same code under AOLserver, Apache, Microsoft IIS, Netscape Enterprise, and Sun Java Server.

One nice thing

Because compiling Java is so difficult, application servers out of necessity usually enforce a hard separation between people who do design (build templates) and those who write programs to query the database (write and compile Java programs). Generally, people can only argue about things they understand. Thus, a bunch of business executives will approve a $1 billion nuclear power plant without any debate, but argue for hours about whether the company should spend $500 on a party. They've all thrown parties before, so they have an idea that maybe paper cups can

be purchased for less than $2.75 per 100. But none of them has any personal experience purchasing cooling towers.

Analogously, if you show a super-hairy transactional Web service to a bunch of folks in positions of power at a big company, they aren't going to say, "I think you would get better linguistics performance if you kept a denormalized copy of the data in the Unix file system and indexed it with PLS." Nor are they likely to opine that "You should probably upgrade to Solaris 2.6 because Sun rewrote the TCP stack to better handle 100-plus simultaneous threads." Neither will they look at your SQL queries and say, "You could clean this up by using the Oracle tree extensions; look up CONNECT BY in the manual."

What they will say is "I think that page should be a lighter shade of mauve." In an application server-backed site, this can be done by a graphic designer editing a template, and the Java programmer need never be aware of the change.

Do you need to pay $35,000 per CPU to get this kind of separation of "business logic" from presentation? No. You can download AOLserver for free and send your staff the following message:

Note:
PC Week tested Netscape Application Server and Sapphire/Web on June 22, 1998 and found that they weren't able to support more than 10 simultaneous users on a $200,000 eight-CPU Sun SPARC/Solaris E4000 server. Not only did the products crash frequently, but sometimes in such innovative ways that they had to reboot the whole computer (something done once every 30 to 90 days on a typical Unix server).

```
To: Web Developers

I want you to put all the SQL queries into Tcl functions that get
loaded at server startup time.  The graphic designers are to build
ADP pages that call a Tcl procedure, which will set a bunch of local
variables with values from the database. They are then to stick in
the ADP page wherever they want one of the variables to appear.

Alternatively, write .tcl scripts that implement the business logic
and, after stuffing a bunch of local vars, call ns_adp_parse to drag
in the ADP created by the graphic designer.
```

Similarly, if you've got Windows NT, you can just use Active Server Pages with a similar directive to the developers: "Put the SQL queries in a COM object and call it at the top of an ASP page; then reference the values returned within the HTML." Again, you save $35,000 per CPU, and both AOLserver and Active Server Pages have much cleaner templating syntax than the application server products.

Furthermore, if there are parts of your Web site that don't have elaborate presentation, such as admin pages, you can just have the programmers code them up using standard AOLserver .tcl or .adp style (where the queries are mixed in with HTML).

Finally, you can use the Web standards to separate design from presentation. With the 4.x browsers, it is possible to pack a surprising amount of design into a cascading style sheet. If your graphic designers are satisfied with this level of power, your dynamic pages can pump out rat-simple HTML.

From my own experience, some kind of templating discipline is useful on about 25 percent of the pages in a typical transactional site. Which 25 percent? The pages that are viewed by the public (and hence get extensively designed and redesigned) and also require at least a screen or two of procedural language statements or SQL. Certainly templating is merely an annoyance when building admin pages, which are almost always plain text. Maybe that's why I find application servers so annoying; there are usually a roughly equal number of admin and user pages on the sites that I build.

Note:
For a more detailed discussion of application servers, see *http://photo.net /wtr/application -servers.html.*

SERVER-SIDE WEB/RDBMS PRODUCTS THAT WORK

Let's try to generally categorize the tools that are available. This may sound a little familiar if you've recently read the options and axes for evaluating server-side scripting languages and environments that I set forth in Chapter 10, Sites that Are Really Programs. However, there are some new twists to consider when an RDBMS is in the background.

Before selecting a tool, you must decide how much portability you need. For example, the PL/SQL script discussed earlier (page 380) will work only with the Oracle RDBMS. The AOLserver Tcl scripts at page 378 would work with any RDBMS if SQL were truly a standard. However, Oracle handles datetime arithmetic and storage in a nonstandard way. So if you wanted to move an AOLserver Tcl application to Informix or some other product that uses ANSI-standard datetime syntax, you'd most likely have to edit any script that used datetime columns. If you were using Java Servlets and JDBC, in theory you could code in pure ANSI SQL and the JDBC driver would translate it into Oracle SQL.

Why not always use the tools that give the most portability? Because portability involves abstraction and layers. It may be more difficult to develop and debug portable code. For example, my friend Jin built some Web-based hospital information systems for a company that wants to be able to sell to hospitals with all kinds of different database management systems. So he coded it in Java/JDBC and the Sun JavaWebServer. Though he was already an experienced Java programmer, he found that it took him 10 times longer to write something portable in this environment than it does to write AOLserver Tcl that is Oracle-specific. I'd rather write ten times as many applications and be stuck with Oracle than labor over portable applications that will probably have to be redesigned in a year anyway.

Speaking of labor, you have to look around realistically at the programming and sysadmin resources available for your project. Some tools are clearly designed for MIS departments with 3-year development schedules and 20-programmer teams. If you have two programmers and a three-month schedule, you might not even have enough resources to read the manuals and install the tool. If you are willing to bite the bullet, you might eventually find that these tools help you build complex applications with some client-side software. If you aren't willing to bite the bullet, the other end of this spectrum is populated by "litely augmented HTML for idiots" systems. These are the most annoying Web tools because the developers invariably leave out things that you desperately need and, because their "litely augmented HTML" isn't a general purpose programming language, you can't build what you need yourself.

AOLserver

All of the sites that I build these days are done with AOLserver, which has been tested at more than 20,000 production sites since May 1995 (when it was called NaviServer). I have personally used AOLserver for more than 100 popular RDBMS-backed services (together they are responding to about 400 requests a second as I'm writing this sentence). AOLserver provides the following mechanisms for generating dynamic pages:

- CGI, mostly good for using packaged software or supporting legacy apps

- Java Servlets

- a gateway to ATG's Dynamo system (Java embedded in HTML pages)

- AOLserver Dynamic Pages (ADP; Tcl embedded in HTML pages)

- "*.tcl" Tcl procedures that are sourced by the server each time a URL is requested

- Tcl procedures that you can register to arbitrary URLs, loaded at server startup and after explicitly reinitializing Tcl

- Tcl procedures that you can register to run before or after serving particular URLs

- C functions loaded into the server at startup time

The last five mechanisms provide access to the AOLserver's continuously connected pools of connections to relational databases and thus provide users with the fastest possible Web service.

I personally have never needed to use the C API and don't really want to run the attendant risk that an error in my little program will crash the entire AOLserver. The AOL folks swear that their thousands of novice internal developers find the gentle-slope programming of ADPs vastly more useful than the .tcl pages. I personally prefer the .tcl pages for most of my applications. My text editor (Emacs) has a convenient mode for editing Tcl, but I'd have to write one for editing ADP pages. I don't really like the software development cycle of "sourced at startup" Tcl, but I use it for applications like my comment server where I want DB-backed URLs that look like /com/philg/foobar.html ("philg" and "foobar.html" are actually arguments to a procedure). These are very useful when you want a site to be dynamic and yet indexed by search engines that turn their backs on CGI-like URLs. I've used the filter system to check cookie headers for authorization information and grope around in the RDBMS before instructing AOLserver to proceed either with serving a static page or with serving a login page.

You can build manageable complex systems in AOLserver by building a large library of Tcl procedures that are called by ADP or Tcl pages. If that isn't sufficient, you can write additional C modules and load them in at run-time.

AOLserver has its shortcomings, the first of which is that there is no support for sessions or session variables. This makes it more painful to implement things like shopping carts or areas in which users must authenticate themselves. Since I've always had an RDBMS in the background, I've never really wanted to have my Web server manage session state. I just use a few lines of Tcl code to read and write IDs in magic cookies.

The second shortcoming of AOLserver is that, though it started life as a commercial product (NaviServer), the current development focus is internal AOL consumption. This is good because it means you can be absolutely sure that the software works; it is the cornerstone of AOL's effort to convert their 11-million–user service to standard Web protocols. This is bad because it means that AOL is only investing in things that are useful for that conversion effort. Thus, there aren't any new versions for Windows NT. I've found the AOLserver development team to be much more responsive to bug reports than any of the other vendors on which I rely. However, they've gone out of the handholding business. If you want support, you'll have to get it for free from the developer's mailing list or purchase it from a third party (coincidentally, my own company is an authorized AOLserver support provider: *http:// www.arsdigita.com/aolserver-support.html*).

You can test out AOLserver right now by visiting *www.aol.com,* one of the world's most heavily accessed Web sites. Virtually the entire site consists of dynamically evaluated ADP pages.

Apache

Ex Apache semper aliquid novi.
—Pliny the Hacker, *Historia Digitalis,* II, viii, 42, c. AD 77

"Out of Apache, there is always something new."

The folks who wrote Apache weren't particularly interested in or experienced with relational database management systems. However, they gave away their source code and hence people who were RDBMS wizards have given us a constant stream of modules that, taken together, provide virtually all of the AOLserver goodies. By cobbling together code from *http://modules.apache.org,* a publisher can have a server that

- authenticates from a relational database

- runs scripting languages without forking

- pools database connections

- serves HTML with an embedded scripting language

Rather than stew at the end of a 24×7 support line, the publisher can hire a programmer to wade into the source code and fix a bug or add a feature.

Personally, I don't use Apache. I have a big library of AOLserver code that works reliably. I don't want to look at someone else's C code unless I absolutely have to.

Microsoft Active Server Pages

Active Server Pages (ASP) are a gentle-slope Web scripting system. An HTML document is a legal ASP page. By adding a few special characters, you can escape into Visual Basic, JavaScript, or other languages such as Perl (via plug-ins). If you edit an ASP page, you can test the new version simply by reloading it from a browser. You don't have to compile it or manually reload it into Internet Information Server (IIS). Microsoft claims that IIS does "automatic database connection pooling." You ought to be able to use almost any RDBMS with ASP, and all the communication is done via ODBC (discussed in the last two sections of this chapter), so you won't have to change your code too much to move from Solid to Sybase, for example.

ASPs can invoke more or less any of the services of a Windows NT box via Microsoft's proprietary COM, DCOM, and ActiveX systems. The downside of all of this is that you're stuck with NT forever and won't be able to port to a Unix system if your service outgrows NT. Microsoft maintains some reasonably clear pages on ASP at *http://www.microsoft.com/iis/*.

Don't switch

You can build a working Web site in AOLserver, Apache, or IIS/ASP. If you read an advertisement for what sounds like a superior product, ignore it. However superior this new product is, be sure that it will probably be a mistake to switch. Once you build up a library of software and expertise in Tool X, you're better off ignoring Tools Y and Z for at least a few years. You know all of the bugs and pitfalls of Tool X. All you know about Tools Y and Z is how great the hype sounds. Being out of date is unfashionable, but so is having a down Web server, which is what most of the leading edgers will have.

How much can it cost you to be out of date? Amazon.com has a market capitalization of $5.75 billion (August 10, 1998). They built their site with compiled C CGI scripts connecting to a relational database. You could not pick a tool with a less convenient development cycle. You could not pick a tool with lower performance (forking CGI then opening a connection to the RDBMS). They worked around the slow development cycle by hiring very talented programmers. They worked around the inefficiencies of CGI by purchasing massive Unix boxes ten times larger than necessary. Wasteful? Sure. But insignificant compared to the value of the company that they built by *focusing on the application and not fighting bugs in some award-winning Web connectivity tool programmed by idiots and tested by no one.*

Things that I left out and why

Netscape is unique in that they offer a full selection of the worst ideas in server-side Web programming. In May of 1997, I looked at Netscape's server products and plans, and wrote the following to a friend:

Netscape would be out of the server tools business tomorrow if Microsoft ported IIS/ASP to Unix and/or if NT were more reliable and easier to maintain remotely.

Since then Netscape has acquired Kiva and renamed it Netscape Application Server. A friend of mine runs a Web server complex with 15 Unix boxes, multiple firewalls, multiple RDBMS installations, and dozens of Web sites containing custom software. His number-one daily headache and source of unreliability? Netscape Application Server.

Nobody has anything bad to say about Allaire's Cold Fusion, but I can't see that it offers any capabilities beyond what you get with Microsoft's ASP. History has not been kind to people who compete against the Microsoft monopoly, particularly those whose products aren't dramatically better.

I used to take delight in lampooning the ideas of the RDBMS vendors. But since they never even learned enough about the Internet to understand why they were being ridiculed, it stopped being fun. The prevailing wisdom in Silicon Valley is that most companies have only one good idea. Microsoft's idea was to make desktop apps. They've made a reasonably good suite of desktop apps and inflicted misery on the world with virtually everything else they've brought to market (most of which started out as some other company's product, e.g., SQL Server was Sybase, Internet Explorer was NCSA Mosaic, DOS was Tim Paterson's 86–DOS). Netscape's idea was to make a browser. They made a great browser and pathetic server-side stuff. The RDBMS vendors' idea was to copy the System R relational database developed by IBM's San Jose research lab. They all built great copies of IBM's RDBMS server and implementations of IBM's SQL language. Generally everything else they build is shockingly bad, from documentation to development tools to administration tools.

BRING IN 'DA NOISE, BRING IN 'DA JUNK

Now that everything is connected, maybe you don't want to talk to your RDBMS through your Web server. You may want to use standard spreadsheet-like tools. There may even be a place for (dare I admit it?) junkware/middleware. First a little context.

An RDBMS-backed Web site is updated by thousands of users "out there" and a handful of people "back here." The users out there participate in a small number of structured transactions, for each of which it is practical to write a series of Web forms. The people back here have less predictable requirements. Perhaps they might need to fix a typo in a magazine title stored in the database or delete a bunch of half-completed records because the forms-processing code wasn't as good about checking for errors as it should have been.

Every RDBMS-backed Web site should have a set of admin pages. These provide convenient access for the webmasters when they want to do things like purge stale threads from discussion groups. But unless you are clairvoyant and can anticipate webmaster needs two years from now, or you want to spend the rest of your life writing admin pages that only a couple of coworkers will see, it is probably worth coming up with a way for webmasters to maintain the data in the RDBMS without your help.

Canned Web server admin pages

Some RDBMS/Web tools provide fairly general access to the database right from a Web browser. AOLserver, for example, provides some clunky tools that let the webmaster browse and edit tables. These won't work, though, if you need to do JOINs to see your data, as you will if your data model holds user email addresses and user phone numbers in separate tables. Also, if you would like the webmasters to do things in structured ways, involving updates to several tables, then these kinds of standardized tools won't work.

Spreadsheet-like access

Fortunately, the RDBMS predates the Web. There is a whole class of programs that will make the data in the database look like a spreadsheet. This isn't all that difficult because, as discussed in the previous chapter, a relational database really is just a collection of spreadsheet tables. A spreadsheet-like program can make it very convenient to make small, unanticipated changes. Microsoft Excel and Microsoft Access can both be used to view and update RDBMS data in a spreadsheet-like manner.

Forms builders

If you need more structure and user interface, then you might want to consider the junkware/middleware tools discussed in Chapter 11, Sites that Are Really Databases. There are literally thousands of these tools for Macintosh and Windows machines

that purport to save you from the twin horrors of typing SQL and programming user interface code in C. With middleware/junkware, it is easy to build forms by example and wire them to RDBMS tables. These forms are then intended to be used by, say, telephone sales operators typing at Windows boxes. If you're going to go to the trouble of installing a Web server and Web browsers on all the user machines, you'll probably just want to make HTML forms and server-side scripts to process them. Some of the people who sell these "easy forms for SQL" programs have realized this, as well, and provide an option to "save as a bunch of HTML and Web scripts." The plus side of these forms packages is that they often make it easy to add a lot of input validation. The down side of forms packages is that the look and user interface might be rather clunky and standardized. You probably won't win any awards if you generate your public pages this way.

Connecting

Both spreadsheet-like database editors and the applications generated by "easy forms" systems connect directly to the RDBMS from a PC or a Macintosh. This probably means that you'll need additional user licenses for your RDBMS, one for each programmer or Web content maintainer. In the bad old days, if you were using a forms building package supplied by, say, Oracle, then the applications generated would get compiled with the Oracle C library and would connect directly to Oracle. These applications wouldn't work with any other brand of database management system. If you'd bought any third party software packages, they'd also talk directly to Oracle using Oracle protocols. Suppose you installed a huge data entry system, then decided that you'd like the same operators to be able to work with another division's relational database. You typed the foreign division server's IP address and port numbers into your configuration files and tried to connect. Oops. It seems that the other division had chosen Sybase. It would cost you hundreds of thousands of dollars to port your forms specifications over to some product that would generate applications compiled with the Sybase C library.

From your perspective, Oracle and Sybase were interchangeable: Clients put SQL in; clients get data out. Why should you have to care about differences in their C libraries? Well, Microsoft had the same thought about five years ago and came up with an *abstraction barrier* between application code and databases called ODBC. Well-defined abstraction barriers have been the most powerful means of controlling software complexity ever since the 1950s. An abstraction barrier isolates different levels and portions of a software system. In a programming language like Lisp, you don't have to know how lists are represented. The language itself presents an abstraction barrier of public functions for creating lists and then extracting their elements. The details are hidden and the language implementers are therefore free to change the implementation in future releases because there is no way for you to depend on the details. Very badly engineered products, like DOS or Windows, have poorly defined abstraction barriers. That means that almost every useful application program written for DOS or Windows depends intimately on the details of those operating systems. It means more work for Microsoft programmers because they can't clean up the guts of the system, but paradoxically a monopoly software supplier can make more money if its products are badly engineered in this way. If every program a user has bought requires specific internal structures in your operating system, there isn't too much danger of the user switching operating systems.

Relational databases, per se, were engineered by IBM with a wonderful abstraction barrier: Structured Query Language (SQL). The whole raison d'être of SQL is that application programs shouldn't have to be aware of how the database management system is laying out records. In some ways, IBM did a great job. Just ask Oracle. They were able to take away most of the market from IBM. Even when Oracle was tiny, their customers knew that they could safely invest in developing SQL applications. After all, if Oracle tanked or the product didn't work, they could just switch over to an RDBMS from IBM.

Unfortunately, IBM didn't quite finish the job. They didn't say whether or not the database had to have a client/server architecture and run across a network. They didn't say exactly what sequence of bytes would constitute a request for a new connection. They didn't say how the bytes of the SQL should be shipped across or the data shipped back. They didn't say how a client would note that it only expected to receive one row back or how a client would say, "I don't want to read any more rows from that last SELECT." So the various vendors developed their own ways of doing these things and wrote libraries of functions that applications programmers could call when they wanted their COBOL, Fortran, or C programs to access the database.

ODBC

It fell to Microsoft to lay down a standard abstraction barrier in January 1993: Open Database Connectivity (ODBC). Then companies like Intersolv (*www.intersolv.com*) released ODBC drivers. These are programs that run on the same computer as the would-be database client, usually a PC. When the telephone operator's forms application wants to get some data, it doesn't connect directly to Oracle. Instead, it calls the ODBC driver, which makes the Oracle connection. In theory, switching over to Sybase is as easy as installing the ODBC driver for Sybase. Client programs have two options for issuing SQL through ODBC. If the client program uses ODBC SQL, then ODBC will abstract away the minor but annoying differences in SQL syntax that have crept into various products. If the client program wants to use a special feature of a particular RDBMS, like Oracle Context, then it can ask ODBC to pass the SQL directly to the database management system. Finally, ODBC supposedly allows access even to primitive flat-file databases like FoxPro and dBASE.

You'd expect programs like Microsoft Access to be able to talk via ODBC to various and sundry databases. However, this flexibility has become so important that even vendors like Oracle and Informix have started to incorporate ODBC interfaces in their fancy client programs. Thus you can use an Oracle-brand client program to connect to an Informix or Sybase RDBMS server.

The point here is not that you need to rush out to set up all the database client development tools that they use at Citibank. Just keep in mind that your Web server doesn't have to be your only RDBMS client.

SUMMARY

- It takes a long time to fork a CGI process and watch it connect to an RDBMS server; fast Web sites are built with already connected database clients.

- Running a relational database is a security risk; you may not want to allow anyone on the Internet to connect directly as a client to your RDBMS server.

- Writing the HTML/SQL bridge code in Perl, Tcl, or Visual Basic is straightforward.

- Encapsulating SQL queries in Java, CORBA, or COM objects will make your site slower, less reliable, more expensive to develop, and more difficult to debug or extend.

- Most Web/RDBMS software does not perform as advertised and will shackle you to an incompetent and uncaring vendor; just say "No" to middleware (becoming my personal "Delenda est Carthago").

- One of the nice things about using an RDBMS, the standard tool of business data processing since the late 1970s, is that you can just say "Yes" to off-the-shelf software packages if you need to do something standard behind the scenes of your Web site.

MORE

- Chapter 15, Case Studies, documents a number of AOLserver/ Oracle–backed sites, with full source code that's mostly available for download from *http://arsdigita.com.*

- See *www.php.net* for examples of server-side scripting with Open Source tools.

- *Professional Active Server Pages* (Homer et al., 1997; Wrox Press) will introduce you to the dark side.

- I think you'll enjoy reading my application server article at *http://photo.net /wtr/application-servers.html,* if only to prove to yourself that all the smart people in your college class really did go into law and medicine.

14

ecommerce

"Electronic commerce" conjures up visions of product catalog sites and shopping baskets, things that were passé back in 1995. Why then a chapter on ecommerce?

First, because so few people are doing it right. A friend of mine said that he wouldn't buy an airplane ticket from the United Airlines Web site. He wasn't paranoid about his credit card number being compromised. Drawing an inference from their sluggish and badly programmed Web service, he didn't believe that his reservation would be made or a ticket issued.

Second, because people are spending obscene amounts of money to do trivial things. Sometimes the money is spent on buying packaged junkware and then on figuring out how to debug/integrate it. Sometimes the money is spent on madly writing, compiling, and debugging Java programs that replicate capabilities already present in sets of Perl or Tcl scripts three years ago.

Finally, because even a bland ecommerce site may occasionally blossom into an interesting site with community or Web service angles.

STEP 1: DECIDE IF YOU'RE SERIOUS AND RESPONSIBLE

Curious to see if some intervening months had sufficed for United Airlines to get their programming act together, I tried to buy a ticket online on April 22, 1998. Even at 2:00 A.M., the site was sluggish, to be sure, but I managed to find a $300 San Francisco/Boston roundtrip. When I tried to buy the ticket, I got a server error message with instructions to try later. A few hours later, the site was operational but the $300 fare was no longer listed. I called United and they said they'd be happy to sell me a ticket, but it would be $1,900. The $300 fare had only been available earlier in the day. When I noted that the only thing that had prevented me from buying the ticket was their broken site and would they consider honoring the fare, they said I should call their customer relations number, which I did. I reached a recording that said, "32-10 you have dialed an invalid number."

Ultimately I did reach customer relations, where they also refused to honor the fare, mumbling something about how the Web was just an experimental thing, anyway. In one transaction, United had managed to simultaneously demonstrate incompetence and unwillingness to take responsibility for its incompetence.

Can you learn from United's mistakes? Yes. Before you set up an ecommerce site, decide (1) whether you are serious about building a working service and (2) whether you are going to take responsibility for your programming and administration mistakes.

STEP 2: THINK ABOUT YOUR ACCOUNTING SYSTEM

Though one of my leitmotifs is "packaged software probably won't solve your problem," accounting software is an exception. Web services tend to be new and varied. It would be a hopeless fantasy for me to go down to CompUSA and try to buy a birthday reminder server that accomplishes what the custom Tcl/SQL scripts at *http:// www.arsdigita.com/remindme/* do. But if ArsDigita, LLC wanted to keep track of invoices, payments, and taxes, it would be insane to write an accounting system from scratch. Our Web publishing goals aren't shared by too many other people, but our accounting problem is the same as that of any other business.

Thus, at the end of the day, you're going to have a custom-developed Web application talking to a standard accounting system of some sort. If the accounting system is powerful and running out of the same RDBMS installation as the Web site, then you might well not need to confront any of the allegedly tough ecommerce technology decisions.

STEP 3: WHERE DO YOU PARK THE DATABASE?

In the past four years, a particular kind of ecommerce site development project seems to cross my desk repeatedly. A manufacturing company has been selling to retailers for decades. The Web site will be the first time that they've sold directly to customers. Customers will get the ability to order semicustom products and the factory will get real-time access to information about what customers want.

An obvious first cut at the problem involves three database installations:

1. an RDBMS on the Web server to hold catalog info, user personalization information, and orders

2. an RDBMS at a bank or service bureau that holds credit card numbers to be billed

3. an RDBMS in the factory that collects orders in batches from the Web server

There are some good things about this solution. You aren't responsible for keeping customer credit card numbers secure. Data that are needed for real-time decisions are kept close to the programs that use the data.

Suppose, however, that the Web server needs a lot of data from the factory tables before it can offer delivery information. It is possible to keep copies of the necessary factory tables in the Web server's RDBMS. Every time an update or insert is made on the factory RDBMS, the transaction is duplicated on the Web server RDBMS. This is called *database replication* and companies like Oracle produce software to facilitate replication. However, you have to budget extra time and money to develop and maintain a replication strategy. So you might consider eliminating the RDBMS next to the Web server and configuring the Web server program to make an encrypted connection to the factory RDBMS.

Suppose that you are quickly turning out custom goods. You can't wait for batches of orders to be sent to the factory because products are supposed to be built and shipped on the same day as orders placed before 2:00 P.M. This means that the factory RDBMS must have rapid access to the relevant tables from the Web server RDBMS. Again, you have the option of replication or eliminating the factory

database installation and having the factory client programs talk directly to the Web server RDBMS.

Suppose that you want to offer customers the option to "bill the same credit card as on your last order, ending in 4561." In that case, you either need to keep the old credit card numbers yourself or have some means of communication between your database and your transaction vendor (bank).

Suppose that your accounting system can run the credit card numbers. In that case, you will probably want to eliminate the RDBMS at the bank and tightly couple the Web site to whatever RDBMS installation is running the accounting system.

There are no correct answers to the questions "how many RDBMS installations and where are they" but you need to address them nonetheless.

STEP 4: LIFETIME CUSTOMER VALUE MANAGEMENT

Companies that are selling direct for the first time will immediately realize that they now have access to their dream data. They can figure out, down to the individual consumer, who is buying what and how often. About two days after the business folks realize this, they will turn to the nerds and say, "Build us a lifetime customer value management system."

The "lifetime" in the above phrase reflects the fact that you have to engineer the system to track particular customers' activities over many years. As soon as Joe Smith shows up on the site, you need to know how many times this person has placed an order, returned a product, demanded a refund, come to the site and not ordered, ad infinitum.

The engineering in a system like this is a straightforward matter of SQL tables and Web scripts. What's hard are the business rules. Here are some examples:

- Rachael Supergreat has ordered 10 times before. Though we're running low on inventory, push her order to the front of the list and quote her a 24-hour delivery time.

- Tristan Pretty Good has ordered once before. However, it was a year ago, so he's probably not going to turn into the best possible customer. If the factory is behind schedule, quote him a three-week delivery time and see if he still wants to place the order.

- Phoebe Unknown has never ordered before. She might become a very valuable customer, so give her order medium priority and quote her a one-week delivery time. We don't want to risk turning her away.

- David Difficult has ordered custom products eight times before and returned them each time. He did not include the original packing material on six of those returns and damaged the product cosmetically three times. Give him a "server busy, please try again later" page.

As a Web developer, I don't think there are customer value management *technical* issues that are distinct from those associated with personalization on noncommercial sites. But as a publisher or service designer, you should at least be aware that you'll have to spend a few weeks thinking about what rules to implement.

CASE STUDY: MIT PRESS

MIT Press is a publisher of books and academic journals. Since 1993, they'd been putting progressively more catalog info and content on their Web site, which was developed and maintained by Terry Ehling. She originally worked part time, but by 1996 being webmistress was a full-time job. In 1996, Terry came to me with the following goals for her Web site (*http://mitpress.mit.edu*):

- Serve up a catalog of 6,000 books and 40 journals in a consistent fashion; the existing collection of static files was becoming too cumbersome to maintain.

- Collect comments on the catalog items.

- Collect names and contact information for readers who wished to be on various mailing lists.

- Collect orders for products.

- Allow MIT Press personnel to spam groups of readers with announcements, e.g., "those readers who've signed up to the cognitive science mailing list".

Decision 1: How much to change the business?

MIT Press maintained overlapping catalog data in several separate systems. Their accounting/ordering system was a turnkey software package for academic publishers. It was coded originally for the Data General Nova, 16-bit minicomputer. As these computers were no longer manufactured, the software was running on an IBM PC emulating the old Nova instruction set. To someone raised in the Oracle/Unix tradition, this sounds kind of insane, but in fact nearly all academic publishers run the same software. None of them do enough volume to justify developing a replacement package. Anyway, this turnkey system had some information on each book. The production folks had a FoxPro database with information on current and past projects. The legacy Web site had pretty good information on the last few years' worth of books, but these data were merely arranged in Unix file system files.

Installing and maintaining an RDBMS is a fair amount of work. If we were going to all that trouble to make the Web service work, it seemed like a good idea to eventually run production and accounting from the same database. Of course, what seems like a good idea to an engineer doesn't always seem like a good idea to a business person. The management of the Press wasn't ready to consider fundamental changes to the rest of the business.

One side effect of this decision was that it got us out of the online credit card verification business. We'd just have to pipe credit card numbers along with orders to the existing accounting system and let those folks handle them the way they handled other credit card orders. If a customer gave us a bad number, we'd email him.

Decision 2: Shopping baskets?

A primary purpose of the Web site was to facilitate online shopping. Everyone else on the Internet at the time was implementing shopping-basket systems. I had built some for clients in 1995, but by 1996 had soured on the idea. It wouldn't have been a horrible concept if every site used the same shopping cart system. But each site had its own user interface. Why should you have to learn how to "check out" when all you wanted was one book?

I argued for an invisible shopping cart. A user would click on a product and get an order form. After submitting it with shipping address and credit card number, a magic cookie would be written back to his browser. The user would be offered the opportunity to continue shopping. If he clicked on an "order" link again, he'd be offered the opportunity to add the item to his previous order. The system would degrade gracefully. If the user's browser didn't adhere to the Netscape magic cookie spec, he'd still be able to place orders for products, but it would be a little more cumbersome. If an order had already been transmitted to the old Data General Nova system, then the user wouldn't be offered the "add to old order" option. If the user quit his browser and restarted, he wouldn't get the "add to old order" option.

We decided to go for the invisible cart. Orders initiated the previous day would be transmitted in a batch from the RDBMS to the legacy system every morning at 7:00 A.M. That meant a user had between 7 and 31 hours to complete an order using the invisible cart.

Choosing technology

We elected to use AOLserver talking to the Illustra database. MIT Press had a puny SPARC 5 Web server and had not budgeted for a larger machine, yet we knew that we'd have to serve about 200,000 hits a day from this computer, some of them requiring RDBMS queries. I knew from bitter experience that Illustra would not scale very well and that it was likely to periodically wedge itself. However, I had a fairly good-sized library of AOLserver Tcl scripts with embedded Illustra queries, the PLS Blade for Illustra was a brilliantly useful tool, and MIT Press did not have the budget to install or maintain an enterprise-class RDBMS such as Oracle.

Moving the legacy data

It turns out that working in the publishing world is a programmer's dream. The industry has been forced for many years to key everything by the International Standard Book Number (ISBN). So there are very few thorny data modeling issues.

To avoid typing 6,000 book titles, we got a text-file dump of the data in the Data General Nova system. Then we wrote some Perl scripts to convert these into SQL inserts and fed the whole batch to Illustra's Unix shell client. We wrote some AOLserver Tcl scripts to semiautomatically transfer over book jacket images and long descriptions from files on the old Web server. We decided not to store book and journal images in the RDBMS. Instead, we kept a Unix file system directory for each catalog item. For books, the AOLserver Tcl script would look in the directory for `cover-sm.gif` or `cover-sm.jpg`. If present, it would be displayed on the book catalog page (see *http://mitpress.mit.edu/book-home.tcl?isbn=0262650398*). If not, we'd serve a page with a slightly different design (see *http://mitpress.mit.edu/book-home.tcl?isbn=0262560631*).

Integrating the graphics

MIT Press brought Ben Williams (*www.blueperiod.com*) up from New York to do the graphic design. I showed him that each book page had the following computational structure:

1. Query the `books` table for basic title and description for the ISBN key in the URL.

2. Stream out the top part of the catalog page.

3. Query the `reader_comments` table to pull out reader comments for display right on the page.

4. Stream out the reader comments, if any.

5. Query the `books` table again to find related items, such as a paperbound version of the same title.

6. Stream out the related items (as hyperlinks).

7. Do an expensive LIKE query against the `books` table to find other books by the same author(s).

8. If found, stream out the list of books.

I explained that, of the four queries, the last one would take the longest. If we wanted to have a site that felt responsive, we'd absolutely have to avoid making the entire page an HTML table. The user shouldn't notice that the LIKE query was taking a second or two, because he'd be reading the top part of the page.

Ben eventually figured it all out and designed a beautiful-looking site with stacked tables. The first table contained the information from the first three RDBMS queries and the last contained the "books by the same author" content plus the page footer. It was fast and looked great. Despite my general blame-the-graphic-designer philosophy, I had to admit that overall it was a huge improvement.

Note:
I went over to *http://mitpress.mit.edu* just now (August 10, 1998) to make sure of exactly where in the page Ben had put in the split table. I found that the site has been redesigned a bit since that meeting. Each book page is a navigation header plus one big HTML table so that the user stares at a blank screen while Illustra grinds. Oh well....

Maintaining the service

What's the bottom line? Site traffic has grown steadily, partly because of new content developed by Terry Ehling, Marney Smyth, and Ken Overton (MIT Press's current Web staff), but also because the catalog information is deeper and more complete. The product catalog turned out to be a failure as a community Web site; only a handful of readers commented on books. There is no obvious technical reason for this failure, since the comment facility is similar to that offered by amazon.com, where readers engage in lively debate (check the comments for *Database Backed Web Sites* at *http://www.amazon.com/exec/obidos/ISBN=1562765302*). It can't be explained by a total lack of reader interest, since nearly 1,000 readers per month are signing up to be notified of new books in various categories.

The invisible shopping-cart system and sending orders to the legacy system turned out to work just fine. The site has processed many thousands of orders without imposing an undue burden on folks at MIT Press.

The AOLserver/Illustra combination turned out to require minimal maintenance. MIT Press did not have to hire full-time computer science geeks, database administrators, or Unix system administrators. They've been able to concentrate almost all of their efforts on developing new Web content.

Should anyone be impressed by these results?

Yes! We put about four person-weeks of programming into the site and it has the same functional capabilities as amazon.com circa 1997 (Amazon had more than 10 full-time programmers). We did not waste server resources with CGI scripts that reopened the database, and hence MIT Press did not have to invest $150,000 in a monster Unix box. We did not use an application server or otherwise invest programmer resources in layers of abstraction to insulate the site from Illustra-specific SQL. Consequently, a variety of people without formal computer science backgrounds have been able to edit and adapt the AOLserver Tcl scripts to their needs, extend the administration section, or get me to swoop in and make the occasional surgical change.

It wouldn't be so impressive if there weren't so many folks out there who spend $1 million on infrastructure, packaged software, and software development before they can take their first order.

Could we do it in 1998 with packaged junkware?

There are many more ecommerce and catalog server packages available in 1998 than there were in 1996. Could we build the site now with packaged software? Perhaps, but not very elegantly. Though the MIT Press product line is very easy to character-ize formally (books have unique ISBNs and journals have unique ISSNs), there are some screwy items. The user interface would become horribly clunky if there weren't a clean way to present multivolume sets and relate paper and hardcover editions of the same title. There are also two completely separate categorization systems for books, one for ordinary consumers and one for professors seeking books to use as textbooks.

Each journal needs to have institutional, individual, and student subscription rates. Back issue prices need to be similarly trifold. Finally, there are separate prices for back issues that are double issues. In a turnkey catalog system, you'd probably have to represent one journal as nine separate products in order to offer these nine separate prices. That would mean MIT Press personnel would have to change journal titles or editorial board info in nine separate database rows.

Because we did not use packaged software, we were able to program in lots of shortcuts on the admin side. The administration home page for a book has the stuff you'd expect from a commercial software package, for example, links to all the orders for the book and the readers who've expressed interest in the book. But it also has one-click catalog maintenance shortcuts, like "Record this title as being out of print" or "Change the price by editing the old price here and hitting carriage return."

For the hard-core nerd

If you're a hard-core nerd, you'll probably be interested to read my annotated data model file: *http://photo.net/wtr/thebook/mitpress-data-model.txt.*

MIT Press summary

With good people, good management, reasonable goals, and reasonable judgment, we managed to develop, operate, and maintain a moderately high-volume and full-featured ecommerce system at minimal cost.

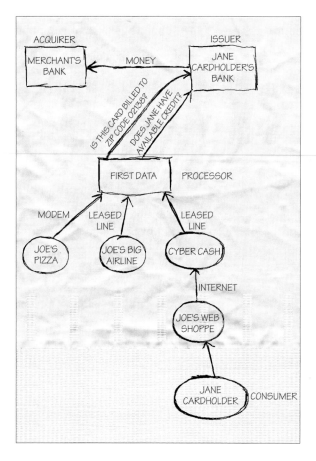

Labels in figure:

ACQUIRER — MERCHANT'S BANK

ISSUER — JANE CARDHOLDER'S BANK

MONEY

IS THIS CARD BILLED TO ZIP CODE 02138?

DOES JANE HAVE AVAILABLE CREDIT?

FIRST DATA   PROCESSOR

MODEM   LEASED LINE   LEASED LINE

JOE'S PIZZA   JOE'S BIG AIRLINE   CYBER CASH

INTERNET

JOE'S WEB SHOPPE

JANE CARDHOLDER   CONSUMER

Figure 14-1:
The processing
system.

MUNDANE DETAILS: RUNNING CREDIT CARDS

If you knew nothing about banking, you'd probably think that every bank in the world had a transaction server on a network. If a merchant wanted to figure out whether a credit card was valid or whether a cardholder's billing address was as stated, the merchant would send a packet of information to its favorite bank's server and that bank would come up with the answer, possibly doing queries to other bank's servers.

It turns out that banks never wanted to do anything like this. They left credit card processing to a handful of third-party companies such as First Data (*http://www.firstdata.com*), NOVA (*http://www.novainfo.com*), and Paymentech (*http://www.paymentech.com*). When a consumer's card gets swiped at the supermarket, the little terminal talks to NOVA, for example, and NOVA talks to the consumer's bank and the supermarket's bank. (See Figure 14-1.)

Okay, so now the obvious thing would be for each of these third-party companies to park a transaction server on the Internet. Then a merchant could choose to contact NOVA or Paymentech by sending encrypted packets rather than dialing up. But it apparently turned out that even NOVA and Paymentech didn't want to wade into the public Internet.

Drop a dime

The most direct and obvious way to bill credit cards is to stick a modem on the back of your Unix machine and have it dial up a credit card processor such as First Data. Your Web site looks to the world's banking system just like the pizza shop around the corner. If you want fast connections, you can get a frame relay or ISDN line to the processor. If you don't want to figure out the protocol that is being used by the little terminal in the pizza shop, you can pick up some software such as HKS's CCVS (see *http://www.hks.net*) for about $1,000.

One downside of this approach is that you'll be forced to maintain a highly secure Web server/database containing customer credit card numbers.

412

Two Internet architectures

For people who don't want to stick modems on the backs of their computers, there are companies like CyberCash (*http://www.cybercash.com*), ICOMS (*http://www.icoms.com*), and Verifone (*http://www.verifone.com*) that operate transaction servers that then talk to First Data, NOVA, or Paymentech (that then talk to the banks' computer systems).

CyberCash and ICOMS exemplify two very different Web service architectures. In the CyberCash case, the merchant server collects credit card numbers from consumers. The merchant server then talks to CyberCash to find out if the card is valid and bills the card. This lets the merchant offer the customer options like "Use the same credit card as your last order?" If the merchant becomes unhappy with CyberCash, this architecture lets the merchant switch transaction vendors without consumers ever knowing.

What's the downside of the CyberCash architecture? It imposes a programming and security burden on the merchant. For example, if the merchant's programmers aren't competent, customers may get billed for orders that are never entered or

shipped. Alternatively, orders may get entered for customers whose credit cards failed authorization. Customer credit card numbers may reside in the merchant database. So if the merchant's database is compromised, not only can the intruder determine who purchased what, but he will get a big table of credit card numbers as well.

The ICOMS architecture assumes that the merchant is incompetent to write programs. A merchant can only embed "digital offers" (little blocks of HTML) in static .html Web documents. As soon as the customer wants to add something to a shopping basket or place an order, the digital offers bounce the customer over to a transaction server run by ICOMS. ICOMS will eventually notify the merchant server that an order was placed. The big advantage of ICOMS is that you don't have to be constantly paranoid about security. Your customers' credit card number might be compromised, but it will be someone else's fault!

A big disadvantage of the ICOMS architecture is that your overall Web service may become unreliable and slow due to factors beyond the merchant's control. For example, under the CyberCash architecture, even if the merchant's server couldn't reach CyberCash, it could be programmed to continue to take orders and then process them in a batch when CyberCash became reachable again. But with ICOMS, the customer can't even type in a credit card number or address if ICOMS is down. Furthermore, it is the ICOMS server that offers customers a "use the same credit card as before" option. So the consumer becomes tied to the ICOMS network and not to the merchant. Finally, you might not be able to achieve your user interface and customer service pages goals with the ICOMS-style architecture.

If you're tempted to use the ICOMS architecture and let another server handle the collection of payment and shipping information, why not go whole-hog and let another server handle the distribution of sales information as well? If your payment pages don't need a custom flow, then maybe your whole shop doesn't need a custom flow. You can go over to *store.yahoo.com,* configure a shop using a Web browser, and pay them $100 a month to present offers and collect orders for you. Yahoo Store offers an interesting comment on the state of ecommerce:

> *Although Yahoo! Store supports real-time credit card authorizations through Cybercash,* **we do not recommend it for most merchants.** . . . *using Cybercash tends to be more trouble than it is worth.*
> — *http://store.yahoo.com/vw/cybercash.html* (August 10, 1998)

A gazillion vendors

If there are only two architectures, how come there are so many listings in *http:// www.yahoo.com/Business_and_Economy/Companies/Financial_Services/Transaction_ Clearing/*?

Some of these listings are deceptive in that they are really front ends to more basic services. If you don't want to grapple with CyberCash's CGI scripts, there are a few dozen ISPs and Web development companies who will sell you simpler, less general scripts. However, it is hard to tell from reading their Web sites that what they've developed is a 100-line Perl script and not a complete system to compete with CyberCash or Verifone.

An annoying future: The SET protocol

Since 1996, the credit card companies and banks have been working on the Secure Electronic Transaction (SET) protocol. If you're a practical-minded Web merchant, all you really need to know about SET is that it requires your customers to have a Web browser, credit card, special vWallet software, and a certificate issued by their bank. They will only be able to make purchases from their desktop machine where the vWallet software and certificate are installed. Your competitors will be selling to folks who have the Web browser and credit card. Your competitors' customers will be ordering from their desktop machines, friends' computers, network computers in public libraries, etcetera.

In the long run, the SET protocol could potentially bring the world closer to the "consumers dealing with merchants dealing with banks as peers on the Internet" model that you'd naively assume was the way everything had always worked. However, if you're a Web publisher, "potentially" and "long run" aren't very interesting ideas. Furthermore, all of the payment APIs to which you can write code in 1999 claim to be SET-compliant. So if the great SET day ever arrives, you might not have to change even one of your scripts.

An extra layer of transactions

Generally, you can rely on the relational database management system (RDBMS) sitting behind your Web service to handle transactions. You can tell Oracle to "change all of these things and if any of them fail, then undo all the changes and insertions that suceeded." Oracle is extremely reliable at rolling back transactions, but your Oracle system isn't capable of rolling back a change on an uncooperative foreign system, such as CyberCash's server or the First Data computer system into which your Web server dialed.

Suppose that you decide to implement the following architecture:

1. Check data from order form.

2. Make a request to CyberCash (or make a phone call to First Data) to authorize credit card.

3. If CyberCash says "authorized", insert a row into your orders table.

Suppose that someone pulls the power plug on your server right after the request to CyberCash gets sent but before your program has had a chance to receive the result or insert anything into your local database. You would have billed someone's card for $X and yet have no record of the order. The way to get around this is to

1. Check data from order form.

2. Insert a row into your orders table with a status of "confirmed".

3. Make a request to CyberCash to authorize credit card.

4. If CyberCash says "authorized", then update the row in the orders table with a status of "authorized" or, if Cybercash doesn't respond or returns "failed", then update the row with a status of "failed".

Someone can still pull the plug in the middle of these steps, leaving you with a confirmed order in your database and no idea whether or not CyberCash authorized the credit card transaction. So you need a process that runs every hour or so to look for confirmed orders that are older than, say, 30 minutes. The cleanup process will then try to connect to CyberCash and see whether or not the order was authorized. If so, the status is updated to "authorized". If CyberCash has no record of the order, the order can be retried (assuming you elected to save credit card numbers) or pushed into the "failed" state.

Reload 5 times = 5 orders?

The obvious way to implement an ecommerce system is the following:

1. Serve user a static order form pointing to an "insert-order" page.

2. When the user hits Submit, the insert-order page will run and
   - generate a unique order ID
   - insert a row in the database
   - run the credit card
   - update the row in the database to say "authorization succeeded"
   - print a thank-you page back to the user's browser
   - send email thanking the user for the order

The problem with this approach is that various aspects of step 2 may be slow, prompting the user to hit Reload. At which point another unique order ID is generated and another row is inserted into the database and the credit card number is authorized again. If the user hits Reload five times, it looks to the merchant's database just the same as five actual orders. The merchant can only hope that the user will notice the duplicate email messages and alert the merchant's customer service department.

There are potentially many ways of getting around this problem, but I think the simplest approach instead is to serve the user a dynamically generated order form that includes a unique order ID, pointing to an "insert-order" page. When the user hits Submit, the insert-order page will run and insert a row into a database table with a primary key constraint on the order ID. If the insert fails (Oracle won't allow two rows with the same primary key), catch it and look to see if there is already an order in the database with the same ID. If so, serve the user an order status page instead.

Eve Andersson, Jin Choi, and I distribute some example software that implements this approach from *http://arsdigita.com/freetools/shoppe.html*.

CASE STUDY: ARSDIGITA, LLC

A *Fortune 500* clothing manufacturer came to my friends and me (ArsDigita, LLC) and asked us to build them an ecommerce site. Consumers would type in some personal data, the order would get sent to a factory, a custom-made item would get shipped to the consumer, and the customer's credit card would be billed.

Our response? Too boring. We specialize in community Web sites and grand public services like *www.scorecard.org* that satisfy our bloated egos when the sites are featured on network TV news.

"We want you to process a few million orders in the next two years. At around $50 each. We have the budget to make this work."

Oh, well, gee, that sounds like an interesting challenge after all . . . .

No modem

We decided early on that we didn't want to talk directly to the card processors via modem. We needed to have a reliable IP connection to talk to Web customers, so why not use that to talk to the banking system as well? We'd have to engineer defensively to handle the times when the Internet gateway to the credit card system was unavailable, but we'd also be eliminating two potential points of failure: the modem and the phone line.

Another motivation behind this decision was that we expected to be able to avoid keeping cleartext credit card numbers in our database if we used one of these fancy Internet commerce gateway services.

Deciding between ICOMS-style and CyberCash-style

Given that we weren't going to bring in a phone line, we had to pick between the ICOMs-style architecture and the CyberCash-style system. Our *Fortune 500* client was picky about the customer experience and that necessitated the customer talking only to our server, which would in turn talk to the banking network; therefore, we decided on the CyberCash-style architecture.

We looked at the vPOS system from VeriFone and rejected it immediately because (1) it only works with Microsoft Internet Information Server (We don't know anyone who understands NT well enough to run a Web service from Windows NT), (2) Netscape Enterprise Server (We aren't willing to suffer with Netscape's programming tools, such as LiveWire), and (3) Oracle Web Server (Our code library is in AOLserver Tcl).

We looked at *http://www.cybercash.com.* It offers three options for building "your online store":

1. Hire an officially sanctioned programming team to build you a site.

2. Buy some packaged online store junkware from a collection of officially sanctioned vendors.

3. Download their core C and Perl software (the CyberCash API), plus some unsupported examples that use the core API calls, then start integrating them into "your existing on-line store."

We don't even like to look at our own source code sometimes, much less anyone else's. So that ruled out option 1. We thought it would take longer to read the marketing literature for all the packaged junkware than it would to just write everything from scratch, so that ruled out option 2. We chose option 3 and registered to download the Merchant Connection Kit 3.2.

Due to a combination of bad programming and user interface design on the CyberCash site, plus sluggish customer service personnel, we weren't even able to download the software for 48 hours. The downloaded kit was a gzipped Unix tar file, but it bore no extension, so it took a bit of Unix expertise to (1) figure out what kind of file it was and (2) rename it to foobar.tar.gz and gunzip it.

At this point, we had to decide whether to use the Perl interface or the C library. In general, we prefer to use interpreted languages for Web software development. However, since we were building the entire site in AOLserver Tcl, it seemed tasteless to maintain some of the pages in Perl CGI. Jin spent a night writing a 200-line C program (see *http://photo.net/wtr/thebook/cybercash.c*).

The CyberCash API consists of exchanging key-value pairs. There is really only one basic C procedure that one needs to call and Jin's code is a bridge between the CyberCash key-value data structure and AOLserver's `ns_set` data structure. All the

interesting information about the API is in Appendix B of *http://www.cybercash.com /cybercash/merchants/docs/dev.pdf.*

To the extent that CyberCash is tricky, it is mostly because the credit card world is archaic and tricky. There are two fundamental steps in processing a credit card order. The first step is authorization. The merchant gives the processor a card number, expiration date, name on card, street address, and zip code. The processor is fundamentally checking that the card number is valid and that the cardholder has sufficient credit to handle the amount authorized. Given the religious zeal with which merchants collect your card expiration dates, you'd think that processors did something clever with this. In fact all they do is make sure that it is a date in the future. So if a consumer's card expires in 06/00 and he gives you 01/00, First Data will not reject the transaction. The address verification service (further discussed at page 428) is purely to help merchants assess the risk of sending out a product and then later finding out that the credit card number was purloined. The processor says, "Zip code matched but address did not" or "Nothing matched". The merchant has to decide whether or not to take the risk of shipping the good.

The second step in processing a credit card order is settlement or "capture." With a hard good, the merchant would typically authorize when it gets an order and capture when it ships the product. With a soft good, for example, the sale of access to a Web service or document, the merchant would typically capture immediately after authorization.

Complicating matters somewhat is the fact that processors try to conserve their network and server resources by coercing merchants into performing settlements in batches of five or more. A merchant can kick CyberCash into autosettlement mode, whereby Cybercash periodically sweeps its database to find transactions that are authorized *and* marked for settlement. So the hard goods merchant's two basic operations become "mauthonly" (to authorize; done when order is received) and "postauth" (to mark for settlement; done when good is shipped). A soft goods merchant can put Cybercash into auto-mark, auto-settle mode, whereby authorized transactions are immediately marked for settlement.

Our honeymoon with CyberCash

What's great about CyberCash is that it is so centered on the merchant's order ID. We give CyberCash a card number and a unique order ID, and from then on we can do all of our transactions merely by referencing this order ID. These transactions include "void" (halt the settlement process), "return" (refund a consumer's money for a settled transaction), and "card-query" (get the full cleartext card number back for a particular order).

Another nice thing about Cybercash is that they have a full Web site where a merchant can go to review all the orders, do refunds, run cards one at a time, and so on.

The end of the honeymoon?

Our brilliant scheme would founder if Cybercash did not keep order data around for a long time. It might take a customer 10 days to receive a good and 45 days to decide that he didn't like it and send it back. We don't want to have to ask him for his card number again. If it took us more than seven days to mark an authorized

transaction for settlement, then the cardholder's bank might reject the settlement and we'd have to reauthorize (using the card number). So we absolutely depend on CyberCash to keep the card numbers around for a fairly long time in *their* database. Currently, they state privately that they will keep these data for 90 days, which seems long enough for most purposes.

That leaves one big remaining hole: If CyberCash were unreachable or could not reach the card processor or the card processor were down, we'd have to either bounce the customer or keep his card number and retry later.

What would plug this last hole is for CyberCash to give us a public key. We'd encrypt the consumer's card number immediately upon receipt and stuff it into our Oracle database. Then if we needed to retry an authorization, we'd simply send them a message with the encrypted card number. CyberCash would decrypt the card number with their private key and process the transaction normally. If a cracker broke into our server, the handful of credit card numbers in our database would be unreadable without Cybercash's private key. The same sort of architecture would let us do reorders or returns six months after an order.

CyberCash has "no plans" to do anything like this.

Disputed charges

Disputed charges or chargebacks are a much greater risk in the mail-order telephone-order (MOTO) world than in the pizza shop face-to-face world. Many banks don't even like to give merchant accounts to companies who say they want to take telephone or Internet orders. What happens is that 45 days after the transaction is authorized, the cardholder writes to his bank and says, "I didn't receive my goods" or "I don't know what this charge is for." The merchant finds out about this in a report from his bank; there is no indication of a charge dispute in the CyberCash database.

What particularly scares a bank about this is that they've already given the merchant the money. Consider the case of a Times Square camera shop. They take $1 million in credit card orders for cameras that they promise to ship in four weeks. The money gets piped into their bank account immediately. They take the money to Brazil. Two months later, their merchant bank is forced to refund $1 million to various cardholders' banks, with no recourse to the merchant.

Before inflicting our software on the *Fortune 500* company, we decided to open a test merchant account through which we'd run charitable contributions to a couple of animal shelters (see *http://photo.net/samantha/gift-shop.html*). We thought it would be easy to get an account from BankBoston. They'd recently discovered that Ricardo S. Carrasco, one of their senior lending officers, had written $73 million in fraudulent loans in Latin America and then disappeared. We therefore figured that ArsDigita would look great by comparison. We'd been customers since 1979, had $175,000 on deposit, and no connections to Argentinian businessmen with "histories of criminal and financial problems."

It turned out that we weren't quite BankBoston's dream customer as we'd envisioned, but five weeks later we had our merchant account. If you're setting up a site, it is probably unwise to rely on service faster than that from a typical bank.

Fees

Getting rich on the Internet isn't cheap. Here's what it cost us to get set up with BankBoston plus CyberCash:

- $375 to set up a merchant account with BankBoston (plus it will cost us another $100 to terminate our account)

- $40 a month to BankBoston or 4.8 percent of the total transactions, whichever is larger

- $595 setup fee to CyberCash

- $40 a month to CyberCash *plus* 20 cents per authorization

Compounding the horror of these payments is the fact that we have three separate companies with which to deal: BankBoston (our bank), First Data (their card processor), CyberCash (our gateway to First Data). If there is a problem with our merchant account, we have to first figure out whose fault it might be and who might have the expertise to fix the problem.

Sales tax

Our *Fortune 500* client has "nexus" in all 50 states, meaning that in each state they are considered to be "engaged in business" and therefore required by law to collect sales tax. Note that they weren't actually selling goods direct-to-consumer nationwide, but had warehouses and salespeople in every state.

This doesn't sound so bad, does it? We just need an Oracle table with 50 rows, each one containing the tax rate for a particular state. Actually it turns out that there are about 7,000 taxing jurisdictions in the United States and 17,000 different tax rates. Okay, that's no problem either. Oracle can handle a 17,000-row table quite easily. We can buy the data for $3,000 a year from *http://www.salestax.com*. A few straightforward Tcl scripts and SQL queries and we can compute the amount of tax to collect based on the zip code of the shipping address.

So what's the problem?

We've *collected* the tax. We haven't *paid* the tax. We now need to write checks and fill out forms for those 7,000 taxing jurisdictions nationwide. Most states let you remit your local jurisdiction taxes to the state along with a schedule, and then the state revenue folks distribute the appropriate amounts periodically to local governments. Still, assuming that our sales are initially light, we could be writing one or two checks and filling out one or two forms for every product that we sell. We will be hiring a big staff of people to sit in front of a forms CD-ROM from *http://www.salestax.com* or a more automated software package from *http://www.corptax.com, http://www .taxware.com,* or *http://www.vertexinc.com.*

The interesting thing to note here is that big companies that have always sold wholesale may initially see the Internet as a great opportunity to cut through layers and get directly to the consumer. Yet the cost of building a sales tax compliance department may wipe out many years of profits from Internet sales.

Accounting

Periodically we have to tell the accounting folks what happened on the Web site, so that they can finish the company's financial statements and taxes. You'd think that an easy way to do this would be just to hand over the merchant bank's monthly statements showing the flux of money going to and from consumers' credit cards. That's sort of like the cash-basis accounting that individuals and very small companies do. Large companies, though, are required to use *accrual basis.* They are supposed to recognize revenue when they know that they're going to get it, rather than when they actually get it.

Should we thus build accounting reports that show orders when they were confirmed by a consumer? No. It turns out that this makes accounting way too hard because assets can be double-counted. For example, the consumer on December 30, 1998 says he wants to buy a widget for $100. You ship the widget on January 3, 1999. At the end of 1998, your books will show that you have a widget in inventory, value $90, *plus* an order for the same widget, value $100.

Companies get around this problem by recognizing revenue when the product ships. The widget gets removed from inventory and the order gets added to revenue. There is never a risk of double-counting.

ArsDigita Shoppe

We decided that we'd have to go live with a full-scale charity shop at least one month before going live with the "big custom clothing shop." Our first product was a $20 donation to Angell Memorial Animal Hospital, a local veterinary research center. People who contributed $20 would receive a pair of prints from my Italian collection (*http://photo.net/italy/*). Ever since the inception of my site, I'd been giving away prints to people who donated money, but the prices were higher ($100 to $250) and donors had to put a check in the mail. However, for the first time we would have a link right at the top of photo.net, a price suited to impulse purchasing, and online ordering.

For the charity test, we used our ArsDigita Shoppe product, a comprehensibly small set of AOLserver Tcl scripts that merchants are expected to customize. There are only a handful of database tables in the system. Note that they are all prefixed with sh_ so that they can be installed in an existing Oracle database without much chance of name conflicts with previously defined tables. Here are the basics of the data model:

- sh_products—containing product descriptions and prices, keyed by product_id

- sh_orders—containing customer information such as shipping address, whether or not the order was shipped, and records of conversations with CyberCash

- sh_problems_log—to record transactions where CyberCash failed or did not return

- sh_country_codes—used to enforce an integrity constraint on the country field of sh_orders

ArsDigita Shoppe is designed for maximum simplicity and security. It does not ever store credit card numbers and must therefore reject any order that cannot be immediately authorized through CyberCash.

We decided that we'd build the system assuming the merchant had put CyberCash into auto-settle, manual-mark mode. For products flagged as soft goods in the sh_products table, we'd do a "mauthonly" and then an immediate "postauth". For regular products, we'd have a fulfillment section among the admin pages, where whoever was doing shipping could mark orders as shipped when they went out the door. The order status would be updated to "shipped" and CyberCash would be sent a "postauth".

The finite-state machine for orders

For both customer service and accounting, a merchant needs to know whether an order has been paid for, shipped, returned, or otherwise. As far as I can tell, the world of business software operates either via recording lines in tabular ledgers or via messages sent from one "system" to another. So you can tell whether or not an order has been shipped depending on whether or not there are rows with that order_id in particular ledgers or in particular systems.

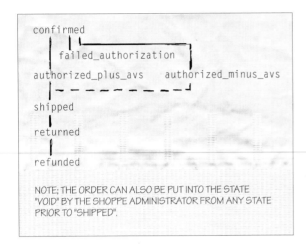

NOTE; THE ORDER CAN ALSO BE PUT INTO THE STATE "VOID" BY THE SHOPPE ADMINISTRATOR FROM ANY STATE PRIOR TO "SHIPPED".

Figure 14-2:
The finite-state
machine.

Though I'm sure the ledger- and message-based approaches feel natural to people in the business data processing world, they feel awkward to me. I visualize an order as being in one of a finite number of states. For example, confirmed means the customer has pressed the Submit button and indicated a desire to place the order. From confirmed, it is possible to get to one of three states: failed_authorization, authorized _plus_avs, and authorized_minus_avs. Whether a state transition occurs and to which new state depends on what our software gets back from CyberCash. Figure 14-2 is a graphical representation of the finite-state machine (FSM).

An authorized order is put into the shipped state when the merchant clicks on the admin fulfillment form's "confirm that this has been shipped" box. As these transitions occur, we are simply updating the order_state column in the sh_orders table. That doesn't mean we're losing information versus the ledger approach. There are extra columns in the sh_orders table to hold the data that accumulate upon state transitions.

For example, after the Tcl order-handling procedure talks to CyberCash to do the initial authorization, it records the CyberCash transaction ID, authorization code from the credit card processor, and Address Verification Service code returned by CyberCash.

Address verification service

The credit card processing system was designed to quickly figure out, "Is this a currently valid credit card and does it have enough available credit to handle this purchase?" Through CyberCash and First Data, we've had no trouble getting authorizations for orders when we supplied the wrong name on the card or the wrong expiration date. This presumably isn't such a bad problem in the face-to-face world. The cardholder has physical possession of the card. If he loses it, he will probably call the bank and have it canceled. So if a merchant sees a customer waving a card, it is almost certain to be the cardholder. However, in the mail-order telephone-order world, the merchant never has the opportunity to verify that the customer has physical possession of the card, only that the customer knows the number of a valid credit card. The number could have been obtained in many ways without the cardholder ever knowing.

If a merchant ships a $1,000-widget to a crook and the real cardholder complains, the merchant has to give $1,000 back to the bank. In order to help mail-order telephone-order merchants manage this risk, the card processors run what

seems to be an essentially separate system called Address Verification Service. They take the first 20 characters of the street address and the billing zip code and return a one-character code:

Code	Interpretation
Y	five-digit zip code and address both match
A	address matches, zip code does not
Z	zip code matches, address does not
N	neither address nor zip code matches
R	system unavailable or timed out
S	card type not supported

As a merchant, you have to decide what to do in these various cases. ArsDigita Shoppe encapsulates this business decision in a single procedure containing a list of codes that are deemed sufficient to put an order into `authorized_plus_avs`. The merchant also needs to make a business decision for every order that lands into authorized_minus_avs. To ship or not to ship? That is the question. ArsDigita Shoppe by default will solicit a customer's telephone number and presumably the merchant will be advised to email or telephone the customer for verification.

Note that in our experience AVS is not very reliable. For our first few successful orders, all of which were from legit folks, here are our stats:

AVS Code	Count
N	2
R	1
S	1
Y	11
Z	28

The 11 cases in which both address and five-digit zip codes match looks pretty good until you look at our source code and note that we neither solicit the card billing street address from the customer nor do we ever provide any street address to CyberCash. We only solicit card billing zip from the customer and send that through to Cyber-Cash. Consequently, the 28 cases of "zip code matches" are to be expected. In two cases, the AVS code raises an unreasonable suspicion ("no match"), and in two more cases we couldn't get an AVS code at all. The one "card type not supported" (S) was a friend's Mastercard. Oddly enough, it was issued by BankBoston, our merchant bank.

Integrity

We assume that the following components could fail at any instant:

- our server hardware or software
- our communication with CyberCash
- CyberCash's servers
- CyberCash's communication with the card processor (First Data)
- the card processor's network or systems

Later in this section, I will discuss the software that we built to recover from failures on the above list. Meanwhile, we assume that the following components are 100 percent reliable:

- transactions committed to our Oracle database
- orders recorded by CyberCash

The consequences of the merchant's Oracle database losing a transaction might include the merchant billing a customer and never knowing that product needed to be shipped or the merchant shipping product to the same customer twice. Recall

that ArsDigita Shoppe does not store credit card numbers. Therefore, if CyberCash lost an already shipped order, the merchant would be unable to issue a refund if the customer returned a product. If CyberCash lost a to-be-shipped order, the merchant would be unable to mark the order for settlement and therefore would not be able to fulfill the order. If CyberCash lost an order that was shipped and marked for settlement but was still to be settled, the merchant would have already shipped the product and would not get any money for it.

I've written a little bit elsewhere in this book about how to make an Oracle installation that never loses committed transactions, even if a disk drive fails. Suffice it to say that you probably need at least eight physical disk drives, plus a full-time staff person who has read every book on my Oracle bookshelf (*http://photo.net/wtr /bookshelf.html*).

How to make sure that CyberCash never loses committed orders? This is something you hope you won't ever have to do. CyberCash runs a database server and therefore is subject to the same DB/sysadmin challenges as everyone else. I haven't talked to enough of CyberCash's internal people to say whether I believe that they'll never screw up their database administration.

ArsDigita Shoppe defends against failures to communicate with CyberCash by periodically running cleanup processes looking for orders in intermediate states. Scheduled by AOLserver's `ns_schedule_proc` (like the Unix cron facility, but it schedules a procedure to run inside AOLserver where it has access to all the AOLserver API calls), we have the following procedures:

- `sh_sweep_for_cybercash_zombies`—Runs every hour. Looks for orders in the `confirmed` state that are older than 30 minutes. Queries CyberCash to find out whether or not an authorization request was received and, if so, whether it succeeded. If CyberCash is reachable, the procedure will always push the order either into `failed_authorization` or one of the authorized states.

- `sh_sweep_for_unmarked_shipped_orders`—Runs every hour. Looks for orders in the shipped state that are older than 30 minutes but for which we have not recorded a "postauth status" code back from CyberCash (i.e., those orders that should be marked for settlement but might not be). Queries CyberCash to find out whether or not the order is marked. If not, the procedure will try again to mark it.

- `sh_query_for_settled_and_setlret`—Runs at 3:14 A.M. every day (if the time seems strange, see Eve Andersson's site at *http://eveander.com*). By 3:14 A.M. eastern time, CyberCash theoretically should have settled all the previous day's marked orders. This procedure grabs those settlement codes and updates the `sh_orders` table.

Going live

We launched our charity shop at around 2:00 A.M. on Thursday, June 18, 1998. Here is our experience to date:

- 3:45 A.M., June 18: Matthew Haughey of UCLA is our first customer, donating $20 to Angell Memorial; we have a total of 24 successfully authorized orders by the end of the day.

- 2:37 A.M., June 19: CyberCash begins rejecting authorization for legitimate cards, reporting "invalid card number" to the customer. We send email to merchant-support@cybercash.com; it has yet to be answered.

- midday, June 19: CyberCash is unreachable. Their API returns, "Could not open socket to connect to Merchant Payment Server". It is impossible to ping or traceroute to cr.cybercash.com (the host that processes payment requests and also lets a merchant log in). Nearly 20 orders are rejected due to inability to communicate with CyberCash. We send email to merchant-support@cybercash.com; it has yet to be answered.

- 8:30 P.M., June 20: We are trying to fulfill the 33 successful orders in our database. CyberCash fails our requests to mark the orders for settlement, saying either "PostAuth: There is no previous authorization for this order" or "DataBase error #-901: System error, RDM runtime memory may be corrupted." We go to *https://cr.cybercash.com* and log into the Merchant maintenance pages. All of the orders we'd received on June 18 and 19 have disappeared from CyberCash's records.

- 10 P.M., June 20: CyberCash fails to process two orders, returning "DataBase error #-901: System error, RDM runtime memory may be corrupted." (I later learned that RDM stands for Raima Database Manager, a system that is cheaper than Oracle but apparently not bulletproof. CyberCash says that they are moving to Oracle.)

- 11:48 P.M., Sunday, June 21: *https:// cr.cybercash.com* is reachable again, but all of our orders from June 18 through 20 are missing. We telephone CyberCash merchant support at (703) 295-0888. They're closed but we push 0 to wake up an oncall support guy. We supply him with the transaction IDs (given to us by Cyber-Cash) of a few of the authorized-by-them-and-now-lost orders. He says that it looks like we'll need "technical support" and they're not available until Monday morning.

- 2:30 P.M., June 22: Gale from CyberCash calls to say that she expects the missing data to be restored by the morning of June 23.

- 10:23 A.M., June 23: A couple of orders fail from CyberCash, with "failure-q-or-cancel; Premature EOF read from socket. HTTP body is missing. A likely reason: server did not respond or dropped a connection." Our software is programmed to retry these once, but apparently that was not enough.

- 1:30 P.M., June 23: Our orders are still missing. No word from CyberCash.

- 4:40 P.M., June 23: Eve telephones Greg at CyberCash to find out why our *Fortune 500* customers' tests were failing earlier:

    E: Why did this valid credit card fail with error message 'Invalid Credit Card Number' today between 10:30 and 10:49 A.M., even though it has since been tested and found to be valid?
    G: It could be because of Internet traffic.

    E: Why would that cause the message 'Invalid Credit Card Number'?
    G: Maybe it got garbled in transmission.

    E: How could it get garbled 12 times?
    G: Maybe the system was down. Let me check . . . . Yes, it was down shortly before 11 this morning.

- 1:30 P.M., June 24: Our orders from June 18 through 20 have reappeared. The card types are missing from standard reports and the AVS codes have been garbled (they no longer fit into our char(3) Oracle column), but we're able to settle transactions.

- 6:00 P.M., June 29: Our first customer of the day (Sales at our charity shop have slowed!) tries to place an order but our machine can't reach Cyber-Cash, so the customer gets hit with a "cannot connect to payment server" message. We start testing *https://cr.cybercash.com* and it responds, albeit very slowly. The customer retries the order five minutes later and succeeds. I call customer support and, after keeping me on hold for 10 minutes, they verify that their payment server was down, but can't say why. They very helpfully give me a service status page: *http://merchant.cybercash.com/cgi-bin/status /cyber/status.cgi*. This page doesn't give a cumulative history, however, for CyberCash or any of its card processors.

- 9:00 P.M., June 30: We take a closer look at the CyberCash status page. The data on the page appear to be incomplete. For example, the payment server's outage on June 29 is not shown. The last outage is instead listed as June 26. Their last problem with Internet connectivity is shown as having been on February 19. Yet we were unable to reach CyberCash on May 18 and narrowed the problem down to a routing loop (either their fault or their ISP's):

```
www: ~% traceroute cr.cybercash.com
traceroute to hcr2.cybercash.com (204.178.186.35), 30 hops max, 40 byte
packets
```

```
 1  main-98.sjc.above.net (207.126.98.4)  6.86 ms  14.535 ms  20.903 ms
 2  main-98.sjc.above.net (207.126.98.4)  1.336 ms  1.209 ms  1.243 ms
 3  paix-main-oc3.above.net (207.126.96.122)
    5.883 ms mae-east-paix.above.net (207.126.96.86)  85.714 ms  84.983 ms
 4  Hssi0-1-0.GW1.TCO1.ALTER.NET (157.130.33.113)  76.284 ms  70.12 ms
    71.111 ms
 5  421.atm10-0-0.cr2.tco1.alter.net (137.39.13.6)  71.226 ms  70.655 ms
    77.131 ms
 6  Fddi0-0.Vienna3.VA.Alter.Net (137.39.11.4)  78.618 ms  164.081 ms
    85.963 ms
 7  CyberCash-gw.customer.ALTER.NET (137.39.154.226)  98.223 ms  74.49 ms
    72.549 ms
 8  204.149.69.253 (204.149.69.253)  79.065 ms  80.27 ms  75.728 ms
 9  cust-gw.cybercash.com (204.178.187.250)  80.119 ms  81.686 ms  79.392 ms
10  ans-gw.cybercash.com (204.178.187.253)  84.779 ms  85.597 ms  83.998 ms
11  cust-gw.cybercash.com (204.178.187.250)  83.425 ms  81.273 ms  88.299 ms
12  ans-gw.cybercash.com (204.178.187.253)  87.992 ms  87.012 ms  89.312 ms
13  cust-gw.cybercash.com (204.178.187.250)  84.027 ms  84.861 ms  85.051 ms
14  ans-gw.cybercash.com (204.178.187.253)  90.975 ms  90.937 ms  87.995 ms
15  cust-gw.cybercash.com (204.178.187.250)  85.138 ms  90.371 ms  84.609 ms
16  ans-gw.cybercash.com (204.178.187.253)  93.612 ms  93.498 ms  93.073 ms
```

- 3:00 P.M., July 8: Fulfilling a few orders, we get hit with "Could not connect to Merchant Payment Server" on one, but the others succeed.

- August 1998: CyberCash seems to have settled down and is working fairly reliably for both ArsDigita Shoppe and our *Fortune 500* customer. Our biggest problem is the confusion generated by the reports that we get from BankBoston. Money seems to get dumped into our bank account and then, about half the time, taken back the next day. It isn't clear whether this is a First Data/BankBoston problem or a CyberCash/First Data problem. In any case, reconciling these reports with our order database would require a team of five Talmud scholars.

ArsDigita summary

So far, we've learned that, if you aren't willing to keep credit card numbers temporarily, you lose orders while your means of billing credit cards is unavailable. We've also seen that, if you aren't willing to keep credit cards permanently, you had better pray that CyberCash keeps its Oracle database together.

For our *Fortune 500* client, we built a fancy system that is robust to CyberCash failures. If CyberCash is unreachable or returns an inconclusive answer, we assume that the credit card number is valid and have cleanup cron jobs that keep trying to authorize the card in hopes that CyberCash has come back to life. This code turns out to be pretty complicated, especially since it has to deal with the case of "that guy who placed an order 18 hours ago is over his credit limit, but we didn't find out until just now because CyberCash was down."

An alternative architecture that we haven't explored would rely on at least two IP-based services like CyberCash. When a new order came in, we'd try to authorize via Credit Card Gateway A. If it was unreachable or inconclusive, we'd try to authorize via Credit Card Gateway B.

Something Interesting

Now that I've bored you to death with all of that ecommerce stuff, is it possible that there is anything interesting here? I think so. Karl Marx may not have been an accurate prophet, but he remains the world's greatest analyst of the industrial revolution. Why was the factory worker's life so miserable? One reason was that the worker never got to talk to a customer, never got to see how his work was used.

Can we fix all of the ills of the modern age with ecommerce? Probably not. In fact, it seems likely that ecommerce will add to the discontents of civilization ("We already killed downtown; now let's go after the mall"). But I think it is possible to use technology to ameliorate the problem identified by Marx. A company can use its Web site to let consumers talk to the people who make the products, and vice versa.

Instead of working an eight-hour factory floor shift, why can't a worker spend six hours a day building products, one hour a day answering customer tech support email, and one hour a day answering sales inquiries? For semicustom goods, why can't the people building the product answer the "When is it going to be done" questions? Or directly ask the "Are you sure you want it with two screws on top, because it would look much nicer fastened from the edges" questions?

Note that this kind of direct customer-worker contact could become a competitive advantage for companies manufacturing domestically. Could I communicate effectively with the 14-year-old Indonesian girl who made my Nike sneakers? Perhaps not. But my Toyota Sienna minivan was built in Kentucky. I'd love to email the folks who built it a picture of Alex in the driver's seat.

Summary

Ecommerce is at once mind-numbingly boring and terrifyingly difficult. It turns out to be a miracle that most businesses operate successfully at all. With ecommerce, people start demanding that all the business systems that have been up eight hours a day, five days a week with human intervention now be available 24×7 and be fully automated. The worst thing about building ecommerce systems is that nobody will notice if you do the job right.

MORE

- For a look at how Microsoft has tried to solve some of the same problems, visit *http://www.microsoft.com/siteserver/* or get *Microsoft Site Server 3.0 Bible* (Harris et al., 1998; IDG).

- If you're working in this area, it is useful to understand business data processing software, the most successful example of which is SAP (*www.sap.com*). Popular books on SAP include *Sap R/3 Business Blueprint : Understanding the Business Process Reference Model* (Curren et al., 1997; Prentice Hall) and *The Sap R/3 Handbook* (Hernandez, 1997; McGraw-Hill).

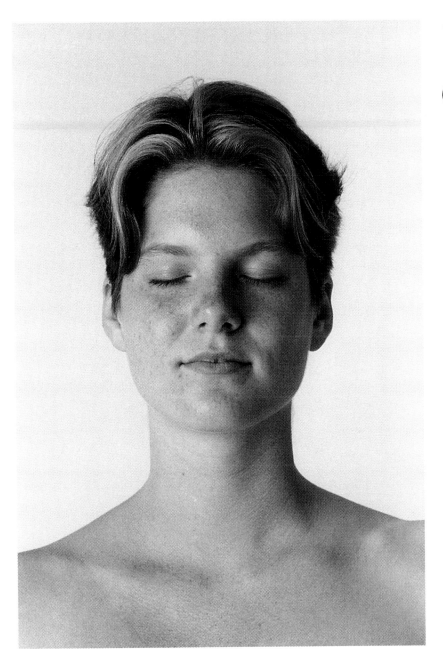

15
Case Studies

This chapter contains six case studies, each with some actual source code. I present user interface, interaction design, and data modeling ideas that should be useful to you in many contexts. This chapter is not a step-by-step guide. If it were, it would be 800 pages long, absurdly boring, and extremely tool-specific.

Because I'm afraid that your eyes will glaze over and you'll skip this, I'll try to give you a hint of what is in store. Case 1 is straightforward and dull. It is intended to help you understand how AOLserver Tcl works with a simple mailing list registration application. Feel free to skip it. Case 2 shows how to generalize this application so that many static Web services can share a single RDBMS-backed service. It is a powerful idea that I have used at least a dozen times. Case 3, the birthday reminder system, introduces the idea that less can be more. It does less than a calendar management program but is easier to use. Case 3 also demonstrates how to build a back end to loop through a database table and send email when necessary. In doing so, it addresses in a practical way an important question about concurrency and RDBMSs.

Case 4, the bulletin board system, shows how important it is to have all of your services run from the same database management system and users table. It also raises the interesting issue of whether a 99 percent reliable system isn't better than a 100 percent reliable system. Case 5, ArsDigita Quizze, shows how to use a server-side database to keep session state, preserve a user's ability to go back and forward on pages, yet keep the user from using the Back button to cheat on a quiz. Case 6 covers the Uptime server monitoring system and brings up issues of maintainability for public Internet services.

I hope that you're inspired. If you don't have the patience to read the source code, then please at least skim the text underneath each new case headline.

CASE 1: THE MAILING LIST

We went through this in the first chapter on RDBMS-backed sites (see Chapter 12), but now let's do it over again with actual code. Remember that you want a mailing list system for your site. Users can add and remove themselves, supplying email addresses and real names. You want to be the only one who can view the list and the only one who can send mail to the list.

Step 1: The data model

```
create table mailing_list (
    email     varchar(100) primary key,
    name      varchar(100)
);
```

Step 2: Legal transactions

Here are examples of the two types of transactions:

```
insert into mailing_list (email,name)
values ('philg@mit.edu','Philip
        Greenspun');
delete from mailing_list where email =
'philg@mit.edu';
```

Step 3: Mapping transactions onto Web forms

Here is a form to add someone to the list:

```
<html>
<head>
<title>Add yourself to the mailing list</title>
</head>
<body bgcolor=#ffffff text=#000000>
<h2>Add yourself to the mailing list</h2>
<form method=post action=add.tcl>
<table>
<tr><td>Name<td><input name=name type=text size=35>
<tr><td>email<td><input name=email type=text size=35>
</table>
<p>
<input type=submit value="Add Me">
```

```
</form>
</body>
</html>
```

(See Figure 15-1 for this form rendered by a Web browser.) And a form so that someone can delete himself from the list:

```
<html>
<head>
<title>Remove yourself from the mailing
list</title>
</head>
<body bgcolor=#ffffff text=#000000>
<h2>Remove yourself from the mailing list</h2>
<form method=post action=remove.tcl>
<table>
<tr><td>email<td>
<input name=email type=text size=35>
</table>
<p>
<input type=submit value="Remove Me">
</form>
</body>
</html>
```

(See Figure 15-2 for this form rendered by a Web browser.)

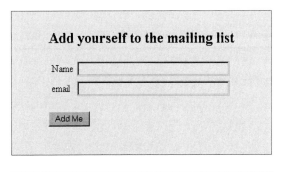

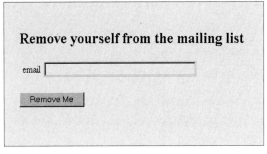

Figure 15-1 (top): Add Me form rendered by a Web browser.

Figure 15-2 (bottom): Delete Me form rendered by a Web browser.

Step 4: Writing code to process those forms

This is supposed to be the easy part, and it really is. However, looking at someone else's source code is always confusing. Don't infer from your confusion that these are complex programs. The only real art to them is how they handle errors and ill-formed input.

Here is an AOLserver Tcl script to process the "add me" form. The script will

1. check for user input errors in Tcl before sending anything to the database, so that more attractive error messages can be returned

2. formulate an SQL INSERT

3. send the INSERT to the database

4. report success or failure to the user

Here's the full program:

```
# call philg's magic functions to set local variables
# to what the user typed into the form
set_the_usual_form_variables
```

443

```
# name, email, QQname, QQemail are now set
# get an open database connection from the AOLserver
set db [ns_db gethandle]
# Check for errors in user input before doing anything else
# we use the Tcl REGEXP command to see if the email variable
# has the following form:  1 or more ASCII characters (.+) followed
# by the "at sign" (@) then 1 or more ASCII characters (.+)
# followed by at least one period (\.) then 1 or more ASCII characters
(.+)
if { ![regexp {.+@.+\..+} $email] } {
    # the REGEXP didn't match
    ns_return 200 text/plain "Your email addresss doesn't look right to
us.  We need your full Internet address ..."
    # RETURN terminates the AOLserver source.tcl command
    # so none of the code below this point will be executed
    # if the email address had an incorrect form
    return
}
# if we got here, that means the email address was OK
if { $name == "" } {
    # the variable NAME was an empty string
    ns_return 200 text/plain "You didn't give us your name..."
    # this terminates the AOLserver source.tcl command
    return
}


# Error checking complete; ready to do real work
# construct the SQL query using the versions of the form
# variables where apostrophes have already been doubled
# so that names like "O'Grady" don't cause SQL errors
set insert_sql "insert into mailing_list (email, name)
                values ('$QQemail','$QQname')"

# we execute the insert inside the Tcl function CATCH
# if the database raises an SQL error, the AOLserver API
# call ns_db dml will raise a Tcl error that would result
# in a "Server Error" page being returned to the user.  We
# don't want that, so we catch the error ourselves and return
# a more specific message
if [catch { ns_db dml $db $insert_sql } errmsg] {
        # the insert went wrong; the error description
        # will be in the Tcl variable ERRMSG
        ns_return 200 text/plain "The database didn't accept your
insert, most likely because your email address is already on
the mailing list..."
} else {
    # the insert went fine; no error was raised
    ns_return 200 text/html "<html><head><title>$email Added</title>
</head>
```

```
<body bgcolor=#ffffff text=#000000>
<h2>$email Added</h2>
<hr>
You have been added to the <a href=/index.html>www.greedy.com</a>
mailing list.
<hr>
<address>webmaster@greedy.com</address>
</body>
</html>
"
```

The AOLserver Tcl script to process the "remove me" form is much simpler:

```
set_the_usual_form_variables

# now email and QQemail are set as local variables

# ask for a database connection
set db [ns_db gethandle]

# note that the dual calls to the SQL UPPER function
# ensure that the removal will be case insensitive
set delete_sql "delete from mailing_list
                where upper(email) = upper('$QQemail')"

# execute the delete statement in the database
ns_db dml $db $delete_sql

# call the special AOLserver API call ns_ora resultrows
# to find out how many rows were affected by the delete
if { [ns_ora resultrows $db] == 0 } {
    # 0 rows were affected
    ns_return 200 text/plain "We could not find <code>\"$email\"</code> on
the mailing list ..."
} else {
  # the delete affected at least one row so removal must
  # have been successful
  ns_return $conn 200 text/html "<html><head><title>$email Removed</title>
</head>
<body bgcolor=#ffffff text=#000000>
<h2>$email Removed</h2>
<hr>
You have been removed from the <a href=/index.html>www.greedy.com</a>
mailing list.
<hr>
<address>webmaster@greedy.com</address>
</body>
</html>
"
}
```

Note:
I was feeling pretty good about this code until Jeff Friedl, author of the superb book *Mastering Regular Expressions* (1997, O'Reilly), pointed out that "philg@mit.edu" or "5 @ $1.95" would slip through my caveman regexp. If I didn't want to adopt the three-page regexp in Appendix B of his book, then at least I could do "^\[^@\t] +@\[^@.\t]+ (\.\[^@.\n]+) +$".

CASE 2: THE MAILING LIST

"Mailing list"? This sounds vaguely like case 1. It is. Vaguely. Suppose it turns out that you need mailing lists for four other services that you offer. Also, 10 of your friends want to run mailing lists for their sites. You'd be happy to give them your code, but you know that they aren't willing to endure the pain of maintaining a relational database management system just for this one feature. They are grateful, but, "Oh, while you're at it, would you mind allowing us also to store snailmail information?"

So can you make the code generic? You just need an extra table to store information about each of your and your friends' services:

```
create table spam_domains (
    domain                      varchar(100) primary key,
    backlink                    varchar(200),
    -- a URL pointing back to the user's static site
    backlink_title              varchar(100),
    -- what to say for the link back
    blather                     varchar(4000),
    -- arbitrary HTML text that goes at the top of the page
```

```
challenge                        varchar(200) default
                                     'Your mother''s maiden name',
response                         varchar(50),
maintainer_name                  varchar(100),
maintainer_email                 varchar(100),
-- send email when a person adds himself?
notify_of_additions_p            char(1) default 't' check
                                     (notify_of_additions_p in ('f','t')),
-- booleans to decide which information will be collected; name &
    email are always done
title_and_company_p              char(1) default 'f' check
                                     (title_and_company_p in ('f','t')),
snail_mail_p                     char(1) default 'f' check
                                     (snail_mail_p in ('f','t')),
demographics_p                   char(1) default 'f' check
                                     (demographics_p in ('f','t')),
-- people who are distributing software, for example, want the
-- post-add-me page to give download instructions, if NULL, we just
-- cough up the usual text
custom_confirm_after_add_me varchar(4000),
-- if they are storing extra columns then the next item will non-NULL
extra_columns_table_name     varchar(100)
);
```

Each domain is identified with a string, for example, photonet for the magazine photo.net. Then you store the URL http://photo.net/photo/ in the backlink column and the title "photo.net" in backlink_title. You provide a space for some descriptive HTML for the top of the "add me" form, such as, "You will get mail once every month describing new articles in photo.net".

Rather than a password, which your friends might forget and then bug you to manually retrieve from the database, you store a challenge question of their choice, such as "mother's maiden name" and their responses.

You keep track, per domain, of the name and email address of the list maintainer. If the notify_of_additions_p column is set to true, then your "add me" script will send email to the maintainer when someone new adds himself to the list. You keep track of how much data is to be solicited in the Boolean columns, such as snail_mail_p (the "add me" form will ask for postal mail address). For publishers who are using the system to collect registration info before offering software to download, you provide the custom_confirm_after_add_me column. Those folks might want to solicit information that you never anticipated, such as operating_system, so you build into the system the ability for forms and reports to have extra columns, stored in a separate table. That table's name is kept in a domain's extra_columns_ table_name column.

Once the new spam_domains table is defined, you need to beef up the mailing list table as well. It would be possible to build this system so that it defined a separate table for each new domain, but I think it is cleaner to add a domain column to the mailing list table, as long as we're adding all the extra columns for physical mail and demographics:

```
create table spam_list (
    domain                  varchar(100) not null references spam_domains,
    email                   varchar(100) not null,
    name                    varchar(100),
    -- info for 'snail_too'
    title                   varchar(100),
    company_name            varchar(100),
    line1                   varchar(100),
    line2                   varchar(100),
    city                    varchar(50),
    state                   varchar(50),
    postal_code             varchar(20),
    country                 char(2),        -- ISO country code
    phone_number            varchar(20),
    -- info for snail_plus_demographics
    birthday                date,
    sex                     char(1) check(sex in ('m','f')),
    primary key( domain, email )
);
```

Note that you have to remove the primary key constraint on the email column. There is no reason why philg@mit.edu can't be in the mailing list table 10 times, each time for a different domain. However, you don't want philg@mit.edu on the photo.net list 10 times. Thus the `primary key( domain, email )` constraint at the end of the table definition.

How does all this work? If you visit *http://www.greenspun.com,* you can see the whole system in action. Here's an example of how the add-me.html form has been replaced by a Tcl procedure:

```
set_the_usual_form_variables

# QQdomain

set db [ns_db gethandle]

set selection [ns_db 1row $db "select *
                              from spam_domains
                              where domain='$QQdomain'"]
set_variables_after_query

set form_fields "<tr><td>Name<td><input name=name type=text size=35>
<tr><td>email<td><input name=email type=text size=35>"

if { $title_and_company_p == "t" } {
    append form_fields "<tr><td>Title<td>
        <input name=title type=text size=35>
```

```tcl
<tr><td>Company Name<td><input name=company_name type=text size=35>"
}

if { $snail_mail_p == "t" } {
    append form_fields "<tr><td>Address Line 1<td><input name=line1
type=text size=35>
<tr><td>Address Line 2<td><input name=line2 type=text size=35>
<tr><td>City, State, Postal Code<td><input name=city type=text size=12>
<input name=state type=text size=6>
<input name=postal_code type=text size=8>
<tr><td>Country<td><input name=country type=text size=3 limit=2> (ISO
    Code, e.g., \"us\", \"fr\", \"ca\", \"au\", etc.)
<tr><td>Phone Number<td><input name=phone_number type=text size=20>"
}

if { $demographics_p == "t" } {
    append form_fields "<tr><td>Birthday<td><input name=birthday type=text
        size=12> (YYYY-MM-DD format must be exact)
<tr><td>Sex<td><input name=sex type=radio value=M CHECKED> Male
<input name=sex type=radio value=F> Female"
}

ns_return 200 text/html "<html>
<head><title>Add Yourself to the Mailing list</title></head>

<body bgcolor=#ffffff text=#000000>
<h2>Add Yourself</h2>

to <a href=\"home.tcl?domain=[ns_urlencode $domain]\">the mailing list</a>
for <a href=\"$backlink\">$backlink_title</a>

<hr>

$blather

<form method=post action=add-2.tcl>
<input type=hidden name=domain value=\"$domain\">
<table>
$form_fields
</table>
<input type=submit value=Submit>
</form>

<hr>
<address><a href=\"mailto:$maintainer_email\">
    $maintainer_name ($maintainer_email)</a></address>
</body>
</html>
"
```

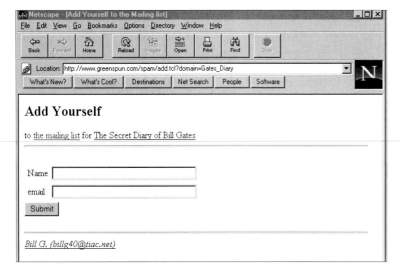

Note how the final HTML page is strewn with values from the database, such as $maintainer_email, $backlink, and $backlink_title. Thus, it looks for all intents and purposes like it is part of your friend's service and you won't be getting email from the confused. See Figure 15-3 for an example.

CASE 3: THE BIRTHDAY REMINDER SYSTEM

A couple of years ago, Olin refused to give Alex (*http://photo.net/photo/alex.html*) a sample off of his plate at brunch. "You're just a dog, Alex," Olin said. We pressed Olin as to his reason for feeling superior to Alex. Olin thought for a few minutes; all he could come up with was, "I have a Ph.D. and he doesn't."

Olin demonstrated the practical value of his Carnegie Mellon computer science degree in 1994 by turning down Jim Clark's offer to become Employee number 3 at a little startup called Mosaic Communications (grab *http://www.netscape.com* if you want to see how Jim and Company are doing now). Consequently, his resort to credentialism set off howls of laughter throughout the room.

"Let's see what value society places on your Ph.D., Dr. Shivers," I said. "We'll take both you and Alex to Harvard Square and hang signs around your necks. Alex's sign will read 'Needs home.' Your sign will read 'Needs home. Has Ph.D.' Which one of you do you think will have to sit out there longer?"

"Nooooo contest," opined Olin's girlfriend.

Anyway, Olin clung to his belief that his Ph.D. was worth something, despite the fact that the marketplace was crushing him under a burden of poverty to correspond to his burden of ignorance of how to build an RDBMS-backed Web service.

I kept offering to show Olin, but he was too busy writing papers for academic journals that even he didn't bother reading. We began to joke that Olin was "afraid to be rich." Then one night Olin came over to my house and said, "Let's jack into this World Wide Cybernet thing."

We sat down to build a toy AOLserver/RDBMS–backed birthday reminder system. Sure, there are plenty of fancy calendar management systems that incorporate one-time events, recurring events, and reminders. But most of these calendar

Figure 15-3: Here my mailing list system is being used by another Web publisher (billg40@ tiac.net). If users looked carefully at the location box, they might notice that they were being bounced from *www.tiac.net* to *www.greenspun.com* after clicking the "join mailing list" link. Billg40 can keep his Secret Diary of Bill Gates at Tiac, where they don't run an RDBMS, and yet look just like a high-tech Web publisher with a staff of programmers and a database administrator.

management programs require you to maintain them on a Macintosh or Windows machine. If you switch from computer to computer, then they don't do you much good. We all read our email, no matter where we are, so why not build a system that feeds reminders into our emailbox? Again, it turns out that there are Web-based calendar management systems that will do just that. But these programs are very complicated. I don't have a job. I don't make appointments. I don't plan in advance. I don't want to invest in learning and using a calendar management program. I just want an email message a week before my friend's birthday so that I can send him a card.

Olin and I sat down at 9:00 P.M. to build RemindMe (*http://www.arsdigita.com /remindme/*). We were finished by midnight (see Figure 15-4). Then we showed the text-only system to Ulla Zang (*http:// www.ullazang.com*) and asked her to do a spiffy graphic design. Now we have a nice public service to offer (see Figure 15-5).

Figure 15-4 (top): The text-only welcome page, built by Olin and me.

Figure 15-5 (bottom): The welcome page, designed by Ulla Zang; we saved a lot of time and heartache by completing our interaction design with a text-only site before consulting a graphic designer. Ulla turns out to be one of the few graphic designers I've worked with who is also an excellent interaction designer. Nonetheless, by having finished the programming beforehand, we were able to use Ulla's time to maximum advantage.

Step 1: The data model

Note that the syntax is now for the Oracle 8 RDBMS, thanks to a noble conversion effort by our partner, Tracy Adams.

```
--
-- this table has one row for each person using the system
-- the PRIMARY KEY constraint says that there can't be two
-- rows with the same value in the EMAIL column
--

create table bday_users (
    email               varchar(100) primary key,
    password            varchar(100) not null
);

create sequence reminder_id_sequence start with 1;
```

```
create table bday_reminders (
    reminder_id             integer primary key,
    email                   varchar(100) references bday_users,
    event_description       varchar(400),
    event_date              date,
    remind_week_before_p    char(1) check (remind_week_before_p in
                                            ('t','f')),
    remind_day_before_p     char(1) check (remind_day_before_p in
                                            ('t','f')),
    remind_day_of_p         char(1) check (remind_day_of_p in ('t','f')),
    last_reminded           date
);

create index bday_reminders_idx on bday_reminders(email);
```

The first item of interest in this data model is the integrity constraint that values in the email column of bday_reminders must correspond to values in the email column of bday_users. That's what references bday_users tells the database management system. After a row in bday_reminders is inserted or updated, the RDBMS will check to make sure that this integrity constraint is true. If not, the transaction will be aborted. Also, nobody will be able to delete a row from bday_users if any rows in bday_reminders still contain the same email address.

Integrity constraints are critical if you have users typing data into a shell database tool. But here users will only be able to access the RDBMS through our Web pages. Why can't we just write our forms-processing software so that it never allows bad data into the database? Well, we can and we will. But unless you are the rare programmer who always writes perfect code, it is nice to have the RDBMS's integrity constraint system as a last line of defense.

Thomas Jefferson did not say, "Eternal vigilance is the price of liberty." That's because he wasn't John Philpot Curran (Irish statesman who never set foot in the United States). Nor did Jefferson say, "Eternal sluggishness is the price of integrity." That's because he wasn't an RDBMS programmer.

Step 2: Legal transactions

You'd think that the most obvious legal transaction would be "add user to bday_users table." However, I decided not to make that one of the legal transactions. I don't want a table full of email addresses for people who aren't really using the system. Thus, it is only legal to add a user atomically with at least one reminder:

```
begin transaction;
insert into bday_users
(email, password)
values
('philip@greenspun.com','hairysamoyed');
```

```
insert into bday_reminders
(reminder_id, email, event_description,
event_date, remind_week_before_p, remind_day_before_p, remind_day_of_p)
values
(reminder_id_sequence.nextval, 'philip@greenspun.com', 'remember to finish PhD',
'1993-06-01', 't', 't', 't');
end transaction;
```

This transaction inserts the user "philip@greenspun.com" with password "hairysamoyed" and an annual reminder to finish his Ph.D. by June 1 (starting from 1993 when he got his masters). Reminders will be sent a week before, a day before, and the day of. Note that each reminder is assigned a unique `reminder_id` using the nonstandard (but very useful) Oracle sequence generator.

Suppose the user doesn't want to be reminded the day of? That's another legal transaction:

```
update bday_reminders
set remind_day_of_p = 'f'
where reminder_id = 5347
```

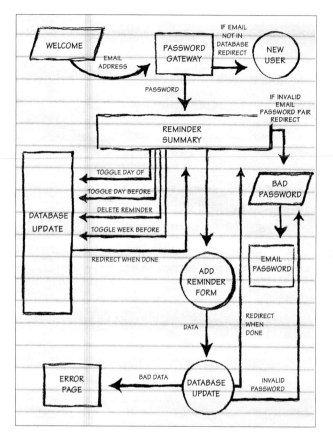

Figure 15-6:
Interaction for the
RemindMe system.
Note the extensive
use of redirects
when bad input is
received and/or after
a simple update.

A reminder system with only one reminder isn't anything to write home about. We ought to be able to add new events:

```
insert into bday_reminders
(reminder_id, email, event_description,
event_date, remind_week_before_p,
remind_day_before_p, remind_day_of_p)
values
(reminder_id_sequence.nextval,
'philip@greenspun.com',
'Wash dog whether he needs it or not',
'1997-12-01','t','f','t')
```

A week before December 1, I'll be reminded to buy shampoo for my Samoyed (he usually requires an entire bottle). I disabled the day before reminder, so that's "f". Then I'll be reminded on December 1, itself.

One last legal transaction: deleting a reminder. Suppose that I finish my Ph.D. thesis (to which supposition my friends invariably respond, "Suppose the sun falls out of the sky"):

```
delete from bday_reminders where
reminder_id = 5347
```

Step 3: Mapping transactions onto Web forms

My general philosophy is to have as few pages as possible. This keeps the user interface simple. Figure 15-6 shows the interaction flow for the RemindMe system.

Often the system uses redirects to pages that reflect current status rather than separate confirmation pages. For example, after a user disables a "week before" alert, there is no confirmation page. Instead, after doing the database update, the Tcl script issues a 302 redirect back to the reminder summary page, where the alert is shown to be disabled.

Step 4: Writing code to process those forms

Here is the .tcl page that summarizes a user's reminders (see Figures 15-7 and 15-8):

```
set_the_usual_form_variables

# email, password
```

454

Reminders

for philg@mit.edu, held by RemindMe
_____

- Mom's Birthday : May 20, 1934 [Week Before: On][Day Before: Off][Day Of: On][DELETE]
- Most Glorious Day Ever : September 28, 1963 [Week Before: On][Day Before: On][Day Of: On][DELETE]

- Add new reminder
_____

remindme@greenspun.com

Figure 15-7: The reminders summary page. Core of the user interface. Olin and I weren't satisfied with this design but decided to dump the user interface issue onto Ulla.

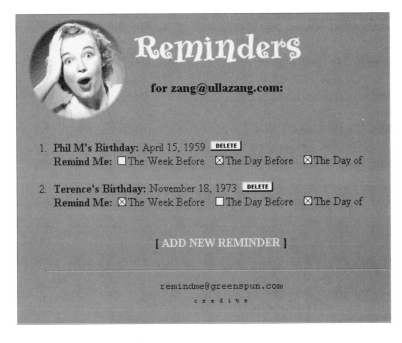

Figure 15-8: Ulla's reminders summary page. Much bigger than our text-only version but also much cleaner. We'll be able to take her simplifications and translate them back into the text-only site as well. (That's another advantage of doing a full text-only site first; you always have something to satisfy the 28.8 K modem crowd, even if your graphic designer doesn't go wild with huge images.)

```
set db [ns_db gethandle]
if { [database_to_tcl_string $db "select unique upper(password) from
        bday_users where upper(email) = upper('$QQemail')"] != [string
        toupper $password] } {
    ns_returnredirect "bad-password.tcl?email=[ns_urlencode $email]"
    return
}

# if we got here it means that the password checked out OK
# we're going to use this a bunch of times so let's save some work
set emailpassword "email=[ns_urlencode $email]&password=[ns_urlencode
    $password]"
```

```
ns_write "HTTP/1.0 200 OK
MIME-Version: 1.0
Content-Type: text/html
Pragma: no-cache

<html>
<head>
<title>Reminders for $email</title>
</head>

<body bgcolor=#ffffff text=#000000>
<h2>Reminders</h2>

for $email, held by <a href=\"credits.tcl\">RemindMe</a>

<hr>

<ol>
"

set selection [ns_db select $db "select bday_reminders.*,
    to_char(event_date,'Month DD, YYYY') as formatted_date,
    to_char(event_date,'MM') as event_month, to_char(event_date,'DD') as
    event_day
from bday_reminders
where upper(email) = upper('$QQemail')
order by event_month, event_day"]

while {[ns_db getrow $db $selection]} {
    set_variables_after_query
    ns_write "<li>$event_description :  $formatted_date
\<[a href=\"delete.tcl?reminder_id=$reminder_id&$emailpassword\">DELETE</a>\]

<br>
Remind me:   "

    # it would have been cleaner to think more and come up with
    # a general-purpose action.tcl function, but I think it is
    # also OK to do what we've done, use a separate .tcl page for
    # each kind of action
    # for each reminder, we test to see if it is already set,
    # then present an appropriate current status hyperlinked to
    # a URL that will toggle the state of that reminder
    if { $remind_week_before_p == "t" } {
        ns_write "\[Week before: <a href=\"week-before-
                off.tcl?reminder_id=$reminder_id&$emailpassword\">yes</a>\]
                " } else {
```

```
              ns_write "\[Week before: <a href=\"week-before-
                      on.tcl?reminder_id=$reminder_id&$emailpassword\">no</a>\]  "
                      }
          if { $remind_day_before_p == "t" } {
              ns_write "\[Day before: <a href=\"day-before-
                      off.tcl?reminder_id=$reminder_id&$emailpassword\">yes</a>\]
                      " } else {
              ns_write "\[Day before: <a href=\"day-before-
                      on.tcl?reminder_id=$reminder_id&$emailpassword\">no</a>\]  "
                      }
          if { $remind_day_of_p == "t" } {
              ns_write "\[Day of: <a href=\"day-of-
                      off.tcl?reminder_id=$reminder_id&$emailpassword\">yes</a>\]
                      " } else {
              ns_write "\[Day of: <a href=\"day-of-
                      on.tcl?reminder_id=$reminder_id&$emailpassword\">no</a>\]  "
                      }

      ns_write "\n<p>\n"

}

ns_write "

</ol>

<center>
<a href=\"add-reminder.tcl?$emailpassword\">Add new reminder</a>
</center>

<hr>
<a href=\"mailto:[bday_system_owner]\"><address>[bday_system_owner]
  </address></a>
</body>
</html>"
```

Most of the interesting points about this procedure are documented in the comments above. The only thing worth stressing is that this is the meat of the user interface. The links from this page mostly just update the RDBMS and then redirect back to this page. For example, here's week-before-off.tcl:

```
set_form_variables

# email, password, reminder_id

set db [ns_db gethandle]

# ... password check as in code above ...
```

```
ns_db dml $db "update bday_reminders set remind_week_before_p = 'f'
             where reminder_id = $reminder_id"
```

```
ns_returnredirect "domain-top.tcl?email=[ns_urlencode
$email]&password=[ns_urlencode $password]"
```

This procedure just checks the password, updates the row in bday_reminders, then redirects back to the reminder summary page.

Step 5: Step 5?

Yes, there is a step 5 for this system: making it work. If you are an Internet entrepreneur who has just raised $40 million for your WebJunkware System 2001, then step 5 is optional. You only need a front end good enough to show to venture capitalists and then to grab some screen shots for an initial public offering prospectus. If, however, you are a cringing little engineer whose ego is pathetically dependent upon producing a useful service, then you need to write a back end to send out reminders.

Almost all back ends require that a function be run every day at a set hour. I like to write my back end code using the same tools as the rest of the system. In the old days, I would write the nightly sweeper, or whatever, as a dynamic Web page. Then I'd use the Unix cron facility to run a shell script every night (the Windows NT equivalent is the At command). The shell script would call htget (a Perl script) to grab this dynamic Web page.

AOLserver, however, has a built-in cronlike function. I prefer to use it rather than an operating system facility, because it means less system administration when moving a service from one physical computer to another. Also, my code is portable across operating systems and I won't need to install Perl scripts like htget.

It should be easy:

```
ns_schedule_daily 5 0 bday_sweep_all
```

This tells the AOLserver to run the function bday_sweep_all at 5:00 A.M. every day.

The first and most obvious problem with this statement is that the server might be down at 5:00 A.M. If we are careful to define bday_sweep_all so that it won't send out duplicates, we can just schedule it for a bunch of times during the day:

```
ns_schedule_daily 5 0 bday_sweep_all
ns_schedule_daily 9 0 bday_sweep_all
ns_schedule_daily 13 0 bday_sweep_all
```

The second problem is an AOLserver bug (my opinion) or feature (Doug McKee's opinion; he's one of the server's authors): If these statements are executed

multiple times, the function will be multiply scheduled. For example, if you put these schedule requests in the Tcl directory that gets sourced on server startup, then reinitialize Tcl five times (to test changes in other code), you will find that bday_sweep_all is called six times at 5:00 A.M.

Here's my workaround:

```
ns_share -init {set bday_scheduled_p 0} bday_scheduled_p
if { !$bday_scheduled_p } {
    set bday_scheduled_p 1
    ns_schedule_daily -thread 5 0 bday_sweep_all
    ns_schedule_daily -thread 9 0 bday_sweep_all
    ns_schedule_daily -thread 13 0 bday_sweep_all
}
```

I say that the variable bday_scheduled_p is to be global among all the AOLserver threads and intialized to 0. If it has not been set to 1 yet (!$bday_scheduled_p), I schedule the sweep at 5:00 A.M., 9:00 A.M., and 1:00 P.M. Then I set the flag to 1 so that subsequent loads of this Tcl file won't result in redundant scheduling.

All we have to do now is write the `bday_sweep_all` procedure. We can expect the algorithm to be more or less for all three reminder types, so we posit a basic `bday_sweep` procedure that takes the reminder type as an argument:

```
proc bday_sweep_all {} {
    bday_sweep "day_of"
    bday_sweep "day_before"
    bday_sweep "week_before"
}
```

Now we just have to write the sweeper per se:

```
proc bday_sweep {message_type} {
    # message_type can be "week_before", "day_before", "day_of"

    switch $message_type {
        week_before { set sql_clause "remind_week_before_p = 't'
and to_char(event_date,'MM') = to_char(sysdate + 7, 'MM' )
and to_char(event_date,'DD') = to_char(sysdate + 7, 'DD' )"
                    set subject_fragment "NEXT WEEK"
                    set body_fragment "next week"
            }
        day_before { set sql_clause "remind_day_before_p = 't'
and to_char(event_date,'MM') = to_char (sysdate + 1, 'MM' )
and to_char(event_date,'DD') = to_char (sysdate + 1, 'DD' )"
                    set subject_fragment "TOMORROW"
                    set body_fragment "tomorrow"
            }
        day_of { set sql_clause "remind_day_of_p = 't'
and to_char(event_date,'MM') = to_char (sysdate, 'MM' )
and to_char(event_date,'DD') = to_char (sysdate, 'DD' )"
                    set subject_fragment "TODAY"
                    set body_fragment "today"
                }
    }

    set db_connections [ns_db gethandle [philg_server_default_pool] 2]
    set db [lindex $db_connections 0]
    set db_sub [lindex $db_connections 1]

    set email_count 0
    set start_stamp [database_to_tcl_string $db "select to_char(sysdate,
        'DD-MM-YYYY HH24:MI:SS') from DUAL"]
    set selection [ns_db select $db "select reminder_id, bday_reminders.*,
        to_char(event_date,'Month') as formatted_month,
        to_char(event_date,'DD, YYYY') as formatted_dayyear
```

```
from bday_reminders
where $sql_clause
and (trunc(last_reminded) <> trunc(sysdate)  or last_reminded is null)"]

    while {[ns_db getrow $db $selection]} {
        set_variables_after_query
        if [catch { ns_sendmail $email [bday_system_owner]
"$event_description is $subject_fragment" "Reminder:

$event_description ([string trim $formatted_month] $formatted_dayyear)

is $body_fragment.

This message brought to you by [bday_system_name].

If you don't want to receive these reminders in the future,
just visit [bday_system_url].
"
    } errmsg] {
        # failed to send email
        ns_log Error "[bday_system_name] failed sending to $email:
                     $errmsg"
    } else {
        # succeeded sending email, mark the row as reminded
        ns_db dml $db_sub "update bday_reminders
set last_reminded = sysdate
where reminder_id = $reminder_id"
        incr email_count
    }
  }

  ns_db dml $db "insert into bday_log (message_type, message_count,
              start_stamp, end_stamp)
values
('$message_type',$email_count, to_date('$start_stamp', 'DD-MM-YYYY
   HH24:MI:SS'),sysdate)"
  # we call these directly because bday_sweep_all calls this fcn
  # three times in succession and otherwise NaviServer won't allow
  # the ns_db gethandle to go through
  ns_db releasehandle $db
  ns_db releasehandle $db_sub

}
```

An interesting highlight of this sweeping function is that we are reading from the same table that we're updating. Why don't these two activities conflict?

MY CONCURRENCY QUESTION

Suppose I have two database connections open.

Connection 1: It does a SELECT * FROM BIG_TABLE and then is slowly sweeping through it. The value of the FOOBAR column is 56 for all rows.

Connection 2: Just as Connection 1 is reaching row 1,000, Connection 2 does an UPDATE BIG_TABLE SET FOOBAR = 15 WHERE ROW_ID = 2000;

Connection 1 eventually reaches row 2,000, maybe one minute later. Does Connection 1 find that the FOOBAR column has the old value of 56 or the updated value of 15? And is this behavior required by the SQL standard?

Answer from my friend who works at Oracle

Okay. When you execute a query, the first thing the kernel does is take note of the time you started the query. As the query progresses through the table, it will look at the SCN (system change number) of each row, which indicates when it has last been updated. If it finds that the row was updated after the query began, the kernel goes to the rollback buffer to fetch the last value the row held *before* the query began. So in your example, Connection 1 will not see the update made by Connection 2 if the update is done after the query begins.

In fact, even after the query finishes and you start another, it *still* won't see the change... not until you explicitly commit the update. (I shouldn't say "explicitly," since closing the connection cleanly will also perform a commit.) But even if you commit while the query is running, it still won't get the new value. However, the next time you query, it will catch the change.

But wait, there's more. Let's say you don't do a "commit" in Connection 2, but you enter the same query as before, this time in Connection 2. While that's running, you also run the query in Connection 1. The results will differ. Why? Because the query running in Connection 2 *knows* you've made an update and sees those SCNs rather than the ones stored in the permanent table structure. (Technically: Before a commit, the results of a write operation are stored in the ITL [Interested Transaction Layer]. A session has access to the portion of those results performed in that session *only;* these operations are "presumably committed" for the purposes of whatever you do in that session. It cannot, however, see anything in other sessions, which is why Connection 1 has no clue what you've done until you truly commit it.) This illustrates one of the challenges of concurrent programming with databases. Lesson: Always commit your changes as soon as you know they're permanent. (Corollary: Always have frequent backups for those plentiful occasions when they weren't and aren't reversible.)

Regarding locks (a subject which I know for a fact varies among database vendors), Connection 1 will not lock the table, unless the person executing the query has explicitly done so beforehand by doing "select * from table_name for update". If so, it would be released after an explicit "commit" is typed, and Connection 2 would wait or time out while the lock is held.

Most likely, you would not want to lock an entire table for a query. The only reason I can dream of doing this is if (1) you need to run a very long query (many hours), (2) there are tons of transactions going on simultaneously, (3) those transactions are less important than the query results, and (4) you have a *very* small amount of rollback space. Remember that point at which it finds a newer SCN and fetches the old value from the rollback? If the rollback doesn't go back far enough, the query errors out with an ORA-1555: snapshot too old error. So as long as the entire table isn't locked, and no other connections are locking the rows you need to update, Connection 2 will do its update right away.

When Connection 2 does update, it will either lock the entire table or just the row it

is trying to update, depending on the database's system and session parameters, e.g., if something like "ROW_LOCKING=ALWAYS" is in your oracle.ini file. I think the default is to lock the table, but don't quote me on that (it would be silly if we did, since row locking is a big thing for Oracle).

The question of yours regarding the SQL standard: That I don't know. I've never read the ANSI standards for SQL or SQL92, but I do not believe there are any rules regarding the behavior of concurrent sessions. If there is, though, I'm fairly confident we're doing what it says. (If we weren't, we'd be fixing it, and I've heard of no intentions to do so.)

My conclusion
Thank God I don't have to write my own RDBMS.

CASE 4: THE BULLETIN BOARD

The Internet is not starved for discussion software. The 20-year-old USENET (Net News) system alone has more than 50,000 active forums. There are some shallow reasons why you might want to build a database-backed bboard system. To

- have an optional "mail me when a response is posted" field
- let people subscribe to email summaries or instant alerts
- provide full-text indexing (assuming your RDBMS supports it)
- control access via all the usual HTTP mechanisms
- do secure transmission of data to and from the bboard via SSL
- use the admin pages to delete stale/ugly/whatever messages
- sort older postings by category
- build (since you have the source code) a collaboration environment that suits your users

The deep reason to run a DB-backed bboard system is that the users table in your RDBMS is your lifeblood. Level and nature of activity in discussion groups are two of the most important things that you can ask about a Web community member. You want to be able to ask, "Show me users who've submitted questions that were deleted by the moderator as redundant" (so that you can have the server welcome them back with a page explaining how to search and browse archived threads). You want to be able to ask, "Show me users who've submitted answers that were deemed definitive by the moderators" (so that you can consider promoting them to co-moderator status). When Reader X is looking at Reader Y's comment on one of your static pages, he ought to be able to say, "Please show me Reader Y's history as a community member" and see forum contributions.

The nuts and bolts (not)

I covered the nuts and bolts of building a threaded discussion group system in Chapter 13 of my last book (*http://photo.net/wtr/dead-trees/53013.htm*) and I gave away the source code for my initial implementation from *http://demo.webho.com.* Thus, rather than talk about how to use a computed sort key to cut the $O[n^3]$ operation of organizing into threads down to $O[n \log n]$, I'll devote this chapter to some lessons I've learned more recently.

Microsoft helps defend against bozos

One of my motivations for building the fancy software described in Chapter 3, Scalable Systems for Online Communities, was the difficulty of moderating the Q&A forum for photo.net. With about 10,000 participants, deleting duplicate postings and uninteresting threads was time-consuming but bearable. One day in

1997, Martin Tai showed up. He contributed some useful information about black-and-white film development and the Minox spy cameras. He also added some eyebrow-raising statements, like a print from a Minox was as good as that from a 4 × 5–inch view camera in 8 × 10–inch enlargements. Since a Minox negative is less than one-tenth the area of a standard 35-mm negative, which is in turn laughably poor quality compared to what you get out of a view camera, this generated some skepticism. Martin pointed to some Web sites displaying Minox photos that allegedly proved his point, but to my eyes you could clearly see the failure in lens and film resolution right on screen.

Personally, I didn't mind having Martin as a community member, despite his eccentric belief in the quality of the Minox's 8 × 11–mm negatives. However, he'd apparently previously annoyed folks in rec.photo.* (USENET) exchanges, and even the slightest error on Martin's part provoked a volley of vitriolic responses from other photo.net readers. Every day I'd have to go in and clear out 50 postings, plus respond to private email complaints.

My forums at the time were backed by the Illustra relational database management system, the child of some self-professed computer science geniuses at UC Berkeley. They spent a lot of time writing papers for academic journals about how stupid the engineers at Oracle were. Indeed, Illustra did quite a few things that Oracle could not. For one user at a time. If you wanted to update an Illustra row, you had to wait for all the readers to stop reading. If you wanted to read from an Illustra row, you had to wait for all the writers to stop writing. The bottom line was that, as soon as you had more than one person using Illustra, the system tended to deadlock. Under the best of circumstances, users posting to the forum would get a page saying,

```
please wait while we try to insert your message ..... message inserted.
```

Under heavy usage, the users would see

```
please wait while we try to insert your message ..
```

```
*** 60 second pause ***
```

```
... deadlock, transaction aborted.
Please hit Reload in five or ten minutes.
```

I felt humiliated by the situation, but for a variety of annoying reasons, it was taking me months to move my services to Oracle. Then it hit me: Sometimes a system that is 95 percent reliable is better than a system that is 100 percent reliable. If Martin was accustomed to seeing the system fail 5 percent of the time, he wouldn't be suspicious if it started failing all of the time. So I reprogrammed my application to look for the presence of "Martin Tai" in the name or message body fields of a posting. Then Martin, or anyone wanting to flame him, would get a program that did

```
ns_write "please wait while we try to insert your message ..."
ns_sleep 60
ns_write "... deadlock, transaction aborted.
Please hit Reload in five or ten minutes."
```

The result? Martin got frustrated and went away. Since I'd never served him a "you've been shut out of this community" message, he didn't get angry with me. Presumably inured by Microsoft to a world in which computers seldom work as advertised, he just assumed that photo.net traffic had grown enough to completely tip Illustra over into continuous deadlock.

I've used this trick a few more times in the photo.net forums with users who wouldn't take gentle suggestions from the moderators. Even though I've subsequently converted to Oracle so that message insertion is 100 percent reliable and takes one-tenth of a second, no user has ever suspected foul play when presented with a "database error" page.

The general rule to be extracted here is to take advantage of the world that Microsoft has created. Don't tell users that you hate them. Just program your server so that it can pretend to be broken.

Case 5: Brutal Truth Industries

I wish that I could say it was my passion for distributing knowledge that inspired me to construct online quiz software. However, the truth is more complex. In fact, it is sometimes brutal. In *The Game,* at *http://db.photo.net/dating/,* the truth is always brutal.

Conceived as an extension of my systematic, five-year,

The Game

designed, photographed, and programmed by Adriane Chapman and Philip Greenspun

Pick Your Date

Figure 15-9:
The Game, where your "date" may look more or less friendly, depending on how high you score.

Web-based program to demonstrate the futility of graduate school in science and engineering (*http://photo.net/philg/careers.html*), *The Game* puts the user in a heterosexual dating situation (see Figure 15-9). The human user is asked a series of questions by the database-driven date. Depending on the answer, the user's score goes up or down and the date becomes more or less friendly. The date's level of friendliness is indicated visually by a photograph.

What are the challenges in building software like this? There is the obvious one of making it easy to add quizzes merely by adding rows to relational database tables. A more interesting challenge is presented by the fact that the Web is inherently stateless. Users expect to be able to back up or reload at any time. However, they shouldn't thereby be able to improve their score. There are probably clever cryptographic ways to accomplish this. But if I paid $100,000 for an Oracle license, I shouldn't have to be clever. So this software, which we call ArsDigita Quizze, keeps updating a row in the database with the quiz-taker's history.

Here are the central features of ArsDigita Quizze:

- tracks users by issuing them a cookie when they start playing

- keeps a linked list of questions as rows in a questions table

- as users play, updates statistics in the answers table

- when users finish, offers them feedback on their performance, drawn from the history generated by other users

- is able to show administrators (and users if so desired) overall statistics on the relative popularity of different answers to each question

I'll sketch out some of the more important items below. Note that you can download the complete source code and data model from *http://arsdigita.com/free-tools /quizze.html.*

The data model

The trickiest part of this data model is the linking. Each quiz points to its first question. Each question points to the next question in a given quiz, as well as back to the quiz of which it is a part.

```
create table quizzes (
    quiz_id             integer primary key,
    title               varchar(100),
    first_question_id   integer not null,
    min_image_number    integer,
    max_image_number    integer,
    -- the sum of all the plays
    total_score         integer default 0,
    -- how many plays (so we can compute the average)
    total_trials        integer default 0
);

create table questions (
    question_id         integer not null primary key,
    -- this will be NULL for the last question
    next_question_id    integer references questions,
```

```
    quiz_id            integer not null
                       references quizzes,
    preamble           varchar(4000),
    text  varchar(4000) not null
);
```

Answers point only to questions:

```
create table answers (
    answer_id          integer primary
                       key,
    question_id        integer not null
                       references
                       questions,
    text               varchar(4000) not
                       null,
    score_delta        number not null,
    responses          integer default 0
);
```

Note that each answer contains a
score_delta column to indicate how much
the player's score should be adjusted in the
event that it is chosen, plus a responses
column for tallying the number of players
who've chosen it.

Each play of the game gets a row in the
players table. The same person playing four
times results in four row insertions. Note
that we're using the Oracle sequence generator to create unique player_id values.

```
create sequence player_id_sequence;

create table players (
        player_id            integer not null primary key,
        start_time           date,
        quiz_id              integer not null references quizzes,
        questions_answered   varchar(4000),
        score                number default 15
);
```

The interesting column here is questions_answered. We keep a space-separated
list of all the question_ids that the user has answered, for example, "23 45 67 81".
This facilitates checking for already answered questions in Tcl, which stores lists as
space-separated tokens in a string.

The new player

Once a user chooses to play a particular quiz (in our case by clicking on the photo of the preferred date), the start.tcl page is invoked with an argument of `quiz_id`:

```
set_form_variables

# quiz_id is now defined

set db [ns_db gethandle]

set player_id [database_to_tcl_string $db
    "select player_id_sequence.nextval
    from dual"]

ns_db dml $db "insert into players
(player_id, start_time, quiz_id)
values
($player_id, sysdate, $quiz_id)"

ns_write "HTTP/1.0 302 Found
Location: question.tcl
MIME-Version: 1.0
Set-Cookie:  player_id=expired; path=/;
             expires=Fri, 01-Jan-1990
             01:00:00 GMT
Set-Cookie:  player_id=$player_id;
path=/;

You should not be seeing this!
"
```

The first thing to note is that we go to Oracle to get the next `player_id` value before doing the INSERT. We do this because the Tcl script needs to have the value to put into the `Set-Cookie` header. The next thing to note is that this page doesn't return intended to be read by the user; it issues a 302 Redirect instructing the user's browser to visit question.tcl. AOLserver has a convenient `ns_returnredirect` API call that will write out a similar collection of bytes, but we also want to write the `Set-Cookie` headers. The first `Set-Cookie` instructs the browser to delete any previous `player_id` cookie value by giving an expiration date in the past (see *http://home.netscape.com/newsref/std/cookie_spec.html* for where this is promulgated as the preferred method of deleting a cookie). The second `Set-Cookie` instructs the browser to send our server back a `player_id` header on every subsequent page request, regardless of where on the server the page is (`path=/`). Because we did not specify an expiration date, the cookie will expire when the user quits Netscape Navigator.

The blank lines after the last header are very important and part of the HTTP standard. Browsers are usually relaxed about such things, but Web proxies are not. If you terminate your script with the last header, you'll find that users behind corporate firewalls generally can't use your service. I try to remember to put in a couple of blank lines plus some text that I don't expect the user to see.

The new answer

```
set_form_variables 0

# answer_id may or may not have been defined, depending on
# whether this is the user's first question

set headers [ns_conn headers $conn]
set cookie [ns_set get $headers Cookie]
if { ![regexp {player_id=([^;]+)} $cookie {} player_id] } {
    ns_return 200 text/html "no cookie :-( "
    return
}

# we have player_id from the cookie header

set db [ns_db gethandle]

set selection [ns_db 0or1row $db "select * from players where player_id =
    $player_id"]

if { $selection == "" } {
    ns_return 200 text/html "no entry in the RDBMS :-( "
    return
}

# we have a row from the database, now turn the columns into Tcl local
# variables

set_variables_after_query

# going to use quiz_id, questions_answered, score

# process answer to previous question

set reanswering_note ""

if { [info exists answer_id] } {
    # we only know the answer_id; we have to ask Oracle to
    # which question this answer corresponds
```

```
        set selection [ns_db 1row $db "select question_id as
            corresponding_question_id, score_delta from answers where
            answer_id = $answer_id"]
        set_variables_after_query
        if { [lsearch $questions_answered $corresponding_question_id] == -1 }
            {
                # the current question is not among those previously answered
                set current_score [expr $score + $score_delta]
                # record the question as answered by this player
                ns_db dml $db "update players
set questions_answered = '[lappend questions_answered
    $corresponding_question_id]',
score = $current_score
where player_id = $player_id"
                # update the statistical tally for this answer
                ns_db dml $db "update answers set responses = responses + 1 where
                    answer_id = $answer_id"
                set next_question_id [database_to_tcl_string $db "select
                    next_question_id from questions where question_id =
                    $corresponding_question_id"]
        } else {
            # re-answering a question
            set next_question_id [database_to_tcl_string $db "select
                next_question_id from questions where question_id =
                $corresponding_question_id"]
            set current_score $score
            set reanswering_note "<p>(not updated because you already answered
                the previous question)"
        }
    } else {
        # not answering a question (presumably this is the first iteration)
        # set score according to what was in the database (presumably the
        # default value of 15)
        set current_score $score
        if { $questions_answered == "" } {
            # we're on the very first question
            set next_question_id [database_to_tcl_string $db "select
                first_question_id from quizzes where quiz_id = $quiz_id"]
        } else {
            # we will only get to this code if the user backs up to the very
            # first question.tcl (with no form vars)
            set last_question_id [lindex $questions_answered [expr [llength
                $questions_answered]-1>
            set next_question_id [database_to_tcl_string $db "select
                next_question_id from questions where question_id =
                $last_question_id"]
        }
    }
}
```

```
if { $next_question_id == "" } {
    # there are no more questions and we've recorded their
    # answer and updated their score, so redirect them to the
    # "thanks for playing" page
    ns_returnredirect final-score.tcl?reason=no_more_questions
    return
}

# prepare to display the next question, finding it in the database
# by using the next_question_id that we previously looked up
# we have to JOIN with the quizzes table in order to get the minimum
# and maximum image numbers.  Logically this should simply be a separate
# query (to the quiz table alone) but realistically it is much faster to
# only go to the Oracle kernel once.

set selection [ns_db 1row $db "select preamble, text as question_text,
    min_image_number, max_image_number
from questions, quizzes
where question_id = $next_question_id
and questions.quiz_id = quizzes.quiz_id"]
set_variables_after_query
```

```
# we know the max possible score now, so let's check to see if this
# guy should be bounced

if { $current_score >= $max_image_number } {
    ns_returnredirect final-score.tcl?reason=player_won
    return
}

# we assume that we have integer images in the /images/**quiz_id**/ dir
# named 0.2.jpg through 30.2.jpg (these will be the 2nd PhotoCD
# resolution, i.e, 256x384

# each image will be a hyperlink to bigger.tcl?quiz_id=n&image_number=m
# the bigger.tcl file will display the .3 PhotoCD res and offer a
# hyperlink to the .4 res.

# < min we round up to min; > max and they should not have gotten here
# (if statement above) but we handle the case anyway so we don't ever
# risk showing a broken image icon

set image_number [expr round($current_score)]
if { $image_number < $min_image_number } {
    set image_number $min_image_number
}
if { $image_number > $max_image_number } {
    set image_number $max_image_number
}

if { $preamble == "" } {
    set full_blurb $question_text
} else {
    set full_blurb "$preamble\n<br><br>\n$question_text"
}

# return standard HTTP 200 headers but with a no-cache directive
# so that the user's browser doesn't just pull a page from its
# cache (with an old score) if he goes back

ns_write "HTTP/1.0 200 OK
MIME-Version: 1.0
Content-Type: text/html
pragma: no-cache

<html>
<head>
<title>$question_text</title>
</head>

<body bgcolor=#ffffff text=#000000>
```

```
<center>

<a target=bigpicture href=
   \"bigger.tcl?quiz_id=$quiz_id&image_number=$image_number\">
<img border=0 src=\"images/$quiz_id/$image_number.2.jpg\">
</a>

<h3>$full_blurb</h3>

</center>

<blockquote>

<ul>

"

# note that we wrote all the stuff above so that the user would have
# something to look at before we hit Oracle again (to get all the
# possible answers)

set selection [ns_db select $db "select answer_id, text as answer_text
from answers
where question_id = $next_question_id"]

while { [ns_db getrow $db $selection] } {
    set_variables_after_query
    ns_write "<p><li><a href=\"question.tcl?answer_id=
            $answer_id\">$answer_text</a>\n"
}

ns_write "

</ul>
</blockquote>

<center>

<h3>Your current score:  $current_score</h3>

$reanswering_note

</center>

<hr>

<a href=index.tcl>The Game</a>

</body>
</html>"
```

Nearly all of the interesting ideas in the above script are covered in the comments. Note, however, that we never put the answer score_deltas in hidden variables in the outgoing page. The scoring of the quiz remains secret from users who "view source" with their browsers. Another thing to observe is the extent to which we are hammering Oracle. On an average page load we

1. query to get the player's history
2. query to get the question_id to which this answer corresponds
3. update the player's history
4. update the answer's stats
5. query to get the next question text
6. query to get the answers to the next question

Yet pages from my quiz server (db.photo.net) load just about as fast as static HTML pages! The code is currently simple enough to understand and believe in. I'm disinclined to strive to reduce the amount of Oracle activity, given that the server is so fast with the current load (10,000 games a month on a four-CPU server that is also handling 25,000 daily photo.net users plus some miscellaneous Web collaboration services).

Lesson: Write your code as cleanly as possible; use the database where elegant; optimize if the performance isn't adequate.

Statistics

The real fun of a system like this is seeing what people pick. For example, with our installation of ArsDigita Quizze, Adriane and I have established that 17 percent of the men on the Internet think that when a woman asks, "If I gained 10 pounds, would you still find me attractive?" the correct response is, "If you went to the beach, I bet little kids would shout out 'Free Willy'" (see Figure 15-10).

How is this done? First, we query the quizzes table to find the first question's id:

```
select title, first_question_id
from quizzes
where quiz_id = $quiz_id;
```

Then we use the magic Oracle CONNECT BY clause to pull out the linked list of questions in one query:

```
select question_id, text as question_text
from questions
where quiz_id = $quiz_id
start with question_id = $first_question_id
connect by question_id = PRIOR next_question_id
```

In order to do the percentage math in SQL rather than Tcl, we have to first query the answers table to get the total responses to a particular question:

```
select sum(responses) as
    total_responses
from answers
where question_id =
    $question_id
```

Now we can grab the rows that you see in the report:

```
select text as answer_text,
    responses, score_delta,
        round((responses/
        $total_responses)
        *100) as percentage
    from answers where
    question_id = $question_id
```

Boy Meets Girl Statistics

- total trials: 41,518
- average score: 25.39

What do you do for a living?

I'm a radiologist. (2)	4979	17%
I'm an anesthesiologist. (2)	5026	17%
I'm a graduate student in physics. (-5)	9275	31%
I'm an anesthesiologist/radiologist. (4)	10626	36%

What do you like to do in your free time?

I enjoy watching Star Trek and reading science fiction novels. (-4)	4573	16%
I spend most weekends racing on my uncle's yacht. (2)	9544	34%
I like to upgrade my Microsoft-brand (TM) desktop software. (-6)	2546	9%
Sometimes I go to the ski condo that I share with the other partners in my corporate law firm. (2)	11347	41%

Figure 15-10: You're so tall and have such beautiful bone structure, nobody would notice if you gained 20 lbs.

We will be doing the last two queries for every question.

Note that CONNECT BY is not part of standard SQL, and that to make it run fast on a large table, you will need to create two concatenated indices:

```
create index questions_idx1 on questions(question_id,next_question_id);
create index questions_idx2 on questions(next_question_id,question_id);
```

See *Oracle 8: The Complete Reference* (Koch and Loney, 1997; Osborne) for more detail on CONNECT BY. If you're not using Oracle, check under "tree extensions" to see what your RDBMS vendor has provided.

Adriane's mom

We got a fair amount of feedback on the pictures and the text of the questions and answers. But our favorite came from Adriane's mom: "You are going to get arrested."

Oh, yes, the name. We took the name "Brutal Truth Industries" from the inspired Cement Cuddlers piece reprinted at *http://photo.net/philg/humor/cement-cuddlers.html*.

CASE 6: UPTIME

For those cases where the cure is worse than the disease, my friends and I built *http://uptime.arsdigita.com/uptime/*. Users type in their email address and a URL. The Uptime server tries to grab the URL every 15 or 20 minutes and sends them email if their server doesn't return "success".

It sounds absurdly simple, but after a few minutes you realize that there are some tough challenges:

- If someone goes on vacation for a week and trips over his server's power cord on the way out, he shouldn't come back to find hundreds of messages from Uptime clogging his inbox (so maybe we should only send one message when we notice that the server has gone down).

- If someone is asking Uptime to email his pager service and isn't within pager range the first time his server is unreachable, he should still be notified (so maybe we should send out notifications every hour or two).

- If someone has a pager service that requires a PIN number in the subject line or body, Uptime won't work (so maybe we have to let users also specify a custom subject or body).

- If someone shuts down a server permanently but neglects to delete his Uptime monitor, how does my server avoid wasting one minute every sweep testing a machine that is never going to come back to life?

- If there is major trouble with some of the Internet backbone providers, how does my server avoid spamming all of its users with email?

- What do we do about privacy? Should a server's uptime record be private or public?

Let's start by looking at the data model:

```
create table uptime_urls (
    monitor_id                    integer not null primary key,
    url                           varchar(200) not null,
    name                          varchar(100) not null,
    email                         varchar(100) not null,
    password                      varchar(30) not null,
    homepage_url                  varchar(200),
    first_monitored               date,
    -- the following are for people who have beepers
    -- and need a special tag or something in the subject
    custom_subject                varchar(4000),
    custom_body                   varchar(4000),
    -- we always send email when the server is down, we can
    -- also send email when the server comes back up
    notification_mode             varchar(30),
    -- 'down_then_up', 'periodic'
    -- these two are only used when notification_mode is 'periodic'
    notification_interval_hours   integer default 2,
    last_notification             date,
    -- if this is NULL, it means that we've sent a BACK UP notification
    time_when_first_unreachable   date,
    unique(url,email)
);

create table uptime_log (
    monitor_id                    not null references uptime_urls,
    event_time                    date,
    event_description             varchar(100)
);

create index uptime_log_idx on uptime_log (monitor_id);
```

Remarkably simple, eh? Note that a server's reachableness is entirely encapsulated in the time_when_first_unreachable column. We set this to sysdate when we notice that a site is newly unreachable. We set this to NULL when we are able to successfully grab the URL again. Note that for periodic notification, the state of our having notified a user is entirely encapsulated in the last_notification column. Note finally that the uptime_log table has no primary key. Events are merely logged with the expectation that they will never be deleted or updated. In order to make reporting for a particular URL fast, we define an index on the table by monitor_id.

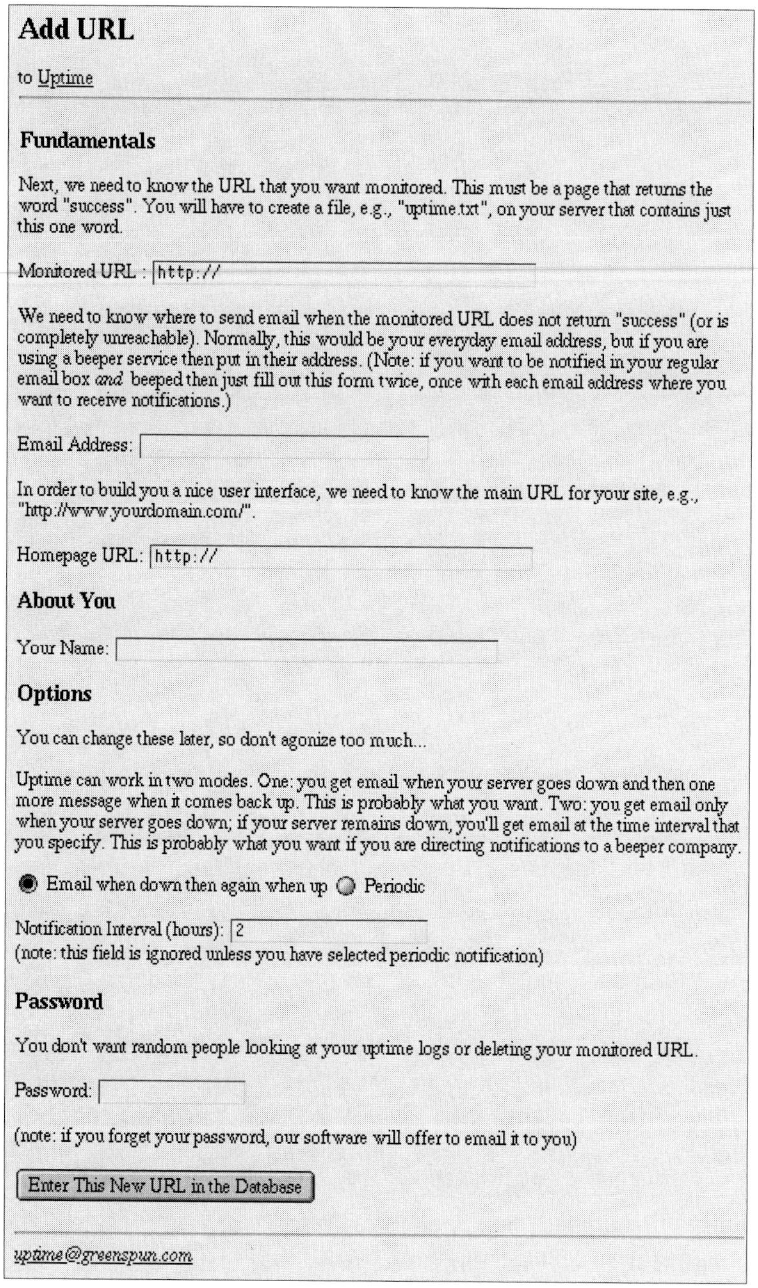

Add URL

to <u>Uptime</u>

Fundamentals

Next, we need to know the URL that you want monitored. This must be a page that returns the word "success". You will have to create a file, e.g., "uptime.txt", on your server that contains just this one word.

Monitored URL : `http://`

We need to know where to send email when the monitored URL does not return "success" (or is completely unreachable). Normally, this would be your everyday email address, but if you are using a beeper service then put in their address. (Note: if you want to be notified in your regular email box *and* beeped then just fill out this form twice, once with each email address where you want to receive notifications.)

Email Address:

In order to build you a nice user interface, we need to know the main URL for your site, e.g., "http://www.yourdomain.com/".

Homepage URL: `http://`

About You

Your Name:

Options

You can change these later, so don't agonize too much...

Uptime can work in two modes. One: you get email when your server goes down and then one more message when it comes back up. This is probably what you want. Two: you get email only when your server goes down; if your server remains down, you'll get email at the time interval that you specify. This is probably what you want if you are directing notifications to a beeper company.

(•) Email when down then again when up (○) Periodic

Notification Interval (hours): `2`
(note: this field is ignored unless you have selected periodic notification)

Password

You don't want random people looking at your uptime logs or deleting your monitored URL.

Password:

(note: if you forget your password, our software will offer to email it to you)

[Enter This New URL in the Database]

uptime@greenspun.com

Figure 15-11:
A successful form:
2,000 people
have registered
and hardly anyone
sent me email.

The first challenge in building a free service is designing forms that are self-explanatory and yet powerful enough to let users take advantage of all the system's capabilities. See Figure 15-11 for what I think is a successful form (2,000 people have registered to use the service and hardly anyone has sent email to clear up confusion). Basically, the goal is to quickly separate those who are having email sent to a pager from those who are receiving email personally. The pager crowd can later edit their monitors to add a custom subject or body.

Privacy has presented an interesting dilemma. If my server is down all of the time, do I want the rest of the world to know? Probably not. But what if I have good uptime and want to prove it to a skeptics? Then I want to be able to direct these skeptics to a trusted source (i.e., Uptime) and let them see the record for themselves. Although we still use the password to authenticate people who want to delete or edit monitors, I decided to make Uptime event records public. Why? Anyone on the Internet can monitor an arbitrary URL. Hence, there is no practical way for a site to hide its downtime. For example, joe_nerd@stanford.edu can spend five minutes with AOLserver or *Web Client Programming* (Wong, 1997; O'Reilly) to build a monitor for *http://www.ai.mit.edu* and then release the results.

With this kind of openness, what kinds of users has the system attracted? My favorite is Online Privacy (*http://www.privacy.nb.ca/*), "a nonprofit group of computer professionals who intend to educate and help the general public preserve their personal privacy while online."

Scanning the rest of the list, I'm gratified to see that, after more than one year of operation, only one of ArsDigita's customers has signed up to monitor a site that we built! Also, though I built Uptime with the expectation that sysadmins would be the primary users, as of July 12, 1998, six GeoCities "customers" are using my service. I'm not really sure what they do if Uptime reports that their site is unreachable. Do they complain to GeoCities that they aren't getting their money's worth?

I'd expected most of the folks using Uptime to be operators of complex, database-backed Web services. Thus, the URL being monitored would be some kind of script that tried to connect to the RDBMS and would report "success" if everything was fine. In fact, as I scan through *http://uptime.arsdigita.com/uptime/search-list-of-urls.tcl,* I note that many of the URLs monitored are plain vanilla .txt files (this is true even for the big companies using the service, e.g., ARCO, LSI Logic, Metropolitan Opera, MGM, Seagate, and the United Way).

How does it work? (the big picture)

```
# tell AOLserver to run uptime_monitor_once every 20 minutes
# the -thread option instructs AOLserver to spawn a new thread
# for this procedure, i.e., that the procedure probably won't
# return quickly
ns_schedule_proc -thread 1200 uptime_monitor_once

# tell AOLserver to run uptime_monitor_stale every night at 11:45
ns_schedule_daily -thread 23 45 uptime_monitor_stale

proc uptime_monitor_once {} {
    set db [ns_db gethandle]
    set monitor_ids [database_to_tcl_list $db "select monitor_id
from uptime_urls
where uptime_stale_p(time_when_first_unreachable) = 'f'"]
    ns_log Notice "Uptime starting to test [llength $monitor_ids] URLs"
    uptime_monitor_list_of_ids $db $monitor_ids
    ns_log Notice "Uptime finished sweeping."
}

proc uptime_monitor_stale {} {
    set db [ns_db gethandle]
    set monitor_ids [database_to_tcl_list $db "select monitor_id
from uptime_urls
where uptime_stale_p(time_when_first_unreachable) = 't'"]
    ns_log Notice "Uptime working on the stale URLs ([llength
            $monitor_ids] of them)"
    uptime_monitor_list_of_ids $db $monitor_ids
    ns_log Notice "Uptime finished with the stale URLs."
}
```

Note that these procedures both rely on uptime_monitor_list_of_ids to do all the real work, passing a database connection and a list of keys into the uptime_urls table. Note further that both write something into the AOLserver error log when they start and stop. This makes it easy to look at the log and find out how long sweeps are taking.

The use of uptime_stale_p bears some explaining. This is a PL/SQL function that takes in a date and returns true or false (Oracle lacks the Boolean data type; hence, these are presented by the letters "t" and "f"). The concept of a URL having gone stale is sufficiently fundamental to the system that I wanted to make sure it was consistent across all the monitoring scripts, reporting scripts, etcetera. In fact, it would have been easier to simply include

```
where time_when_first_unreachable is null
or time_when_first_unreachable  (sysdate - 10)
```

in the query than put

```
create or replace function uptime_stale_p (time_when_first_unreachable IN
        date) return varchar
is
begin
        IF time_when_first_unreachable is null THEN
          return 'f';
        ELSIF time_when_first_unreachable  (sysdate - 10) THEN
          return 'f';
        ELSE
            return 't';
        END IF;
end;
```

in the data-model.sql file. However, I personally get a warm and fuzzy feeling knowing that all of my Tcl scripts will rely on this procedure to determine staleness (in this case, we've set it for 10 days).

What's under the hood of that uptime_monitor_list_of_ids procedure?

```
proc uptime_monitor_list_of_ids {db monitor_ids} {
    foreach monitor_id $monitor_ids {
        set selection [ns_db 0or1row $db "SELECT uu.*,
to_char(time_when_first_unreachable,'YYYY-MM-DD HH24:MI:SS') as
full_unreachable_time,
to_char(sysdate,'YYYY-MM-DD HH24:MI:SS') as full_sysdate,
round((sysdate - time_when_first_unreachable)*60*24) as n_minutes_downtime
FROM uptime_urls uu
WHERE monitor_id = $monitor_id"]
        if { $selection == "" } {
            # this row got deleted from the database while we were
            # running our script; this presumably
            # happens very rarely (user chooses to delete his monitor)
            # but we must handle it for cleanliness
            # jump to next iteration
            continue
        }
        # there was a row in the database
        set_variables_after_query
        # now url, email, a bunch of other stuff are set
        ns_log Notice "Uptime testing $url for $email ..."
        # we do the ns_httpget inside a Tcl catch because we don't
        # want one URL that raises a Tcl error to make the sweep halt
        # for everyone else; ns_httpget wil raise an error when a server
        # doesn't respond, when a URL is badly formed, e.g., "htttp" or
        # "https" (doesn't handle SSL), etc.
```

```
            if [catch {set grabbed_text [ns_httpget $url]} errmsg] {
                ns_log Notice "Uptime failed to reach $url"
                set grabbed_text "GETURL failed"
                # let's try once more before raising the alarm
                if [catch {set grabbed_text [ns_httpget $url]} errmsg] {
                    ns_log Notice "Uptime failed to reach $url
                            (second attempt)"
                    set grabbed_text "GETURL failed"
                }
            } else {
                ns_log Notice "Uptime grabbed something from $url"
            }
            if { [regexp -nocase "success" $grabbed_text] } {
                # we got it
                if { $time_when_first_unreachable != "" } {
                    # we have the URL on record as having been dead
                    ns_db dml $db "update uptime_urls
set time_when_first_unreachable = NULL
where monitor_id = $monitor_id"
                    ns_db dml $db "insert into uptime_log
(monitor_id, event_time, event_description)
values
($monitor_id, sysdate, 'back_up')"
                    if { $notification_mode == "down_then_up" } {
                        ns_sendmail $email [uptime_system_owner] "$url
                                back up" "$url returned \"success\".

It was last reached by [uptime_system_name] at $full_unreachable_time
    ([uptime_system_timezone]).
Currently our Oracle database thinks it is $full_sysdate.
In other words, your server has been unreachable for approximately
$n_minutes_downtime minutes.

Does this mean your server was down?  No.  Our server could have lost ITS
network connection.  Or there could have been some problem on the
wider Internet.

Does this mean your server was actually unreachable for all of those
minutes?  No.  We only sweep every 15 minutes or so
"
                    }
                }
            } else {
                # we did NOT successfully reach the URL (or the page we got
                # back did not contain the word "success")
                if { $time_when_first_unreachable == "" } {
                    # this is the first time we couldn't get it
                    ns_db dml $db "update uptime_urls
set time_when_first_unreachable = sysdate,
```

```
last_notification = sysdate
where monitor_id = $monitor_id"
                ns_db dml $db "insert into uptime_log
(monitor_id, event_time, event_description)
values
($monitor_id, sysdate, 'down')"
                set subject "$url is unreachable"
                set body "[uptime_system_name] cannot reach $url.

You may want to check your server.

Does this mean that your server is down?  No.  But as of $full_sysdate
([uptime_system_timezone]), our server is having trouble reaching it.

Oh yes, if you are annoyed by this message and want to desubscribe
from [uptime_system_name], visit

  [uptime_url_base]delete.tcl?monitor_id=$monitor_id

"
                if { ![string match $custom_subject ""] } {
                      set subject $custom_subject
                  }
                if { ![string match $custom_body ""] } {
                      set body $custom_body
                  }

                ns_sendmail $email [uptime_system_owner] $subject $body
              } else {
                    # site is unreachable, but we already knew that
                    if { $notification_mode == "periodic" &&
[database_to_tcl_string $db "select count(*)
from uptime_urls
where (last_notification + notification_interval_hours/24)
```

Is Uptime up?

How do I know that Uptime itself is working? By having programmed AOLserver
to send me email every night at 11:30 noting the number of events logged:

```
ns_schedule_daily -thread 23 30 uptime_notify_system_owner

proc uptime_notify_system_owner {} {
    set db [ns_db gethandle]
    set total_entries [database_to_tcl_string $db "select count(*)
from uptime_log
where trunc(event_time) = trunc(sysdate)"]
    ns_sendmail uptime@arsdigita.com uptime@arsdigita.com "Uptime sent
              $total_entries messages" ""
}
```

The one odd thing to note about this query is the use of trunc. In most Oracle installations, if you ask Oracle to print out the date, you'll get precision down to the day:

```
SQL select sysdate from dual;

SYSDATE
----------
1998-07-12
```

However, Oracle internally records precision down to the second. This makes naive comparisons fail:

```
create table test_dates (
        the_value       varchar(20),
        the_date        date
);

insert into test_dates values ('happy',sysdate);
insert into test_dates values ('happy',sysdate);
insert into test_dates values ('joy',sysdate);
insert into test_dates values ('joy',sysdate);

*** brief pause ***

SQL select * from test_dates where the_date = sysdate;

no rows selected
```

We didn't get any rows because none matched down to the second. Are we stuck? No. We can rely on the fact that Oracle stores dates as numbers:

```
SQL select * from test_dates where trunc(the_date) = trunc(sysdate);

THE_VALUE    THE_DATE
---------    ----------
happy        1998-07-12
happy        1998-07-12
joy          1998-07-12
joy          1998-07-12
```

Note:
For more about
Oracle and dating
see *http://photo.net
/wtr/oracle-tips.html.*

An arguably cleaner approach is to use to_char:

```
select * from test_dates where to_char(the_date,'YYYY-MM-DD') =
        to_char(sysdate,'YYYY-MM-DD');
```

What I learned about the Internet

As of July 12, 1998, Uptime had 55,486 server-days of monitoring under its belt. It had observed 10,760 unreachability incidents that weren't corrected by the next sweep. So from a particular browser's point of view, the average Web site would appear to be unreachable 5.8 times a month.

What are the sources of these problems? If you scan through *http://uptime.ars-digita.com/uptime/rank.tcl,* network connectivity doesn't seem to be the overwhelming determining factor. The machines inside MIT Net (where the Uptime server resides) should be at the top of the list. Yet a little playing around with traceroute shows that the top machines are in Houston, Minnesota, New York, and so on. Some of the most reliably reachable servers seem to be BBN Planet customers (MIT's ISP), but others require hops to other backbones.

ISP diligence seems to be a factor. Many of the best servers are operated by Mindspring, for example. It looks like even a diligent ISP cannot conquer technology, however. For example, my main static site seems to have suffered 1.6 outages per month. It relies only on HP-UX. But db.photo.net is down at 7.2 outages per

month. It relies on Solaris, Illustra (for all of the monitored period), and Oracle 8 (for some of the monitored period).

The RDBMS seems to be implicated in many of the worst performing sites in the Uptime service. Nearly in last place are www.greenspun.com and lavsa.com, both hosted at America Online's Primehost facility. The folks at Primehost run the Illustra RDBMS and they stop answering tech support calls at 9:00 P.M. eastern time. This combination is apparently capable of producing between 27 and 35 outages a month.

Note: After computing these stats, I moved greenspun.com to MIT and an Oracle backend.

What I learned about operating an Internet service

As with my community software, the Achilles heel of a service like this is bouncing email. Without some kind of automated system for absorbing bounced notifications and eventually deleting those folks from the database of users, operating Uptime eventually will become a living hell for the maintainer (me and my friends). Looking around Yahoo, I found that there are some commercial companies (such as *http://www.netmechanic.com* and *http://www.redalert.com*) offering Uptime-like services. They charge $10 to $20 a month. Now I know why! What I'd love to do is tell people that Uptime is a free service, but take their credit card number on condition that I get to feed it into ArsDigita Shoppe (see Chapter 14, ecommerce) if I'm forced to edit or delete their monitors.

SUMMARY

Here's what you should have learned from reading this chapter:

- Interaction design is the heart and soul of a good service (all the cases).

- When you manage a project the way that I suggested in Chapter 11, Sites that Are Really Databases—programmers do a text-only site; graphic designer makes it pretty—you end up with a site that works well, looks good, and costs very little to develop (the RemindMe system).

- Oracle is very, very fast, and you can probably afford to abuse it (ArsDigita Quizze).

- It is indeed tough to hang yourself with the software if you start out with a decent data model (all the cases).

If you don't like staring at my software, you'll be pleased to learn that the next two chapters take us back to the tone and level of the beginning of the book.

MORE

- For an overview of one proven method of keeping Web services up and running, see the ArsDigita Server Architecture (*http://photo.net/wtr/arsdigita-server-architecture.html*).

- "Sites that Don't Work (And How to Fix Them)," a chapter from my old book, contains several interesting system-design case studies. You can find it at *http://photo.net/wtr/dead-trees/53014.htm.*

- *http://photo.net/philg/research/monitoring.html* talks more generally about monitoring/reminding systems like Uptime and RemindMe.

- The hard-core Oracle concurrency story is explained nicely in Chapter 23 of *Oracle 8 Concepts, Volume 2,* part of the Oracle server documentation (Someday Oracle will put this on their Web site), which also contains the *Oracle 8 Server Application Developer's Guide,* very useful when you are making high-level decisions about an Oracle-backed system.

16
Better Living Through Chemistry

his chapter explores two Internet
applications. The first tells you
whether your neighborhood is being
polluted and, if so, by whom. The
second helps groups of citizens communicate with politicians and other decision
makers. We will examine the technical
challenges presented by these applications,
but first let's look at how the service ideas
themselves fit into the modern conception
of the Internet.

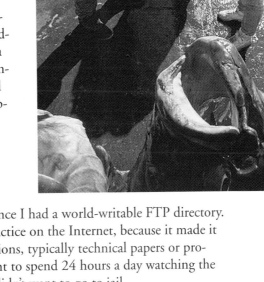

TWO WAYS OF LOOKING
AT A BLACKBIRD

In 1994, the U.S. Department of Justice
indicted David LaMacchia, an MIT undergraduate, for the crime of operating a world-
writable FTP server. User A could upload a
file and then User B would be able to download the file. Although the government did
not allege that David had personally distributed any copyrighted material, the indictment asserted that others had done so and
that his server facilitated the exchange.

I was upset by the indictment, for a
variety of reasons:

1. I was guilty of the same crime, since I had a world-writable FTP directory.
   It was more or less a standard practice on the Internet, because it made it
   easy for folks to accept contributions, typically technical papers or programs, from authors. I didn't want to spend 24 hours a day watching the
   activity of my FTP server and I didn't want to go to jail.

2. The evidence that the government claimed to have obtained seemed far too
   easy to forge. I didn't want to go to jail because someone who gained shell
   access to one of my Unix machines decided to spend a few minutes in
   Emacs forging some log files and email.

3. David was a nice kid who had worked in our lab.

Mostly for the last reason, I started a legal defense fund to ensure that David got the best lawyers possible. The Web was already sufficiently mature in 1994 that most of the people who might have been interested in the case had browsers on their desktops. I built a page (*http://photo.net/dldf/*) that distributed documents about the case and accepted on-line pledges.

Philip Elmer-Dewitt showed up at MIT to interview me for the *McNeil-Lehrer Report*. Elmer-Dewitt would later achieve fame as the author of *Time*'s "Cyberporn" cover story (July 3, 1995), in which the Internet was deemed 83.5 percent porn, a figure subsequently adjusted (July 24, 1995) to "less than one-half of 1 percent." However, in 1994 he was a relative unknown.

For the interview, I got my hair cut, dressed up a bit with a button-down shirt and khakis, and sequestered the dog in my office. On camera in an MIT conference room, I patiently explained the ease with which someone could forge electronic evidence against an enemy. I noted the absurdity of the government's claim that software publishers had suffered more than a $30-million-dollar loss. That someone would spend five minutes downloading the Adobe Photoshop binary wasn't evidence that the person was ready to spend $500 for a boxed supported documented version of the product. In fact, software publishers might be *profiting* from the copying of binaries. Many of the students who learned an application by trying out a pirate binary would eventually get jobs where their company bought them a legal copy. Software publishers had already developed many clever marketing methods for making sure that people weren't satisfied with "just the binary." If they didn't have these methods, they'd be in trouble in 1997, because everyone would have cable modems and be able to email each other the entire contents of CD-ROMs: software binaries, music, etcetera. In Microsoft's ideal world, the Internet would be a place where people shared their stories about how much they loved Microsoft products and where to purchase them. But since commercial software publishers hadn't contributed anything to the development of the Internet, they couldn't very well expect the tool to serve their interests exclusively. They would find that high-speed Internet connections made it easier to copy binaries but created other opportunities. (I know that these statements sound pathetically banal now, but remember that this was April 1994.)

A few days later, I rushed home with some friends to watch the show. I'd been cut! The case against David was presented by a three-piece suited lawyer from the Software Publishers Association. Software pirates were bad and threatened to destroy an essential industry. For contrast, the producers had dredged up a long-haired, tie-dyed hippie in San Francisco who argued that all software should be freely shared.

Sitting on the sofa with my nerd friends, we railed against the absurdity of this polarized view of the Internet. Yet four years later, I think there is some truth in the *McNeil-Lehrer* segment. Mining my email archives, I find the following:

Tie-Dyed Hippie

"I heard from Mr. Rowe and will be talking to him later this week. Thank you for bringing us together...."
—Holocaust researcher in Iowa who found an original source at *http://photo.net/bp/*

"...a really nice guy, who had previously sold me a used tripod, works a few blocks from Wall Street Camera and offered to go inspect the [used $4,000 lens for sale]. I was delighted, particularly because he is a professional photographer, and was someone whose judgement I would really trust."
—Texan reader of photo.net who found a New Yorker willing to help

SPA Stuffed Shirt

"the joy of the Internet is feeling like I can buy exactly what I want"
—Employee of Open Market, makers of software that supposedly does ecommerce (though for me it only dumps core)

"I found the very article that nudged me into test driving an NSX (I bought it—you're assessment is spot on. I don't want or need the penile enhancement factor of a prancing horse on my hood...)."
—Guy who came to my site looking for information about the Lisp programming language and ended up buying an $85,000 Acura NSX sports car

Tie-Dyed Hippie

"Picture an evening with your mom just diagnosed with terminal cancer and you are leaving the next day after a 3 week stay. You both are big ELVIS fans, but have never been to graceland and wanted to go. Now you know that dream with your mom can never be, she is too sick. You find the sight of the Graceland Tour and help her to the room. You and her are sharing this moment quietly in private. Looking at the pictures and holding each other."
—Reader of *http://photo.net/summer94/graceland.html*

"I went to Edward Tufte's [world's leading authority on information presentation] seminar in San Francisco, and he basically said if you are looking for examples of good information display on the web, don't." Then he went on to say that he could only recommend two sites, one of which was photo.net."
—Email received on same day as *Wall Street Journal* article

"As a 75+ senior and a native son of a 97 yr. old native of the San Diego area. I must say I really enjoyed your photos. When younger I hiked all those places either with the Boy Scouts or family. It is nice to sit in a easy chair and redo them without the sweat that went with it. I WANT TO THANK YOU FOR A VERY PLEASANT REVIEW OF THE PAST. I have a webtv and a h.p. printer. . . ."
—WebTV user who'd been printing my images

SPA Stuffed Shirt

"Under the heading "Where to buy a camera?", there is a sub-heading "I want to get f*****" and a highly objectionable picture. To say that it is outrageous is a gross understatement. It is obscene, vulgar, and deserves to be removed rightaway. At the same time the author owes an apology to all the readers/contributors to this forum. I can't even believe that such an absurd matter got its way here. I also appeal to all the rightminded viewers to register their protests against this indecency. . . ."
—Reader of *http://photo.net/photo/where-to-buy.html*

"The site's style isn't glitzy—the front page is one long menu of options."
—The *Wall Street Journal*'s opinion of photo.net's design

"I've run classified ads to sell three Nikon F4S bodies, and three F3 bodies. Thus far, I have successfully sold all the F4's, and two of the F3's . . . . two cameras went to Singapore, two to Malaysia, and the fifth went to Houston. I never would have imagined it possible to sell my cameras overseas . . . let alone across the US from my tiny office in Alaska!"
—User of the photo.net classifieds

Tie-Dyed Hippie

Gary was truly a very funny and engaging man. I repaired his cameras while he taught at the University of Texas. I loved the guy, he was a typical NY'er if I ever met one. I have several of his photos which are quintessential Americana of the "70. It may be street photography, but what about the photos of Mohammed Ali, Diane Arbus, and Monkey in the Bronx Zoo. You could stand on a street corner for a very long time and never be in the right place at the right time with a camera and know what to do with it. He was a master technician with Tri X and D76, plus he could see the pathos of a seemingly humdrum existence and give it timelessness. He was my friend.
—Reader of *http://photo.net/photo/wino-grand.html*

"Philip is one of my heroes. His blatant arrogance and self-promotion are the perfect mask for this sweet bodhisattva; it discourages worship and promotes critical thinking.... A therapist once told me that people change because of a lover, a guru, or being thrown against a wall. Philip is all three, I think, to thousands of us."
—Reader

"I was searching the net seeking information for a paper I'm doing on Narcissistic Personality Disoder, and I came across your web page."
—My favorite comment ever

SPA Stuffed Shirt

"I really think it would be better, much better, to leave comments about the size of someone's genitalia out of items you publish on the web. Yes, I suppose that it's your so-called "right" to do this in our great country...."
—Reader of *http://photo.net/photo/what-camera-should-I-buy.html*

"Why would anyone want to view a computer book online? Computer books are used beside your computer to help you. We present visuals and step by steps to assist actual work. I don't want to . . . hope for royalties for a book I have no way of knowing if anyone actually used (i.e., bought)...."
—Professional computer book author (see *http://photo.net/wtr/thebook /globnet.html* for my response)

"While looking for some Aristotle I found a source with links to great books, including such classics as Aristotle's *Poetics,* Kant's *Critique,* Marx's *Manifesto,* The King James Bible, etc. There's one odditiy, though: Greenspun's *Travels with Samantha.*"
—From my friend Ted

WHO IS WINNING?

After all these years, who is winning on the Internet? The tie-dyed radicals or the stuffed business suits?

In *U.S. v. LaMacchia,* both sides won. David won when a federal judge dismissed the government's case against him at the earliest possible moment. It turned out that, even if one accepted as true all of the government's assertions, David had not committed a crime. Criminal copyright infringement required a profit motive. Wealthy copyright holders won on December 16, 1997 when Bill Clinton signed the No Electronic Theft Act and it became Public Law 105-147. It is now a criminal act to trade a copyrighted work with a friend. It is now a criminal act to reproduce or distribute, during any 180-day period, copyrighted works with a total retail value of more than $1,000. The statute of limitations for such acts was extended to five years. Senator Orrin Hatch said, "This bill plugs the '*LaMacchia* Loophole' in criminal copyright enforcement."

As noted in Chapter 3, Scalable Systems for Online Communities, a lot of noncommercial activity on the Internet collapsed because the software and the systems used to support it did not scale well. Meanwhile, the expense of operating a Web site has grown dramatically. In 1994, you could park a bunch of static files on a server and call yourself an innovator. Total cost: $50 a month. In 1998, if you don't want people to laugh at your effort, you need to acquire a collaboration infrastructure (e.g., a relational database management system), hire someone to encourage and moderate online collaboration, and even (sigh) hire a graphic designer every year to rethink your look and message. Total cost: $50,000 a month.

My public antidote to the increasingly commercialized Web is to offer a bunch of collaboration software for free and, more importantly, to offer a bunch of collaboration *services* for free (see *http://photo.net/philg/services.html*). I want to make sure that Web publishers can adopt the modern collaboration religion without selling their souls to the banner ad devils.

My private antidote to the increasingly commercialized Web is to spend some of my time working on sites with the Environmental Defense Fund (EDF; *www.edf.org*).

GOVERNMENT REGULATION PROTECTING YOU

In the bad old days there was no government regulation of pollution. If you were a farmer and the paper mill upstream was poisoning the river, you couldn't complain that the mill was violating statutes and administrative rules. Your only remedy was to sue the mill under common law (legal precedent going back to Germanic tribal law).

How effective could that be?

It turns out that under common law, people have an absolute right to clean air and water. If the paper mill was polluting the river, they had to pay for all the damage they did to downstream users of the water. If a plaintiff proved damage and causality

(the difficulty of which is chronicled in *A Civil Action* [Harr, 1995; Random House]), a court would order the mill to compensate the farmer for killed livestock, vet bills, and less plentiful crops.

Under the current legal system, the government regulates pollution by promulgating state and federal laws and making administrative decisions. If your cows are dying and your fields won't support crops, you can still sue the paper mill. However, they don't have to pay you anything if they can show that their output of filth is not in excess of the statutory limit.

Note: Workman's compensation laws grew out of the same kind of situation. When a factory worker was killed because of the company's negligence, the relatives of the deceased would sue the owners for megabucks. The owners didn't want to invest in making the factories safe and they didn't want to pay big jury awards. So they got politicians to pass workman's compensation laws limiting their liability to $X for the loss of an arm or $Y for a worker who was killed. That's why you find injured workers suing the companies that make the machines on factory floors rather than the factories themselves.

If a factory isn't legally required to reduce pollution beyond the limits established by statute, how then to nudge them into reducing discharges?

IS INFORMATION POWER?

Although the EDF is probably best known for convincing McDonald's to eliminate its wasteful packaging, the 175-person organization has been working for 30 years to increase the amount of information available about pollution, environmental hazards, and waste generation.

Is distributing information sufficient to cut pollution? Remarkably, it seems to be. In 1988, the Environmental Protection Agency began collecting and publishing data on chemicals released from manufacturing facilities. If you check the nationwide report (*http://www.scorecard.org/env-releases/us.tcl*), you'll see a dramatic reduction in releases of chemicals covered by the federal Toxic Release Inventory (TRI).

What could a consumer learn from the TRI data? That Ford Electronics in Connersville, Indiana released 605,000 pounds of trichloroethylene into the air in 1995 (see *http://www.scorecard.org/env-releases/facility.tcl?tri_id=47331FRDLCSTATE*). Is that good or bad? Is trichloroethylene hazardous? Carcinogenic?

In California, voters passed Proposition 65 in 1986. This requires industry not only to disclose but also to warn the public about exposure to known carcinogens

and reproductive toxicants. Thus, a resident of California would be warned that a local factory was releasing trichloroethylene and that it was a recognized carcinogen and reproductive toxicant.

The result? California companies cut emissions of TRI chemicals roughly in half, just as manufacturers did elsewhere in the nation. But California companies cut emissions of Prop. 65 chemicals to one-quarter of their previous usage. Apparently, disclosure plus interpretation is more powerful than disclosure alone.

WOULD 750 MB OF DATA HELP YOU OUT?

Thanks to the Internet, it turns out to be pretty easy to pull together 750 MB of data on toxic releases and the health effects of various chemicals. This is *potentially* useful and interesting. How do we make it *actually* useful and interesting?

- Interpret. Show users how a chemical is used, by which industries, and how hazardous it is.

- Localize. Let users type in their zip code and see what's being released in their neighborhood.

Note: Trichloroethylene is the villain, along with W. R. Grace and Beatrice Foods, in the gripping book *A Civil Action* (Harr, 1995; Random House), which covers the litigation by families in Woburn, Massachusetts whose children had died of leukemia.

- Rank. Show users how their county compares to others in the state or nation; show users which factories put out the most toxins.

- Slice. Let users see which chemicals are harmful to the development of children.

- Facilitate. Help users contact the companies operating these facilities by letting them send faxes to the top-ranking polluters.

Our attempt to do all of these things is *http://www.scorecard.org*. Did we succeed? Bill Pease at the Environmental Defense Fund would probably point to the 40 users a second who showed up on the very first day (April 15, 1998) or Dupont's "The Goal is Zero" advertising campaign. Personally, I look to user feedback:

> *What makes you think that normal nonbrainwashed average americans care about your alarmist, victim-minded, advocacy-pseudoscientific, anti-profit, anti-success, anti-business, anti-American, emotion over logic, big brother, landgrabbing, legal enemy of landowners large and small, mankind hating, pantheistic, gaia worshippping, tree-hugger drivel?*
> —Email received July 23, 1998 as I wrote this chapter

If a site doesn't make people angry enough to sue, then it probably isn't saying much.

PERSONALIZATION

I decided that Scorecard would be a showcase for personalization. Users would tell us

- where they lived

- whether they were pregnant

- whether they preferred a text-only or graphics site

- whether they wanted to see chemicals displayed as upper- or lowercase

- whether they wanted longer lists to display as HTML tables (slow) or bullet lists (fast)

Nearly every page on the site would be able to use these personal data to increase the relevancy of the information. I came up with what I thought was a clever idea: Have the "personalize" link target a separate Netscape window (`<a target=personalize href=personalize.tcl>`). This way a user would be able to play with personalization settings and reload a Scorecard page to see the effects.

What percentage of Scorecard users took advantage of this fancy system? To a first approximation, 0 percent. Though we only asked for email address and name, most people apparently didn't understand how the "personalize" form would help them. Only about 1,000 people per month were personalizing. So we augmented our database-backed system with simpler one-click "text-only" or "graphics-site" links that set a persistent cookie on the user's browser:

```
Set-Cookie:
scorecard_graphics_default=f; path=/;
expires=Fri, 01-Jan-2010 01:00:00 GMT
```

SENDING FAXES

One of the key elements of Scorecard is that users can fill out a form on our site and then send a fax to the factory down the street. This turned out to require only about one hour of programming. There are lots of companies that will take a carefully formatted email message and send out a fax on your behalf. We use *http://www.interpage.net*.

```
set subject "fax -extword codes"
set body "<extended begin codes>
-select fax -code **accnt-number** -
    font courier -fontsize 10
-nocover -confsucc **admin-email-
    address** -conffail **admin-email-
    address**
$fax_digits_only
<extended end codes>

<<begin fax>>
$final_letter
<<end fax>>
"

ns_sendmail "**clientaddr**@interpage.net" "postmaster@scorecard.org"
$subject $body
```

Note that the actual sending of the email is left to the AOLserver API procedure `ns_sendmail`.

MAKING IT FAST

Thanks to the EDF's public relations savvy and the public's interest in toxic exposure data, we found ourselves in the business of hosting one of the Internet's most popular DB-backed Web sites on a two-year-old computer whose performance would not satisfy a Quake-addicted 10-year-old. Yet even when handling 20 requests a second, the page loading times from scorecard.org are faster than those from many static Web sites.

How did we accomplish this? By not doing anything clever, modern, or advanced. We used Unix rather than NT. We kept the data in Oracle 8 and gave Oracle enough RAM to cache most of the data set. We used AOLserver, an extremely simple Web server program that is designed to connect Web users to relational databases as quickly as possible.

THE BOTTOM LINE

Aside from my personal site, Scorecard is probably the most satisfying project that I've done to date. It has made lots of people angry. It has made lots of people think. It has helped school kids and university students learn about toxics and environmentalism.

It has made lots of companies pay attention to their neighbors. Bill Pease and David Abercrombie at EDF did all the hard work of collecting and cleaning the data; Oracle does all the hard work of caching blocks of data; we (*arsdigita.com*) look like geniuses for making the Web site work, though really it was painless stuff that we could have done in our sleep.

If Scorecard is something that looks hard but was easy, the Action Network is something that sounds easy but was in fact way hard.

INFLUENCING DECISION MAKERS

Christopher Alexander argued in his 1977 classic *A Pattern Language* (1977, Oxford University Press) for countries of no more than a few million people:

> *It is not hard to see why the government of a region becomes less and less manageable with size. In a population of N persons, there are of the order of N^2 person-to-person links needed to keep channels of communication open. Naturally, when N goes beyond a certain limit, the channels of communication needed for democracy and justice and information are simply too clogged, and too complex; bureaucracy overwhelms human process. . . .*

> *We believe the limits are reached when the population of a region reaches some 2 to 10 million. Beyond this size, people become remote from the large-scale processes of government. Our estimate may seem extraordinary in the light of modern history: the nation-states have grown mightily and their governments hold power over tens of millions, sometimes hundreds of millions, of people. But these huge powers cannot claim to have a natural size. They cannot claim to have struck the balance between the needs of towns and communities, and the needs of the world community as a whole. Indeed, their tendency has been to override local needs and repress local culture, and at the same time aggrandize themselves to the point where they are out of reach, their power barely conceivable to the average citizen.*

Note:
For an illustration of the limits of government power in the Microsoft Age, see the July 13, 1998 issue of *Government Computer News* (*http://www.gcn.com /gcn/1998/July13 /cov2.htm*), which describes the Navy's $1-billion Aegis missile cruiser *Yorktown* being towed into port after some problems with its Windows NT cluster.

The United States is 100 times larger than Alexander thought prudent, and indeed most people feel like inhabitants rather than citizens participating in decision-making.

If you have a huge bank account, you don't need a Web server to influence politicians. You can go to Capitol Hill and hand out checks. However, if you forgot to get rich during the Great Internet Boom (see the next chapter), then you might have to explore other options.

At least in theory, a politician is responsive to constituents. If a large number of constituents call, write, or fax the politician, then the politician's vote might be influenced. An advocacy group will traditionally contact its members by telephone or mail asking them to contact their congressmen and senators. Since only a few percent of people will respond to this appeal, it is extremely expensive to get one constituent to contact one politician. Furthermore, many of those contacts will occur after the vote has occurred; many of the most destructive laws are passed within just a few days.

In order to really make this effective, we need:

- a cheap way of alerting group members to the impending decision, before it is too late for the members to voice their opinion

- a way of saving group members the trouble of figuring out who their politicians are and how to contact them

- a way of telling professional lobbyists, before they walk into a politician's office, that "15 faxes have been sent by group members to this person so far"

- a way of informing members who responded that "your response was communicated to Jane Senator and she voted the right way" or "your response was communicated to Fred Congressman and he voted the wrong way"

- a way of reminding Jane and Fred, after they've voted, that their performance was conveyed to X thousand members of the group

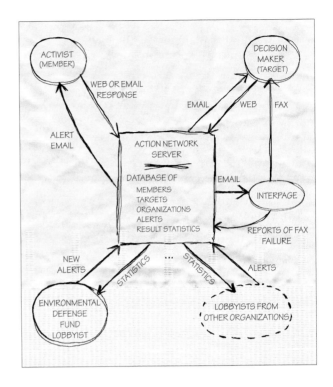

Figure 16-1:
A Web server–based communication system.

Suppose that one advocacy group was able to do this for themselves? They would necessarily have to run some kind of computing system, plus go to the effort of maintaining politician contact information. Why not then add one more system requirement?

- a way of letting other advocacy groups use the same system

OUR SOLUTION

We have a cheap way of contacting members: email. It also happens to be fast enough so that members will be alerted well before decisions are made. We can send email notes to members asking them to come to our Web site and draft a note to their representatives. How do we know which these are? We keep a database of politicians, their states and district numbers, and their contact information. For each activist, we ask for a street address and five-digit zip code. Using software lifted from the Bill Gates' Personal Wealth Clock, we can use these data to query a variety of other Web sites and get the member's zip+4 and congressional district. To deliver the communications, we use the same Interpage email-to-fax service that we used in Scorecard. (See Figure 16-1.)

The rest is mere programming! How do we make this technology available to like-minded advocacy groups? By using the same division-by-domain techniques that I used three years before when building *www.greenspun.com,* my collaboration server that works on behalf of hundreds of Web publishers.

WHAT IF I DON'T WANT TO TALK TO MY POLITICIANS?

If you've ever testified before the Senate (see *http://photo.net /philg/politics-and -litigation.html*) or read John Jackley's book, *Hill Rat* (1992, Regnery Gateway), you might not want to communicate with politicians. Is this software then useless?

No! I built it so that it could also be used any time a large number of people need to influence a small number of people. For example, a large company might decide to use the software to assist in collaborative decision-making. Joe Employee would contribute his opinion to the system and that opinion would get shown to Joe's boss, Joe's boss's boss, and on up the line. However, Joe's opinion would not be shown to managers in sister divisions. Thus, managers would get a feel for what their own employees had to say. In this intranet example, the executives being lobbied are presumably cooperating in the process. There would thus be no need to fax opinions to decision makers; email or Web delivery of summaries would be preferred.

HOW DOES IT WORK? (SHORT)

We keep the following in a database:

- a table of all the organizations using the system: an_domains (note the an_ prefix; it lets these tables coexist in a database that is also used for other applications). For each organization, we need to know whether or not they are U.S.-based (in which case things like the state or zip+4 matters), how much information they wish to collect from new members, and how much we're going to charge them to send faxes and email messages on their behalf (we'll have to recycle the software from Chapter 14, ecommerce).

- a table of all the activists: an_members. For each member, we store contact information; whether or not email has started bouncing from his address; what congressional, state senate, and state house districts he is in; and his history of responding to alerts.

- a table recording to which advocacy groups particular members belong: an_member_domain_map. Note that this table can also contain a "member ID" key into a group's private database on their own computer system (on the assumption that most groups using the system will have their own systems for keeping track of members).

- a table recording which members are authorized to administer a domain: `an_maintainer_domain_map`. If there is a row present in this table, a person will be permitted to send out alerts, view statistics from old alerts, etc.

- a table of decision makers: `an_targets`. This contains contact information, including the fax number, but more importantly, the state and a `filter_value` column that can be used to match a target with members from, for example, only one congressional district.

- two tables to group decision makers: `an_target_groups` and `an_target_group_map`

- a table of all the alerts that have been sent out: `an_alerts`

- a table specifying that alerts are to be sent to particular members: `an_alert_member_map`

- a table specifying that alert responses are to be sent to particular targets: `an_alert_target_map`. A row in this table can say, "Send all responses from members in any state to the EPA District Administrator," or "Send responses from members to the group of U.S. senators, matching by state," or "Send response from members to the group of U.S. congressmen, matching by state and then congressional district."

- tables recording mass uploads of members, with enough information to remove some or all of those members, if, for example, a domain administrator uploaded 10,000 records with the first and last names reversed

Then, uh, we write some AOLserver Tcl scripts.

How Does It Work? (Long)

The Action Network gives us an opportunity to talk about a bunch of interesting ideas:

- database triggers
- PL/SQL
- Oops-proof Batch Upload
- high-efficiency/high-security user authentication

Database triggers

One of the things that we record about an Action Network member is his or her original registration date:

```
create table an_members (
        member_id integer not null primary key,
        email                   varchar(100) not null unique,
        password  varchar(50) not null,
        registration_date    date,
    ...
);
```

There may be lots of application programs, in our case, typically AOLserver .tcl pages, that add members. If we want to make sure that registration_date is always set, we could either inspect every application program and write documentation instructing future programmers that this column must always be set to the current date. Or we could add an Oracle trigger:

```
create trigger
an_member_registration_date
before insert on an_members
for each row
when (new.registration_date is null)
begin
 :new.registration_date := SYSDATE;
end;
```

It is now Oracle's job to make sure that member insertions that don't have a registration date will get one. Whom would you rather trust? Oracle or the pimply-faced kid that is likely to take over the system that you developed?

PL/SQL

Suppose that a computation is needed in a variety of places on your site. You want it to be consistent everywhere: The answer for inputs X, Y, and Z is the same on every Web page that performs the computation. Novice programmers think this is easy. They will just put the same mathematical expression in all the Web pages. Expert programmers know that one day someone will change seven out of eight of those pages, leading to subtle inconsistencies because of that one unmodified page.

Depending on your Web server, there are various ways to encapsulate this computation so that you only need to change the formula in one place. If you were using Microsoft IIS you'd use a COM object. If you were using AOLserver, you could define a Tcl procedure. However, what if a variety of applications all talk to the same Oracle database? Perhaps your public Web site is AOLserver, but someone else has kludged together a little maintenance application in IIS/.asp, and still other folks use Crystal Reports and Microsoft Access to query the tables?

Oracle lets you write little programs and run them inside the database server. Thus, any application that is querying the Action Network tables can also invoke these little programs. If you change your mind about the formula, you only have to change it in one place. With the most modern databases (Oracle 8.1, Informix Dynamic Server), you can write these programs in Java. With older versions of Oracle, you have to use Oracle's proprietary PL/SQL language:

```
create or replace function probability_of_response (
n_times_notified IN integer,
n_times_responded IN integer)
return number
as
begin
  if n_times_notified < 5 then
    -- not enough experience, just use a default
    return 0.1;
  else
    return n_times_responded/n_times_notified;
  end if;
end probability_of_response;
```

Note:
For more on
PL/SQL, read
Oracle 8 PL/SQL
Programming
(Urman, 1997;
McGraw-Hill) and
the O'Reilly books
by Feuerstein:
Oracle PL/SQL
Programming and
Advanced
Oracle PL/SQL:
Programming with
Packages (1997 and
1996, O'Reilly).

This function takes two inputs, both integers, that say how many times a member has been alerted and how many times that person has responded. The `return number` tells Oracle that this function must always return a number, in this case the estimated probability of a member responding to a new alert. If the activist hasn't been notified at least five times, we assume that we don't have enough data for statistical significance. Thus, the function returns a default value of 0.1. Otherwise, it does the division. Note that the presence of `n_times_notified < 5` prevents this function from generating a divide-by-zero error.

Oops-proof batch upload

I've been building a bunch of Web systems lately that allow users to upload huge tables of information, formatted as comma-separated values (CSV) files. The CSV format is convenient for users because it is native to popular desktop spreadsheet applications such as Lotus 1-2-3 and Microsoft Excel. The format is convenient for me because AOLserver has lots of API support for reading information from uploaded CSV files.

Here are a few applications for user-uploaded structured data:

■ The administrator of an advocacy domain in Action Network ought to be able to upload a database of several thousand members.

■ A participant in the photo.net community ought to be able to upload a table of captions of the photos that he has taken (thus enabling a student or art director to say, "Show me people who have photos of the Eiffel Tower").

- After you are discharged, a hospital ought to be able to upload your visit history to your personal medical record server, thus making these data available 10 years later if you go for treatment to a doctor in a foreign city.

There are a couple of strategies for mapping these data into your tables. I'll call the first strategy AOLserver-style, because it is what AOLserver gives you out of the box when you request a URL of the form "foobar.csv". What AOLserver does is show you the first 20 rows of the CSV file and, at the top of each row, lets you pick a database table column into which you'd like the input data column to be stuffed (see Figure 16-2).

Upload CSV file

The contents of this CSV file are shown in the table below:

/scratch/cong-with-phone.csv

Select a column name for each column, and press the **Upload** button to upload the data into the **an_test_targets** table.

- ● First line of file is data.
- ○ First line of file is column names.

- ● Add data in file to data in table **an_test_targets**.
- ○ Delete all data in table **an_test_targets** before inserting from file.

[Upload]

Warning: The table below contains only the first 50 lines of this file. You may want to download the entire file and examine it locally before loading it into your database.

usps_abbrev	filter_value	first_names	last_name	email
DS	FST	lname	fname	Pty
1	HI	Abercrombie	Neil	D
5	NY	Ackerman	Gary L.	D
4	CO	Allard	Wayne	R
1	NJ	Andrews	Robert E.	D
7	TX	Archer	William	R
26	TX	Armey	Richard K.	R
6	AL	Bachus	Spencer	R
6	KY	Baesler	Scotty	D
6	LA	Baker	Richard H.	R
10	CA	Baker	Bill	R
2	ME	Baldacci	John	D

Figure 16-2: AOLserver-style strategy for data mapping.

The second strategy is to be lazy/mean. The Web site publisher specifies a format and the user is expected to manipulate his data in a desktop app until the data fit the specification. For the Action Network system, the lazy/mean approach would be to say, "Here is a list of columns for each row (* fields are required to be nonempty)"

foreign_key	a unique key in your database system, e.g., "member id"
Source	where you got this member, e.g., "bread_and_puppet_booth"
Member_type	e.g., "inner_circle"
Email *	must be a full Internet email address, e.g., "foo@bar.com"
First_names *	e.g., "Lisa Marie"
Last_name *	e.g., "Presley"
...	

and then let the user do his or her best to get the data into this format.

In the AOLserver-style case, you have to anticipate the domain administrator who chooses "last name" for the column containing first names. In the lazy/mean case, you have to anticipate the domain administrator who produces a CSV file in which the columns are not in the expected order or in which a column is left out by mistake.

In both cases, it is possible that 10,000 bogus records will be inserted into the database.

Oops.

Shouldn't we be able to solve this problem with SQL transactions? We'll just tell Oracle to open a transaction before inserting the first record and won't tell Oracle to commit the transaction until after the 10,000th record has gone in and been inspected. An insurmountable problem with this idea is that the person uploading the data might not realize for a few days that something was wrong, particularly if the error was swapping two, little-used columns.

My first idea was "As my program is inserting a new member, stuff some crud into the database recording the insertion as part of this upload." I didn't really like this idea because it seemed that I'd need to write slightly different software for the photo-captioning upload, the Action Network upload, and the medical record upload. Couldn't I write a general piece of software that would work for all three applications?

It seemed to me that the problem was very similar to the transaction-processing monitors (TP monitors) in use throughout Corporate America. Suppose that taking an order from a customer involves inserting records into a factory-scheduling database in Indiana (Oracle), a billing database in Pennsylvania (old IBM mainframe with nonrelational database), a management reporting system in New York (Informix), and a shipping-scheduling system in California (Sybase). If any one of these systems is down or unreachable, you want all the other systems to be untouched. Yet you can't ask the Oracle system in Indiana to roll back changes made to the old IBM mainframe database in Pennsylvania.

As far as I can tell, the TP monitor works kind of like the software described in Chapter 14, ecommerce: Before trying to do anything on a foreign system, it records what it is about to try to do. Afterward, if something bad happens on any of the foreign systems, it can use this record to undo what it did.

Not wishing to buy and install one of these systems or read the white papers for BEA Tuxedo and M3 at *http://www.beasys.com,* I decided to take advantage of my privileged position as an academic computer scientist. I went to the world's leading authorities on transaction processing, folks who teach on this subject every semester and publish scholarly articles in refereed journals, and asked, "Can you suggest a general algorithm that, given an SQL insert statement, will produce another SQL insert that writes enough information into the database to undo the first insert? Is this how commercial TP monitors work?"

I learned a few things from their answers. First, academic experts on transaction processing do not know how to solve this problem. Second, academic experts on transaction processing are unaware of the existence of commercial TP monitors. Third, if academic experts on transaction processing could be fired for inability to

sit down at Oracle and type a single legal SQL statement, there would be plenty of job openings for new Ph.D.s.

My ultimate solution to this problem? As my program is inserting a new member, stuff some crud into the database recording the insertion as part of this upload:

```
create sequence an_csv_upload_sequence;

create table an_csv_uploads (
        upload_id integer primary key,
        upload_time            date,
        -- who did the upload and from where
        member_id integer not null references an_members,
        originating_ip         varchar(50),
        -- for which domain
        domain                 varchar(20) not null references an_domains,
        -- the original file name on local disk
        original_filename   varchar(300)
);
```

```
-- this table records which members were added during an upload

create table an_csv_upload_rollback (
        upload_id integer not null references an_csv_uploads,
        member_id integer not null references an_members
);
```

What about the Tcl code that populates these tables? First, the file upload form:

```
<form method=POST enctype=multipart/form-data action=members-upload-2.tcl>
<input type=hidden name=domain value="$domain">
Pick a file: <input type=file name=csv_filename size=50><br>
<p>
<center>
<input type=submit value="Upload">
</center>
</form>
```

Note the use of the enctype specification in the form tag. This tells the user's browser to MIME-encode the file chosen with the input type=file widget. How do we process this MIME-encoded file? AOLserver decodes it automatically and puts it in a .tmpfile on the server. Calling ns_queryget csv_filename.tmpfile will get the temporary filename, which can then be read using the standard Tcl language commands.

Here's the main loop of the upload processor:

```
set upload_id [database_to_tcl_string $db "select
an_csv_upload_sequence.nextval from dual"]

ns_db dml $db "insert into an_csv_uploads (upload_id, upload_time,
member_id, originating_ip, domain, original_filename)
values
($upload_id, sysdate, $member_id, '[DoubleApos [ns_conn
peeraddr>','$QQdomain','[DoubleApos [ns_queryget csv_filename>')"

# let's grab the csv file

set stream [open [ns_queryget csv_filename.tmpfile] r]

set first_iteration_p 1

# we call the AOLserver API procedure ns_getcsv to read the next line from
# the CSV file, decode it, and put the values into the Tcl list one_line

while { [ns_getcsv $stream one_line] != -1 } {
    if { $first_iteration_p && ([lindex $one_line 0] == "foreign_key") } {
        ns_write "<li>skipping the first line because it looks like
            column headers\n"
```

```
        continue
    }
    set first_iteration_p 0
    # let's destructure the list first, using the magic
    # procedure an_destructure_record_list that will set
    # a bunch of local variables
    an_destructure_record_list
    # now all the column vars are defined in our local env,
    # including $QQ versions for use with the RDBMS
    ns_write "<li>Working on $first_names $last_name... \n"
    # look for existing members either by foreign_key or email address
    # (code removed for clarity)
    ...
    # if we got here, we didn't find a record with the same email
    # address or foreign_key
    set new_id [database_to_tcl_string $db "select
        member_id_sequence.nextval from dual"]
    # one of the few tricks below is the "string to upper" on the state
    # code we want to forgive folks who use "ma" or "Ma"
    if [catch { ns_db dml $db "begin transaction"
                ns_db dml $db "insert into an_members (member_id, email, ...)
values
($new_id,'$QQemail', ...)
                ns_db dml $db "insert into an_member_domain_map
                    (member_id, domain, foreign_key, source, member_type)
values
($new_id, '$QQdomain', [ns_dbquotevalue $foreign_key text],
    [ns_dbquotevalue $source text], [ns_dbquotevalue $member_type text])"
                ns_db dml $db "insert into an_csv_upload_rollback
                    (upload_id, member_id)
values
($upload_id, $new_id)"
                ns_db dml $db "end transaction"
    } errmsg] {
        ns_db dml $db "abort transaction"
        ns_write ".. ouch!  Here was the error from Oracle:
    \n$errmsg\n
"
    } else {
        ns_write ".. inserted"
    }
}

close $stream
```

At any time after an upload, a domain administrator can

- review upload history
- remove all the members added by a particular upload
- remove some of the members added by a particular upload (using checkboxes)

User authentication

On a site like Action Network you want to be pretty sure that a guy who says he is Joe Smith, authorized maintainer of a domain, is actually Joe Smith. Although Rush Limbaugh is one of my heroes (because he met his wife online), I would not want him using my server to send out messages to thousands of environmentalists.

I'm fairly convinced that by the year 2002, standard computers will be augmented with authentication hardware that talks to a card or a key that users carry around. The physical device plus a PIN will then suffice to authenticate them all over the Internet, much as an ATM card plus PIN are used in our current banking system.

For now, we have passwords. Here's the simplest reasonable way to do authentication:

- Ask the user for an email address and password combination.
- Look up the person's user_id in the database (by the email address) and then check to see if the password matches (I like to do this case-insensitive).
- If the password matches, write the password from the database plus the user ID into a browser cookie.
- On subsequent page requests for URLs that require authentication, look for the user_id cookie and then query the database to see if the password matches.

Using a cookie saves the user from having to enter his password repeatedly. If you use HTTPs, all the transmissions of cookies are encrypted so that the password/user_id combo is not subject to packet-sniffing attacks. We have a potential performance problem in that we're querying the database on every page load. Oracle will have cached the query plan and the data, but still it seems ridiculous to ask Oracle 100 times on 100 page loads for "user 456's password."

Although my servers are probably more than powerful enough to handle the extra Oracle queries, I prefer to save the power for more interesting applications or those big days when a site gets into the news (see Chapter 8, So You Want to Run Your Own Server). Thus, my solution is to cache retrieved passwords in a Tcl global variable (stored in AOLserver's virtual memory). When a request comes in, my server will check the cache first. If there is no entry or if the passwords don't match, then it asks Oracle for the password. Note that this algorithm works, even if a user changes his password. Here's the code, lifted from the ArsDigita Community System:

```
# we tell AOLserver to run our cookie checker procedure before
# serving any request for a URL that starts with "/pvtm"
ns_register_filter preauth GET /pvtm/* an_verify_member_filter
ns_register_filter preauth POST /pvtm/* an_verify_member_filter

proc an_verify_member_filter {args why} {
    set member_id [an_verify_member]
    if { $member_id == 0 } {
        ns_returnredirect /
        # returning "filter_return" causes AOLserver to abort
        # processing of this thread
        return filter_return
    } else {
        # got a member_id and the password matched
        # returning "filter_ok" causes AOLserver to proceed
        return filter_ok
    }
}


# return member_id if happy, 0 otherwise

proc an_verify_member {} {
    set headers [ns_conn headers]
    set cookie [ns_set get $headers Cookie]
    if { [regexp {an_member_id=([^;]+)} $cookie {} member_id] } {
        if { [regexp {an_password=([^;]+)} $cookie {} \
            urlencoded_password] } {
            # got member_id and password, let's check it
            # we urlencode/decode passwords so that users are free to
            # put in semicolons and other special characters that might
            # mess up a cookie header
            set password [ns_urldecode $urlencoded_password]
            # the ns_share API call instructs AOLserver to treat
            # an_password_cache as a global variable; note that we're
            # using it as a Tcl associative array
            ns_share an_password_cache
            if { [info exists an_password_cache($member_id)] && \
                ([string compare $password
                    $an_password_cache($member_id)] == 0) } {
                # we had a cached password and it matched
                return $member_id
            } else {
              # we need to talk to Oracle
                set db [ns_db gethandle subquery]
                set an_password_cache($member_id)
                    [database_to_tcl_string $db \
                    "select password from an_members where member_id =
                        $member_id"]
                # we explicitly release the database connection in case
```

```
        # another filter or the thread itself needs to use one
        # from this pool
        ns_db releasehandle $db
        if { [string compare $password
              $an_password_cache($member_id)] == 0 } {
            # passwords match
            return $member_id
        }
    }
  }
}
# we didn't get a match or a member_id or something...
return 0
}
```

Paul Holbrook, one of the guys who makes *www.cnn.com* so fast, sensibly asked me, "How would you prune such a cache? If you have a large number of users, such a cache could grow very large." Here was my response:

```
Paul, you will be impressed by my advanced cache pruning algorithm: I
have another AOLserver running that kills my primary server once/day!
So the cache builds up over only a 24-hour period.

Generally I architect all of my Web services so that AOLserver or Oracle
can be restarted at any time without even affecting a current user
"session". So in theory the server could be restarted every two hours
or whatever.  In practice, a server restart can affect a handful of
users.  When AOLserver gets a kill signal, if it is in the middle of
serving files to users, it may stay alive for a configurable period of
time (default 60 seconds) to finish serving them.  So anyone connected
by a reasonably fast link shouldn't notice that the server was killed
halfway through serving their request.  However, during this shutdown
period, AOLserver does not respond to new requests.  Browsers generally
time out after 30 seconds so if a very busy AOLserver serving large
files to at least some modem users is killed, a few users will get a
"server did not respond" message and have to retry.

Let's talk about the cache size, though. Suppose that each userid +
password takes up 100 bytes. If I have one million users visiting
during my 24-hour period, the cache would only be 100 MB in size.
Given that AOLserver runs as a single process (i.e., these data aren't
duplicated in multiple processes, as they might be with Apache),
this wouldn't be an unsupportable load on my HP-UX box (with its
4 GB of RAM).

In practice, my pathetic site is only visited by at most 25,000 people
per day :-( And probably only half would be users who've registered in
some way (e.g., by posting a Q&A forum message). So my daily cache would
never be more than about 1 MB.
```

I don't think there are ways of achieving higher performance and simplicity than my system, which was particularly easy to implement because of AOLserver's filter facility. However, for higher security over unencrypted connections, it would probably be better to issue encrypted tickets that are good for a limited period of time and only from a particular IP address.

Something else I learned

I learned one more thing while building the Action Network: If you've signed a book contract, do not promise to do anything for anyone, no matter how small the task may seem, until the book is done.

SUMMARY

As Philip Elmer-Dewitt wrote in TIME magazine, "The Internet is more than a place to find pictures of people having sex with dogs." The Internet is also more than a place to buy exactly what you want. The Internet is a tool that we can use to make our world a better place.

I hope that the example applications here will inspire you to go out and build something that changes people's minds. The most educational, the most irritating, and the most useful sites are yet to be built.

MORE

- Wallace Stevens' "Thirteen Ways of Looking at a Blackbird" is available from *http://www.poets.org/poets/lit/POEM/wsteve04.htm*.

- An archive of the documents in the *David LaMacchia* case is at *http://photo.net/dldf/*.

- *Cyber Rights* (Godwin, 1998; Times Books) covers the *LaMacchia* case, the controversy over *Time*'s Cyberporn story, and the litigation over the Communications Decency Act of 1996.

- *A Civil Action* (Harr, 1995; Random House) documents the litigation by leukemia victims in Woburn, Massachusetts against W. R. Grace and Beatrice Foods, whose factories released trichloroethylene. The book-on-tape version is very compelling and requires an investment of only a couple of hours.

- *A Pattern Language* (Alexander, 1977; Oxford University Press).

- *Hill Rat* (Jackley, 1992; Regnery Gateway) chronicles a few years in the life of a congressional staffer; you won't know whether to laugh or to cry.

- If you're an Oracle user, you'll probably want *Oracle 8 PL/SQL Programming* (Urman, 1997; McGraw-Hill) and *Oracle PL/SQL Programming* and *Advanced Oracle PL/SQL: Programming with Packages* (Feuerstein, 1997 and 1996; O'Reilly).

17

A Future So Bright You'll
Need to Wear Sunglasses

E ric Rabkin, professor of English at University of Michigan, surveyed science fiction and found only one case in which a science fiction writer had accurately predicted an invention: Arthur C. Clarke's 1945 proposal for geostationary communication satellites, the first of which were launched in 1965. All the other writers credited with scientific invention were merely extrapolating implications of technologies that had already been invented.

The most successful Internet punditry is a lot like Rabkin's survey of science fiction. University labs got corporate money in the 1980s to invent virtual reality. Magazines and newspapers got advertising dollars in the 1990s to tell the public about the amazing new development of virtual reality. All of this was greatly facilitated by Ivan Sutherland and Bob Sproull. They placed an array of sensors in a ceiling to track the user's head postion and attitude. With a head-mounted display and real-time information about the user's position, Sutherland and Sproull were able to place synthetic chairs in the room (Sutherland joked that the ultimate computer display would let the user sit down in the chair). They built a completely functioning virtual reality system, using government research funds, and published the results to the world with papers, photographs, and movie demonstrations. The year? 1966.

I did a careful study of book and magazine Internet punditry, graphing the authors' wealth and fame versus the novelty of the ideas presented. Based on this research, here are my predictions for the future:

- Have you ever picked up a small plastic device and heard a voice from the other side of the planet? You will. (Alexander Graham Bell, 1876)

- Have you ever had a friend in the office next door type a message and watched an image of the typed letters form seconds later on a cathode-ray tube in front of your eyes? You will. (Various email systems of the 1960s)

Note:
You can read more about Ivan Sutherland at *http://www.eu.sun.com/ 960710/feature3/*.

- Have you ever cooperated with a friend in another city, each of you typing on a computer keyboard, drawing with a mouse, talking to each other, and looking at a little inset video picture of your collaborator on the screen? You will. (Douglas Engelbart at the December 1968 Fall Joint Computer Conference in San Francisco; demonstrated to a live audience of 2,000 people)

- Have you ever clicked a mouse on a hypertext document or graphic? You will. (Engelbart, same 1968 demo)

- Have you ever imagined that the mouse click could grab a file from halfway across the Internet? You will. (Engelbart, same 1968 demo)

Can we learn anything general from my results? Absolutely. Armies of hardware engineers will work anonymously in cubicles like slaves for 30 years so that the powerful computers used by pioneers in the 1960s will be affordable to everyone. Then in the 1990s, rich people and companies will use their PR staffs to take credit for the innovations of the pioneers in the 1960s, without even having the grace to thank the hardware geeks who made it possible for them to steal credit in the first place. Finally, the media will elect a few official pundits who are (a) familiar enough with the 1960s innovations to predict next year's Cyberlandscape for the AOL crowd, but (b) not *so* familiar with the history of these innovations that they sound unconvincing when crediting them to the rich people and companies of the 1990s.

Where does that leave me? I'm not one of the pioneers of the 1960s—I was born in 1963. I'm not a rich person of the 1990s—I forgot to get rich during the Great Internet Boom. I'm not an official pundit, except once for an Italian newsweekly (see *http://photo.net/philg/narcissism/narcissism.html* for the full story)—I guess I must have done a bad job for those Italians.

I may be a failure, but they can't take away my aspirations. There isn't much point in aspiring to be a pioneer of the 1960s. The 60s are over, even if some folks in my hometown (the People's Republic of Cambridge, Massachusetts) haven't admitted it. There isn't much point in my aspiring to be an official, real, dead-trees media pundit. My friends would only laugh at me if I started writing for *Wired* magazine. However, being a rich person of the 1990s has a certain indefinable appeal for me. Perhaps this comment I made in *http://money.rules-the.net/materialism/* sums it up: "Not being a materialist in the U.S. is kind of like not appreciating opera if you live in Milan or art if you live in Paris. We support materialism better than any other culture. Because retailing and distribution are so efficient here, stuff is cheaper than anywhere else in the world. And then we have huge houses in which to archive our stuff."

Materialism is definitely more fun when one is rich. How to get there, though. Conventional wisdom in Italy has it that: "There are three ways to make money. You can inherit it. You can marry it. You can steal it." Based on my survey of the computer industry, the third strategy seems to be the most successful. With that in mind, I'm going to present the following ideas (mostly stolen from smarter people):

- At work, people will stop using desktop apps in favor of collaborative Web-based apps.

- Society's rush to develop Web-based apps puts a stiff premium on the skills of great programmers.

- Collaboration technology will make it possible to manage corporate and workgroup structures that are impossible for us to conceive.

- The idea of trundling down to the computer store to buy a box full of software will seem as absurd as the idea of playing amateur sysadmin.

- At home, every appliance will have an IP connection and thus be a potential Web browser.

- Computer systems will start talking to each other via collaboratively exchanged data models.

- We will harness the power of the Web to develop data models that solve our problems.

- *Delenda est Junkware.*

DELENDA EST DESKTOP APPS

Marcus Porcius Cato (234 BC to 149 BC) went onto the floor of the Roman Senate every day and decreed "*Delenda est Carthago*" ("Carthage must be destroyed"). My personal crusade since 1993 has been against desktop applications. Desktop apps promised to deliver the power of computers to the ordinary citizen; in fact, they delivered the pain of a corporate system administration job right into the ordinary citizen's home or office. Desktop apps promised to help people collaborate; in fact, they have imprisoned individual contributions on individual machines.

What people need and, with the ubiquitous Internet, can finally get are collaborative Web-based applications. Web-based apps let people use computers without becoming mired in system administration. Web-based apps help people collaborate. Web-based apps can weave an individual's contribution into a larger work produced by many people over the decades.

The future is WimpyPoint (*wimpy.arsdigita.com*), not PowerPoint.

If Web-based apps are so great, why aren't we all using them now? Desktop apps serve one user at a time and tend to be copies of systems from the 60s and 70s.

Web-based apps serve thousands of users simultaneously and oftentimes are based on completely new service ideas. Thus, Web-based apps require programmers with great skill, imagination, and taste.

SHOULD SOFTWARE DEVELOPMENT BE CHEAP?

As noted in Chapter 11, Sites that Are Really Databases, the compensation of the best programmers has varied over the decades. When computers were new, expensive, and obscure, the wizards commanded high salaries. As software technology stagnated, project schedules grew extended and managers

became skilled at yoking together mediocre talents. The wizards were thrust into cubicles along with everyone else.

Are we moving into an era in which wizards will be overpaid or underpaid? Here's a thought experiment:

You're managing the information system for the British gas pipeline company. Thanks to Margaret Thatcher, customers get to buy their gas from their choice of 20 vendors. However, since each household only has one physical gas line, these purchasing choices are really an accounting fiction maintained in a relational database. How big a database? The pipeline company divides the country into eight regions, each of which is supported by an HP Unix box running a 400-GB Oracle database. If a sloppy programmer leaves out an AND clause in a SQL statement that does JOINs against a 400-GB database, query time will rise from one-tenth of a second to one million seconds, and the entire server may be effectively frozen while the query is executing. If an inexperienced programmer can't elegantly solve the little logic puzzles that writing SQL presents, your system may be delivering the correct answers, but perhaps by chewing up 1,000 times as many computing resources as necessary. How much are you willing to pay for a programmer who is guaranteed to be careful and experienced?

Here's a real-life example drawn from this installation: Reports from the 400-GB Oracle databases were being generated every night and FTP'd out to regional offices. A good programmer spent a few weeks writing a Web application to deliver these reports only on demand. How much did this guy save the company? Let's just say that they'd previously been FTP'ing 180,000 reports every night.

Modern computing systems, which generally incorporate massive relational databases, greatly amplify the benefits delivered by good programmers and the mistakes made by bad ones.

The compressed development schedules in the Web/DB world also contribute to high programmer salaries. *Fortune 500* customers come to my little consulting company (arsdigita.com) with absurdly ambitious projects. They want to take an entire existing business with thousands of customers and make the whole thing Web-based. In three months. Having always sold to retailers, they now want to sell products direct to consumers. Starting in two-and-a-half months. The inherently conservative IT departments of these companies would laugh these guys out of the glass room. Three months? That's not enough time to call up Andersen Consulting and pay for them to write a project plan, much less write any code, do any testing, or install a production system. The only programmers who can do something in three months are programmers who've built a substantially similar system before.

Suppose that you're a business executive with an important new idea. The Web/DB application has to be live in three months. Your internal IT people have refused to touch the project. If you picked up one of those "business secrets from Microsoft" books at the airport, you'd hire a bunch of kids fresh out of college, let them spend a few years working through their mistakes, and be a little late to a market in which you already had a monopoly. Sadly, however, you realize that nobody has a monopoly in the Web service world. If you don't go live soon, someone else will, and then you'll have to spend millions of dollars advertising your way into users' thoughts. The answer? Find the best and most experienced Web-service developers that you can and pay them whatever they ask. What if you can get 500 competent programmers in Banglor for the same price? That's great, but it will take you at least three months just to develop a management plan to yoke those 500 programmers together. Save them for a three-year project.

The above picture may seem a bit bleak for the manager, who won't enjoy scrambling to find a competent and *available* Web/DB developer. Nor will the manager enjoy paying programmers $250 an hour. However, think about it from the programmer's point of view. When I graduated from MIT in 1982, my classmates and I had but one choice if we wanted to get an idea to market: Join a big organization. When products, even software, needed to be distributed physically, you needed people to design packaging, write and mail brochures, set up an

assembly line, fill shelves in a warehouse, fulfill customer orders, and so on. We went to work for big companies like IBM and Hewlett-Packard. Our first rude surprise was learning that even the best engineers earned a pittance compared with senior management. Moreover, because of the vast resources that were needed to turn a working design into an on-sale product, most finished designs never made it to market. "My project was killed" was the familiar refrain among Route 128 and Silicon Valley engineers in 1982.

How does the Web/DB world circa 1998 look to a programmer? If Joe Programmer can grab an IP address on a computer already running a well-maintained relational database, he can build an interesting service in a matter of weeks. By himself. If built for fun, this service can be delivered free to the entire Internet at minimal cost (see *http://photo.net/philg/services.html* for my own efforts in this direction). If built for a customer, this service can be launched without further effort. Either way, there is only a brief period of several weeks during which a project can be killed. That won't stop the *site* from being killed months or years down the road, but very seldom will a Web programmer build something that never sees the light of day (during my entire career of Web/DB application development, 1994 to 1998, I have never wasted time on an application that failed to reach the public).

So is this the Golden Age for programmers? We work at a high level of abstraction and rely on powerful subsystems (for example, Oracle, the Internet, and ubiquitous browsers) and therefore get a lot done in brief periods. Companies want things done within weeks rather than years, and hence are willing to pay huge bucks to programmers with good track records. Development schedules are so short and it is so easy to release a Web application to the world that very rarely do we work hard to develop something that doesn't get released.

All of the foregoing is true, and yet what makes this the Golden Age for programmers is that Web publishers are often willing to distribute source code. Deeply ingrained in the culture of engineering companies is that the way to get rich is to keep technology from falling into the hands of competitors. You make your engineers sign over all their intellectual property rights and you sit on that intellectual property, even if you can't find a use for it. The goal is to achieve Bill Gates–style world domination where nobody else can think of competing with you. Publishing doesn't work this way. Companies explicitly recognize that their main assets are name recognition, readers, graphics, and the like. Publishers don't realistically think that they can get 100 percent of the book market, 100 percent of the movie market, 100 percent of the magazine readers, or 100 percent of the TV viewing audience.

They can give away all of their source code to a publisher with a slightly different demographic and not be any worse off. As George Bush said to Michael Dukakis, "A short man never got any taller by sawing the legs off of a tall man."

When people share source code, it means that programmers spend more time doing the interesting work of solving new problems and less time doing the uninteresting work of reverse-engineering a solution to an old problem. Source-code sharing also means that programmers have more chances to become personally recognized for their achievement, rather than their corporate bosses getting the credit.

Does that mean all software will become free? No. But I predict a continued growth in the popularity and power of free software for Web applications. Later in this chapter, we look at whether the nonfree software can't be sold in a way that is less destructive for users and software developers.

WHAT IS A BIG COMPANY?

East Cambridge is filled with brick industrial buildings dating from around 1900. Each is large enough to hold a company of 50 to 100 people. I was walking around with a friend, pointing to these buildings, and said, "Isn't it interesting that there were a lot of small companies in East Cambridge even a century ago?"

"Those weren't small companies," he replied. "In 1900, a company with 100 employees would have been considered large. Without the telephone, it wasn't really practical to manage a larger organization."

People are bad at extrapolating from the early years of a technology. Edison thought the phonograph would be used for recording business dictation, not the Bee Gees singing, "Saturday Night Fever." In July 1998, I heard a computer science professor say, "The Web is really good for distributing papers, but I don't see it being used for collaboration."

Suppose Professor Forwardthinker is wrong and we are able to engineer truly great Web-based collaboration tools. At that point, it might become feasible to drop some of the assumptions about corporate and project management. Here are some of the things that shape current corporate structures:

- It is difficult to benefit from work by someone who isn't in the same building.

- It is difficult to benefit from work by someone who doesn't labor at least 40 hours per week.

- It is easier to deal with fellow employees versus outside contractors, because one doesn't have to negotiate prices for every little job, in other words, one can just walk into Jill Fellowslave's office and ask, "Would you please help me for 15 minutes with this problem?"

- Training people requires physically assembling them in a room with an expert.

Though we might not be aware of most of them, there are probably dozens more assumptions that go into today's corporate structures. If technology changes those assumptions, corporate structures will change.

How does that change the work that Web technologists must do? Right now we tend to see projects in terms of *Internet* or *intranet*. People say, "We have some really great applications, but we can't show them to you because they're behind the firewall." If work gets organized more along project lines than corporation lines, this kind of thinking becomes a serious impediment to progress.

For example, in 1998 if people from Companies A, B, and C need to work together, they'd expect to be able to call up the phone company and ask it to set up a conference call in 15 minutes. In 2018, it is possible that cross-company collaboration will be far more prevalent. In that case, people will expect to be able to ask the phone company to set up a Web-based collaboration environment, *in 15 minutes.*

SHOULD SOFTWARE REALLY BE SOLD LIKE TABLES AND CHAIRS?

In a world so advanced that people can get the phone company to do *anything* in 15 minutes, that people can muster significant computing resources without having to purchase or maintain a desktop computer, and that people can engage in computer-mediated collaboration on a scale that we can't imagine, isn't it absurd to imagine that people will be driving down to the local computer store and purchasing a physical box full of software?

Absolutely.

If you think about it a bit more, it begins to seem absurd even without the box. Users are out of the system administration business. Why need they be consciously paying for, downloading, and installing software products?

If you think about it yet still more, it begins to seem absurd even in the primitive world of the 1990s.

THE NUB

Software developers live in a preindustrial age. We don't build on each other's work, we reinvent the wheel over and over again, and the bumps in the wheel. Ultimately, it is the user who gets the stuffing beaten out of him.

It is the way that software is sold that keeps software technology mired in the 1950s. We put it into packages and sell it like tables or chairs because we have a highly efficient distribution and retail system for tables and chairs and because we've been buying things like tables and chairs for centuries. It would all work out beautifully for everyone if only tables and chairs needed periodic upgrades, if tables and chairs required documentation and support, if tables and chairs could be downloaded over networks, if users developed significant investments in the interfaces of tables and chairs, and if it cost $30 million to develop a slightly better table or chair from scratch.

Look at the choices that current software pricing forces people to make.

Johnny the user

Johnny the user is a university student. He wants to use Adobe Photoshop for a class project and has a Macintosh on the Internet in his dorm room. He can buy Photoshop for $500, he can steal it from a friend, or he can drive to Kinko's to rent a Macintosh for a few hours.

Suppose that Johnny buys Photoshop. Adobe gets $500 and is happy. Johnny gets manuals and support and he's working efficiently. Johnny doesn't have to drive anywhere, so society doesn't suffer from increased pollution and traffic congestion. Unfortunately, probably not too many people would pay $500 for software that they're only going to use for a day or two. Also, when Johnny next wants to use the software, he'll probably find that the version he has no longer runs with Apple's new operating system, or that Apple has gone belly-up and his version doesn't run on his new Linux machine, or that the instructor wants him to use a program feature that is only in the latest version of Photoshop.

Let's be realistic. Johnny probably isn't going to buy Photoshop. He's going to steal it from Adobe by borrowing the CD-ROM from his friend's friend. He'll spend his $500 on a spring-break trip to Florida. Unfortunately for Johnny, Photoshop is almost impossible to use without the manuals. Johnny drives to the bookstore and spends $30 on an "I stole the program and now I need a book on how to use it" book. Johnny wastes some time; Adobe gets no money; society has to breathe Johnny's exhaust fumes and wait behind his jalopy at intersections.

If Johnny is remarkably honest, he may go to Kinko's and rent a Macintosh running Photoshop. This is great, except that the network was supposed to free users from having to physically move themselves around. Johnny is inconvenienced and society is inconvenienced by the externalities of his driving.

Amanda the user interface programmer

Amanda is writing some user interface code for an innovative new spreadsheet program. She wants it to appeal to the users of Microsoft Excel and Lotus 1-2-3, but knows that they have spent years learning the user interface quirks of those programs. Amanda has to choose between copying the user interface and spending 10 years in federal court or making her new program work in a gratuitously different manner (in which case each user has to spend several days relearning commands that they already knew in their old programs).

Joey the image editor programmer

Joey wants to make a nice program for quickly converting all the images on a PhotoCD. Adobe Photoshop does 99 percent of what his program needs to do. Unfortunately, lacking that last 1 percent, Photoshop is useless for the task at hand. Adobe had no incentive to make the pieces of Photoshop callable by other programs, so Joey has to start from scratch or abandon his project. Should Joey succeed, his program will contain duplicates of code in Photoshop. Joey's software, though, will have bugs that Adobe stamped out in 1991.

Adobe the software publisher

Adobe wants to maximize its revenue under the "tables and chairs" software vending model. It will do this by keeping manuals and documentation out of the hands of users who don't pay, by not putting full documentation up on the Web, for example. Adobe will withhold support from users who stole the binary. Adobe will sue companies who copy the Photoshop user interface. Adobe will not share its internal program design with anyone.

CHOICES SUMMARY

Selling software like tables and chairs forces users to make a buy/steal choice with a threshold of $500. It forces thousands of confusing new user interfaces into the marketplace every year. It forces programmers to start from scratch if they are to market anything at all.

A BETTER WAY

Suppose that Jane's Software Consortium (JaneSoft) negotiated deals with a bunch of software authors. Users would pay a fixed amount per year to JaneSoft for the right to use any software they wished. Each user's computer would keep track of which company's programs were actually executed and file a report once a month with JaneSoft. Based on those usage reports, JaneSoft would apportion its revenues to software publishers and authors.

 Let's revisit the same people under the new model....

Johnny the user

Johnny can decide whether to (a) pay his $X a year and get everything or (b) buy a few important packages under the tables-and-chairs model and steal or rent everything else. Assuming he pays the $X a year, Johnny may legally run any software that he finds useful. It gets delivered via the Internet to his machine, along with any documentation and support that he may need.

Amanda the user interface programmer

Amanda still wants her users to be able to employ the familiar Lotus user interface. It is now in Lotus's interest to tell other programmers how to call their user interface code. Because licensing consortium revenues are apportioned according to usage, every time a Lotus menu is displayed or command is run, Lotus is going to get some extra money from the consortium. Amanda's company will get paid when her new spreadsheet core program is executing. Lotus and Amanda's company are sharing revenue, and it is in both of their interests to make the user productive.

Joey the image editor programmer

Adobe now has an incentive to document the internal workings of Photoshop. Joey can tap into these and add his 1 percent. Because Photoshop is an old and well-debugged program, the user gets a much more reliable product. Joey only gets 1 percent of the revenue derived from any user's session with "his" software, but he had to do only 1 percent as much work, so he can move on to other projects. Furthermore, because he doesn't have to come up with an attractive physical package, his cost of entering the software market is considerably reduced.

Adobe the software publisher

Adobe's main goal now is to get as many people as possible to run Photoshop and for as long as possible. Remember that a user who runs Photoshop frequently won't pay extra, but if a user spends a greater percentage of his time in Photoshop, then Adobe will get a greater percentage of the licensing consortium's revenues. Adobe's first likely action would be to put the Photoshop manuals on the Web, possibly open only to people who are licensing consortium subscribers. Making telephone and email support fast and effective becomes a priority because Adobe doesn't want any user to give up on Photoshop and run a flight simulator instead. Hardcopy manuals are mailed out free or at nominal cost.

Adobe sponsors conferences to help other software developers call Photoshop's internals. Adobe will not file any look-and-feel lawsuits, because they're getting paid every time someone uses their user interface code.

New World Order

Five years after software licensing consortia are in place, the world looks very different. Fewer programs are written from the ground up, fewer users stab away cluelessly at stolen programs for which they lack documentation, fewer look-and-feel lawsuits are filed, fewer bugs are created. Roughly the same amount of money is flowing to the software publishing industry, but the industry has better information about who its customers are and how useful they find their products.

My personal prediction is that two kinds of consortia would emerge in this New World. One kind would cater to business. Users would pay $X per year and get the old familiar software. Consortia catering to home users, however, would offer a $0 per year deal: You can use any software you want, but we're going to replace those startup screens and hourglasses with ads for McDonald's and Coke. Ask for a spell-check in your word processor? While it is loading, an ad for Rolaids will ask you how you spell relief. Ask Photoshop to sharpen a big PhotoCD scan? That thermometer progress bar will be buried underneath an ad reminding you how sharp you'd feel if you were dressed from head to toe in L. L. Bean clothing. Visit *www.llbean.com.*

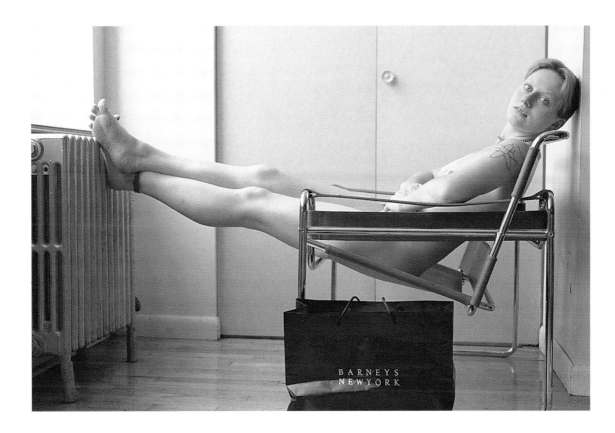

A Less Radical Approach

Renting *software* rather than the physical machines on which it is installed would achieve some of the same goals as blanket licensing and metering. Certainly a casual user would prefer to spend $1 an hour trying out Photoshop than $500 for "the package" and then $100 a year for updates. Adobe would then have many of the same incentives to make documentation and support readily available.

However, renting software would not solve the deeper problem created by software developers standing on each other's toes rather than each other's shoulders.

Privacy

I probably wouldn't want my employer to know that I spent 95 percent of my time running Netscape and Doom when I was supposed to be using Word and Excel. So I want to make sure that a public-key encryption system can be designed so that nobody can figure out which programs were run on my machine. Anonymity is good, but it opens the door to fraud by software publishers. Suppose that I write a

text-editing program. It isn't nearly as good as Emacs, so nobody uses it. But if I can figure out a way to file false usage reports that fool the consortia into thinking that 100,000 people ran my text editor for 2,000 hours each, I'll get a much larger-than-deserved share of license revenue. Again, public-key encryption and digital signatures can be used to fraud-proof the system.

WE HAVE A NETWORK; WE CAN DO BETTER

Selling software like tables and chairs is a fairly new idea. In the mainframe decades, customers rented software so that they could be sure of getting support and updates. The idea of selling software like tables and chairs was an innovation that came with the personal computer, and it worked pretty well for a while. However, it doesn't make sense in a networked world.

Web publishers will need to operate in a world where the typical client is not a desktop PC running a manually installed browser. That doesn't have many implications for service design, as long as most of the clients still have the familiar keyboard, mouse, and monitor. Oops.

Your User's Browser: A GE Range

Your reader's house will be a Class C subnet. Every device in the typical American home will have an IP address. The washing machine, the microwave oven, the VCR, the stove, the clock radio, the thermostat. Any device with an IP address is a potential Web client. As a Web publisher, you have to think about how your content can be used by browsers that aren't keyboard, mouse, and monitor.

Do I believe in this explosion of Internetworking because I'm a technology optimist? Have I decided to write for *Wired* magazine after all? No. I believe this because I've become a technology *pessimist*.

Product engineering: Theory versus reality

When I graduated from MIT in 1982, I was a technology optimist. I was a genius doing brilliant engineering. My work would go out the door into the arms of an adoring public whose lives would be enriched by my creations. Experience taught me that I had at least the first part of this right: New products indeed go out the doors of companies. As to the rest, well, sometimes those products work. Sometimes the documentation is adequate. Sometimes the consumer can figure out how to make it work. But mostly every time consumers buy a new gizmo they are in for a few days of misery and waiting in tech support phone queues. Our society can engineer lots of things that it can't support.

An engineer's age is thus determinative of his or her attitude toward home networking. Young engineers think that we'll have home appliance networking because it will make life easier for consumers. Gerry Sussman, my former advisor at MIT, is a bit grizzled and probably wouldn't argue with my characterization of him as an old engineer. Gerry loves to pull a huge N (Navy) RF connector out of his desk drawer to show students how it can be mated with the small BNC (Bayonet Navy Connector) for expediency. "These were both designed during World War II," Gerry will say. "You don't get strain relief, but it makes a perfectly good contact in an emergency. The guys who designed these connectors were brilliant. On the other hand, there has been a commission meeting in Europe for 15 years trying to come up with a common power-plug standard."

The problems of home appliance networking are human and business problems, not technical problems. There is no reason why a Sony CD player shouldn't have been able to communicate intelligently with a Pioneer receiver 10 years ago. Both machines contain computers. How come when you hit Play on the CD player, the receiver doesn't turn itself on and switch its input to CD?

Why can't a Nikon camera talk to Minolta's wireless flash system? Or, for that matter, why can't this year's Nikon camera talk intelligently to last year's Nikon flash?

Computer engineers are confused into thinking that companies care about interoperability. In fact, the inherently monopolistic computer industry was dragged kicking and screaming toward interoperability by the United States federal government, the one buyer large enough to insist on it. Many of the standards in the computer industry are due to federal funding or conditions in government purchasing contracts. Buyers of home appliances are too disorganized to insist on standards. General Electric's appliance division, the market leader in the United States, isn't even a sponsor of the Consumer Electronics Bus consortium. IBM is. AT&T Bell Labs is. Hewlett-Packard is.

Does this mean you have to figure out how to fry an egg on your PC or telephone before you'll have a really smart house? No. As I have hinted, I think that companies such as GE will start to put Internet interfaces into their appliances as soon as about 20 percent of American households are wired for full-time Internet, for example with cable modems (see Chapter 6). But they won't do it because they think it is cool for your GE fridge to talk to your Whirlpool dishwasher. They'll do it because it will cut the cost of tech support for them. Instead of paying someone to wait on the 800 line while you poke around with your head underneath the fridge looking for the serial number, they'll want to ping your fridge across the Internet and find out the model, its current temperature, and whether there are any compressor failures.

What kinds of things can happen in a networked house?

My GE Profile range (see *http://photo.net /materialism/kitchen.html*) already has a tall backsplash with an LED display. If GE had put a 10base-T outlet on the back to provide technical support, the next logical step would be to replace the LED display with a color LCD screen. Then I would be able to browse recipe Web sites from my stove top. Once I'd found the desired recipe, I would press Start Cooking. A dialog box would appear: "JavaScript Alert: Preheat oven to 375?" After I'd confirmed that, the recipe steps would unfold before me on the LCD.

What does this mean to me as a Web publisher?

Ubiquitous Internet, and therefore ubiquitous Web browsers, suggest that publishers should adhere to Tim Berners-Lee's original vision of the Web: The browser renders the content appropriately for the display. This idea seemed laughable when the "weirdo displays" were VT100 terminals in the hands of physics post-docs. Who cares about those

pathetic losers? They don't have enough money to buy any of the stuff we advertise on our site, anyway.

So I watched as the sites I'd built for big publishers got tarted up with image maps and tables and frames and flashing GIFs and applets. If it looks okay in Netscape Navigator on a Mac or a PC, then ship it. Don't even worry whether it is legal HTML or not. Then one day WebTV came out. Suddenly there was a flurry of email on the group mailing lists. How to redesign their sites to be compatible with WebTV? I had to fight the urge to reply, "I looked at my personal site on a WebTV the other day; it looked fine."

WebTV was a big shock to a lot of publishers. Yet WebTV is much more computerlike than any of the other household appliances that consumers will be connecting to the Internet. Be ready: Focus on content. Standard HTML plus

semantic tags can make your content useful to household devices with very primitive user interface capabilities.

This chapter started off by saying that average users shouldn't be forced to maintain computer systems. Then we threw rocks at the 100-MB desktop apps that people buy in computer stores. Then we looked at whether people might not just browse Web content from their stoves and microwave ovens. Does that mean that corporate information systems staffers will be attacking the challenge of reformatting Web content to fit 8×80 character displays? No. They will be busy attacking the challenge of meaningfully communicating with other companies.

COLLABORATIVELY EXCHANGED DATA MODELS

As discussed briefly in Chapter 2, corporations have been squandering money on computers for years and don't have too much to show for their investment. Suppose that Spacely Sprockets wants to buy widgets from Acme Widgets. Spacely Sprockets has an advanced computerized purchasing system. An employee in purchasing works through some online forms to specify that Spacely needs 2,500 widgets—Spacely part number W147, Acme model number A491—to be delivered on June 1. The order is stored in a relational database.

Acme is also a modern company. They have an integrated order entry, inventory, and billing system backed by an RDBMS. As soon as the order goes into the system, it sets into motion a synchronized chain of events in the factory.

How does the data for the 2,500-widget order get from Spacely to Acme? Each decade had its defining technology:

- In the 1970s, a Spacely employee printed out the order from the advanced Spacely system, stuck it into an envelope, and mailed it to Acme. An Acme employee opened the envelope and keyed the order into the Acme system, typing "25,000" instead of "2,500."

- In the 1980s, a Spacely employee printed out the order from the advanced Spacely system and faxed it to Acme. An Acme employee grabbed the order from the fax machine output bin and keyed the order into the Acme system, typing "25,000" instead of "2,500."

- In the 1990s, a Spacely employee pulls the order out of the advanced Spacely system and emails it to Acme. An Acme employee grabs the order from his or her inbox and rekeys the order into the Acme system, typing "25,000" instead of "2,500."

If this all sounds a little more efficient than the business world with which you're familiar, keep in mind that the whole process is repeated in the opposite direction when Acme wants to invoice Spacely for the 25,000 widgets.

What stops Spacely's computer from talking directly to Acme's?

In the old (pre-Internet) days, we would say that it was the impossibility of getting the bits from Acme's glass room to Spacely's. Now we have an Internet and any computer in the world can talk to any other. But sadly, it turns out that they have nothing to say.

Security is the first thing that worries most companies when they hook critical systems to the Internet. Can we be sure that Spacely's computer won't attempt any naughty transactions on Acme's computer? For example, if Spacely had full access to Acme's RDBMS, it could mark lots of invoices as having been paid. The issue of security is an anthill, however, compared to the craggy mountain of data model incompatibility.

Column names may be different. Acme's programmers choose "part_number" and Spacely's use "partnum". To humans they look the same, but to the computer they might as well be completely different. Worse yet are differences in the meaning of what is in that column. Acme has a different part number for the same widget than does Spacely. Nor need there be a one-to-one mapping between columns. Suppose Spacely's data model uses a single text field for shipping address and Acme's breaks up the address into line_1, line_2, city, state, postal_code, and country_code columns? Nor, finally, need there be a one-to-one mapping between tables. Spacely could spread an order across multiple tables. An order wouldn't contain an address at all, just a factory ID. You'd have to JOIN with the factories table if you wanted to print out one order with a meaningful shipping address. Acme might just have one wide table with some duplication of data. Multiple orders to the same factory would just contain duplicate copies of the factory address.

We could fix this problem the way GM did. Go over to Germany and buy some data models from SAP (*www.sap.com*). Then make every division of the company use these data models and the same part numbers for the same screws. Total cost? About $1 billion. A smart investment? How can you doubt GM? This is the company that spent $5 billion on robots at a time when they could have purchased all of Toyota for about the same sum. Anyway, the bureaucrats at MIT were so fattened by undergrads paying $23,000 a year and so impressed by GM's smart move that they bought SAP data models, too. My advisor was skeptical that data models designed for a factory would work at a university. "Sure they will," I said, "You just have to think of each major as an assembly line. You're probably being modeled as a painting robot."

Was my faith in SAP shaken when, two calendar years and 40 person-years into the installation process, MIT still wasn't really up and running? Absolutely not. SAP is the best thing that ever happened to computer people. It appeals to businesses that are too stupid to understand and model their own processes but too rich to simply continue relying on secretaries and file cabinets. So they want to buy SAP or a set of data models from one of SAP's competitors. But since they can't understand their business processes well enough to model them themselves, they aren't able to figure out which product is the best match for those processes. So they hire consultants to tell them which product to buy. A friend of mine is one of these consultants. If you take what you've learned from this book and score a $2,000-per-day Web consulting gig, don't bother to gloat in front of David. His time is worth $6,500 a day. And he doesn't even know SQL! He doesn't have to do any programming. He doesn't have to do any database administration. He doesn't have to do any systems administration. David just has to fly first class around the world and sit at conference tables with big executives and opine that perhaps PeopleSoft would be better for their company than SAP.

There are plenty of rich stupid companies on the Web. Is it therefore true that the same "convert everyone to one data model" approach will achieve our objective of streamlined intercompany communication? No. There is no central authority that can force everyone to spend big bucks converting to a common data model. Companies probably won't spend much voluntarily, either. Company X might have no objection to wasting billions internally, but management is usually reluctant to spend money in ways that might benefit Company Y.

What does that leave us with? n companies on the Web technically able to share data but having n separate data models. Each time two companies want to share data, their programmers have to cooperate on a conversion system. Before everyone can talk to anyone, we'll have to build $n*(n-1)$ unidirectional converters (for each of n companies we need a link to $n-1$ other companies, thus the $n*(n-1)$). With just 200 companies, this turns out to be 39,800 converters.

If we could get those 200 companies to agree on a canonical format for data exchange, we'd only need to build 400 unidirectional converters. That is a much more manageable number than 39,800, particularly when it is obvious that each company should bear the burden of writing two converters (one into and one out of its proprietary format).

The fly in the ointment here is that developing canonical data models can be extremely difficult. For something like hotel room booking, it can probably be achieved by a committee of volunteer programmers. For manufacturing, it apparently is tough enough that a company like SAP can charge tens of millions of dollars for one copy of its system (and even then they haven't really solved the problem, because they and their customers typically customize about 20 percent of their systems). For medical records, it is a research problem (see *http://www.emrs.org*).

That's why the next section is so interesting.

COLLABORATIVELY EVOLVED DATA MODELS

When I was 14 years old, I was the smartest person in the world. I therefore did not need assistance or suggestions from other people. Now that I've reached the age of 35, my mind has deteriorated to the point that I welcome ideas from other minds with different perspectives and experience.

Suppose I wanted to build a database for indexing photographs. When I was 14, I would have sat down and created a table with precisely the correct number of columns and then used it forever. Today, though, I would build a Web front end to

Note:
If this example
sounds insufficiently
contrived, it is
because it is one
of my actual back-
burner projects;
check *http://
photo.net/photo/*
to see if I've
actually done it.

my database and let other photographers use my software. I'd give them the capability of extending the data model just for their images. After a few months, I'd look at
the extensions that they'd found necessary and use those to try to figure out new features that ought to be common in the next release of the software.

Ditto for my SPAM mailing list manager system (*http://www.greenspun.com
/spam/*), described *ad nauseum* in Chapter 13. The interesting thing to do with it
would be to let each publisher add extra columns to his or her private data model,
and then see what people really wanted to do with the system.

A much more challenging problem is building a computer system that can find
commonality among the extensions that users have made to a data model and automatically spit out a new release of the canonical data model that subsumes 85 percent
of the custom modifications. (You want as much capability in the canonical data
model as possible, because off-the-shelf software will only be convenient when
working with the standard portions of the model.)

Why this obsession with data modeling? Computers can't do much to help us if
we can't boil our problems down to formal models. The more things that we can
formally model, the more that computers can help us. The Web is the most powerful tool that we've ever had for developing models. We don't need focus groups. We
don't need marketing staff reading auguries. We don't need seven versions of a product before we get it right. We have a system that lets users tell us directly and in a
formal language exactly what they need our data model to do.

DELENDA EST JUNKWARE

Junkware must be destroyed. Serverside Web junkware in particular. It breaks my
heart to see a Web publisher clutching boxes of software that are in no way specific
to the desired application. Consider Joe Pathetic with

- a packaged ad server
- off-the-shelf discussion group software
- a fancy log analyzer
- a personalization engine
- an ecommerce system

In the time that it takes Joe to read the manuals for these products and think
about how they might be made to work together, Jane Intelligent will have thought
about her users and built a data model that captures everything important about
their relationship to her business and to each other. Jane's site and service will grow in
a natural way, while Joe Pathetic will be scrambling to hire ad server administrators.

Hog farmers are smarter than Web publishers. A hog farmer would not spend $500,000 on a state-of-the-art payroll software system, the market-leading purchasing package, and an award-winning accounts receivable management system. A hog farmer would buy Hogfarmix, the same integrated software package used by other smart hog farmers. Hogfarmix represents the information that is critical to the hog farming business. If its payroll, purchasing, and receivables components are less than state of the art, they still work better for a hog farmer than the market leading products. All the information in these components is interpreted in a hog-farming light.

Does that mean that publishers must build everything from scratch? Not necessarily.

A retail bank that wishes to start offering online services should try to find an "online bank in a box" package. If it can't find adequate software, it should team up with banks in other regions to fund the construction of a good package that they can all use.

A magazine should ask itself whether the community software package outlined in Chapter 3 wouldn't be better than starting from scratch. As noted in the case studies in Chapter 15, it doesn't matter whether or not the discussion forum software in the community system is better or worse than that in a standalone package. It is integrated with the users table and enables the publisher to ask, "Show me the documents that people were reading immediately before asking questions" or "Show me users who've answered more than 50 questions and who've read at least 60 percent of our static content" (these are people who might be promotable to co-moderators).

A company with an existing information system should find Web applications that will run from their current data model. It is insanely costly to maintain multiple sets of the same data.

The Last Word

Chapter 1 instructs publishers to give readers the last word. The intervening chapters make some hardware and software recommendations. Combining those themes, let's close the book with a submission to the comment server for *http://photo.net /philg/humor/bill-gates.html:*

> *I must say, that all of you who do not recognize the absolute genius of Bill Gates are stupid. You say that bill gates stole this operating system. Hmm.. i find this interesting. If he stole it from steve jobs, why hasn't Mr. Jobs relentlessly sued him and such. Because Mr. Jobs has no basis to support this. Macintosh operates NOTHING like Windows 3.1 or Win 95/NT/98. Now for the mac dissing. Mac's are good for 1 thing. Graphics. Thats all. Anything else a mac sucks at. You look in all the elementary schools of america.. You wont see a PC. Youll see a mac. Why? Because Mac's are only used by people with undeveloped brains.*
> —Allen (chuggie@geocities.com), August 10, 1998

More

- If you miss seeing the interview with Noam Chomsky, you'll find it at the end of the old book (*http://photo.net/wtr/dead-trees/53015.htm*).

GLOSSARY

Application server   See Middleware.

AOLserver   Released in early 1995 as NaviServer, AOLserver remains the most powerful Web server program on the market and it is free). It is a multi-threaded server that provides a lot of support for connecting to relational database management systems. Nearly all of the programming examples in this book are written in the AOLserver Tcl API. AOLserver is documented at *www.aolserver.com*.

Apache   The world's most popular Web server. Originally not nearly as powerful as AOLserver, Apache had one huge advantage: The source code was available right from the start (NaviServer was initially a commercial product). This, coupled with the failure of Windows NT to work reliably and the failure of Netscape to have any clue about what Web publishers need, has made Apache dominant. See Chapter 8 for some discussion of Apache's pros and cons.

API   Application Programming Interface. An abstraction barrier between custom/extension code and a core, usually commercial program. The goal of an API is to let you write programs that won't break when you upgrade the underlying system. The authors of the core program are saying, "Here are a bunch of hooks into our code. We guarantee and document that they will work a certain way. We reserve the right to change the core program, but we will endeavor to preserve the behavior of the API call. If we can't, then we'll tell you in the release notes that we broke an old API call."

ASP   Active Server Pages, developed by Microsoft. This is the standard programming system for Web sites built on Windows NT. It is bundled with Internet Information Server (IIS) when you buy the Windows NT Server operating system. The fundamental idea is that you write HTML pages with little embedded bits of Visual Basic that are interpreted by the server. See Chapter 10 for more information.

Cable modem   A cable modem is an Internet connection provided by a cable TV operator, typically with at least 1.5 Mbits per second of download bandwidth (50 to 100 times faster than modems that work over analog telephone lines).

Cache   Computer systems typically incorporate capacious storage devices that are slow (e.g., disk drives) and smaller storage devices that are fast (e.g., memory chips, which are 100,000 times faster than disk). File systems and database management systems keep recently used information from the slow devices in a cache in the fast device.

CGI   Common Gateway Interface. This is a standard that lets programmers write Web scripts without depending on details of the Web server program being used. Thus, for example, a Web service implemented in CGI could be moved from a site running AOLserver to a site running Apache. See Chapter 10.

Client/Server   In the 1960s, computers were so expensive that each company could have only one. "The computer" ran one program at a time, typically reading instructions and data from punch cards. This was batch processing. In the 1970s, that computer was able to run several programs simultaneously, responding to users at interactive terminals. This was time-sharing. (It would be nice if modesty prevented me from noting that this was developed by my lab at MIT circa 1960.)

In the 1980s, companies could afford lots of computers. The big computers were designated servers and would wait for requests to come in from a network of client computers. The client computer might sit on a user's desktop and produce an informative graph of the information retrieved from the server. The overall architecture was referred to as client/server. Because of the high cost of designing, developing, and maintaining the programs that run on the client machines, Corporate America is rapidly discarding this architecture in favor of intranet: Client machines run a simple Web browser and servers do more of the work required to present the information.

Community site   A community site exists to support the interaction of an online community of users. These users typically come together because of a shared interest and are most vibrant when there is an educational dimension, i.e., when the more experienced users are helping the novices improve their skills.

Compression When storing information in digital form, it is often possible to reduce the amount of space required by exploiting regular patterns in the data. For example, documents written in English frequently contain "the". A compression system might notice this fact and represent the complete word "the" (24 bits) with a shorter code. A picture containing your friend's face plus a lot of blue sky could be compressed if the upper region were described as "a lot of blue sky". All popular Web image, video, and sound formats incorporate compression.

Data model A data model is the structure in which a computer program stores persistent information. In a relational database, data models are built from tables. Within a table, information is stored in homogeneous columns, e.g., a column named `registration_date` would contain information only of type date. A data model is interesting because it shows what kinds of information a computer application can process. For example, if there is no place in the data model for the program to store the IP address from which content was posted, the publisher will never be able to automatically delete all content that came from the IP address of a spammer.

Dynamic site A dynamic site is one that is able to collect information from User A, serve it back to Users B and C immediately, and hide it from User D because the server knows that User D isn't interested in this kind of content. Dynamic sites are typically built on top of relational database management systems because these programs make it easy to organize content submitted by hundreds of concurrent users. An example of a simple dynamic site would be a classified ad system.

EDI Electronic Document Interchange. A standard for exchanging business documents, such as invoices and purchase orders.

Emacs World's most powerful text editor, written by Richard Stallman (see *RMS*) in 1976 for the Incompatible Timesharing System (ITS) on the PDP-10s at MIT. Subsequently, Emacs has been ported to virtually every kind of computer hardware and operating system between 1976 and the present (including the Macintosh, Windows 95/NT, and every flavor of Unix).

Good programmers tend to spend their entire working lives in Emacs, which is capable of functioning as a mail reader, USENET news reader, Web browser, shell, calendar, calculator, and Lisp evaluator. Emacs is infinitely customizable because users can write their own commands in Lisp. You can find out more about Emacs at *ftp://publications.ai.mit.edu/ai-publications /pdf/AIM-519A.pdf* (Stallman's 1979 MIT AI Lab report), at *www.gnu.org* (where you can download the source code for free), or by reading *Learning Emacs* (Cameron et al., 1996; O'Reilly). If you want to program Emacs, then you'll want *Writing Gnu Emacs Extensions* (Glickstein, 1997; O'Reilly).

Firewall A computer that sits between a company's internal network of computers and the public Internet. The firewall's job is to make sure that internal users can get out to enjoy the benefits of the Internet while external crackers are unable to make connections to machines behind the firewall.

Flat file A flat file database keeps information organized in a structured manner, typically in one big file. A desktop spreadsheet application is an example of a flat file database management system. These are useful for Web publishers preparing content because a large body of information can be assembled and then distributed in a consistent format. Flat file databases typically lack support for processing transactions (inserts and updates) from concurrent users. Thus collaboration or ecommerce Web sites generally rely on a relational database management system as a backend.

GIF Graphical Interchange Format. Developed in 1987 by CompuServe, this is a way of storing compressed images with up to 256 colors. It became popular on the Web because it was the only format that could be displayed inline by the first multiplatform Web browser (NCSA Mosaic). The use of GIF versus JPEG is discussed in Chapter 6.

HTML Hyper Text Markup Language. Developed by Tim Berners-Lee, this specifies a format for the most popular kind of document distributed over the Web (via HTTP). You can find HTML documented sketchily in my HTML chapter (Chapter 5), documented badly at *http://www.w3.org,* and documented well in *HTML: The Definitive Guide* (Musciano and Kennedy, 1998; O'Reilly)

HTTP Hypertext Transfer Protocol. Developed by Tim Berners-Lee, this specifies how a Web browser asks for a document from a Web server. Questions such as "How does a server tell the browser that a document has moved?" or "How does a browser ask the time that a document was last modified?" may be answered by reference to this protocol, which is documented badly at *http://www.w3.org* and documented well in *Web Client Programming* (Wong, 1997; O'Reilly).

IIS Internet Information Server. A Web server program that is included by Microsoft when you purchase the Windows NT Server operating system. As Larry Ellison notes, this is not the same as "free." Rather than compete with other vendors of Web server programs, Microsoft puts its product into the operating system that everyone has to buy (unless they free themselves with Linux) and then raises the price of the operating system. The best part about IIS is Active Server Pages (ASP), described in Chapter 10. The worst part about IIS is the comparative unreliability of Windows NT.

Java Java is, first, a programming language, developed by Sun Microsystems around 1992, intended for use on the tiny computers inside cell phones and similar devices. Java is, second, an interpreter, the Java virtual machine, compiled into popular Web browsers such as Netscape Navigator. Java is, third, a security system that purports to guarantee that a program downloaded from an untrusted source on the Internet can run safely inside the interpreter. Java is the only realistic way for a Web publisher to take advantage of the computing power available on a user's desktop. Java is generally a bad language for server-side software development (see Chapter 10). For more background on the language, see the Java chapter from *Database Backed Web Sites* at *http://photo.net/wtr/dead-trees/53008.htm.*

JPEG   Joint Photographic Experts Group. A bunch of guys who sat down and designed a standard for image compression, conveniently titled, IS 10918-1 (ITU-T T.81). This standard works particularly well for 24-bit color photographs. C-Cube Microsystems came up with the JFIF standard for encoding color images in a file. Such a file is what people commonly refer to as "a JPEG" and typically ends in ".jpg" or ".jpeg". See Chapter 6 for tips on producing JPEGs for the Web. See *www.jpeg.org* for more about the standard.

Linux   A free version of the Unix operating system, primarily composed of tools developed over a 15-year period by Richard Stallman and Project GNU. However, the final spectacular push was provided by Linus Torvalds who wrote a kernel (completed in 1994), organized a bunch of programmers Internet-wide, and managed releases. Currently, because it can be installed on any Wintel box, Linux is the most likely vehicle by which users can free themselves from the Microsoft monopoly (see *http://photo.net/philg/humor/bill-gates.html*). I discuss Linux in Chapter 8. Linux is free but you'll save yourself a lot of pain if you buy a well-organized and easy-to-install version from *www.redhat.com*. A good example of how commercialization and banner ads have disfigured even the unlikeliest corners of the Web is *www.linux.org*.

Lisp   Lisp is the most powerful and also the easiest to use programming language ever developed. Invented by John McCarthy at MIT in the late 1950s, Lisp is today used by the most sophisticated programmers pushing the limits of computers in mathematical physics, computer-aided engineering, and computer-aided genetics. Lisp is also used by thousands of people who don't think of themselves as programmers at all but as people who want to define shortcuts in AutoCAD or the Emacs text editor. The best introduction to Lisp is also the best introduction to computer science: *Structure and Interpretation of Computer Programs* (Abelson and Sussman, 1996; MIT Press).

Log analyzer   A program that reads a Web server's log file (one line per request served) and produces a comprehensible report with summary statistics, e.g., "You served 234,812 requests yesterday to 2,039 different computers; the most popular file was /samoyed-faces.html".

Magic cookie   The magic cookie protocol allows a Web service to conveniently maintain a "session" with a particular user. The Web server sends the client a magic cookie (piece of information) that the client is required to return on subsequent requests. The original specification is at *http://home.netscape.com/newsref/std/cookie_spec.html*.

Magnet content   Material authored by a publisher in hopes of establishing an online community. In the long run, a majority of the content in a successful community site will be user authored.

Middleware   Software sold to people who don't know how to program by people who know how to program. In theory, middleware sits between your relational database management system and your application program and makes the whole system run more reliably. M.B.A.s are lining up right now to buy the Netscape Application Server middleware for $35,000 per CPU.

Without the benefit of middleware, I'm able to support a few hundred simultaneous users on a cheap desktop Unix box running AOLserver. The mainframe studs are usually able to get a few thousand transactions per second through systems like the airline reservations systems. With Netscape Application Server and a $200,000 eight-CPU Unix box, though, the testers at *PC Week* were able to support . . . 10 simultaneous users. To achieve this performance, it was necessary to restart the servers constantly and reboot the Unix box occasionally (see *http://photo.net/wtr/application-servers.html*).

MIME   Multi-Purpose Internet Mail Extensions. Developed in 1991 by Nathan Borenstein of Bellcore so that people could include images and other non–plain-text documents in email messages. MIME is a critical standard for the World Wide Web because an HTTP server answering a request always includes the MIME type of the document served. For example, if a browser requests "foobar.jpg", the server will return a MIME type of "image/jpeg". The Web browser will decide, based on this type, whether or not to attempt to render the document. A JPEG image can be rendered by all modern Web browsers. If, for example, a Web browser sees a MIME type of "application/x-pilot" (for the .prc files that PalmPilots employ), the browser will invite the user to save the document to disk or select an appropriate application to launch for this kind of document.

Operating system   A big complicated computer program that lets multiple simultaneously executing big complicated computer programs coexist peacefully on one physical computer. The operating system is also responsible for hiding the details of the computer hardware from the application programmers, e.g., letting a programmer say, "I want to write ABC into a file named XYZ" without the programmer having to know how many disk drives the computer has or what company manufactured those drives. Examples of operating systems are Unix and Windows NT. Examples of things that try to be operating systems but mostly fail to fulfill the "coexist peacefully" condition are Windows and the Macintosh OS.

Oracle   Oracle is the most popular relational database management system (RDBMS). It was developed by Larry Ellison's Oracle Corporation in the late 1970s. All of the example applications in this book were built using Oracle.

Perl   Perl is a scripting language developed by Larry Wall in 1986 to make his Unix sysadmin job a little easier. It unifies a bunch of capabilities from disparate older Unix tools. Like Unix, Perl is perhaps best described as "ugly but fast and useful." Perl is free, has particularly powerful string processing operators, and quickly developed a large following and therefore a large library for CGI scripting. For more information, see *www.perl.com* or *www.perl.org*.

Historical Note: Lisp programmers forced to look at Perl code would usually say, "If there were any justice in this world, the guys who wrote this would go to jail." In a rare case of Lisp programmers getting their wish, in 1995 Intel Corporation persuaded local authorities to send Randal Schwartz, author of *Learning Perl* (O'Reilly, 1997), to the Big House for 90 days (plus 5 years of probation, 480 hours of community service, and $68,000 of "restitution" to Intel). Sadly, however, it seems that Schwartz's official crime was not corrupting young minds with Perl syntax and semantics. At MIT, our Unix sysadmins periodically run a program called "crack" that tries to guess our passwords. When crack is successful, the sysadmins send us email saying "your password has been cracked; please change it to something harder to guess." Obviously they do not need our passwords since they have root access to all the boxes and can read any of our data. At MIT, you get paid about $50,000 a year for doing this. In Oregon if you do this for a multibillion dollar company that has recently donated $100,000 to the local law enforcement authorities, you've committed a crime. See *http://www.lightlink.com/spacenka /fors/* for more on *State of Oregon v. Randal Schwartz.*

PhotoCD   A Kodak standard for scanning and storing images. Every image on a Kodak PhotoCD is available in five resolutions, the highest of which is 2,000 × 3,000 pixels (Pro PhotoCD contains one extra resolution: 4,000 × 6,000 pixels). These disks are made from original slides or negatives by specially equipped labs, the best of which can be linked to from *http://photo.net/photo/labs.html.*

RDBMS   Relational database management system. A computer program that lets you store, index, and retrieve tables of data. The simplest way to look at an RDBMS is as a spreadsheet that multiple users can update. The most important thing that an RDBMS does is provide transactions. See Chapter 12 for more information.

RMS   Richard M. Stallman. In 1976, he developed Emacs, the world's best and most widely used text editor. He went on to develop gcc, the most widely used compiler for the C programming language. In 1990, he won a $240,000 MacArthur fellowship. Stallman is the founder of the free software movement (see *www.fsf.org*) and Project GNU, which gave rise to Linux. *See also Emacs.*

Robot   In the technologically optimistic portion of the 20th century, robots were intelligent, anthropomorphic machines that understood human speech, interpreted visual scenes, and manipulated objects in the real world. In the technologically realistic 21st century, robots are absurdly primitive programs that do things like "Go look up this book title at three different online bookstores and see who has the lowest price; fail completely if any one of the online bookstores has added a comma to their HTML page." Also known as intelligent agents (an intellectually vacuous term but useful for getting tenure if you're a university professor). Some simple but very useful examples of robots are the spiders or Web crawlers that fill the content database at public search engine sites such as AltaVista.

Scalable   A marketing term used to sell defective software to executives at wealthy Web publishing companies. The Web is fundamentally about processing updates from thousands of concurrent users. This is for what database management systems were built. Smart engineers build Web services so that if the database is up and running, the Web site will be up and running. Period. Adding more users to the site will inevitably require adding capacity to the database management system, no matter what other software is employed. The thoughtful engineer will realize that a provably scalable site is one that relies on no other software besides the database management system (or that cheats with a thin layer of simple, reliable opensource software such as AOLserver or Apache).

Semantic tag   The most popular Web markup language is HTML, which provides for formatting tags, e.g., "This is a headline" or "This should be rendered in italics." This is useful for humans reading Web pages. What would be more useful for computer programs trying to read Web pages is a semantic tag, e.g., "The following numbers represent the price of the product in dollars," or "The following characters represent the date this document was initially authored". XML and SGML are examples of systems that support communities of people who wish to exchange semantically tagged documents.

SGML   Standard Generalized Markup Language. Standardized in 1980, a language for marking up documents so that they can be parsed by computer programs. Each community of people that wishes to author and parse documents must agree on a Document Type Definition (DTD), which is itself a machine-parsable description of what tags a marked-up document must or may have. HTML is an example of an SGML DTD. See Chapter 5.

Spider   A spider or Web crawler is a program that exhaustively surfs all the links from a page and returns them to another program for processing. For example, all of the Internet search engine sites rely on spider robots to discover new Web sites and add them to their index. Another typical use of a spider is by a publisher against his or her own site. The spider program makes sure that all of the links function correctly and reports dead links.

SQL   Structured Query Language. Developed by IBM in the mid-1970s as a way to get information into and out of relational database management systems. A fundamental difference between SQL and standard programming languages is that SQL is declarative. You specify what kind of data you want from the database; the RDBMS is responsible for figuring out how to retrieve it. I include a tutorial on SQL in Chapter 12.

Static site   A static Web site comprises content that does not change with the identity of the user, the time of day, or what other users might have contributed recently. A static Web site typically is built using static documents in HTML format, with graphics in GIF format and images in JPEG format. Collectively, these are referred to as static files. Contrast this with a dynamic site, in which content can be automatically collected from users, personalized for the viewer, or changed as a function of the time of day.

Tcl   Tool Command Language. An interpreted computer language designed for rapid prototyping and maximum flexibility, Tcl was developed in the late 1980s by John Ousterhout, a professor at UC Berkeley. Personally, I'd much rather use Lisp, but AOLserver has a compiled-in Tcl interpreter. In Chapter 10, I explain why I think Tcl has been effective for Web/DB application development. Tcl is documented at *www.scriptics.com* and *www.tclconsortium.org*.

TCP/IP   Transmission Control Protocol and Internet Protocol. These are the standards that govern transmission of data among computer systems. They are the foundation of the Internet. IP is a way of saying, "Send these next 1,000 bits from Computer A to Computer B." TCP is a way of saying, "Send this stream of data reliably between Computer A and Computer B" (it is built on top of IP). TCP/IP is a beautiful engineering achievement, documented beautifully in *TCP/IP Illustrated, Volume 1* (W. Richard Stevens, 1994; Addison-Wesley).

Transaction   A transaction is a set of operations for which it is important that all succeed or all fail. On an ecommerce site, when a customer confirms a purchase, you'd like to send an order to the shipping department and simultaneously bill the customer's credit card. If the credit card can't be billed, you want to make sure that the order doesn't get shipped. If the shipping database can't accept the order, you want to make sure that the credit card doesn't get billed. RDBMSs such as Oracle provide significant support for implementing transactions.

Unix   An operating system developed by Ken Thompson and Dennis Ritchie at Bell Laboratories in 1969, vaguely inspired by the advanced MULTICS system built by MIT. Unix really took off after 1979, when Bill Joy at UC Berkeley released a version for Digital's VAX minicomputer. All the competent computer hackers used to hate Unix but, through some combination of Unix being enhanced and the rest of the world slipping into darkness (Windows, Mac OS), the Unix haters have all lumped it and brought Linux boxes into their homes.

URL   Uniform Resource Locator. A way of specifying the location of something on the Internet, e.g., *http://photo.net/wtr/thebook/glossary.html* is the URL for the online version of this glossary. The part before the colon specifies the protocol (HTTP). Legal alternatives include encrypted protocols such as HTTPS and legacy protocols such as FTP, news, gopher, etc. The part after the "//" is the server hostname (photo.net). The part after the next "/" is the name of the file on the remote server.

USENET   A threaded discussion system that today connects millions of users from around the Internet into newsgroups such as rec.photo.equipment.35mm. The original system was built in the late 1970s and ran on one of the wide area computer networks later subsumed into the Internet.

WebTV   A pioneering Internet appliance, based on the premise that a consumer would be delighted to enjoy email and Web browsing without having to suffer with the complexity and system administration overhead of running a Microsoft operating system. WebTV also provided an illustration of the staying power of unregulated monopolies as Microsoft used its supranormal profits from desktop applications to acquire WebTV along with Hotmail, two of the best examples of a future beyond Windows.

Windows NT   A real operating system that can run the same programs with more or less the same user interface as the popular Windows 95/98 system. Windows NT was developed from scratch by a programming team at Microsoft that was mostly untainted by the people who brought misery to the world in the form of Windows 3.1/95. The final system works surprisingly well, though not as reliably as moldy old Unix. See Chapter 8 for a comparison between these two warhorses.

WYSIWYG   What you see is what you get. A WYSIWYG word processor, for example, lets a user view an onscreen document as it will appear on the printed page, e.g., with text in italics appearing onscreen in italics. This approach to software was pioneered by Xerox Palo Alto Research Center in the 1970s and widely copied since then, notably by the Apple Macintosh. WYSIWYG is extremely effective for structurally simple documents that are printed once and never worked on again. WYSIWYG is extremely ineffective for the production of complex documents and documents that must be maintained and kept up to date over many years. Thus QuarkXPress and Adobe Frame facilitated a tremendous boom in desktop publishing, while Microsoft FrontPage and similar WYSIWYG tools for Web page development have probably hindered the development of interesting Web services.

XML   Extensible Markup Language. A simplifed version of SGML with enhanced features for defining hyperlinks. As with SGML, it solves the trivial problem of defining a syntax for exchanging structured information but doesn't do any of the hard work of getting users to agree on semantic structure.

INDEX

About the Author

Philip Greenspun runs the Scalable Systems for Online Communities group at the Massachusetts Institute of Technology. He is the founder of ArsDigita, a Web development and hosting firm that distributes open-source toolkits for building community and ecommerce Web sites.

Philip Greenspun started his career in Web publishing with *Travels with Samantha*, a 210-page story about a trip from Boston to Alaska, illustrated with 300 photographs (winner of Best of the Web '94). Although the Bill Gates Personal Wealth Clock appears regularly in the mass media, more people probably know Philip Greenspun because of photo.net, his photography page that has grown to the point of requiring a 3,000-pound Hewlett-Packard Unix box to serve all the requests.

The Web boom hasn't changed certain things about Philip Greenspun. He is still at the same email address he's had since 1976 (philg@mit.edu). He is still teaching at the Massachusetts Institute of Technology, which he describes as "regarded by people worldwide as the finest engineering school in East Cambridge."

Like most dogs these days, Alex Greenspun has a personal Web site, but he also has his own email address and links to other Samoyeds with their own email addresses. Alex and Philip live in Cambridge, Massachusetts, with Pi goddess Eve Andersson, who takes care of them both.